THE BUY-IT-RIGHT BUSINESS PRODUCTS GUIDE

THE
BUY-IT-RIGHT
BUSINESS
PRODUCTS GUIDE

RATINGS, RANKINGS, AND EVERYTHING YOU NEED TO KNOW ABOUT THE BEST PRODUCTS FOR ALMOST EVERY BUSINESS NEED

LES KRANTZ & ADRIENNE BROWN

AMACOM
American Management Association
New York • Atlanta • Boston • Chicago • Kansas City • San Francisco • Washington, D.C.
Brussels • Mexico City • Tokyo • Toronto

This book is available at a special discount when ordered in bulk quantities. For information, contact Special Sales Department, AMACOM, a division of American Management Association, 1601 Broadway, New York, NY 10019.

The publication is designed to provide accurate and authoritative information in regard to the subject matter covered. It is sold with the understanding that the publisher is not engaged in rendering legal, accounting, or other professional services. If legal advice or other expert assistance is required, the services of a competent professional should be sought.

The images on the front cover of this book are courtesy of Click Art ® Incredible Image Pack; ©1996, T-Maker Company, a wholly owned subsidiary of Broderbund Software, Inc. All rights reserved. Used by permission.

Library of Congress Cataloging-in-Publication Data

Krantz, Les.
    The buy-it-right business products guide : ratings, rankings, and everything you need to know about the best products for almost every business need / Les Krantz & Adrienne Brown.
    p.   cm.
    Includes index.
    ISBN 0-8144-7972-3
    1. Purchasing—Handbooks, manuals, etc. 2. Office equipment and supplies—Purchasing—Handbooks, manuals, etc. 3. Business—Communications systems—Purchasing—Handbooks, manuals, etc.
    I. Brown, Adrienne. II Title.
    HF5437.k7 1998   97-42449
    658.7'2—dc21   CIP

Printing number
10 9 8 7 6 5 4 3 2 1

Contributors:

The authors wish to thank the following individuals for their contributions to this book:

Craig Bobchin, *Contributing Writer*
Bob Kalish, *Contributing Writer*
Sue Sloan, *Contributing Writer*
Melissa Ulloa, *Manuscript Editor*
Marjorie Glass, *Photo Editor*

Acknowledgments:
The authors are grateful to have been associated with the following individuals at Amacom Books. They were a pleasure to work with and valuable assets to the project.
Hank Kennedy, Publisher
Ellen Kadin, Editor
Kate Pferdner, Managing Editor

CONTENTS

CONTENTS

COMPUTERS AND PERIPHERAL DEVICES

CONTENTS

PRESENTATION DEVICES & AIDES

SOFTWARE

CONTENTS

INTRODUCTION

The Buy-It-Right Business Products Guide is designed to help you purchase business products and services that meet the specific needs of your organization. It can be useful to the biggest *Fortune 500* company or the smallest home-based business. Whichever category you fall into, easy-to-use equipment or accessible outside services that will meet your needs are reviewed in this volume. Both those with the most sophisticated requirements and those with the most basic needs will find myriad solutions in the pages that follow.

EXPLANATION OF RATINGS

All the chapters in your book comparatively rate products and services. Two types of rating systems are used. The most prevalent are "star ratings," a system similar to those used by movie critics. Though simple and understandable at a glance, there's more than meets the eye. The "overall rating," which can range from one to four stars, takes into account other "subratings," which are evaluations of various facets of the products or services. For example, the overall ratings of courier services (the first two chapters of this book) are derived from averaging

various important facets of their service: reliability, cost effectiveness, efficiency and trackability, which are individually rated one to four stars. Evaluations of these facets are presented as subratings and are found in the alphabetical descriptions under the overall rating, which is always computed by averaging the subratings. Many products are also rated this way.

Not all products and services are evaluated with a star rating; another method is employed. This type of rating is more numerically based and is usually presented as a score, which has a maximum numerical value of 100. These are used mainly for products for which something quantifiable is inherent to it. Office copiers, for example, are distinguishable more for their speed, capacity and features, than the quality of their output, which is by-and-large the same from manufacturer to manufacturer. In such a case, points, rather than stars, are awarded for each aspect that is evaluated. The number of points awarded is somehow linked to a quantitative value inherent to the product; for example, copies per minute, capacity, maximum life of use, or other relevant values.

After the points are totaled, they are then indexed with the highest possible score being 100. Based on these figures, the various brands and models are then ranked according to their indexed scores.

USING THE RATINGS

Perhaps the most important thing you need to know is that the product or service with the highest overall rating is not necessarily the one that will serve your needs the best. *Pay attention to the subratings, too.* Sometimes, for example, the fastest machine or the service with the lowest price can be lacking the component or aspect that is most important to you. Or, the opposite can be true: a lower rated product or service might have a facet that, for *your* needs, is essential, but is totally absent in the highest rated product or service. In sum, look at every facet that has been rated, not just the overall rating, which—it bears repeating—is simply the average of each facet that is rated.

CONTACT INFORMATION

A list at the end of each chapter provides the phone numbers—and in some cases the Internet addresses—relevant to getting additional information about the products or services. Local offices, technical information and other pertinent information can be obtained by using these lists. In researching the products and services, we've often found that information provided by sales agents is not always accurate. Technicians or customer services representatives that can be reached by using the Contact Information are likely to be more helpful and we therefore recommend that you contact them with questions, rather than local vendors, even though you eventually might have to contact them to make your purchase.

COURIER SERVICES,

DOMESTIC DESTINATIONS

At last, there are viable alternatives to giant Federal Express (FedEx), once considered by many as the best. Their past promise, "Absolutely, positively overnight," cannot be counted upon now. Under certain conditions, normal first-class U.S. mail can arrive at the same destination at the same time as a FedEx "overnight letter," which they've failed to deliver as promised—and at cost which is 84-times greater than the cost of a 32-cent stamp. United Parcel Service (UPS), is a viable, perhaps better alternative for overnight mail, especially with their standard "by-10:30 am" delivery, whereas FedEx charges extra for delivery by 10:30. Also, be advised to look into the U.S. Postal Service (USPS), which—amazing to "snail mail" haters—can do some things that private couriers cannot. (Delivering on Sundays and holidays are two of them.)

Several other companies have found a place in the courier market and have jumped into the lucrative business both by offering similar services as well as focusing their operations on various specialty services.

UPS leads the list of courier services because they now have an almost comparable range of services to FedEx and have well-established overnight networks. The two giant companies specialize in slightly different areas: FedEx in small envelop/documents, though UPS now does basically the same thing, and does it as well, some say even better. UPS is the undisputed leader in quality when it comes to larger parcels delivered via ground transportation.

Bigness has gone to FedEx's head and if you don't want to deal with an "attitude" try UPS, which offers similar services, and seems to value customer satisfaction more than FedEx. If you have been inadvertently misinformed by an FedEx agent or representative, the company will not always make amends. Be careful! FedEx can deliver good service, but sometimes not as good as UPS. If FedEx doesn't deliver when an agent has promised, for example, they can demand payment anyway (or refuse to refund your money). One of their agents may tell you delivery by a certain time is guaranteed, and you don't have to pay if it's not, but the onus is on the customer to prove FedEx dropped the ball. If you can't, the decision of who's right and who's wrong is theirs, and FedEx has a history of backing their employees and not necessarily their customers.

Most of the domestic couriers have volume discounts. UPS, in particular, is getting more competitive in this area in order to compete with FedEx for overnight small-package deliveries. Those who haven't checked recently are advised to compare UPS to FedEx. Overall, UPS may fit business needs better than Fed Ex, whose quality service has diminished. UPS on the other hand, is improving service and is historically good in customer relations.

The best services which these two companies offer comes with a price. FedEx and UPS do offer the broadest range of delivery services, but where they hold exclusive delivery rights or offer the "only service available" the prices can be steep or the service inefficient. For the bargain hunters and those who have the time to consider other options, less expensive prices can be obtained by consulting the other services.

New since the UPS strike in the summer of 1997 are early-bird deliveries offered by various couriers and three-day services, the latter apparently designed to compete with UPS, the dominant company for over-the-road, small package deliveries.

Few people know about "Same-Day" service, which, though expensive can be a life saver, if the cost can be justified. Rates for this service generally start at $150 for air service. You can expect to pay $50 and up for over-the-road Same-Day service.

OVERALL RATINGS

United Parcel Service (UPS)	★★★★
Airborne Express	★★★1/2
Burlington Air Express	★★★1/2
Federal Express (FedEx)	★★★ 1/2
U.S. Postal Service	★★★ 1/2
DHL Worldwide Express	★★★
Emery Worldwide	★★★

Roadway Package System (RPS)	★★ 1/2

EXPLANATION OF RATINGS

The companies above were rated from one to four stars for the following aspects of their services: Range of Services, Reliability, Reasonable Cost, Efficiency and Tracking (via their Internet web site). The data shown below was culled at press time from the courier's websites . It is recommended that users consult these websites as things can change quickly in this industry.

ALPHABETICAL DESCRIPTIONS

Airborne Express
Overall Rating ★★★1/2
Range of Services ★★★★
Reliability ★★★
Reasonable Cost ★★★★
Efficiency ★★★
Tracking ★★★★

Airborne Express is third-largest overnight delivery company in the country. It is efficient at delivering to businesses, but not recommended for delivery to private homes or small businesses. One downside pertaining to home delivery is that the company will not allow the parties at the destinations to waive their signature. This can mean that if they are not present when the driver arrives, the package will not be left and usually that translates to an additional day of waiting for redelivery.

For packages up to two lbs. and traveling less than 150 miles, Airborne is the best service for the price. Longer distances and larger packages (up to seven lbs.), are chared at a flat-rate. Recommended when using this service: open an account. Even if shipping infrequently, an open account entitles you to published rates available and discounts. Same-day service is also available.

Burlington Air Express

Overall Rating ★ ★ ★ 1/2
Range of Services ★ ★ ★
Reliability ★ ★ ★ ★
Reasonable Cost ★ ★ ★
Efficiency ★ ★ ★ ★
Tracking ★ ★ ★ ★

Burlington Air Express is one of the largest air freight shippers in the country. The company focuses on delivering heavy and over-sized shipments over 200 lbs, it is still cost-effective for smaller packages, particularly if you can allow two to three days for delivery.

DHL Worldwide Express

Overall Rating ★ ★ ★
Range of Services ★ ★ ★
Reliability ★ ★ ★
Reasonable Cost ★ ★ ★
Efficiency ★ ★ ★
Tracking ★ ★ ★

DHL focused much more of its business on the international scale, which is where it excels. Domestic deliveries, however, are competitive. Extensive networks exist nationally and pricing is comparable with Federal Express and the service DHL offers (USA Overnight) is generally reliable.

Emery Worldwide

Overall Rating ★ ★ ★
Range of Services ★ ★ ★
Reliability ★ ★ ★
Reasonable Cost ★ ★ ★
Efficiency ★ ★ ★
Tracking ★ ★ ★

Emery offers a very competitive pricing plan for package delivery; that is, if it's a heavy package. Small packages are expensive. Best service is notable for morning deliveries of packages over 50 lbs. Less urgent shipments utilizing Emery's Time-Definite Deferred plan with 2-3 day delivery is highly cost-effective and especially recommended for items moving long distance shipments. It's not the choice for small, overnight packages.

Federal Express (FedEx)

Overall Rating ★ ★ ★ 1/2
Range of Services ★ ★ ★ ★
Reliability ★ ★ ★
Reasonable Cost ★ ★ ★ ★
Efficiency ★ ★ ★
Tracking ★ ★ ★ ★

Federal Express is the largest shipping company in the world and acts like it, which has its upside and downside. The downside—primarily an attitude of indifference to their customers—may be annoying if there's been a problem and there are often many when one ships lots of packages.

The company has the most extensive network, and the greatest variety of services (some very expensive). The FedEx "First Overnight" program, which provides delivery before 8:00 am in most major cities, is an exceptional service. It also offers (for not too big of a premium) a 10:30 arrival. However competitor UPS, delivers small packages by 10:30 am as a policy, and not for a premium like FedEX. Same-day service is also available.

FedEx also provides real-time shipping data on an easily accessible web site. Frequent shippers get discounts, but if you are not a heavy user of this service, more cost-effective companies for your needs may be worth researching. In some cities the company does not deliver early (by 8:00 am or 10:30 am), and this limitation is often not communicated well with customers or agents. But you'll still have to pay for it as FedEx is not particularly sensitive to customer complaints about broken promises.

Roadway Package System (RPS)

Overall Rating ★ ★ 1/2

Range of Services ★ ★

Reliability ★ ★ ★

Reasonable Cost ★ ★ ★

Efficiency ★ ★

Tracking ★ ★ ★

Roadway Package System (RPS) is a recent addition in the courier services and offers some limited, but excellent services. RPS does not offer over-night delivery but the two day service offered is quite competitive. Best recommendation is for two day shipping and utilize other carriers if overnight is required.

United Parcel Service (UPS)

Overall Rating ★ ★ ★ ★

Range of Services ★ ★ ★ ★

Reliability ★ ★ ★ ★

Reasonable Cost ★ ★ ★ ★

Efficiency ★ ★ ★ ★

Tracking ★ ★ ★ ★

United Parcel Service (UPS) is the world's largest parcel delivery service and offers overnight service to more locations in the U.S. than all other carriers combined. The extensive range of UPS as well as the number of service options available earns the high rating noted. The most recommended services are second day air and three day select. Also, if your company does a lot of shipping, consolidating all shipping needs utilizing UPS exclusively earns substantial discounts and deals. UPS offers zone pricing which can become expensive as the range increases. Small shippers are encouraged to use UPS strategically and look to other carriers for better bargains when shipping longer distances. Same-Day service is also available.

U.S. Postal Service

Overall Rating ★ ★ ★ 1/2

Range of Services ★ ★ ★ ★

Reliability ★ ★ ★

Reasonable Cost ★ ★ ★ ★

Efficiency ★ ★ ★

Tracking ★ ★ ★

The U.S. Postal Service earns a reasonable rating because of the extraordinary reach of its services. In response to competitive pressure of the above delivery services, the USPS has expanded its offerings to include express mail (overnight) and priority mail (2 - 3 day) along with its regular service. USPS has an absolute lock on regular mail and it is the exclusive server of the U. S. Armed Forces. The postal service is also the best, and sometimes only, choice for holiday and Sunday deliveries.

CONTACT INFORMATION

Airborne Express
(800) Airborne {247-2676]
Same-Day: (Sky Courier)(800) 336-3344
www.airborne-express.com

Burlington Air Express
(800) CALL-BAX (800-225-5229)
www.baxworld.com

DHL Worldwide Express
(800) CALL-DHL (800-225-5345)
Same-Day: (800) DHL-ASAP (800-345-2727)
www.dhl.com

Emery Worldwide
(800) HI-EMERY (800-443-6379)
www.emeryworld.com

Federal Express (FedEx)
(800) GO-FEDEX (800-463-3339)
Same-Day: (800) 399-5999
www.fedex.com

Roadway Package System (RPS)
(800) ROAD-PAK (800-762-3725)
www.shiprps.com

TNT Express
(800) 558-5555
www.tnt.com

United Parcel Service (UPS)
(800) PICK-UPS (800-742-5877)
Same-Day: (800) 451-4550
www.ups.com

U.S. Postal Service
(800) 222-1811
Web Site: www.usps.gov

COURIER SERVICES,

INTERNATIONAL DESTINATIONS

International shipping is significantly different than shipping within the U.S. The issue of passing through customs makes sending items across international borders more complex. The courier services that were rated in the preceding chapter pertaining to domestic service all offer international delivery service, but some have focused specifically on this and therefore rank differently than their domestic operations.

One of the caveats that international shippers need to know is the misnomer pertaining to their services. "Next Day" usually means that a package is delivered in two days, due, in part, to time changes that translate to the very next day (local time overseas) dawning just a few hours after the time it is shipped in the U.S. One must also factor in the time it takes to clear customs. In sum, most international shipments require two calendar days for delivery.

"Same Day" service is the closest thing to getting a package to its destination overnight. However, it *is* possible to get a

Though it's not a familiar sight in the U.S., the trucks of DHL Worldwide Express are ubiquitous overseas. DHL is the number-one choice for international shipments.

package to its destination the same day, if it is shipped early enough in the morning. In real terms, however, "Same Day" means the next calendar day. "Same Day" is also very, very expensive, costing several hundred dollars, on average.

Below are the major international couriers with their overall ratings for international service.

OVERALL RATINGS

DHL Worldwide Express	★ ★ ★ ★
Burlington Air Express	★ ★ ★ 1/2
United Parcel Service (UPS)	★ ★ ★ 1/2
U.S. Postal Service	★ ★ ★ 1/2
TNT Express	★ ★ ★
Federal Express (FedEx)	★ ★ ★
Airborne Express	★ ★ ★
Emery Worldwide	★ ★ ★
Roadway Package System (RPS)	★ ★

EXPLANATION OF RATINGS

The companies above were rated from one to four stars for the following aspects of their services: Range of Services, Reliability, Reasonable Cost, Efficiency, and Tracking (via their Internet web site). The data shown below was culled at press time from the courier's websites. It is recommended that users consult these websites as things can change quickly in this industry.

ALPHABETICAL DESCRIPTIONS

Airborne Express

Overall Rating ★ ★ ★	
Range of Services ★ ★ ★	
Reliability ★ ★ ★	
Reasonable Cost ★ ★ ★	
Efficiency ★ ★ ★	
Tracking ★ ★ ★	

Airborne Express offers competitive international shipping for small packages (up to 70 lbs.) almost everywhere in the world. Their Canada operations are highly developed, therefore, they are recommended for this destination. Though they have no same-day service, their sister company Sky Courier offers this service, though no rating is offered for them.

Burlington Air Express

Overall Rating ★ ★ ★ 1/2	
Range of Services ★ ★ ★ ★	
Reliability ★ ★ ★	
Reasonable Cost ★ ★ ★	
Efficiency ★ ★ ★ ★	
Tracking ★ ★ ★ 1/2	

Burlington Air Express offers a wide range of services in the international arena. The best services are noted for delivering non-dutiable packages to Mexico and most of Western Europe. BAX also offers Time Definite Premiere service which provides fast service to several regions of the world. BAX has more than 100 offices worldwide; however, it should be noted that BAX only delivers to business locations. Residential delivery must utilize another carrier. Shipping heavy packages internationally, business to business, is the best application of this service and is most highly recommended.

DHL Worldwide Express

Overall Rating ★★★★

Range of Services ★★★★

Reliability ★★★★

Reasonable Cost ★★★

Efficiency ★★★★

Tracking ★★★★

DHL is the leader in the international delivery business, which is its main focus. The company has more than 1,600 offices worldwide and has inroads at establishing operations which make it especially efficient in this area. Real-time package tracking is available for all international shipments. DHL can be expensive for certain priority services. Companies that are sending non-urgent materials may find better rates with other services.

Emery Worldwide

Overall Rating ★★★

Range of Services ★★★

Reliability ★★★

Reasonable Cost ★★★

Efficiency ★★★

Tracking ★★★

Emery offers a very cost-effective program for shipping packages internationally. Shipping to Canada is highly recommended via Emery. International Express service is designed to deliver larger packages almost anywhere in the world within two days to one week.

Federal Express (FedEx)

Overall Rating ★★★

Range of Services ★★★

Reliability ★★

Reasonable Cost ★★★

Efficiency ★★

Tracking ★★★★

Federal Express still has a way to go in the international arena. Most notable is their lack of same day service, which translates to their best service taking two days for delivery. Competitor DHL has more connections and offices overseas; however, FedEx operates a very competitive International Priority program, if you can allow two calendar days for delivery. FedEx offers real-time tracking for international packages.

Roadway Package System (RPS)

Overall Rating ★★

Range of Services ★★

Reliability ★★★

Reasonable Cost ★★★

Efficiency ★

Tracking ★

The company primarily specializes in domestic, over-the-road service, in the same vein as UPS ground service. RPS offers shipping to Europe; however, a seven-day ship time does not make it compelling for consideration as a player in the international market.

TNT Express

Overall Rating ★★★

Range of Services ★★★

Reliability ★★★★

Reasonable Cost ★★

Efficiency ★★★

Tracking ★★★

TNT Express offers excellent service from the major U.S. cities to European markets. Guaranteed delivery before 9:00 AM is offered at more than 640 locations throughout Europe. Bulk rates can be arranged to various major cities and is worth looking into for heavy mailers to Europe. The company also offers same day service.

United Parcel Service (UPS)

Overall Rating ★★★1/2
Range of Services ★★★★
Reliability ★★★★
Reasonable Cost ★★★
Efficiency ★★★
Tracking ★★★★

UPS offers a wide range of services in the international market and also will send from more locations in the U.S. than any other carrier. UPS offers a premium service, Worldwide Express Plus, that guarantees delivery before 8:00 AM to many international business centers. Same day service is also available.

U.S. Postal Service

Overall Rating ★★★1/2
Range of Services ★★★
Reliability ★★★★
Reasonable Cost ★★★★
Efficiency ★★★
Tracking ★★★

Since clout is important in international shipping, the U.S. Postal Service has high marks. It also has exclusive reach into APO & FPO addresses as well as Sunday and Holiday delivery services. USPS offers competitive prices for overseas shipping with its International Express Mail

service. Government limitations do not allow the Postal Service to offer corporate discounts; however, for infrequent shippers it should be considered.

CONTACT INFORMATION

Airborne Express
(800) ABX-INTL (800-229-4685
Same Day: (Sky Courier) (800) 789-8988
(800) 336-3344
www.airborne-express.com

Burlington Air Express
(800) CALL-BAX (800-225-5229)
Same Day: 800 DHL-ASAP (800-345-2727)
www.baxworld.com

DHL Worldwide Express
(800) CALL-DHL (800-225-5345)
Same Day: (800) DHL-ASAP (800-345-2727)
www.dhl.com

Emery Worldwide
(800) 323-4685
www.emeryworld.com

Federal Express (FedEx)
(800) 247-4747
www.fedex.com

Roadway Package System
(800) ROAD-PAK (800-762-3725)
Web Site: www.shiprps.com

TNT Express
(800) 558-5555
Same Day: (800) 677-4444
www.tnt.com

United Parcel Service (UPS)
(800) 782-7892
Same Day: (800) 451-4550
www.ups.com

U.S. Postal Service
(800) 222-1811
Web Site: www.usps.gov

LONG DISTANCE CARRIERS,

DOMESTIC SERVICE

Long distance telephone service was expected to get easier to figure out after passage of the Telecommunications Act in 1996. However, the marketplace is even noisier almost two years after passage of the bill than it was before. With the explosion of Internet usage, never has there been a greater reliance on telephone lines to exchange information.

Telephone deregulation began in the 1980s. Before then, the one, single phone company in the United States was AT&T. In 1984 they were forced to split up into what became known as "Baby Bells," which paved the way for major competitors such as MCI and Sprint. The Telecommunications Act of 1996 took deregulation even further, opening local markets to competition and at the same time allowing the Baby Bells to enter other markets. The result has been mergers among the Baby Bells and a refiguring of the market between local and long distance service providers.

There are three categories of long distance service providers: those carriers that maintain their own facilities, such as telephone lines and switching equipment; resellers who lease lines from other companies and resell their use to end us-

ers; and aggregators, who recruit groups of 50 to 100 clients for the purpose of negotiating a contract with a long distance carrier for group discounts. The long distance carriers the public is most familiar with — AT&T, Sprint and MCI — are carriers of the first type, maintaining their own network of lines and switches. Other companies in this category include Cable & Wireless, Frontier, LCI, and LDDS World Com.

This chapter focuses on the larger carriers who maintain their own lines and switches. For a consumer, there isn't much difference in technology between the carriers. The larger companies market themselves based on three criteria: transmission quality, service, and reliability. Transmission quality is that aspect of a telephone call you don't notice unless its quality is degraded. In the early days of deregulation AT&T owned and operated the best lines and switches while its competitors had to patch together the leftovers. Along with the fiber-optic cables came new digital switches to replace the older analog switches. With these new improvements available across the board, it is difficult to distinguish between carriers on the basis of transmission quality.

The same holds true of service. Immediately after deregulation, the newer companies had to play catch-up with the vast experience of AT&T. The result was the weeding out of those companies that couldn't provide adequate service. There are several things to look at now to determine the level of service provided by an individual carrier. One factor is the availability of technical support. Some carriers feature 24-hour service, others are available only during business hours. Another feature worth looking into is operator service. If you don't plan on using such operator-dependent services as international calling or collect dialing, then you might save money by signing with a service that doesn't offer such a feature.

Finally, reliability. Even the biggest, most advanced systems will break down occasionally. Most often it is for no longer than 15 minutes. The key issue is how well the service can fix the problems when they occur. Most of the carriers now feature built-in safeguards that can quickly fix any problem shortly after it occurs. As a last resort, you can always access another carrier by simply dialing their five-digit access code. Trying to compare long distance programs on the basis of cost can be a daunting task. Charges vary according to region and the type of plan offered. Basically, there are three factors that make up long distance costs. One is the basic cost of making the long distance connection, which is composed of the basic cost of leasing the line or maintaining the infrastructure. Another factor is the local access charge, the amount the local telephone company charges a long distance carrier each time you are connected to the long distance network. And the third factor is either profit or costs related to serving the account.

Monthly charges, however, reflect more than the basic costs and are dependent on such factors as monthly volume, average distance of calls, and the percentage of calls during peak time periods. To determine which service is best for you requires a knowledge of your business's calling patterns.

The following ratings were based on criteria discussed in "Explanation of Ratings" and derived from data provided by the individual carriers and Beacon Research Group. Because each carrier's rates are determined by so many vari-ables, the criteria used were those that could be applied across the board.

Below are "low volume" plans (under 3,000 minutes monthly) and "high volume" plans (over 3,000 minutes monthly) distinguish between those services suited to those particular situations.

OVERALL RATINGS

Under 3,000 Minutes Per Month

LDDS World Com/ World One	★★★★
AT&T Small Business Advantage	★★★★
LCI Alternative	★★★

Over 3,000 Minutes Per Month

LCI Simply Business/ Option A	★★★
Sprint Business Sense	★★★
MCI One	★★★
Frontier Clear Value	★★★

EXPLANATION OF RATINGS

Since the primary factor in considering which long distance service is cost, most of the criteria used to rate the carriers weighed the variables that influence charges. The following criteria were used:

Discounts: Most carriers offer three different kinds of discounts. The most advantageous for one kind of user may not be the most advantageous for another. Volume discounts are offered to users who exceed a certain amount of calls per month. For businesses with heavy volumes of calls, this discount would be helpful. Another kind of discount is the term discount, given for those subscribers who sign up for a guaranteed period of time, such as one to three years. A third type of discount is the regional, in which the carrier offers a discount for calls to a particular geographical area. We weighed the volume and regional discounts as more valuable than the term for most users.

Rate Programs: Carriers offer two types of rate programs. The flat-rate program charges a flat rate for calls within the United States, though they may offer discounts for calls between certain times. Banded-rate programs charge calls based on the distance between user and recipient. We weighed the banded programs slightly higher since they offer more control over costs than the flat rate.

Monthly Service Charge: Some programs have a monthly service charge and some don't. Those with no charge scored higher than those with a monthly charge.

Monthly Minimum: Some programs require a monthly minimum billing in order to sign up for a particular program. Those with lower monthly minimums were given higher ratings in this category.

ALPHABETICAL DESCRIPTIONS

AT&T Small Business Advantage
Overall Rating ★ ★ ★ ★

Despite deregulation and the growth of competition, AT&T is still the largest long distance carrier in the country. They market aggressively and are certainly worth checking out when determining which carrier to choose. Their Small Business Advantage offers both volume and term discounts and no monthly minimum requirement. Though in most programs AT&T may have the higher rate per minute, they do offer discounts and a low monthly service charge that is easily waived.

Frontier Clear Value
Overall Rating ★ ★ ★

Frontier is a relative newcomer to the long distance field, the result of the merger between RCI and Allnet in 1995. Originally a local service provider (for Rochester, N.Y.), Frontier has grown primarily by acquisition of other regional carriers. Their Clear Value plan is a flat-rate program that offers discounts for those subscribers able to commit to at least a one year term. The Clear Value plan is most appropriate for those companies with high volume of long distance calls.

LCI Alternative
Overall Rating ★ ★ ★

LCI International is an aggressive long distance service marketer with four calling programs available. Their Alternative program features both volume and term discounts and a low monthly service charge. The Alternative program is suitable for businesses with low calling volumes.

LCI Simply Business
Overall Rating ★ ★ ★

LCI's Simply Business offers several options with varying term discounts. One feature is their six-second billing increments, the lowest in the field. Their Option A program, for examples, features no monthly minimum and attractive pricing structure.

LDDS World Com World One
Overall Rating ★ ★ ★ ★

LDDS World Com is the fourth largest long distance carrier in the country, with a reputation for having consistently low rates. Their World one program features both volume and term discounts with no monthly minimums and no service charge. The program is well suited for low- and mid-volume callers, those with less than 3,000 calls per month.

MCI One
Overall Rating ★ ★ ★

MCI is the country's second-largest telecommunications company. MCI One is one of the company's newer programs and features no monthly minimum, a flat rate and a low monthly service charge. Unlike most other programs, MCI One uses full 60-second billing increments.

Sprint Business Sense
Overall Rating ★ ★ ★

Sprint Communications is right behind number two MCI as the nation's third largest carrier. Sprint Business Sense features term discounts, no monthly service charge, and varying minimums. Business Sense and the other Sprint programs are most suitable for high-volume users.

CONTACT INFORMATION

AT&T
(800) 222-0400

Frontier
(800) 836-0808

LCI
(800) 860-1020

LDDS World Com
(800) 539-2000

MCI
(800) 950-5555

Sprint Communications
(800) 877-4646

LONG DISTANCE CARRIERS,

INTERNATIONAL SERVICE

For businesses involved in the global economy, international telephone and fax calls are critical to their success. Excessive rate charges, poor quality, and unreliable connections are all possible if a company chooses the wrong international calling service. International calls work the same way domestic calls do —there is an international access code, a country code, a city code and maybe one other before you can dial the actual phone number. Those initial numbers direct the call either over phone lines or via satellite to ensure your call gets to its destination and it only takes a matter of seconds.

The international calling scene is undergoing crucial changes in the United States. Legislation is under review that would open up the market even further, with the end result being lower fares for international calls. As it is now, the largest players in the international calling market are the same firms that dominate the domestic calling market—AT&T, Cable and Wireless, Frontier, MCI, Sprint, LCI, and LDDS WorldCom.

There are two alternatives to the usual calling programs. The first option is international callback. International callback works this way: a caller places a call to the service bureau from a previously designated phone number. The caller then hangs up and waits for a call back from the service. When the call comes through, the user picks up the phone and is patched into an available line to complete his or her call. This option works fine for firms large enough to have a specific place and phone to place these calls from, and have enough use for them to make them efficient.

Another option is via the Internet. Most businesses can connect to anywhere in the world via the Internet for no more than a local phone call. Another advantage is that the Internet, even with a relatively slow 14.4 bps modem, can carry much more information than a voice line. With the right hardware, voice calls can be made anywhere in the world for the cost of a local phone call. There are several firms making hardware and software to enable computers to link up with voice. One is VocalTec, which markets a software program that, along with a microphone and a sound card, a PC can use to communicate over the Internet just like a phone. Another program is Webtalk. See the "Additional Information" box at the end of this report for the addresses of these options.

The carriers in this study were evaluated according to four criteria: access, line quality, features and pricing. Access refers to the number of countries reached by a particular carrier. There is little difference between carriers in this category, except when it comes to calling very small, remote countries in the less developed third world. For most businesses dealing with companies in the more developed countries of Europe, South America, and Asia, access is not an issue. Quality is another factor that is not the issue it used to be. Most phone lines are of high quality, even to Europe and Asia. Some carriers offer other features as a selling point, such as call accounting and detailed billing. Interpreters are another feature that can be useful to firms doing business overseas. Pricing is the one aspect of international calling that differs the most from carrier to carrier and from country to country. Therefore, when shopping for an international calling service, it is a good idea to check what features are provided with the service.

Listed below are eight calling programs and their overall scores.

RANKINGS AND OVERALL SCORES

1	Sprint Business Sense	93
2	LDDS WorldCom WorldOne	88
3	Cable & Wireless Business First Int'l	81
4	Sprint Clarity	80
5	LCI Simply Guaranteed	79
6	Frontier Clear Value Int'l Optional	76
7	MCI Preferred Worldwide	71
8	AT&T Global Business Advantage	65

EXPLANATION OF RATINGS

International calling programs were compared using the following criteria, with the highest possible score in parentheses:

Company (40 pts): Telephone carriers that dominate the international market tend to be the same ones that dominate the domestic market. Carriers were judged on access, line quality, features and pricing, with a highest possible score of 40 points.

Single Country Rate (10 pts): Some programs charge a flat rate for calls to each country. These rates are the same no matter where in the country you call or what time of day. This feature was worth 10 points.

Auto Enroll (5 pts): Some companies automatically include enrollment in their international service when you sign up for their domestic service, at no extra charge. Such a service was worth five points.

Billing Increments (5 pts.): Although most carriers base their billing on 30-second increments, the range was from 18 seconds to 60 seconds. Generally the less time the better for the caller being billed, since those extra seconds can add up over a month's time. The highest possible score was five points for this feature.

Monthly Service Charge (10 pts): Some calling services include a monthly service charge that ranges from $3 up to $20. The lower the service charge, the higher the score, with the highest possible score being 10 points.

Monthly Minimum (10 pts): Some programs require a volume minimum to qualify for the plan, ranging from $5 to $15,000. The less required, the higher the score, worth a total of 10 points.

Minimum Term (10 pts): Many plans require a minimum commitment in time to participate in the calling plan, ranging from no minimum to three years. The less time the higher the score, up to 10 points.

Required Domestic Program (10 pts): Some international calling plans are only available with an accompanying domestic program. Those international plans that did not require participation in a domestic plan received the entire 10 points while those requiring such participation received only five points.

ALPHABETICAL DESCRIPTIONS

AT&T Global Business Advantage

Rank 8

AT&T remains the largest long distance carrier in the United States, despite its court-ordered breakup years ago. Their Global Business Advantage is available to participants in their Small Business Advantage Plus and CustomNet domestic plans. The plan results in 15 to 30 percent reductions off AT&T's regular international rates. However, studies have found AT&T rates to be among the highest across the board. Still, their Global Business Advantage makes sense for companies with employees who travel extensively all over the world rather than to the same foreign location repeatedly. The plan requires a $5 monthly minimum and offers no single country rate. AT&T scored high on services, but

whether that is worth the higher rates must be considered.

Cable & Wireless Business First Int'l

Rank 3

Cable & Wireless, despite its lack of name recognition, is the sixth-largest long distance carrier in the United States and one of the leaders in the market in the United Kingdom. Participants in Cable & Wireless's Business First domestic plan are automatically enrolled in the international program. The plan requires a minimum volume of $100 per month, with a $25 service charge for customers who fall below that amount. The Business First International uses a complex discounting structure based on such factors as which phone number, country, or part of the world is most often called. Despite its complexity, the plan is probably best suited for firms with international calling volumes between 150-300 minutes per month, and especially if those calls are predominantly to a single country. The company seems most competitive in their rates to Europe.

Frontier Clear Value Int'l Optional

Rank 6

Frontier started out as a local and long distance provider in the Rochester, NY area, and, after a merger with Allnet is now the fifth-largest long distance carrier in the country. Frontier offers two international plans under the Clear Value banner. Clear Value Basic is the international plan businesses are automatically enrolled in when they sign on for the domestic service. Clear Value International Optional, however, is a better deal, with rates 30 to 40 percent lower than Clear Value Basic with an extra $4.95 monthly service charge. Frontier Clear Value International Optional is a good choice for low-volume users who call most often to Europe and/or South America. Its rates to Mexico are the best at any volume level.

LCI Simply Guaranteed

Rank 5

LCI is one of the fastest growing telecommunications companies in the United States. Their Simply Guaranteed program, unlike others, uses flat rates and no monthly fee, but requires a one- or two-year commitment. However, unlike other companies, LCI does guarantee both the rate and the discounts for the length of the term agreement. Simply Guaranteed is suitable for businesses whose volume exceeds 350 minutes per month, with most of those calls to Europe.

LDDS WorldCom WorldOne

Rank 2

LDDS WorldCom is now the fourth-largest long distance carrier in the United States. It offers two international programs: WorldOne and WorldForce. WorldOne is the plan businesses are automatically enrolled in when they sign on for the LDDS domestic service. WorldForce offers more competitive rates for heavy-volume users who can commit to a minimum term. WorldOne features a single country rate and no monthly service charge or minimum.

MCI Preferred Worldwide

Rank 7

MCI's record in the international market has been spotty, with the company appearing unsure of a marketing strategy. At the time the data were compiled, MCI only offered Preferred Worldwide as its international calling service. This program did not require enrollment in MCI's domestic program, but there was a $5 monthly service charge. Rates in general were not very competitive with other international carriers.

Sprint Business Sense

Rank 1

Sprint is the third-largest carrier in the United States and has only recently focused on the international market. Sprint offers several plans, all of them quite complicated, using different rates depending on volume, time of day, and other variables. Business Sense, however, is a simple plan with outstanding rates for low volume callers. For businesses whose volume is less than 150 calls per month, Sprint Business Sense is the best deal, especially if those calls are predominantly to Europe and Asia. Business Sense offers single country rates for no monthly service charge or minimum.

Sprint Clarity

Rank 4

Sprint Clarity is a bit more complicated than Business Sense, but less complicated than Sprint's massive VPN plans. Clarity offers competitive rates, but at a monthly service charge of between $10 and $20.

For high-volume users, Sprint Clarity is worth investigating.

CONTACT INFORMATION

AT&T
(800) 222-0400

Cable & Wireless
(800) 486-8686
Frontier
(800) 836-8080

LCI
800) 860-1020

LDDS WorldCom
(800) 539-2000

MCI
(800) 950-5555

Sprint
(800) 877-7253

VALUABLE RESOURCES

For more information on international callback services call Telegroup in Fairfield, IA at (319) 469-5000. For more information on Internet calling services you can reach the VocalTec software web site at *http://www.vocaltec.com/* or you can call them at (201) 768-9400. Webtalk is the full duplex package offered by Quarterdeck of Marina del Ray, CA. They can be reached online at *http://www.qdeck.com/* or by telephone at (310) 309-4210.

OFFICE COPIERS,

OVERVIEW

Photocopiers are complex machines that require care and maintenance to perform adequately. In most offices today, copiers are taken for granted and used by everyone, from the secretary to the CEO. Because it is used so often by so many people, it is no surprise that the copier is the one machine in the office most likely to break down. For this reason, choosing a copier can be more complicated than just choosing the model you want, because it is also necessary to consider the company's dealership and service reputation, and perhaps negotiate a service contract or guarantee you can live with.

NEW VS. USED

If the current copier in your office is older than five years, there is a good chance you will need a new one within a year. Especially if the copier has been used moderately, meaning a volume one-half to two-thirds of the manufacturer's maximum rating. Copiers used more than that tend to wear out sooner; those used less than that, later.

If you haven't purchased a copier in several years, you may be in for a shock when you look at the price tag. One cost-saving possibility is to buy a used or remanufactured copier. The primary advantage is cost—used copiers sell for as much as 30 percent less than an equivalent new one. However, before committing yourself to a used copier, there are some questions you should ask.

First, how extensively has the machine been restored? Some companies rebuild the machine from the ground up, replacing dozens of parts, fixing up the exterior, and resetting the copier counter to zero. This is basically a new machine in an old casing. Both Xerox and Kodak remanufacture and sell such machines.

Most dealers, however, prefer to sell refurbished copiers rather than undertaking such extensive rebuilding. This is where the buyer must beware. Determine what the particular dealer's definition of "refurbished" is before buying. Also, make sure your service contract and warranty are from the dealer selling you the machine and not some third party. This will insure that the company servicing the machine is the one most familiar with it.

A good source to review before buying a used or refurbished copier is the Copier Blue Book (Assay Publishing, 800-395-0222), which lists average wholesale and retail prices for used copiers. Each book costs $59, and there is a fax option for $8.95.

Buying a new copier can be just as daunting as buying a used or rebuilt one. Currently, about 18 different companies compete in the office copier industry. Although most of them manufacture their own models, some companies relabel other manufacturers models and sell them under their own name. Because the copier market has been flat for the past five years, some companies, like A.B. Dick and Kodak, have either moved out of the market completely or have sold their sales and service operations.

Most manufacturers focus on a specific market niche. Copiers are categorized by their speed, as measured by copies per minute (CPM), from low to high. At the high end of the market, machines that operate over 45 CPM, are three of the leading manufacturers— Xerox, Kodak and Océ. The mid-range includes copiers that operate at 20 to 45 CPM. Many of the Japanese manufacturers such as Mita, Ricoh, Canon and Konica, aim for this market. At the low end of the scale, below 20 CPM, the market is dominated by Canon, but Sharp, Panasonic and Mita/Copystar are also key players.

One new wrinkle in the copier market is the advent of digital copiers. Digital copiers were designed to replace both the photocopier and the laser printer in large offices. The machine can make copies at speeds of 35 to 70 CPM, collate and staple, and print from any desktop or network computer. The quality of the copies is no better than analog copiers, since they usually output at 400 dots per inch (dpi) which is less than the standard 600 dpi of analog copiers. The advantage of digital copiers is their reliability. Since the copier only has to scan each original once, there is less wear on the feeder and originals. Also, digital copiers don't need sorter bins to collate and finish multiple sets of one document. Digital copiers cost about 20 to 30 percent more than standard copy machines.

Until digital copiers take over, you'll need to determine what standard copier to buy. The crucial feature here is speed. Low-speed copiers often have the same features as high-speed models, but they take longer to perform their functions. This can mean lower productivity if you have a busy office. The entire spectrum of speed runs from a low of 10 CPM to as fast as 100 CPM. Most experts agree there are 2 important points to remember: a) speed ratings should not be taken at face value but figured at about 70 percent of manufacturer's rating; and b) added features and options can dramatically slow copier performance.

The other major factor in determining what size copier to buy is the volume. Volume refers to the maximum number of copies the machine is rated to make per month without breaking down. Volume figures range from 800 copies per month on low-end machines to over 150,000 for some of the biggest office copiers.

Once you have determined the speed you want and the volume you need in a new copier, the next choice concerns which of the many features you need. A number of optional features have been added to the basic copier over the years, features that make the machine easier to use and more productive. These options usually cost extra, so it is important to determine which ones you really need.

FEEDERS

Probably the most important option is the feeder. A feeder allows you to make as many copies as you want without having to place each sheet individually on the copy glass. With a feeder, you simply place a stack of originals in the feeder and press a button. Document feeders come in two basic types. The most basic is the automatic document feeder, or ADF, which takes each page from the stack of originals and moves it onto the copying glass, then removes it after copies are made. An ADF option can cost anywhere from $1,200 to $2,500 extra, depending on the size of copier.

The other type is the recirculating automatic document feeder, or RADF. While an ADF is excellent for making one-sided copies, to make copies of both sides you will need an RADF. There are two options when buying an RADF. The basic RADF makes all the required copies of each page before moving on to the next page. An alternative method is that used by a recirculating document handler, or RDH. The RDH makes only one copy of each page but circulates through the document stack to make all copies required.

To produce collated sets using a RADF, you will need the extra expense of sorter bins to finish the job. But with an RDH, because of the way the feeder makes multiple copies, you do not need sorter bins. The disadvantage of the RDH is that because of the way it recirculates the document through the feeder, it can cause damage to the original document. Both RADFs and RDHs can cost up to $3,500, depending on size of copier.

OTHER FEATURES

One feature to consider when buying a copier is its paper supply. Obviously, the copier you buy should be able to hold and use the kinds of paper you use in your business. Some copiers have options for larger-sized paper such as 11-by-17-inch ledger size. In addition to the size of the paper, you want to make sure the copier you buy can hold multiple reams of paper, thus reducing the time spent on refills. If you make transparencies often, it may pay to find a copier that offers a bypass sheet feeder to hold such materials.

Another popular feature is duplex printing, in which the copier can automatically produce two-sided copies from one- or two-sided originals. Duplex printing works by first copying onto one page, and then flipping the copied sheet within the machine to accept an image on the reverse side. Duplex printing is useless without a feeder that can handle two-sided originals for copying.

Potential buyers need to consider the reduction/enlargement option, which allows images to be magnified or shrunk to better fit on the page. Most copiers offer this feature built in with preset levels, but advanced models offer a zoom lens that allows the image to be enlarged or reduced any percentage.

For those businesses which tend to do large outputs of long documents, sorting and collating capability must be considered. Sorters consist of a series of bins, anywhere from 10 to 40 bins to a set, that move up and down to catch the copies as they exit the machine. Some of these sorters come equipped with stapler attachments. Copiers equipped with RDH document feeders do not require sorters to collate copies since copies are automatically collated as they exit the machine.

SERVICE AND WARRANTY

Today's copiers come equipped with a variety of the above features. Choosing the right copier for your office means studying the options and picking the ones most applicable to your needs. However, no matter what options and features you've chosen, if the copier breaks down often and refuses to work smoothly, then it will not be productive and you will not be satisfied. Fortunately, today's copier manufacturers have fixed most technical bugs in their machines. The result is that there are few reliability differences between major manufacturers, but there are differences in each company's service and warranty programs.

All companies offer warranties, but they may differ in their details. The best warranties offer copier replacement if the customer is dissatisfied in any way. Lanier, Pitney-Bowes, and Xerox are companies leading the way in replacement policies. In addition to warranties, most copiers are sold with some kind of service plan, an agreement that the dealer will provide some kind of service on a regular basis. Most copiers require anywhere from eight to 20 maintenance visits a year. Even the best copiers can be expected to break down under heavy workloads three or four times a year.

Not all copiers may need service contracts. Generally, copiers with speeds below 20 CPM usually don't need as much maintenance; neither do copiers with no extra attachments, such as feeders or sorters.

CHOOSING A COPIER

Given all the variables, choosing a copier becomes a process of elimination. The most important factor is size. How many copies a month does your business usually make? How many copies a month will you need in the future? The copiers rated here are categorized by size, as measured by the number of copies a month they are capable of producing.

After deciding the size of machine you need, the next thing to look at is how the copier is used. Do you most often make single copies? Do you make copies of long documents? Do you need to copy onto ledger paper? The answers to these questions are important because they determine which features are needed. If you do a lot of single copies, then the first-copy speed becomes important. If you make copies of many multi-page documents then you need to look at the overall speed of the machine and the speed of the document feeder it comes with.

The copiers rated in the following sections are categorized by size and based on monthly copy volume. At the low end are those machines producing less than 15,000 pages per month, at the high end are copiers producing up to 75,000 pages per month

OFFICE COPIERS,

LOW-VOLUME

It is recommended that you read the chapter titled "Office Copiers, Overview" before reading the following.

Low-volume copiers are those able to turn out up to 15,000 copies per month. The following list contains 12 low-volume copiers, their rankings, and overall scores.

RANKINGS AND OVERALL SCORES

1	Pitney-Bowes Smart Image C170	84.8
2	Canon NP 6025	83.3
3	Mita DC 2355	82.3
4	Sharp SF 2022	80.6
5	Canon NP 6016	76.1
6	Mita DC 1856	76.0
7	Toshiba 1550	74.2
8	Pitney-Bowes 9023	69.3
9	Xerox 5021	67.0
10	Ricoh FT 4022	66.2
11	Konica 1120	59.5
12	Kodak Ektaprint 30	48.7

EXPLANATION OF RATINGS

Copiers in this category were evaluated on several criteria: reputation, service and warranty programs; basic options; and miscellaneous options. The highest possible score was 100 points. The following three "mega-features" were considered and weighted to establish the rankings: 1) *The manufacturer's general reputation* and its particular service and warranty programs were given a possible 40 points. 2) *Options* such as sorter or sorter/stapler, feeder, and duplex capability were each worth 10 points, to make a 30 point total for this set of features. 3) *Other important features* were worth six points each, for a total of 30 points. These features included copies per minute (CPM), feeder speed, standard and maximum paper capabilities, and the first-copy speed.

The specific point breakdown is as follows.

Company (40 points): Companies were rated Excellent, Good, Fair, or Poor based on their reliability, service and reputation. An important factor in a company's rating was the type of replacement guarantee. Pitney-Bowes and Xerox have the best guarantees in the industry, and were rated the highest.

Sorter (10 points): Sorters are necessary to help collate and finish multiple sets of copies. For copiers in this class, all the models charged extra for the sorter or sorter/stapler option. The price of a 10-bin sorter ranged from $1,100 to $1,500, plus extra for the stapler capability. For 20-bin sorters the extra charge ranged from $1,500 to $2,500. For some models the sorters required extra pedestals or cabinets to use.

Feeder (10 points): The feeder is perhaps the most important component of a copier, since it is during the feeding process that a copier can fail mechanically. The basic feeder component is the automatic document feeder, or ADF, which takes each page from the document stack and moves it onto the copying glass. After a copy is made, the document is removed automatically. A recirculating automatic document feeder (RADF) allows the user to copy from both sides of a document without removing it from the machine between copies. Since an RADF allows the user more options, this feature was worth 10 points, while the ADF was worth five.

Duplex (10 points): Duplex copying allows the copier to automatically produce two-sided copies from one or two-sided originals. Such a feature makes for less use of paper. Some models charge extra for the option, from $900 to $2,000.

Copies Per Minute (CPM) (6 points): The speed at which a copier can turn out copies is a crucial factor in a machine's productivity. Most users don't want to spend too much time waiting for their copies. The best on the market in this size made copies at a speed of 30 CPM.

Feeder Speed (6 points): Feeder speed represents the speed in copies per minute (CPM) of either the ADF or RADF feeder, using letter-sized originals. The feeder speed should match the copier's CPM, since a feeder that is faster will slow down the machine's CPM. The fastest on the market in this size had a CPM of 35.

Standard Paper (6 points): This category represents the copier's capacity to hold standard, letter-size paper. The best

on the market in this size could hold 1,200 sheets.

Maximum Paper (6 points): This category represents the capacity of the copier using all optional paper trays installed. The best on the market could hold 4,150 sheets.

First-Copy Speed (6 points) This category represents how many seconds it takes for the first original to be copied. The fastest on the market in this size made a copy in 4 seconds.

ALPHABETICAL DESCRIPTIONS

Canon NP 6016

Price $4,125

Rank 5

The Canon NP 6016 is on the high end of the price range, but it has a lot of features to give it a high ranking. Its 10-bin sorter/stapler option will cost an extra $1,300 ($1,100 for the sorter without stapler) but to use it requires the addition of either a $200 cabinet or a $900 cassette feeding module. An ADF feeder costs an extra $1,500, and an extra paper tray $800.

Canon NP 6025

Price $5,698

Rank 2

The Canon NP 6025 is full of features, although many of them cost extra. For example, duplex capability is available for $1,615, an ADF runs over $1,500 and an RADF just over $1,700. Both 10- and 20-bin sorter/stapler options are available for an additional $1,400 or $3,700 respectively, but the 20-bin sorter does require an optional $300 cabinet or a $1,000 paper deck pedestal. The NP 6025 CPM of 30 makes it one of the fastest, and a first-copy speed of only six seconds boosts its productivity.

Kodak Ektaprint 30

Price $6,770

Rank   12

Kodak has recently been trying to unload its copier operations, so the future of the company's commitment to copiers is uncertain. Traditionally, Kodak's most competitive share of the market was in the high-speed copiers. The Ektaprint 30, though it does have duplex capability, doesn't offer either a ADF or RADF feeder component. Yet its speed of 30 CPM is one of the fastest in its category.

Konica 1120

Price $4,510

Rank   11

Konica is a well-respected company in the copier field which offers both analog and digital models. The 1120, with a copies per minute speed of 20, is a bit slow compared to other in its category. An ADF option is an extra $1,500, but there is no RADF available. But with a standard paper capacity of 550 and a maximum paper capacity of 1,050, it would prove adequate for certain users who don't require duplex capability.

Mita DC 1856

Price $3,995

Rank   6

With a moderate CPM of 18, plus a host of optional features, the Mita DC 1856 is an excellent choice. Standard features include ledger-sized paper capability and a

zoom option. An ADF will cost an additional $1,400, while a second paper tray is an extra $500. The DC 1856 offers both a 10-bin sorter and a 10-bin sorter/stapler option for an additional $1,200 to $1,500.

Mita DC 2355

Price $4,995

Rank   3

Mita Copystar is the fourth largest manufacturer of copiers in the United States. The Mita DC 2355 has all the features necessary for a top ranking, including a maximum paper capacity of 4,550, far ahead of other copiers in its class. An ADF is available for an extra $1,300, and an RADF for an additional $1,600. For duplex capability, figure an additional $950. Mita offers both 10- and 20-bin sorter options for $1,100 and $1,500, respectively. Both sorter options come with added stapler capability. With its many options, the Mita DC 2355 can be customized for any office situation.

Pitney-Bowes Smart Image C170

Price $4,295

Rank   1

Pitney Bowes is well-known as the world's largest manufacturer of postage equipment, but they also make and sell other office equipment including copiers. The advantage of Pitney-Bowes is that they offer a strong replacement guarantee on their machines. This means they will replace any machine a customer is dissatisfied with. The Pitney-Bowes Smart Image C170 offers just about everything in a low-volume copier. It has ledger-sized paper capability. a 20-bin sorter and sorter/stapler option, and a maximum paper capacity of 2,050. The sorter alone will cost an additional $2,000, while the sorter/stapler runs for $3,500.

Pitney-Bowes 9023

Price $4,995

Rank 8

The Pitney-Bowes 9023 is actually a discontinued Mita copier. The 9023 speed of 22 copies per minute, and its first-copy speed of eight seconds (one of the slowest), makes it rather slow. It offers 10 or 20-bin sorter options for $1,300 and $1,700 respectively. An ADF is available for an additional $1,300. If you don't need duplex capability and quick copying, this machine is recommended on the basis of the company's excellent guarantee.

Ricoh FT 4022

Price $4,455

Rank 10

Ricoh is a major manufacturer of copiers, not only under its own name but also for companies like Gestetner and Savin. The FT 4022 offers an RADF for an additional $1,800. Ten- or 20-bin sorters are an option at $1,200 and $1,400, respectively, the 10-bin sorter available with stapler attachment. With a CPM of 27, the FT 4022, is a good choice if you don't need duplex capability. The model FT 4522 is the same as the 4022 but with duplex capability, at a base price of $6,115.

Sharp SF 2022

Price $5,795

Rank 4

Sharp Electronics, the third-largest copier company in terms of total copier placement, is especially strong in low-volume copiers. The SF 2022 is a speedy machine, with a first-copy speed of four seconds, one of the lowest in its category. It offers duplex capability for an extra $910. It offers both 10- and 20-bin sorter options for an additional $1,200 and $2,100, respectively. The SF 2022 comes with both an ADF ($1,100) and RADF ($1,800) option. The number of features, plus a maximum paper capacity of 2,550, make it a strong choice.

Toshiba 1550

Price $3,502

Rank 7

The 1550 is Toshiba' model with the most features in this class. The 1550 has ledger-sized paper capability and a zoom option at no extra charge. An ADF document feeder is available for an additional $1,200 and a 10-bin sorter for under $1,000. A second paper tray is also available for an additional $600. This model is a good choice for those needing ledger-sized capability and multi-page copying.

Xerox 5021

Price $4,950

Rank 9

Xerox is a name long associated with copy machines. The company offers one of the most extensive warranty programs, providing full replacement if a customer is dissatisfied. Though their machines are for the most part competitive with other manufacturers, Xerox models tend to be more expensive than others to operate. The Xerox 5021 offers an an ADF for an additional $1,400, and only a 10-bin sorter for an extra $1,100. Its maximum paper capacity of 3,370 was one of the highest in its category. With its replacement guarantee, this is a fine choice if you don't need duplex capability.

CONTACT INFORMATION

Canon
800-OK-CANON (800-652-2666)

Kodak
800-255-3434

Konica
800-2-KONICA
(800-256-6422)

Mita Copystar
800-ABC-MITA (800-222-6482)

Pitney-Bowes
800-MR-BOWES (800-6672-6937)

Ricoh
800-63-RICOH (800-637-4264)

Sharp
800-529-9600
Toshiba

714-583-3000
Xerox
800-TEAM-XRX (800-832-6979)

VALUABLE RESOURCES

For information on used or refurbished copiers, look for the Copier Blue Book, published by Assay Publishing (800-395-0222). The book compiles and lists average wholesale and retail prices for used copiers and costs $59. If you just want the prices for one brand, you can receive it via fax for $8.95.

OFFICE COPIERS,

MID-VOLUME

It is recommended that you read the chapter titled "Office Copiers, Overview" before reading the following.

Mid-volume copiers are those able to turn out 15,000 to 30,000 copies per month.

The following list contains 10 mid-volume copiers, their rankings and overall scores.

RANKINGS AND OVERALL SCORES

1	Canon NP4050	74.6
2	Pitney-Bowes Smart Image C320	83.1
3	Panasonic FP7750	77.3
4	Xerox 5334	76.9
4	Minolta EP3050 CS/Pro	75.6
6	Toshiba 3550	72.1
7	Mita DC4086	71.8
8	Kodak Ektaprint 90	70.4
9	Ricoh FT6645	67.6
10	Mita DC4056	60.7

EXPLANATION OF RATINGS

Copiers in this category were evaluated on several criteria: reputation, service, and warranty programs; basic options; and miscellaneous options. The highest possible score was 100 points. Three "mega-features" were considered and weighted to establish the rankings.

1) *The manufacturer's general reputation* and its particular service and warranty programs were given a possible 40 points. 2) *Options* such as sorter or sorter/stapler, feeder, and duplex capability were each worth ten points, to make a 30 point total for this set of features. 3) *Other important features* were each worth six points each, for a total of 30 points. These features included copies per minute (CPM), feeder speed, standard and maximum paper capabilities, and the first-copy speed.

The specific point breakdown is as follows.

Company (40 points): Companies were rated Excellent, Good, Fair, or Poor based on their reliability, service and reputation. An important factor in a company's rating was the type of replacement guarantee. Pitney-Bowes and Xerox have the best guarantees in the industry, and were rated the highest.

Sorter (10 points): Sorters are necessary to help collate and finish multiple sets of copies. Copiers in this size range offer only 20-bin sorters, some with a stapler attachment. The price of a 20-bin sorter ranged from $1,300 for the sorter alone to over $3,000 for the stapler capability.

Feeder (10 points): The feeder is perhaps the most important component of a copier, since it is during the feeding process that a copier can fail mechanically. For this size copier, the choices of feeders are two: a recirculating automatic document feeder (RADF) allows the user to copy from both sides of a document without removing it from the machine between copies. A recirculating document handler (RDH) makes only one copy of each page, but will circulate through the document stack as many times as is necessary to complete the job. Since an RDH doesn't require a sorter bin to collate copies, the availability of an RDH was worth 10 points, whereas an RADF was worth five.

Duplex Capability (10 points): Duplex printing enables a copier to automatically produce two-sided copies from one- or two-sided originals. Duplex printing works by first copying onto one page, and then flipping the copied sheet within the machine to accept an image on the reverse side.

Copies Per Minute (CPM) (6 points): The speed at which a copier can turn out copies is a crucial factor in a machine's productivity. Most users don't want to spend too much time waiting for their copies. The best on the market in this size made copies at a speed of 50 CPM.

Feeder Speed (6 points): Feeder speed represents the speed in copies per minute (CPM) of either the ADF or RADF feeder, using letter-sized originals. The feeder speed should match the copier's CPM, since a feeder that is faster will slow down the machine's CPM. The fastest feeder speed on the market in this size was 50.

First-Copy Speed (6 points): This score represents how the copier rates when it comes to the speed with which the first original is copied. The fastest on the mar-ket in this size made a copy in three seconds.

Standard Paper (6 points): This score represents how the copier rates in its capacity to hold standard, letter-size paper. The best on the market in this size could hold 5,221 sheets.

Maximum Paper (6 points): This score represents the capacity of the copier using all optional paper trays installed. The best on the market in this size could hold 6,221 sheets.

ALPHABETICAL DESCRIPTIONS

Canon NP 4050

Price $8,482

Rank 1

Canon makes more copiers than any other company, and it virtually invented the small-size personal copier. But it is strong in the larger models of office copiers also. The NP 4050 offers many features that make it a top choice, including a 20-bin sorter ($2,400), a 20-bin sorter/stapler ($3,500), and an RADF for an additional $1,900. However, sorters with this model require either a cabinet ($350), a cassette feeding unit ($1,200), or a paper-deck pedestal ($1,700), all at extra charge. With a moderately fast CPM of 40 and duplex capability, the NP 4050 is a top choice.

Kodak Ektaprint 90

Price $18,000

Rank 8

Kodak has recently been trying to unload its copier operations, so the future of the company's commitment to copiers is uncertain. Traditionally, Kodak's most competitive share of the market was in the high-speed copiers, one of which is the Ektaprint 90. For a moderately high price of $18,000, the Ektaprint 90 comes with an RDH and duplex capability, plus optional features at extra cost, such as 20-bin sorter and sorter/stapler attachment ($2,300 for sorter, $3,300 for sorter/stapler). The Ektaprint 90 is one of the fastest in its category, with a CPM of 50.

Minolta EP3050 CS/Pro

Price $7,180

Rank 4

The Minolta EP3050 CS/Pro has one feature not found in any other copier: a three-hole punch that comes with the optional 20-bin sorter/stapler, which costs an additional $3,300 ($2,100 for the sorter alone). The model also offers an optional RADF for $1,900, duplex for an additional $1,000, and a CPM of 35. The EP4050 CS/Pro is the same as this model except faster (45 CPM rather than 35).

Mita DC 4056

Price $7,145

Rank 10

The Mita DC 4056 is the low end of the Mita models in this category, selling for just over $7,000. The 4056 offers no duplex capability, but it does offer many other options found on more expensive copiers. An RADF is one option available for an additional $1,600. A 20-bin sorter is an additional $1,500, while a sorter/stapler costs an extra $2,100. In addition, Mita offers a 20-bin sorter/stapler with three staple positions and a three-hole punch for $3,400. Without the three-hole

punch the option costs about $2,500. The 4056 is an excellent choice for a situation in which duplex capability is not needed.

Mita DC 4n086

Price $9,600

Rank 7

The Mita DC 4086 is an enhanced version of the DC 4056 that comes with duplex capability and an RADF. Like the DC 4056, the DC 4086 offers the 20-bin sorter/stapler/three-hole punch option . Its added features and reasonable price make it an excellent choice for those who need duplex capability.

Panasonic FP-7750

Price $13,750

Rank 3

The Panasonic FP-7750 has duplex capability and an RADF included in its base price. A 20-bin sorter costs an additional $2,000, while a sorter/stapler runs about $3,400. The FP-7750 rated high in speed (50 CPM), first-copy speed (three seconds) and its maximum paper capacity (5250), to place it number three in the overall rankings.

Pitney-Bowes Smart Image C320

Price $6,295

Rank 2

The Pitney-Bowes Smart Image C320 carries the name known mainly for postage equipment. But Pitney-Bowes also sells copiers, although they don't manufacture them. They buy copiers from other manufacturers and sell them under their label, guaranteeing them with their excellent warranty program. The Smart Image C320 has loads of options: an RADF for

$1,600; duplex capability for $1,800; and 20-bin sorter ($1,900) and sorter/stapler ($3,500) options.

Ricoh FT6645

Price $12,165

Rank 9

The Ricoh FT6645 is a fast (45 CPM) copier that comes with duplex capability. An additional $2,400 will bring an RADF, and for about the same charge you can add a 20-bin sorter/stapler option. A recommended machine for those needing duplex capability.

Toshiba 3550

Price $9,195

Rank 6

The Toshiba 3550 is a slower version of the 4550, with a CPM of 35 and an optional RADF for $1,800. Toshiba also offers a 20-bin sorter for a little over $2,000 and a sorter/stapler option for $3,600. Its combination of moderate price and available options make it a good choice for those needing duplex capability.

Xerox 5334

Price $10,785

Rank 4

The Xerox 5334 comes with duplex capability and an RADF. An optional 20-bin sorter ($2,700) and sorter/stapler ($3,700) give it enough features to make it a good choice for those needing duplex capability. The Xerox name, of course, is worth a lot, and the company's replacement warranty is one of the industry's best.

CONTACT INFORMATION

Canon
800-OK-CANON (800-652-2666)

Kodak
800-255-3434

Minolta
800-9-MINOLTA (800-964-6582)

Mita Copystar
800-ABC-MITA (800-222-6482)

Panasonic
800-843-0080

Pitney-Bowes
800-MR-BOWES (800-672-6937)

Ricoh
800-63-RICOH (800-637-4264)

Toshiba
714-583-3000

Xerox
800-TEAM-XRX (800-832-6979)

VALUABLE RESOURCES

For information on used or refurbished copiers, look for the Copier Blue Book, published by Assay Publishing (800-395-0222). The book compiles and lists average wholesale and retail prices for used copiers and costs $59. If you just want the prices for one brand, you can receive it via fax for $8.95.

OFFICE COPIERS,

HEAVY-VOLUME

It is recommended that you read the chapter titled "Office Copiers, Overview" before reading the following.

Heavyweight copiers are those able to turn out 30,000 to 75,000 copies per month.

Listed below are 10 popular copiers, their ranks and overall scores.

RANKINGS AND OVERALL SCORES

1	Xerox 5665	81.8
2	Konica 6190	79.2
3	Minolta EP6000CS/Pro	76.6
4	Ricoh FT8680	75.7
5	Mita DC5590	74.5
6	Océ 2475	74.4
7	Toshiba 5540	73.1
8	Konica 4355	69.8
9	Mita DC8090	68.6
10	Minolta EP8010 CS/Pro	67.3

The Xerox 5665, the number one-rated heavy-volume copier, comes with a recirculating automatic document feeder (RADF) and a 20-bin sorter/stapler and has a CPM of 64.

EXPLANATION OF RATINGS

Copiers in this category were evaluated on several criteria: reputation, service, and warranty programs; basic options; and miscellaneous options. The highest possible score was 100 points. Three following "mega-features" were considered and weighted to establish the rankings.

1) *The manufacturer's general reputation* and its particular service and warranty programs were given a possible 40 points. 2) *Options* such as sorter or sorter/stapler, feeder, and bypass tray were each worth 10 points, to make a 30 point total for this set of features. 3) *Other important features* were each worth six points, for a total of 30 points. These features included copies per minute (CPM), feeder speed, standard and maximum paper capabilities, and the first-copy speed.

The specific point breakdown is as follows:

Company (40 points): Companies were rated Excellent, Good, Fair or Poor based on their reliability, service and reputation. An important factor in a company's rating was the type of replacement guarantee it offered. Pitney-Bowes and Xerox have the best guarantees in the industry, and for that reason were rated the highest. **Sorter (10 points):** Sorters are necessary to help collate and finish multiple sets of copies. Copiers in this size range offer only 20-bin sorters, some with a stapler attachment. The price of a 20-bin sorter ranged from well over $2,000 for the sorter alone to as much as $5,000 for the stapler attachment.

Feeder (10 points): The feeder is perhaps the most important component of a copier, since it is during the feeding process that a copier can fail mechanically. For this size copier, the choices of feeders are two: a recirculating automatic document feeder (RADF) allows the user to copy from both sides of a document without removing it from the machine between copies. A recirculating document handler (RDH) makes only one copy of each page, but will circulate through the document stack as many times as is necessary to complete the job. Since an RDH doesn't require a sorter bin to collate copies, the availability of an RDH was worth 10 points, whereas an RADF was worth five.

Bypass Tray (10 points): A bypass tray allows the copier to hold materials such as acetates and card stock that might jam going through the feeder. The bypass utilizes a straighter paper path through the copier. Some bypass trays only hold a single sheet, others allow more.

Copies Per Minute (CPM) (6 points): The speed at which a copier can turn out copies is a crucial factor in its productivity. Most users don't want to spend too much time waiting for their copies. 100 CPM is considered excellent for the purposes of this ranking.

Feeder Speed (6 points): Feeder speed represents the speed in copies per minute (CPM) of either the ADF or RADF feeder, using letter-sized originals. The feeder speed should match the copier's CPM, since a feeder that is faster will slow down the machine's CPM. The fastest feeder speed on the market in this size was 100.

First-Copy Speed (6 points): This score represents how the copier rates when it comes to the speed with which the first original is copied. The fastest on the market in this size made a copy in two seconds.

Standard Paper (6 points): This score represents how the copier rates in its capacity to hold standard, letter-size paper. The best on the market in this size could hold 6,100 sheets.

Maximum Paper (6 points): This score represents the capacity of the copier using all optional paper trays installed. The best on the market in this size could hold 7,500 sheets.

ALPHABETICAL DESCRIPTIONS

Konica 4355

Price $16,950

Ranking: 8

The Konica 4355 is a good choice for those situations where the copier will be used mostly for single copies on a walk-up basis rather than longer runs. Its first copy speed of three seconds makes it one of the fastest in its category. A 20-bin sorter and sorter stapler are available for $2,400 and $3,600, respectively. The 4355's low price make it a good choice.

Konica 6190

Price $41,130

Ranking 2

The Konica 6190 scored high because of its fast CPM and feeder speed, its fast first-copy speed, and a large paper capacity. The 6190 offers a single 20-bin sorter/stapler option for an additional $5,800. A bypass tray holds up to 2,000 sheets, the largest capacity in this category.

Minolta EP6000 CS/Pro

Price $19,725

Ranking 3

The Minolta EP6000 CS/Pro is a good choice for those situations in which the copier will be used mostly for longer runs and not primarily single copies. The EP6000 CS/Pro offers a 20-bin sorter/stapler with a 3-hole punch feature for an additional $3,200. For the 20-bin sorter alone, it's an extra $2,100. A fast first-copy speed of four seconds, a maximum paper capacity of over 6,500, and a continuous form feeder (CFF) option for $1,600 add to its appropriateness for copying long documents.

Minolta EP8010 CS/Pro

Price $26,750

Ranking 10

The Minolta EP8010 CS/Pro is a fast machine ideal for those situations in which the copier will be used heavily on a walk-up basis for single copies. A RADF feeder and a 20-bin sorter/stapler are included in the base price, as is a standard bypass holding one sheet. An optional 100 sheet bypass tray is available, as is a three-hole punch ($850) that operates with the sorter/stapler.

Mita DC5590

Price $19,995

Ranking 5

The Mita DC5590 is recommended as an appropriate choice for those situations in which the copier will be used heavily on a walk-up basis for single copies. A 100-

sheet bypass tray and a RADF feeder are standard features. A 20-bin sorter and sorter/stapler are optional at an additional $2,400 and $3,400, respectively. A continuous form feeder is also an option at $1,600.

Mita DC8090

Price $29,995

Ranking 9

Because the Mita DC8090 has a speedy 80 CPM pace and a first-copy speed of three seconds, it's a good choice for those copiers used heavily on a walk-up basis for single copies. No separate feeder is available. A 20-bin sorter and sorter/stapler option are available for an additional $2,400 and $3,400, respectively. The bypass tray holds 100 sheets, and a continuous form feeder (CFF) is available as an option.

Océ 2475

Price $56,100

Ranking 6

Océ is a U.S. division of the Océ-van der Grinten company headquartered in the Netherlands. Océ concentrates their copier line on the high end of the speed spectrum. The 2475 is recommended for long runs, since its first-copy speed is a sluggish eight seconds, but its CPM rate is a relatively speedy 75. The model comes with a recirculating document handler (RDH) and a finisher as standard features. With an RDH no sorter is needed. A continuous form feeder (CFF) is also standard.

Ricoh FT8680

Price $36,995

Ranking 4

The Ricoh FT8680 is a reasonably priced model that comes with many features other manufacturers charge extra for. The FT8680 has as standard features an RADF, a 20-bin sorter/stapler, and a continuous forms feeder. With a moderately fast 80 CPM and a first-copy speed of four seconds, the FT8680 is recommended for situations in which longer runs predominate.

Toshiba 5540

Price $19,787

Ranking 7

Toshiba copiers are considered among the easiest to use. That's one reason the Toshiba 5540 is recommended for heavy single-copy use in walk-up situations. The model comes with a host of options, including a 20-bin sorter or sorter/stapler for $3,200 and $3,800, respectively, and a continuous form feeder (CFF) for an additional $1,800.

Xerox 5665

Price $35,290

Ranking 1

Xerox has several models in the heavyweight range, probably their strongest market. The 5665 comes with a recirculating automatic document feeder (RADF) and a 20-bin sorter/stapler as standard features. With a CPM of 64 and a first-copy speed of four seconds, it's one of the faster machines. However, its standard paper capacity is only 600 sheets, far below others in its class.

CONTACT INFORMATION

Konica
800-2-KONICA (800-256-6422)

Minolta
800-9-MINOLTA (800-964-6582)

Mita Copystar
800-ABC-MITA (800-222-6482)

Océ
312-714-8500

Ricoh
800-63-RICOH (800-637-4264)

Toshiba
714-583-3000

Xerox
800-TEAM-XRX (800-832-6979)

VALUABLE RESOURCES

For information on used or refurbished copiers, look for the Copier Blue Book, published by Assay Publishing (800-395-0222). The book compiles and lists average wholesale and retail prices for used copiers and costs $59. If you just want the prices for one brand, you can receive it via fax for $8.95.

POSTAGE METERS,

SYSTEMS & BASES

Postage meters are unique in the realm of office products because by federal law they cannot be owned outright, but must be rented or leased from government-approved manufacturers. This leads some buyers to believe there is no choice in postage meters, and that the market is ruled by one name and one name only: Pitney-Bowes. Although Pitney-Bowes is the leader in the industry, and its name has become synonymous with postage meters, there are three other companies providing postage meter systems at a competitive level: Ascom-Hasler, a division of a large Swiss telecommunications company; Neopost (formerly Friden-Neopost), the third-largest supplier with six percent of the market; and Francotyp-Postalia, the U.S. branch of a large German manufacturer. All of these manufacturers offer a wide range of postage meter systems for all levels of use.

Postage meter systems consist of two parts—the base and the meter. The base feeds envelopes through the meter, the meter keeps track of the postage used and stamps each envelope. A separate compo-

The number-one rated Pitney Bowes Paragon II comes with a computer disk-based system and two-thirds fewer parts than conventional mailing machines.

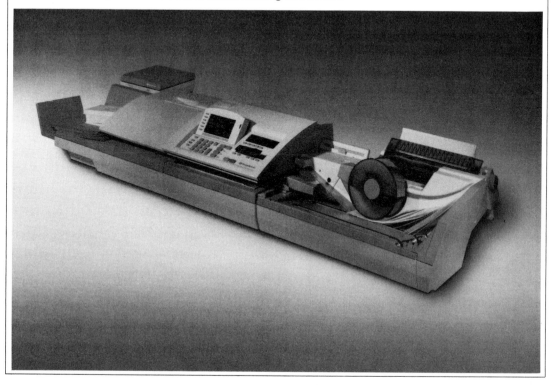

nent consists of a scale to weigh each piece of mail before it is stamped. Some systems are designed to integrate scales into the process. Because of postal regulations, the meter component can only be leased or rented. The base can be purchased outright, although many companies prefer leasing both the meter and base. Bases make using a postage meter easier by automating the mailing process. The primary difference betwen bases depends on how envelopes are fed through the system.

For the ratings below, postage meters and bases have been judged separately. Meters and bases made by the same manufacturer are generally compatible, but buyers should check to make sure.

The following list contains 10 postage meter bases, their rankings, and overall scores.

RANKINGS AND OVERALL SCORES

1	Pitney-Bowes Paragon	100.0
2	Neopost SM78AL	97.0
3	Pitney-Bowes 6105	88.6
4	Neopost SM58HL	82.0
4	Ascom-Hasler 320i	82.0
6	Ascom-Hasler 220	80.0
7	Neopost SM26B	61.6
8	Ascom-Hasler 120i	60.0
9	Francotyp-Postalia 7503	58.1
10	Francotyp-Postalia 7500	41.6

EXPLANATION OF RATINGS

Postage bases were evaluated on the following criteria, with 100 points being the highest possible score.

Company (40 points): There are four major manufacturers of postage meter bases supplying the United States market. Company ratings were based on reliability, service, and availability, with the highest rating of 40 points.

Feeders (10 points): There are three types of feeders available: manual, semiautomatic, and automatic. *Manual Feeders*, which require the user to place each letter onto rollers and guide it through the meter, are the least expensive option, and the slowest. Most manufacturers offer at least a semiautomatic feeder, therefore there were no points given for manual feed postage meter bases. *Semiautomatic Feeders* grab letters in a continuous stream and feed them through the machine. They are capable of processing up to 300 letters a day. Bases equipped with semiautomatic feeders were given five points. *Automatic Feeders* allow the user to place a stack of letters in a tray and leave the machine to stamp and process them without supervision. These fully automatic feeders are more expensive, but can speed up the mailing process considerably for companies that often do heavy mailings. Bases equipped with fully automatic feeders were given the full 10 points.

Sealers (10 points): Sealers automatically wet and seal each envelope as it passes through the base. On most systems they can be used independently of the meter. Sealers often get gummed up because of the presence of glue and water. Postage meter bases equipped with automatic sealers were given 10 points.

Stackers (10 points): Most stackers are simple drop-off trays. These can fill up after a few dozen letters. Bases equipped with a simple stacker were given 10 points.

Power Stackers (10 points): Power stackers use a mechanized wheel that pushes envelopes further away from the meter, thus allowing more envelopes to be processed at one time. Since a power stacker can significantly increase productivity, bases equipped with this option received an extra 10 points.

Roll Tape (10 points): Tape dispensers are handy when mailing something other than envelopes, such as large packages or odd-sized mail. Tape dispensers come in two varieties: pre-cut and roll. Pre-cut dispensers use single pieces of tape loaded into a bin. The other style uses a continuous roll of tape that is cut to the proper length as needed. The roll tape option costs considerably more, but for businesses that send many packages, it may be cheaper over the long run. Therefore, the roll tape option on postage meter bases was worth 10 points, while no points were given for the pre-cut style.

Speed (10 points): The speed of a postage meter base is measured by envelopes per minute. The fastest machine on the market can process 240 envelopes per minute.

ALPHABETICAL DESCRIPTIONS

Ascom-Hasler 120i
Price $895

Ranking 8

Ascom-Hasler manufacturers a full line of postage meter systems that are priced competitively with the industry leader, Pitney-Bowes. The 120i model is a version of the discontinued 101 series that is compatible with electronic meters and comes equipped with a built-in sealer and stacker. The 120i is a good choice for businesses that don't desire phone refills and want a bare-bones system at a reasonable cost. The 120i is compatible with Ascom- Hasler meter models 1441, 1446, and 13313.

Ascom-Hasler 220
Price $1,725

Ranking 6

The Ascom Hasler 220 has more options than the 120i so it is a good choice for those businesses whose mailings are fairly steady in volume. An automatic feeder is available for an extra $1,350 but Ascom-Hasler also offers an extra heavy feeder for heavy packages for $1,795. An optional power stacker costs an additional $1,600. As with all Ascom-Hasler bases, an automatic sealer is included with all feeder options. The 220 base is compatible with meter models 13313 and 13863.

Ascom-Hasler 320i
Price $2,925

Ranking 4

The model 320i is a base model able to work with electronic meters and with a full list of options available, most at extra cost. As with all Ascom-Hasler bases, an automatic sealer is included with any feeder option. The 320i has options for either a semiautomatic feeder for $350 or a fully automatic feeder for $1,350. The model comes with a stacker, but a power stacker option is also available for an additional $1,600. The 320i is recommended for businesses with medium volumes of mail between 70 to 600 letters per day and most of those letters and not packages. The 320i is compatible with meter models 16413, 16463, and 17563.

Francotyp-Postalia 7500

Price $1,275

Ranking 10

Francotyp-Postalia is the American division of Francotyp, a major German postage meter manufacturer. The company is considered rather undistinguished—many of their models are relabeled versions from other manufacturers. However, their 7000 series of systems has plenty of options and could be an adequate choice. The 7500 is the basic model with a manual feeder and a stacker and that's about it. The 7500 series is compatible with Francotyp-Postalia meter models 7100 or 7200.

Francotyp-Postalia 7503

Price $1,980

Ranking 9

The Francotyp-Postalia model 7503 is about the same as the 7500, but comes with a semiautomatic feeder that serves to almost double the speed at which envelopes can be processed (from about 40 per minute with the manual feeder to over 70 with the semiautomatic feeder). The 7500 series is compatible with Francotyp-Postalia meter models 7100 or 7200.

Neopost SM26B

Price $1,495

Ranking 7

The Neopost (formerly Friden-Neopost) Company is second only to Pitney-Bowes

as the largest producer of mailroom equipment in the world. Neopost was started in 1933 and is the longest-running competitor to the Pitney-Bowes dominance. They are known for their innovation, being the first to offer electronic meters and digital scales. Their SM26B replaces the 9000 model and, like its predecessor, is designed for low-volume users. It is a basic machine with a manual feeder and an optional sealer ($275). The SM26B is compatible with only one meter, the SM26A.

Neopost SM58HL

Price $1,795

Ranking 4

Neopost's SM58HL is designed for higher-volume users. Like all SM models, the SM58HL is modular and can be equipped with the features needed: a semiautomatic feeder ($515), a fully automatic feeder ($1,750), plus a power stacker option for an additional $1,025. The SM58HL is compatible with meter models 9647 and 9648, and with the new 964X series.

Neopost SM78AL

Price $4,405

Ranking 2

The Neopost SM78AL is the company's second most expensive model, but a good choice for those businesses which find their mail volume peaking erratically and their outgoing mail laden with odd-sized packages that need roll tape. A fully automatic feeder, plus a sealer and stacker are standard with this model; a roll tape option is also available for $725 and a power stacker for $1,025. Its speed of 170 envelopes per minute make it one of the faster machines in this category. The SM78AL is compatible with the 9250 and 9260 series meter models.

Pitney-Bowes 6105

Price $8,895

Ranking 3

The Pitney-Bowes 6105 is the base model for the entire 6100 series of postage meter bases designed for high-volume users. The 6105 is a good choice for those businesses with high volumes of outgoing mail composed mostly of uniform-sized envelopes. The 6105 comes with a fully automatic feeder, sealer and stacker, plus a roll tape option at no extra cost. With a speed of 207 envelopes per minute it's one of the fastest machines on the market. The 6105 base is compatible with meters 5380, 6500/1, and the A900.

Pitney-Bowes Paragon

Price $11,495

Ranking 1

The Pitney-Bowes Paragon is the Cadillac of postage meter bases with a price tag to prove it. This is Pitney-Bowes' top of the line, and the buyer does get a lot for the money. One of the most advanced features of the Paragon is the scale that is integrated into the feeding mechanism. The company calls this Weigh on the Way, or WOW, and it means that mixed-size mail can be weighed and stamped at speeds up to 90 pieces per minute. This makes the Paragon an excellent choice despite its price tag for high-volume users who send many different sizes and weights. The Paragon is compatible with the meter model E100.

CONTACT INFORMATION

Ascom-Hasler
800-243-6275

Francotyp-Postalia
800-95-NO-INK (800-956-6465)

Neopost
800-624-7892

Pitney-Bowes
800-MR-BOWES (800-672-6937)

POSTAGE METERS

Before reading this chapter it is suggested that you read the preceding one titled "Postage Meters, Systems and Bases."

The purpose of a postage meter is simple and straightforward: to print a postal indicia, which indicates the amount of postage, on each piece of mail leaving the machine. Meters are leased or rented from postal service approved vendors. To use a postage meter, postage must be "filled" by the post office by prepaying an amount at the local post office where the machine is registered. The post office then sets the internal counters on the meter so that with each piece of outgoing mail run through it, the correct amount of postage is deducted. Meters come in two varieties: mechanical and electronic. Mechanical meters use levers and counters to indicate the amount of postage, electronic meters use digital readouts and memory to store and use postage. The postal service is moving towards making all meters electronic, since electronic meters are more difficult to tamper with, thus reducing postage fraud.

Another difference in meters is in the way they can be "refilled." Traditionally, meters had to be brought to the post office to be inspected and filled. Now many meters can be refilled by phone. Phone refills involve sending a check in advance to your vendor (i.e., the meter manufacturer), who then can transfer the funds via telephone. Obviously, this method works best with electronic meters, but both Pitney-Bowes and Ascom-Hasler equip some mechanical meters to accept phone refills.

Other features of postage meters include: auto postage reset, which prevents users from accidentally printing large denominations of postage; postage capacity, the maximum amount to which the meter can be filled; meter setting, the maximum postage the meter can be set at; and decimal, or bulk mail meters, which are able to print postage in fractional amounts.

The following list contains 10 postage meters, their rankings, and overall scores. Two meters tied for first-place; therefore, there is no second-ranked meter.

RANKINGS AND OVERALL SCORES

1	Pitney-Bowes 6500	100
1	Pitney-Bowes E-100	100
3	Neopost 9267A	90
4	Francotyp-Postalia T-1000	85
4	Ascom-Hasler 17563	85
6	Neopost 9247A	80
7	Ascom-Hasler 1441	75
8	Neopost 9212A	70
9	Francotyp-Postalia 7200	65
10	Ascom-Hasler 13313	55

EXPLANATION OF RATINGS

Postage meters were evaluated on the following criteria, with 100 points being the highest possible score.

Company (40 points): There are four major manufacturers of postage meters supplying the United States market: Ascom-Hasler, Neopost, Francotyp-Postalia and Pitney-Bowes. Company ratings were based on reliability and service, with a highest possible rating of 40 points.

Electronic (10 points): Manual meters are being faded out by most manufacturers. Electronic meters are not only faster and more trouble-free, but they are the ones that can take advantage of new technology in the future, such as phone refill capability. Systems equipped with electronic meters received the highest score possible in this category, 10 points.

Decimal (10 points): This feature allows the meter to print decimal amounts of postage for bulk mailings, such as $0.198. This capability can save a company sums of money by preventing unnecessary postage. This capability was given a score of 10 points.

Over $1 (10 points): If the meter can print postage in amounts over one dollar, it earned 10 points. Some meters have a one dollar limit, which would be inconvenient for businesses that send many packages costing more to mail.

Over $10 (10 points): If the meter can print postage in amounts over 10 dollars, it was given an additional 10 points. This capability is important for users sending many sizes of packages, needing a wide range of postage.

Phone Refills (10 points): This capability allows the user to order more postage over the phone rather than have to deliver the meter to the postal service or the vendor.

Scale Interface (10 points): This feature allows the meter to be connected to a scale to automatically print the appropriate postage. A feature such as this speeds the overall time spent in the mailing process.

EXPLANATION OF RATINGS

Ascom-Hasler 13313

Monthly Rental $24.25

Ranking 10

The Ascom-Hasler 13313 is a basic manually operated meter with few extra features, but nevertheless a good choice for those businesses with low mail volumes that aren't expected to grow substantially. All Ascom-Hasler postage systems interface scales through the base.

Ascom-Hasler 1441

Monthly Rental $30.00

Ranking 7

The Ascom-Hasler 1441 is an electronic meter which can print postage in amounts over $1 and over $10. For businesses that want phone refill capability, the 1441TMS model offers that for an additional cost of $7.50 per refill.

Ascom-Hasler 17563

Monthly Rental $37.00

Ranking 4 (tie)

The Ascom-Hasler 17563 is loaded with features that make it a good choice for medium-to high-volume users. The electronic meter has decimal capability and will print postage amounts from pennies to over 10 dollars. For an additional $7.50

per refill, the TMS model adds phone refill capability.

Francotyp-Postalia T-1000
Monthly Rental $30.00

Ranking 4 (tie)

The Francotyp-Postalia T-1000 is an electronic meter that doesn't need a separate base. The T-1000 can be set at amounts over $10 and has phone refill capability. It's a recommended choice for businesses needing a basic postage meter with phone refill capability. It uses thermal transfer printing to apply ink, which avoids smudging.

Francotyp-Postalia 7200
Monthly Rental $30.00

Ranking 9

The Francotyp-Postalia 7200 is one of the company's 7000 series designed for low- to middle-volume users. The 7200 is an electronic meter that can print postage up to $10 but not over that amount, with decimal capability. It doesn't have phone refill capability nor does it interface with scales for automatic processing.

Neopost 9212A
Monthly Rental $25.75

Ranking 8

The Neopost 9212A is an electronic meter designed for low-volume users who want phone refill capability. It prints postage over $1 up to but not over $10. Phone refills cost $8. The Neopost company offers a feature it calls Postage-On-Call service, which is a no-deposit system of phone refills. Customers open their own account with the company. Traditionally, phone refills require that postage be trans-

ferred in advance to the postage system company's account. With Postage-On-Call, postage funds are drawn directly from the user's account.

Neopost 9247A
Monthly Rental $35.75

Ranking 6

The Neopost 9247A is an electronic meter that prints decimals and offers the phone refill option at $8 per refill.

Neopost 9267A
Monthly Rental $55.50

Ranking 3

The Neopost 9267A is similar to the 9247A but has the added feature of a scale interface, making it a recommended choice for higher-volume users. Phone refills cost $8.

Pitney-Bowes 6500
Monthly Rental $48.25

Ranking 1 (tie)

The Pitney-Bowes 6500 is loaded with features which make it a recommended choice for heavy-volume users. They are among the most expensive to rent, but include the scale interface feature, phone refill capability (at $9.50 per refill), decimal printing, and settings up to $99.99.

Pitney-Bowes E-100
Monthly Rental $48.25

Ranking 1 (tie)

The Pitney-Bowes E-100 is the meter used exclusively by their Paragon base system. It is the company's top of the line, able to handle heavy volume with speed and dispatch. The E-100 has every feature in the book and is designed to work with the Paragon's exclusive Weigh-on-the-Way feature that allows mixed-size mail to be automatically processed in one step.

CONTACT INFORMATION

Ascom-Hasler
800-243-6275

Francotyp-Postalia
800-95-NO-INK (800-956-6465)

Neopost
800-624-7892

Pitney-Bowes
800-MR-BOWES (800-672-6937)

ANSWERING MACHINES

Answering machines have become almost as ubiquitous as telephones. Although there are many ways to avoid missing telephone messages, such as voice mail and running special software through your computer, the answering machine remains the most simple and cost-efficient. Answering machines have become much more sophisticated than they were several years ago. Now a potential buyer has many options to choose from, such as mailboxes for each family member or office staffer, automatic paging which can call you at a remote location, and voice memos to other users.

The basic choice today is whether to get a stand-alone answering machine or an integrated one. Integrated machines come with either a cordless or corded telephone. Another choice is between those machines using microcassette tapes to record messages and those using a digital chip. Most manufacturers offer both models, with the tape models generally less expensive than the digital. Stand-alone models

The General Electric 2-9985, the top-rated answering machine, is a digital, integrated phone system that is packed with features: a speed dial feature that holds up to 32 phone numbers, a digital answering chip that records up to 14 minutes, and up to 4 mailboxes.

generally offer fewer features than the integrated models, but for some small businesses and homes the less expensive stand-alone machines may be suitable. One advantage of the integrated machines is that they do allow the user to take advantage of some of the newer services offered by phone companies, such as call waiting and Caller ID.

The following list contains 10 answering machines, their rankings and overall scores.

RANKINGS AND OVERALL SCORES

1	General Electric 2-9985	94.6
2	Toshiba FT9506 BK	86.6
3	AT&T 1830	74.5
4	Toshiba FT8906BK	71.6
5	Sony SPP-AQ600	70.0
6	RadioShack TAD 1005	65.0
7	Panasonic KX-TM2395BW	61
8	AT&T 1314	60.0
8	Sony SPP-A400	60
10	Panasonic KX-TM80W	58.3

EXPLANATION OF RATINGS

A wide range of features come with answering machines, and this is reflected in the wide range of costs. The above machines were rated on the inclusion of certain features that would provide a basic level of service, with 100 points being the highest possible score. The following features were considered in establishing the ratings:

Digital vs. Tape (10 points): The newer and more expensive answering machines have moved beyond microcassettes to digital chip to retrieve and record messages. The digital system is better because there are no tapes to wear out and replace. Because of this, we gave 10 points to those using digital technology and five points for those using microcassetes.

Integrated vs. Stand-alone (10 points): Integrated answering machines, those that come with either a cordless or corded telephone, are becoming more and more popular. The inclusion of a telephone makes the purchase of such a machine an economical choice. However, the low cost of stand-alone machines make them a suitable choice for a home or small office that doesn't expect heavy phone traffic. But since integrated machines generally have more choices and features, they were given the optimum 10 points and stand-alone machines were given 5 points.

Time/Day Stamp (10 points): This feature enables either a voice or LCD readout to inform the user of the day and time a message was recorded. Such a feature is important when heavy volume makes it difficult to sort through messages. Inclusiion of this feature was worth 10 points.

Speed Dial (10 points): This feature allows the user to access and dial a pre-programmed number by touching one or two buttons rather than dialing the entire number. This feature is found only on integrated machines and was worth 10 points.

Toll Saver (10 points): This nifty feature delays answering when there are no messages, thus allowing the user checking for messages to save a toll call by not answering. This feature was worth 10 points.

Mailboxes (10 points): The mailbox feature enables the messages to be divided into two or more sections that can be selected and played back separately. This is necessary if the machine will be used by several people. Mailbox capacity ranges from two or three to 10. This feature was worth 10 points.

Message Capacity (10 points): Tape machines can store messages for as long as the tape holds out. Thus if there is a 45 minute tape, that's how long a message can be. Digital machines differ according to the chip used. Most machines range from seven minutes to 30 minutes. Of the machines rated, the highest rating was 30 minutes, worth the full 10 points.

Remote Access (10 points): This feature allows the user to call from any touch-tone phone to hear the messages stored on the machine and to change messages. This feature was worth 10 points.

Speakerphone (10 points): A speakerphone allows the user to hear the caller without having to lift up the handset. Some machines only allow you to listen, others allow you to listen and speak without having to lift the receiver. This feature was worth 10 points.

Memo Feature (10 points): The memo features allows one user to leave messages to other users without interfering with the machine's answering capability. Worth 10 points.

ALPHABETICAL DESCRIPTIONS

AT&T 1314
Price $45.95
Rank 8

The AT&T remote answering system 1314 is a stand-alone microcassette tape answering machine that has several features common to more expensive machines. One button playback makes it easy for older people to operate. An LED message indicator makes it easy to see if there are messages, and the toll saver feature delays answering when there are no messages. Other features include a time/day stamp, remote playback capability and a memo feature. The 1314 is a suitable choice for those desiring the bare-bones answering system.

AT&T 1830
Price $115
Rank 3

The AT&T 1830 is an integrated phone and answering machine that packs a lot of features in a reasonable price. The digital answering mechanism will store messages on a chip up to nine and a half minutes. The 1830 also features a speakerphone, memo feature, and a speed-dial memory that holds up to nine phone numbers. AT&T's model number 1810 ($95) is the same as the 1830 but without the speakerphone.

General Electric 2-9985
Price $59.95
Rank 1

The General Electric 2-9985 is a digital, integrated phone system packed with features. A speed dial feature holds up to 32 phone numbers, the digital answering chip records up to 14 minutes, and it comes with up to 4 mailboxes. Users can retrieve messages from distant locations with the remote message retrieval feature, and a speakerphone allows one to listen without holding the handset.

Panasonic KX-TM80W

Price $45.95

Rank 10

The Panasonic KX-TM80W is a stand-alone digital answering machine that records messages for up to 10 minutes. It features a remote access feature that allows you to listen to messages, change the outgoing message and erase messages from remote locations. A toll saver lets the user know when calling in if there are any messages before the machine answers. For a stand-alone machine it's a suitable choice for low-volume users.

Panasonic KX-TM2395

Price $69.95

Rank 7

The Panasonic KX-TM2395 is an integrated telephone with answering system that uses the older tape technology. But it does have some features found in the higher-priced and higher-tech models. Panasonic calls its feature that automatically rewinds, plays messages and stops at the last message with just one touch of a button Auto Logic Operation. Add to that a memo feature and an automatic speed dial with up to 12 telephone numbers in memory, and you have a tape machine with many of the features of digital.

Radio Shack TAD 1005

Price $90

Rank 6

Radio Shack considers itself America's electronics store and it does offer workman-like products at reasonable cost. The TAD 1005 is one example, a digital, stand-alone answering machine with plenty of features and a reasonable price tag. The 1005 features four mailboxes, a date/time stamp, and a data compression feature that compresses periods of silence so you can receive up to 60 minutes of messages.

Sony SPP-A400

Price $120

Rank 8 (tie)

The Sony name has been associated with electronics for several generations, so it is no surprise they offer several different models of answering machines. The SPP-A400 is an integrated system with a cordless phone and digital answering system. The answering machine offers a memo feature, remote access, a voice/time stamp, and message capacity of 15 minutes. The phone comes with a speed-dial feature that holds up to 10 numbers in its memory.

Sony SPP-AQ600

Price $180

Rank 5

The Sony SPP-AQ600 is similar to the SPP-A400 but its cordless phone has a speed dial memory of 20 numbers and its message capacity is 30 minutes. It also has a few more features, such as two-way paging/intercom between the handset and base and two-way conversation recording which allows the user to record both voices in a two-way phone conversation.

Toshiba FT8906BK

Price

Rank 4

The Toshiba FT8906BK is an integrated system with a cordless phone and digital answering machine. The answering system features two mailboxes, a pre-recorded answering message, voice time/date stamp and a flash memory feature that saves messages even if there is a power failure without a back-up battery. The machine can store messages up to 20 minutes in length. The cordless phone has a 10-number automatic speed dial feature.

Toshiba FT9506BK

Price $75.95

Rank 2

Toshiba FT9506BK is similar to the FT8906BK but with several more features.

The cordless phone features an automatic speed dial with 23- number memory. The answering system features a voice time/day stamp, pre-recorded message, speakerphone, and it is hearing-aid compatible. One added feature allows the user to set the answering machine to call his or her pager after receiving a message.

CONTACT INFORMATION

AT&T
800-247-7000

General Electric
800-626-2000

Panasonic
800-843-0080

Radio Shack
800-843-7422
(or see *Yellow Pages* for local dealers)

Sony
800-222-7669

Toshiba
800-631-3811

E-MAIL CLIENTS

Electronic mail, or "e-mail," acts like a virtual post office, allowing you to write messages, then transmit them to almost anyone who has an e-mail address whether they are in your office, in another state or in another country. E-mail messages are transmitted in seconds and you can not only send text messages but, in some cases, files can be attached to your message such as a word processing, spreadsheet, graphics files, etc. The application that turns your computer into this virtual post office is called an e-mail client. These e-mail clients are applications that are either stand-alone programs or add-ons to web browsers. With commercial online services providing e-mail accounts, one would wonder why you would need an extra e-mail package. Well, many of these packages offer more features than some of the on-line commercial services, like the ability to send binary files as attachments over the Internet ... a real plus if you're a heavy user.

The list below ranks e-mail clients for Windows 95. Data on these e-mail clients were gathered from our editors and the vendors. To the right of each e-mail client is its Overall Rating. The higher the Overall Rating the better.

RANKINGS & OVERALL SCORES

1	Microsoft Outlook Express 4.0	86
2	Netscape Messenger	76
3	Eudora Pro 3.02	64
4	Pegasus	46

EXPLANATION OF RATINGS

Overall Ratings were given in five categories: ease of use, address book, message handling, Internet features, and advanced options. The highest possible Overall Rating is 100. Ratings in each category range from 20 to 100; therefore, if a particular facet of e-mail is important to you, beware of very low ratings for that particular aspect. Once these five category ratings were achieved, a final overall rating was computed by averaging them.

Eudora Pro 3.02

Price: $89
Overall Rating 64
Ease of Use 70
Address Book 70
Message Handling 100
Internet Features 20
Advanced Options 60

Eudora Pro is a popular standard whose message handling and basic e-mail features are first-rate. The interface may not be as slick as other programs but it's simple and easy to navigate. It divides into two panes, with mailboxes on the left and messages headers on the right. Clicking on a message header opens it, but it would be nice if there was a message preview pane. Basic functions such as creating, replying, moving, and deleting messages are straightforward. A detachable mailbox display and customizable toolbar round out the interface. You can schedule Eudora to sign on and send and retrieve mail at preset intervals. Attaching files is as easy as dragging and dropping them onto messages. Also BinHex, MIME, and UUencode formats are supported. Eudora supports multiple address books, separate categories, and remote sharing of address books. Addresses can be entered manually, copied from an incoming message, and dragged from one address book to another. When creating a message the address book can be accessed from the menu or the To, cc, or Bcc field. A few drawbacks include the limitation of the additional data that can be entered about the addressee and the mailing list creation is awkward.

If you get a ton of mail you'll be pleased with Eudora's top-notch message handling. Filters can be used on both incoming and outgoing messages, including contents of the message body. Five actions can be applied per message. Messages can be redirected, forwarded, moved, copied, and automatic replies can be sent. Some of the program's drawbacks includes its lack of Internet integration and advanced options. Eudora can't handle newsgroups nor can it display HTML web pages. You can click on a URL in a message and start your browser, but that's it. Multiple POP accounts can be set up and mail can be simultaneously sent and received from them. Multiple signatures can be created and used as you wish. It supports Extended Messaging Services API for third-party plug-ins. The program lacks IMAP, LDAP, and built-in encryption.

Microsoft Outlook Express

Price: Free (bundled with Microsoft Internet Explorer 4.0)

Overall Rating 86

Ease of Use 90

Address Book 80

Message Handling 60

Internet Features 100

Advanced Options 100

Outlook Express comes bundled with Microsoft Internet Explore 4.0, so of course it would offer excellent Internet integration and a slick interface, which is Microsoft's forte. To make sure this program catches on quickly, it's free and can easily import addresses from Eudora, Messenger and Netscape Mail. The interface uses three-panes, which include mailboxes left, message headers right and message contents lower right. This makes it easy to drag and drop messages to folders. Attachments can be dragged and dropped onto messages and MIME, UUencode, and BinHex (receive only) formats are supported. To view an attachment, right-click on the icon and Windows 95 will launch and show you the attached file's contents. You can automatically spell check your messages if you have Microsoft Word or Works installed. Since its included with Internet Explorer 4.0 its Internet features are top-notch. URLs are live and complete web pages sent by other Outlook or Messenger users can be displayed, and you can edit HTML messages. If you want certain Internet content sent to your in-box, then Internet Explorer's subscription function can be used to funnel user-specified web pages directly to your in-box. Outlook also works with newsgroups.

The address book is similar to Messenger and can hold a wealth of information. There can only be one address book, but it can query public directories like Four11 using LADP support and mailing lists can quickly be created by choosing names from a master list of addresses. Address books cane imported from other e-mail clients like Eudora or Messenger. Filtering features work rather well. You can set up rules for incoming messages only for either copying or moving messages to a folder, deleting mail from the server, or replying and forwarding. Multiple filtering actions can be set up with unlimited criteria attached. Advanced support includes IMAP, LDAP, S/MIME encryption, digital signaling, multiple POP or IMAP accounts with automatic send/receive from all of them.

Netscape Messenger

Price: $59; 90-day free trial

Overall Rating 76

Ease of Use 80

Address Book 60

Message Handling 40

Internet Features 100

Advanced Options 100

Netscape Messenger has been transformed to a better e-mail client with a slicker interface, support for IMAP and LDAP all combined with its tight integration with the Internet. This e-mail client is integrated into the Netscape Navigator browser. The two-panel interface holds message headers on top and message contents on bottom. Mailboxes aren't displayed but can be accessed from a pull-down list or the Message Center. To file messages just right-click on it to move it to a file. An spellchecker is integrated. Multiple attachments can be dragged and dropped on messages and there is support for BinHex, MIME and UUencode formats for incoming messages only on the PC. Only one address book is allowed, but it can hold a ton of information. The address book can be sorted and you can search Internet directories like Bigfoot and Four11 via Messenger's LDAP support. Message handling is fair. You can use filters only for incoming messages and can only delete, move messages to specify folders, change priority and mark as read. Some complex filters can be set up using up to five criteria, such as filtering mail from a certain sender with certain text in the message body. You can't set filters for reply or forwarding and unattended mail handling is not possible. Automatic mail retrieval is kind of clumsy, to get e-mail from multiple accounts the program must be restarted.

Since this e-mail client is from the same folks who make Netscape Navigator it's no surprise it integrates so well with the Internet. You can have web content such as newspapers or stock prices sent directly to your e-mail account. HTML links are live, web pages can be sent via Navigator or Messenger, or you can create a web page with the Communicator, a built-in web page creator. Messenger supports newsgroups, digital signatures, offline operation, IMAP, LDAP, and S/MIME encryption.

Pegasus Mail

Price: Free

Overall Rating 46

Ease of Use 50

Address Book 60

Message Handling 80

Internet Features 20

Advanced Options 20

If you're on a budget you can't beat this price—free. This freeware can be downloaded from its web site (see "Contact Information" immediately following). It offers many features found on other packages such as drag and drop capability, multiple address books, mailing lists, extensive filtering options, and multiple accounts. During setup you can create multiple accounts, but mail can't be sent and received from multiple accounts at once. The interface is rather cluttered with separate windows for messages and there is no preview window. Quite impressive are the filters, which can be used for in-

bound and outbound messages. Filters can be set for a variety of actions including sending files and starting a program. Attaching files is a mixed bag. You can either drag and drop attachments onto messages or you can try to use an archaic DOS-like selection process. However, MIME, UUencode and BinHex formats are supported. Pegasus does not support HTML (but you can launch a browser by clicking on a URL), or other advanced features like IMAP and LDAP.

CONTACT INFORMATION

Eudora Pro
Qualcomm Inc.
800-238-3672
www.qualcomm.com

Pegasus Mail
www.pegasus.com

Netscape Messenger
Netscape Communications Corp
415-937-3777
www.netscape.com

Outlook Express 4.0
Microsoft Corp
800-426-9400
www.microsoft.com

FAX MACHINES, OVERVIEW

It's difficult to imagine doing business today without a fax machine. Originally, fax technology's anticipated use was for the postal service. A customer could bring a letter to the post office in Chicago and have it faxed to Los Angeles and delivered the same day. But business had a better idea, which was to eliminate the middle man and send your document directly to the person, bypassing the postal service. The market took care of the rest, and today few businesses do without a fax machine. They provide an easy way to send documents to any phone number equipped with a similar machine. And they are cost effective, usually less expensive than overnight delivery and faster than regular mail.

Facsimile machines send and receive documents over telephone lines. They work by scanning each outgoing page, converting the image into a series of light and dark dots. This pattern is translated into audio tones, which are then transmitted over the phone lines. The receiving fax "hears" the tones and decodes them back into the original image.

One reason for the success of fax machines is the establishment of worldwide standards which allow different brands of fax machines to communicate with each other. These standards group fax machines into Group 1 through Group 4. Currently, most fax machines are Group 3, which means these machines can transmit information at 9,600 bits per second (bps). Group 4 standard is up to eight times faster, but requires special digital phone lines, so the standard for the foreseeable future should remain Group 3, especially since technological advances now allow such machines to transmit at higher speeds, such as 14.4 bps. More and more high-end fax machines are now capable of transmitting at the higher speed. Although such fax machines are more expensive than the slower ones, their faster transmission times should result in overall reduction of phone costs.

Another way of reducing transmission time is by using advanced data compression protocols. All Group 3 machines are equipped with the Modified Huffman (MH) compression protocol, but more advanced machines are equipped with faster protocols such as Modified Read (MR) and Modified Modified Read (MMR). This faster technology allows the machine to read more images using fewer bits of data.

METHODS OF PRINTING

The oldest and least expensive fax printing technology was thermal printing. A small heating element in the machine marks heat-sensitive paper. The advantages of thermal paper printing are that it is simple and reliable, since there are almost no moving parts to wear out. The disadvantage is that most people do not like using thermal paper. The rolls of paper often curl up and are difficult to write on, plus the thermal image fades over time.

Most manufacturers now offer plain paper fax machines at prices not too much more than thermal machines. The least expensive of these plain paper faxes use ink-jet printing, similar to computer printers. However, ink-jets are rather slow, so manufacturers of high-volume fax machines use laser or LED technology.

Laser and LED printing are virtually identical. Laser facsimile incorporates the same technology as a laser printer, using a beam of laser light, to produce high-quality images on plain paper. LED uses LED lights instead of lasers in the printing process. These machines are quite reliable, needing only toner and paper to maintain themselves. On the downside, laser/LED machines are much more expensive than ink-jet machines.

Some machines on the market use thermal transfer technology to print onto plain paper. These machines use heat to transfer ink from a ribbon to a page. They are slow and noisy, and the quality of their image is poor, so they are not recommended.

MEMORY

Memory allows a fax machine to store incoming or outgoing pages. Although this may not directly affect the operating cost, it does affect the productivity by allowing the business to utilize its time more efficiently. Some of the features worth noting, and which are evaluated in the following rankings, were out-of-pa-per-reception, quick-scan, dual access, and the ability to enhance memory.

Out-of-Paper Reception is one of the most useful features of memory. This saves incoming faxes if the machine runs out of paper. When paper is reloaded, the image is then printed. **Quick-Scan** allows you to scan a page into memory before beginning transmission, thus reducing time waiting to retrieve the original. **Dual Access** allows both sending and receiving features to be used at the same time. For example, with dual access you can scan an outgoing fax into memory while receiving an incoming fax at the same time.

RECOMMENDED FEATURES

Like most office machines, faxes now come with many features critical to efficient operation. Features such as automatic document feeding, autodial and auto redial, error correction mode (ECM) and fine and superfine resolution are recommended for most fax users. Automatic document feeder (**ADF**) is a tray that feeds the document pages into the fax machine. Without such a feature, a user would have to wait and feed each page into the machine for transmission. The **Autodial** feature allows a user to program frequently called numbers for dialing with just one or two buttons being touched. Autodial feature should have battery backup so re-programming isn't necessary after a power outage. **Auto Redial** feature allows the user to instruct the fax machine to redial a number repeatedly when it receives a busy signal. **Error Correction Mode (ECM)** allows a fax machine to correct communication errors stemming from poor quality phone lines. **Fine and Superfine Resolution** settings allow the user to send documents containing finely detailed images or small-sized text. Standard fax machines scan at 98 horizontal lines per inch, With fine or super-fine resolution, machines can scan as high as 392 lines per inch. The drawback is that such fine resolution increases transmission time.

Other features worth noting are valuable only for specialized needs. These include machines capable of multifunctionality, delayed transmission, multiple transmission, and confidential faxing. These features add to the cost and unless truly needed do not add much to a machine's productivity.

CHOOSING A FAX MACHINE

In choosing a fax machine, several factors must be considered. The first is whether or not you need a plain paper machine or a thermal. Thermal faxes are more reliable, less expensive initially, and cost less to operate. Despite the advantages of thermal paper, most businesses seem to prefer plain paper faxes. However, for those businesses with minimal faxing needs, thermal machines provide an efficient, low-cost option.

Another factor to consider is volume. How many faxes per day do you expect to send or receive? The fax machines in this report have been categorized by volume of use, from low to high volume, with thermal machines in a separate category.

These two decisions—whether to use thermal or plain paper and which category

of machine—are the most important. Other factors include ease of use, noise levels of the machine, how much space it occupies, and basic maintenance procedures. There are about 30 manufacturers and sellers competing in the fax machine market. The largest manufacturer is Sharp, with more than 25 percent of the market. Other companies with over five percent of the market include Panasonic, Canon, Brother, Muratec, Hewlett-Packard and Toshiba. In the early days of fax technology, most machines were bought direct from dealers. With the decline in price, fax machines can now be bought by mail order and in office superstores such as Staples and Home Office. Make sure warranty agreements are in effect when purchasing.

The fax machines rated in the following sections are divided into four reports. Thermal faxes are one category, the rest have been determined by volume expected. Light-duty fax machines are suitable for those users who expect to fax less than 20 pages per day while heavy-duty machines can be expected to handle more than 35 pages per day.

CONTACT INFORMATION

Brother
(908) 356-8880

Canon
(800) OK-CANON (800-652-2666)

dex
(800) FOR-A-FAX (800 -367-2329)

Hewlett-Packard
(800) HP-HOME-8; ext. 9339 (800-474-6638)

COMMUNICATIONS DEVICES

JetFax
(800) 7-JETFAX (800-753-8329)

Konica
(800)-2-KONICA (800-256-6422)

Lanier
(800) 708-7088

Mita
(800) ABC-MITA (800-222-6482)

Muratec
(214) 403-3300

Okidata
(800) OKIDATA (654-3282)

Panasonic
(800) 843-0080

Pitney-Bowes
(800) MR-BOWES (800-672-6937)

Ricoh
(800) 63-RICOH (800-637-4264)

Samsung
(800) SAMSUNG (800-726-7864)

Sanyo
(201) 641-2333

Sharp
(800) BE-SHARP (800-529-9600)

Toshiba
(800) GO-TOSHIBA (714-583-3000)

Xerox
(800) TEAM-XRX (800-832-6979)

VALUABLE RESOURCES

In addition to conventional fax machines using phone lines, e-mail has become a less expensive alternative to using fax technology. Two companies have begun to offer e-mail pricing for fax transmissions. It works by combining the two technologies. The sender sends his or her message via e-mail to the service, which then sends it to an Internet access near the recipient, and local phone lines are used for the final step. The two firms offering the service are NetCentric at http://www.netcentric.com and FaxSav at http://www.faxsav.com

FAX MACHINES, LIGHT-DUTY,

PLAIN PAPER

Before you read this portion, it is recommended that you read the chapter titled "Fax Machines, Overview."

Light-duty plain paper fax machines include those machines capable of sending and/or receiving more than 20 pages per day without needing large-paper capacity. Many machines in this catagory offer multifunction capabilities such as scanning and printing. Plain paper fax technology at this low-volume end takes two forms: ink jet and thermal transfer, with laser or LED limited to higher volume machines.

The following list contains 10 light-duty copiers, their rankings, and overall scores.

RANKINGS AND OVERALL SCORES

1	JetFax 4	88.2
2	Canon CFX B3801F	86.6
3	Xerox 3006	84.9
4	Ricoh MV74	79.0
5	Panasonic UF 322	73.3
5	Samsung FX 4100	73.3
7	Brother MFC-1950MC+	68.2
8	Sharp FO-1650	63.6
9	HP OfficeJet	49.9
10	Muratec Imagemate CX	35.2

EXPLANATION OF RATINGS

Fax machines in this category were evaluated on several criteria: service and reliability records, document feeder capacity, speed of transmission, data transmission protocol available, quick-scan feature, error correction mode(ECM), dual access capability, standard paper capacity, and the amount of memory provided. Highest possible score was 100.

The specific point breakdown is as follows.

Company (20 points): There are about 30 major manufacturers of fax machines today. Companies were rated Excellent, Good, Fair or Poor based on their reliability, service and reputation, with the best worth 20 points.

Transmission Speed (10 points): As described above, many manufacturers offer the faster 14.4 bps machines instead of the slower standard of 9.6 bps. These faster machines can cut operating costs by using less phone time. Machines with the faster speed were allocated the full 10 points.

Document Feeder Capacity (10 points): Refers to the number of pages that can be held in the document feeder. The highest number of pages in this category was 30, worth 10 points.

Data Compression Protocol (10 points): Machines with Modified Read (MR) were given five points, those with the faster Modified Modified Read (MMR) or with both MR and MMR were given the full 10.

Quick Scan (10 points): This feature allows the machine to quickly scan outgoing faxes into memory before transmission. Availability of this feature counted for 10 points.

Standard Paper Capacity (10 points): For plain paper faxes this represents how many sheets of paper can be held in the standard paper tray. Top capacity in this category is 300, worth the full 10 points.

Standard Memory (10 points): Represents how much memory, measured in kilobytes or megabytes, is standard in the machine. Memory is necessary for features such as out-of-paper capability. The maximum amount of standard memory available in this category was one megabyte.

Error Correction Mode (ECM) (10 points): Error correction mode is a transmission standard that allows the fax machine to correct errors in communication arising from poor phone lines. Inclusion of this feature was worth 10 points.

Dual Access (10 points): This feature indicates the fax is capable of transmitting and receiving at the same time. Inclusion of this feature is worth 10 points.

ALPHABETICAL DESCRIPTIONS

Brother MFC-1950 MC+

Price $444

Rank 7

The MFC-1950 MC+ is another in the line of multifunctional devices (MFC) released by Brother International in recent years. The MFC-1950 MC+ is an ink jet machine that offers quick scan capability, 200-page standard paper capacity and

even scanning capability as part of its multifunctionality. Its transmission speed of 14.4 bps and error correction mode (ECM) should help make it a speedy transmitter, but the absence of either MR or MMR data compression protocols puts it behind others in this category.

Canon CFX-B3801F

Price $695

Rank 2

Canon, the second largest supplier in the fax machine market, is strongest in the low-end category. The CFX-B3801F, with its load of features, is highly recommended for businesses that receive relatively few messages but send more than 35 pages per day. The ink jet machine offers both MR and MMR data compression protocol, a 14.4 transmission speed, quick scan and dual access, plus scanning capability as part of its multifunctionality.

Hewlett-Packard HP OfficeJet

Price $599

Rank 9

Hewlett-Packard has used its success with ink jet computer printing to market a line of fax machines using that technology. Their line of low-volume OfficeJet fax machines has become a major player in the market. The HP OfficeJet transmits at the slower speed of 9.6 bps, but its features include MR and MMR data compression protocols and half a megabyte of memory.

JetFax 4

Price $999

Rank 1

The JetFax 4 is loaded with features, which may explain its high price tag. The

JetFax company is not a big player in the fax market, offering only two models, but the JetFax 4 offers ink jet technology and a host of features to justify its price: 14.4 bps transmission speed, both MR and MMR data compression protocols, quick scan and dual scan capabilities, and scanning and printing options as part of its multifunctionality.

Muratec Imagemate CX

Price $340

Rank 10

The Muratec Imagemate CX is a good example of the Muratec company's commitment to thermal transfer (TT) technology. TT offers plain paper faxing without using ink jet or laser, but the technology is noisy and many businesses would be put off by the security issue. The Imagemate CX, however, does offer plain paper faxing at a price barely more than thermal units, if you don't mind the absence of any features included in other models in this category.

Panasonic UF-322

Price $665

Rank 5 (tie)

The Panasonic UF-322 is an ink jet fax machine transmitting at the slower 9.6 bps speed, but offering such standard features as MR and MMR data compression protocols, and half a megabyte of memory. One feature unique to Panasonic is the conditional dual access offered on this and the UF-315 models. This feature means the machine only scans incoming and outgoing documents into memory when directed to do so by the fax operator.

Ricoh MV74

Price $1,095

Rank 4

Ricoh is another major player in the fax market concentrating on mid- and high-volume models. The MV 74, despite its slow transmitting speed of 9.6 bps and one of the smallest document feed capacities (15), it does offer MR and MMR data compression protocols, quick scan and dual access, and over four megabytes of expanded memory.

Samsung FX4100

Price $899

Rank 5 (tie)

The Samsung FX4100 is an ink jet fax machine loaded with features. The major drawback is the company's weak distribution network that may make their products hard to find. Although burdened with a 9.6 bps transmission speed, the FX4100 offers MR and MMR data compression protocols, quick scan, dual access, error correction mode (ECM), and half a megabyte of memory to offset its drawbacks. Standard multifunctional capabilities include printing.

Sharp FO-1650

Price $699

Rank 8

The Sharp FO-1650 is a thermal transfer fax machine operating at the faster 14.4 bps speed. Along with its speed, it offers standard paper capacity of 300 pages, the top in its category, and 700 kilobytes of memory that can be expanded to one megabyte. It also comes with error correction mode (ECM) and a 20-page document feeder tray.

Xerox 3006

Price $1,395

Rank 3

The Xerox 3006 is one of the more expensive models in this category, but it is full of features and multifunctional capability. An ink jet fax machine with a transmission speed of 14.4 bps, it comes with MR and MMR data compression protocol, quick scan, error correction mode (ECM), dual access, and half a megabyte of memory that can be expanded to 1.5 megabytes. Faxing, printing and scanning capability are available as part of its multifunctional capability.

For the 800 numbers of the manufacturers of the fax machines reviewed in this chapter, refer to the final page of the chapter titled "Fax Machines, Overview."

CONTACT INFORMATION

For the 800 numbers of the manufacturers of the fax machines reviewed in this chapter, refer to the final page of the chapter titled "Fax Machines, Overview."

FAX MACHINES, MID-DUTY, PLAIN PAPER

Before you read this portion, it is recommended that you read the chapter titled "Fax Machines, Overview."

Mid-duty fax machines are plain paper fax machines capable of sending photos, detailed drawings, and oversized documents such as blueprints. These machines offer features not available in smaller machines, such as gray-scale adjustments and larger paper capacities. The machines in this category use laser or LED technology and offer multifunctional capabilities such as printing and copying.

The following list contains 10 mid-duty fax machines, their rankings and overall scores.

RANKINGS AND OVERALL SCORES	
1 Toshiba TF621	88.8
2 Panasonic UF-744	88.7
3 Ricoh FAX2700L	86.9
4 Panasonic UF-550	82.3
5 Mita LDC-720	79.3
6 Konica 7310	76.8

The Toshiba TF621, the top-rated mid-duty fax machine, offers MR and MMR data compression protocols, quick scan, dual access, a 250-sheet standard paper tray with a 500-sheet-maximum tray, and 64-shade gray-scale capability.

7	dex 645	74.5
8	Lanier 1110	62.8
9	Muratec F-76	61.8
10	Sharp FO-3350	56.8

EXPLANATION OF RATINGS

Fax machines in this category were evaluated on several criteria: service and reliability records, document feeder capacity, data transmission protocol available, quick-scan feature, gray-scale resolution, oversize paper capability, dual access capability, standard paper capacity, maximum paper capacity, and the amount of memory provided. The highest possible score was 100. The specific point breakdown is as follows.

Company (10 points): There are about 30 major manufacturers of fax machines today. Companies were rated Excellent, Good, Fair or Poor based on their reliability, service and reputation, with the best worth 10 points..

Document Feeder Capacity (10 points): Refers to the number of pages that can be held in the document feeder. The highest number of pages in this category was 30, worth 10 points.

Data Compression Protocol (10 points): Machines with Modified Read (MR) were given 5 points, those with the faster Modified Modified Read (MMR) or with both MR and MMR were given the full 10.

Quick Scan (10 points): This feature allows the machine to quickly scan outgoing faxes into memory before transmission. Availability of this feature counted for 10 points.

Gray-Scale Resolution (10 points): This feature indicates the range of shades of gray that can be faxed and scanned. The best in this category could scan 64 shades, worth the full 10 points.

Maximum Paper Width (10 points): This feature indicates the maximum width of outgoing documents. The maximum in this category was 11.9 inches, worth the full 10 points.

Standard Paper Capacity (10 points): For plain paper faxes this represents how many sheets of paper can be held in the standard paper tray. Top capacity in this category is 300, worth the full 10 points.

Maximum Paper Capacity (10 points): This represents the number of sheets of paper that can be held in the maximum paper tray, with the most in this category being 750 sheets, worth the full 10 points.

Standard Memory (10 points): Indicates how much memory, measured in megabytes, is standard in the machine. Memory is necessary for features such as out-of-paper capability. The maximum amount of standard memory available in this category was 1.3 megabytes.

Dual Access (10 points): This feature indicates the fax is capable of transmitting and receiving at the same time. Inclusion of this feature is worth 10 points.

ALPHABETICAL DESCRIPTIONS

dex 645

Price $2,999

Rank 7

The dex company has been in business for 28 years, but has gone through a number of owners in recent years. The 645 has quick scan and dual access capability, both MR and MMR data compression protocols and is at the top of its class in standard memory supplied. The 645 is a suitable choice for those businesses not needing oversized document capability or fine gray-scale resolution.

Konica 7310

Price $3,695

Rank 6

The Konica 7310 is actually a copier with fax capability. A multifunctional device, what sets this model apart is its true copier engine, complete with a copier platen, while other fax machines use a sheet-fed scanner to make copies of poorer quality than a dedicated copy machine. The result is that the 7310 offers nothing extraordinary in the fax features, but does offer photocopier-quality copying. This makes the 7310 quite competitive for those businesses looking for a fax machine and copier.

Lanier 1110

Price $1,195

Rank 8

The strongest selling point for the Lanier 1110 is the strong service guarantee the company offers with all their fax machines, a guarantee that promises 98 percent uptime for the machines. The 1110 offers both MR and MMR data compression protocols, quick scan and dual access, plus printing and scanning multifunctional capabilities. Its standard paper capacity of 150 with no maximum paper tray was a minus. The unit comes with 300 kilobytes of memory, but can be expanded to 1.3 megabytes.

Mita LDC-720

Price $1,995

Rank 5

The Mita LDC-720 is loaded with features and is capable of transmitting up to 64 shades of gray, making it a suitable choice for businesses which often fax detailed drawings or photos. The LDC-720 offers both MR and MMR data compression protocols, quick scan, dual access, and its 300 kilobyte memory can be expanded to 2.3 megabytes. Its multifunctionality capability includes printing. A 30-sheet document feeder and a 250-sheet standard paper tray are standard on the LDC-720.

Muratec F-76

Price $1,895

Rank 9

Muratec F-76 is a basic plain paper fax with most, but not all, of the features notable for this category. On the plus side, the F-76 offers both MR and MMR data compression protocols, quick scan, a 30-page document feeder, and a 250-sheet standard paper tray. On the minus side, it has only 300 kilobytes of memory with no room for expansion, no dual access capability, and a minimum 16 shades of gray scale. A suitable choice for businesses interested in a bare-bones mid-volume fax machine on a tight budget.

Panasonic UF-550

Price $1,995

Rank 4

The Panasonic UF-550 is a relatively new model similar to the UF-744. The major difference is that the UF-550 can be upgraded to a full multifunctional device. Like the UF-744, the UF-550 is loaded with features, including both MR and MMR data compression protocols, quick scan, dual access, and a 64-shade gray scale. The UF-550 only accepts standard paper width, making it unsuitable for those users who fax oversize documents.

Panasonic UF-744

Price $2,495

Rank 2

The Panasonic UF-744 is similar to the UF-550 described above, but it accepts oversize paper up to 9.9 inches wide. Its standard paper tray holds 250 sheets, a bit larger than the UF-550. The UF-744, therefore, is a good choice for businesses which fax many oversize documents.

Ricoh FAX2700L

Price $2,795

Rank 3

The Ricoh FAX2700L is a feature-loaded fax machine well suited for those needing to fax oversize documents. The FAX2700L accepts paper up to 11.9 inches, the maximum in this category. In addition, it features both MR and MMR data compression protocols, quick scan and dual access, and comes with 300 kilobytes of memory that can be expanded up to 4 megabytes.

Sharp FO-3350

Price $1,499

Rank 10

Sharp, the largest seller of fax machines, has a wide variety of models across every category. The FO-3350 is a bare-bones model thats main attribute may be its relatively low price. It does have dual access capability, 32-shade gray scale, and 800 kilobytes of memory which can be expanded to 1.5 megabytes. But it doesn't have the newer data compression protocols or the quick scan feature.

Toshiba TF621

Price $2,599

Rank 1

The Toshiba TF621 is a fully-loaded fax machine, similar to the TF601 but with a larger document feedeer and more memory. It offers MR and MMR data compression protocols, quick scan, dual access, a 250-sheet standard paper tray with a 500 sheet maximum tray, and 64-shade gray-scale capability. It can be upgraded to include printing and scanning capability at extra cost.

CONTACT INFORMATION

For the 800 numbers of the manufacturers of the fax machines reviewed in this chapter, refer to the final page of the chapter titled "Fax Machines, Overview."

FAX MACHINES, HEAVY-DUTY,

PLAIN PAPER

Before you read this portion, it is recommended that you read the chapter titled "Fax Machines, Overview."

Heavy-duty fax machines are those capable of faxing over 35 pages a day, with corresponding features to support heavier workloads. These include more memory, larger paper trays, and either standard or optional multifunctional capabilities such as printing and scanning. Generally the price of a high-volume machine is substantially higher than lesser machines, but its many features may well compensate by resulting in less phone costs. These machines use laser or LED technology.

The following list contains 10 popular heavy-duty fax machines, their rankings and overall scores.

RANKINGS AND OVERALL SCORES

1	Xerox FaxCenter Pro 735	83.6
2	Toshiba TF851	80.7
3	Okidata Okifax 2600	72.3
4	Panasonic UF-788	71.7
5	Sharp FO5450	70.2

The FaxCenter Pro 735, the number-one rated heavy-duty fax machine, also offers scanning and printing capability and a 64-shade gray-scale.

6	LanierFax 6500	67.0
7	Sharp FO3850	64.0
8	Pitney-Bowes 9720	59.3
9	Canon CFX6400	55.4
10	dex 665	50.5

EXPLANATION OF RATINGS

Fax machines in this category were evaluated on several criteria: service and reliability records, document feeder capacity, gray-scale resolution, oversize-paper capability, standard paper capacity, maximum paper capacity, the amount of standard memory provided, and the maximum amount of memory available. The highest possible score was 100.

The specific point breakdown is as follows.

Company (30 points): Since many of the high-volume machines are bought through dealers and manufacturers, the company's service and warranty programs were weighted in the rankings, with the highest score possible of 30 points.

Document Feeder Capacity (10 points): Refers to the number of pages that can be held in the document feeder. The highest number of pages in this category of fax machine was 50, worth 10 points.

Gray-Scale Resolution (10 points): This feature indicates the range of shades of gray that can be faxed and scanned. The best in this category could scan 128 shades, worth the full 10 points.

Maximum Paper Width (10 points): This feature indicates the maximum width of outgoing documents. The maximum in this category was 11.7 inches, worth the full 10 points.

Standard Paper Capacity (10 points): For plain paper faxes this represents how many sheets of paper can be held in the standard paper tray. Top capacity in this category is 1150, worth the full 10 points.

Maximum paper capacity (10 points): Indicates the number of sheets of paper that can be held in the maximum paper tray, with the most in this category being 1150 sheets, worth the full 10 points.

Standard Memory (10 points): Indicates how much memory, measured in megabytes, is standard in the machine. Memory is necessary for features such as out-of-paper capability. The maximum amount of standard memory available in this category was two megabytes.

Maximum Memory Available (10 points): The amount of memory available for expansion. In this category the largest amount of memory for expansion was 14 megabytes.

ALPHABETICAL DESCRIPTIONS

Canon CFXL400

Price $1,495

Rank 9

The Canon CFXL400, despite its low ranking, is a good choice mainly because of its low price for all the features it has. What its missing is memory and oversize document capability, but it does feature MMR data compression protocol and a fast speed, plus a 250-sheet standard paper tray. These features and its low price combine to make it suitable for businesses that expect to send and receive a lot of faxes but have no need for the frills.

dex665

Price $2,899

Rank 10

The dex 665 features 1.3 megabytes of memory, enough to handle delayed sending and quick scan. A 500-sheet standard paper tray is one of the largest in this category. Its gray-scale capability is a low 16 shades and the maximum width paper it handles is standard-sized 8.5 inches. This makes the 665 is suitable for those businesses who want basic faxing capabilities but won't be sending or receiving detailed drawings or photos or oversize documents.

Lanier LanierFax 6500

Price $4,195

Rank 6

Like other Lanier products, the strongest selling point for the LanierFax 6500 is the strong service guarantee the company offers with all their fax machines, a guarantee that promises 98 percent uptime for the machines. The 6500 features oversize document capability, up to 11 inches, 64-shade gray-scale capability, and standard memory of one megabyte with four megabytes available for expansion.

Okidata Okifax 2600

Price $3,999

Rank 3

The Okidata company is well known as a strong player in the personal computer peripheral market. Using its experience with LED-based printers, they've built several models of LED-based fax machines for the high-volume market. The Okifax 2600 features 64-shade gray scale, a 750-sheet maximum paper tray, and one megabyte of standard memory with expansion to a maximum of nine megabytes. The company offers a 5-year warranty on its LED print head.

Panasonic UF-788

Price $3,395

Rank 4

The Panasonic UF-788 boasts the most maximum memory in this category, with a full 10 megabytes to back up its standard memory of half a megabyte. Other features include a 250-sheet standard paper tray, a 750-sheet maximum paper tray, and a 50-sheet document feeder. With 64-shade gray-scale capability and a 9.9-inch maximum paper width, the UF-788 is suitable for businesses with some oversized documents to be sent and a modicum of detailed drawings or photos to fax.

Pitney-Bowes 9720

Price $4,195

Rank 8

Pitney-Bowes is synonymous with postage meters, but they do make and sell fax machines. Because they target very large companies and provide a range of services to them, smaller businesses are unlikely to fall into their marketing net. The 9720 fax machine is a pretty basic unit for this category, featuring a 50-sheet document feeder, a 250-sheet standard paper tray and one megabyte of standard memory with a maximum of 5 megabytes available. It does not accept oversize documents.

Sharp FO3850

Price $2,995

Rank 7

The Sharp FO3850 is a fast but very basic machine, suitable for businesses with basic, no-frills faxing needs. The FO3850 features 50-sheet document feeder and 500-sheet standard paper tray. It comes with 3 kilobytes of standard memory which can be increased to 2.3 megabytes. With a moderate price, the FO3850 is a good choice for businesses on a budget who want no-frills faxing capability.

Sharp FO5450

Price $3,695

Rank 5

The Sharp FO5450 differs from the FO3850 primarily in its multifunctional capability, which features scanning and printing capability. Another feature unique to the FO5450 is duplex capability, allowing two-sided faxing. Other features include 1.4 megabytes of standard memory with 3.4 megabytes available for expansion, 500-sheet standard paper tray, and a 50-sheet document feeder.

Toshiba TF851

Price $4,399

Rank 2

The Toshiba TF851 offers a lot of memory and oversize document capability, making it a good choice for heavy users who send many oversize documents. With 2 megabytes of standard memory and 10 megabytes available for expansion, the TF851 also features a 750-sheet maximum paper tray and printing and scanning multifunctional capability.

Xerox FaxCenter Pro 735

Price $4,195

Rank 1

The Xerox FaxCenter Pro 735 is a high-volume workhorse that features 14 megabytes of maximum memory, 2 megabytes standard, and a maximum paper width of 11.7 inches for the top honors in this category. In addition, the FaxCenter Pro 735 offers scanning and printing multifunctional capability and 64-shade gray scale.

CONTACT INFORMATION

For the 800 numbers of the manufacturers of the fax machines reviewed in this chapter, refer to the final page of the chapter titled "Fax Machines, Overview."

FAX MACHINES, THERMAL

Before you read this portion, it is recommended that you read the chapter titled "Fax Machines, Overview."

Generally speaking, thermal fax machines are are for low-volume users and offer a low-cost, low-maintenance option for those users who don't mind working with thermal paper and don't mind making photocopies of faxes they want to keep for a length of time, since one of the major drawbacks of thermal paper is that the image fades over time. The following list contains ten thermal fax machines, their rankings, and overall scores.

RANKINGS AND OVERALL SCORES

1	Muratec F-56	100
2	Panasonic UF V-60	71.3
3	Sharp FO-455	66.6
4	Lanier LanierFax550	66.3
5	Brother MFC 890MC	60.0
6	Sharp FO-355	56.6
7	Brother IntelliFAX 635	55.0
8	Muratec M800	51.3
9	Sanyo 200	41.3
9	Samsung FX 800	41.3

The Muratec F-56, the number-one rated thermal fax machine, has almost every feature available, and a transmission speed of 14.4 bps, making it fast and capable of higher volumes.

EXPLANATION OF RATINGS

Fax machines in this category were evaluated on several criteria: service and reliability records, document feeder capacity, speed of transmission, data transmission protocol available, quick-scan feature, standard paper capacity, memory available, and automatic paper cutting option. The highest possible score was 100.

The specific point breakdown is as follows.

Company (30 points): There are about 30 major manufacturers of fax machines today. Companies were rated Excellent, Good, Fair, or Poor based on their reliability, service and reputation, with the best worth 30 points.

Transmission Speed (10 points): As described above, many manufacturers offer the faster 14.4 bps machines instead of the slower standard of 9.6 bps. These faster machines can cut operating costs by using less phone time. Machines with the faster speed were allocated the full 10 points.

Document Feeder Capacity (10 points): Refers to the number of pages that can be held in the document feeder. The highest number of pages in this category was 30, worth 10 points.

Data Compression Protocol (10 points): Machines with Modified Read (MR) were given five points, while those with the faster Modified Modified Read (MMR) were given the full 10.

Quick Scan (10 points): This feature allows the machine to quickly scan outgoing faxes into memory before transmission. Availability of this feature counted for 10 points.

Standard Paper Capacity (10 points): For thermal machines this represents how many feet in the roll of thermal paper the machine can accomodate. Top number in this capacity was 328 feet, worth the full 10 points.

Memory (10 points): Indicates how much memory, if any, the machine features. For the thermal machine category, having any memory available counted for the full 10 points.

Automatic Paper Cutter (10 points): Indicates the inclusion of an automatic paper cutter which automatically cuts each page as it feeds through the machine. An important feature for thermal faxes, worth 10 points.

ALPHABETICAL DESCRIPTIONS

Brother IntelliFAX 635
Price $250

Rank 7

Brother International is a strong player in the low-end fax machine market. The IntelliFAX 635 is a basic-bones thermal unit, one of the lower-priced models on the market. With an automatic paper cutter and a paper capacity of 164 feet, it's an adequate choice for the low-volume user.

Brother MFC-890MC
Price $300

Rank 5

The MFC-890MC is one of a line of multifunctional devices (MFD) from Brother that the company has recently released. The MFC-890 transmits at the higher 14.4

bps speed and has one-half megabyte of memory. Its lack of the faster data compression protocol pulls it back from the cutting edge of thermal units, as does its lack of an automatic paper cutter.

Lanier LanierFAX550

Price $895

Rank 4

The Lanier company offers a total of eight fax machines, most of them for the high-volume market. The LanierFAX550 is their thermal unit, operating at the slower 9.6 bps transmission speed and offering Modified Read (MR) data compression protocol. Other features include one to three megabytes of memory and an automatic paper cutter.

Muratec M800

Price $599

Rank 8

Muratec is a major manufacturer in the fax market. They are notable for the fact that among the higher volume, plain paper fax machines, they support the newer thermal transfer technology. The M800 is a barebones thermal unit that offers neither of the newer data compression protocol standards (MR or MMR), no memory option, and a transmission speed of 9.6 bps.

Muratec F-56

Price $795

Rank 1

The Muratec F-56 is the strongest model in the thermal paper category, with every feature available. A transmission speed of 14.4 bps, combined with both Modified Read and Modified Modified Read data compression protocols, make it a fast unit

capable of higher volumes. Its hefty paper capacity of 328 feet, plus Quick Scan capability, and one megabyte of memory make it a real workhorse for the office.

Panasonic UF V-60

Price $467

Rank 2

Panasonic is a major maker of fax machines for both businesses and the consumer market. The UF V-60, despite its slower transmission speed of 9.6 bps, has enough features to make it a recommended choice for the thermal market. It offers both Modified Read (MR) and Modified Modified Read (MMR) data compression protocols, standard paper capacity of 30 pages, and one megabyte of memory.

Samsung FX 800

Price $499

Rank 9 (tie)

Samsung Electronics focuses mostly on the low end of the fax machine market. The company's weak distribution network sometimes makes it difficult to locate a dealer. The FX 800 is a bare-bones thermal unit with few notable features. However, its low cost may make it suitable for those offices with a low budget in need of low-volume faxing.

Sanyo 200

Price $450

Rank 9 (tie)

Sanyo is not a strong player in the fax market, but its 200 model offers bare-bones fax capability at a reasonable price. Its paper tray capacity of 10 pages makes it one of the smaller units in that feature. That plus its transmission speed of 9.6 bps make it suitable for those businesses in need of low-budget, minimum faxing capability.

Sharp FO-355

Price $188

Rank 6

Sharp is the largest player in the fax market, with several models in each category. Their FO-355 unit, with its low cost of less than $200, is a bare-bones model with a 20-page document tray, a standard paper capacity of 164, feet and an automatic paper cutter. Its low price makes it a suitable choice for businesses with limited needs and low budgets.

Sharp FO-455

Price $238

Rank 3

The Sharp FO-455 offers the same features as the FO-355 plus 200 kilobytes of memory. With a standard paper capacity of 164 feet, automatic paper cutter, and a 20-page document tray, the FO-455 would be a suitable choice for businesses with limited needs and low budgets.

CONTACT INFORMATION

For the 800 numbers of the manufacturers of the fax machines reviewed in this chapter, refer to the final page of the chapter titled "Fax Machines, Overview."

ONLINE SERVICES

There are many specific—and extremely valuable—business applications that the major online services offer, not to mention Internet access, which includes a link to the World Wide Web. The online services and the Internet can be used to download tax forms, find job applicants, hire consultants, find services or merchandise, not to mention do research, send e-mail, make travel reservations, and do literally thousands, if not a million more things. And all of them can be done from a desktop, usually in a fraction of the time they traditionally took.

Here we a look at the four major online services, America Online (AOL), CompuServe Interactive (CSI), Prodigy Internet and Microsoft Network (MSN) to determine which is the best for business use. The list below shows the overall score for each service

CompuServe offers the business user valuable information including databases and references favored by professionals for years: major references, magazines; dictionaries; financial; medical, and business databases, as well as many other valuable resources.

OVERALL RATINGS

CompuServe Interactive ★★★1/2

America Online ★★★1/4

Prodigy Internet ★★1/2

Microsoft Network ★★1/4

EXPLANATION OF RATINGS

Overall scores were computed using a four-star scale with four stars being the highest score possible and one the lowest. Each online service was scored for four facets: Ease of Use, Business Content, E-mail, and web Access. Different key tasks made up each factor. Ease of use measured installation and connection as well as ease of navigation and customization options. Business Content refers to business and reference resources, the ability to download software, and networking opportunities. E-mail took into consideration the ability to attach and send files over the Internet, address book options and online conferencing. Web access measured how easily integrated the web was with the service, filtering options available and if there was free space for subscribers' web pages.

At the time of this writing it was announced that America Online (AOL) had acquired CompuServe's worldwide online services. AOL stated that its service and CompuServe will still be run as separate services but some time in the future there may be an integration of services.

ALPHABETICAL DESCRIPTIONS

America Online

Price $19.95 per month—unlimited use; other pricing plans available

Overall Rating ★★★1/4
Ease of Use ★★★★
Business Content ★★★
E-mail ★★★★
Web Access ★★

America Online (AOL) is the most popular online service, with over 8 million members. Navigating around AOL is simply a matter of pointing and clicking, since icons on the screen represent all of AOL's areas. Help is readily available online or by telephone. Those new to online services should take the online tutorial that gives you a tour of AOL and its offerings.

AOL is primarily known for its family-oriented content; however, businesses can find valuable resources on this service. AOL offers numerous business resources such as daily stock prices, banking online, online trading, mutual fund services, investment advice, and access to Hoovers Business Resources, a database of over 2,000 company profiles. You also get access to magazines such as Newsweek, Inc., Business Week Daily and the New York Times Magazine. AOL's Your Business area offers business owners and entrepreneurs resources to help them in their business. If you need general reference resources such as dictionaries, encyclopedias, or Yellow Pages they are readily available. AOL offers its members perks such as discounts on office equipment, books, and supplies.

AOL's content is consolidated so you won't have to search endlessly for what you want. The magazines listed in AOL's newsstand may have their own web page but AOL brings this information into one place, thus saving you from endless searching.

Need a break from business? Entertainment is AOL's forte. Even though the entertainment sections were not taken into consideration in this study, it is worth a mention. You can find some sort of diversion on this service.

AOL's mail center is easily accessible. Just click on the Mail Center icon from the main screen and you can send, receive, forward, reply, and file messages with ease. Mail can be composed offline and quickly sent through AOL's Flash sessions which will also download any waiting messages. You can also create group mailing lists. An added feature is the ability to use different fonts, add color, and embed HTML links in an e-mail message, but only other AOL members can read your colorful message. Other AOL-only mail features include the ability to check if mail you've sent has been read and retrieve the messages if it has not been read. Files can be attached to your messages and sent to AOL members and over the Internet. You can also receive binary files.

Instant Messages is an AOL-only feature that lets you send real-time messages to other AOL members. You can send an Instant message to any other AOL member that is online the same time you are. To keep track of your associates online you have to use AOL's Buddy List, which is an address book of your associates. You receive a signal when someone on your Buddy List is online. You then have the option of sending them an instant message to say hello or invite them for an online chat.

AOL's much improved Internet access offers a version of Internet Explorer and 2MB of space for a web page. There are also filtering options per user profile to restrict access to certain web sites.

Because of its increasing popularity, AOL has been plagued with problems. When AOL began advertising its $19.95 unlimited use pricing plan, traffic on the service became so congested, connecting to AOL became impossible. To AOL's credit, they have corrected the problem, adding 150,000 more modems to help ease the traffic jams. However, there are still occasional problems with connecting to the service and being involuntarily disconnected during a session.

CompuServe Interactive (CSi)

Price $9.95 a month—5 hours per month; $2.95 each additional hour; other pricing plans available	
Overall Rating ★★★1/2	
Ease of Use ★★★	
Business Content ★★★★	
E-mail ★★★	
Web Access ★★★★	

One of the oldest online services is still offering more substance than splash. CSi's updated interface is easily integrated through a modified version of Internet Explorer.

The interface can't be customized to the users preference, but essential areas can be easily accessed from the main menu or menu bar. Support is available online or through telephone.

While CompuServe may not offer flashy graphics and hot chats with celebrities, it does offer the business user valuable information. The databases and references found here have been favored by professionals for years. Here you can get information not available on other online service or the Internet. References include magazines; dictionaries; financial; medical, and business databases. The Newspaper Archives is a free service that offers searching of full-text articles from 55 daily newspapers. Many of the databases are fee-based. The Business Database Plus offers over 2 million articles from various magazine and industry newsletters. This fee-based service charges a 25-cent-per-minute surcharge to use the database. For $1.50 you can download an article.

CSi has numerous professional forums where you can network with other users in your business or with users who could use your services. CSi is an excellent place to make business contacts and to drum up new business.

CSi's software libraries offer an in-depth collection of files. Finding and downloading the files is easy. You can do a search of the software libraries by keyword or file name. While you are downloading a file, you can do other tasks. Files can also be marked for retrieval at a later time. If your connection gets interrupted during a download, CSI can resume the download. A timer on the screen tells you how long you've been online.

CSi's e-mail system is straightforward and efficient. You can now send files as attachments to your message, but binary files can't be sent over the Internet. Your mail can be filed in separate folders and you can create a personal Address Book. CSi does not offer any online instant messaging but there are some unique mail features not offered on AOL. You can schedule your messages to be sent at a specific time, send blind copies, and search your mail by subject, recipient, or keyword. Other features include the ability to automatically add addresses to your address book and create group mailing lists.

The version of Internet Explorer offered by CSi allows you to view pages featuring Java, JavaScript and RealVideo. Navigation between the web and CSi is transparent to the user since Internet Explorer is also used to navigate the CSi service also. An external browser can be used for Internet access, but this causes problems when trying to access CSi proprietary content. Each CSi account gets 8 MB of space for web pages. If you've never created a web page, there is software online that will create the web page for you.

Overall, CSi is a good bet for business users because of the depth of their business content.

Microsoft Network (MSN)

Price $19.95 per month—unlimited use; other pricing plans are available.

Overall Rating ★★1/4

Ease of Use ★★

Business Content ★1/2

E-mail ★★★

Web Access ★★★

The latest player in the online service arena is the Microsoft Network (MSN). Originally launched as an online service, MSN has reinvented itself into a web-based service. With a visually appealing interface that skillfully incorporates animation and graphics, MSN uses technology to its fullest. Despite the slick interface, navigating around MSN is cumbersome and excruciatingly slow over a 28.8 modem.

MSN does not have the extensive business and reference content that AOL or CompuServe has. The proprietary content consists of six channels each offering a different show. Other content offerings can be accessed by any browser at www.msn.com. The e-mail function uses the default MAPI mail client you have set up in Windows 95.

Internet access is smoothly integrated into MSN because it is web-based. web links are offered in a hodge podge listing. There seems to be no structure in these web listings. Subscribers do not get any space for web pages, but that is scheduled to change in the future.

Even if you wanted to use MSN to access the Internet, the fact that the web-listings are hard to navigate and the service is so slow, it's not worth the hassle.

Prodigy Internet

Price $19.95 per month—unlimited access; other pricing plans are available.

Overall Rating ★★1/2

Ease of Use ★★1/2

Business Content ★

E-mail ★★★

Web Access ★★★★

Prodigy has undergone a complete transformation from a proprietary online service to a web-based service, called Prodigy Internet. The switch was made after Sears sold the service in 1996. The old online service renamed Prodigy Classic is still operating, but it is not being advertised.

Prodigy Internet's interface is like a personal web page rather than a slick commercial entity. Prodigy uses Netscape Navigator as its services browser. No bells and whistles here. Prodigy Internet offers limited original con-

tent. Reference databases are lacking also. This service opts to organize links to the content already on the web.

E-mail is sent via Netscape Navigator's e-mail client. If you are a Prodigy Classic user and you switch to the new Prodigy Internet service you will lose your Prodigy Classic e-mail address. Your mail is not forwarded to the new service.

Since the Prodigy Internet service is entirely web-based, Internet access is excellent. The Netscape Navigator browser is included free when you subscribe, but you can use any browser you wish.

If you primarily just want to access the web for your business needs, this service could fit that bill, but the networking aspect and the proprietary business content that comes with other online service is missing here for business people.

CONTACT INFORMATION

America Online
Dulles, VA
(800) 826-6364, 703-448-8700
www.aol.com

CompuServe Inc.
Columbus, OH
(800) 848-8990
www.compuserve.com

Microsoft Corp
Redmond, WA
(800) 373-3676, 206-882-8080
www.msn.com

Prodigy Inc.
White Plains, NY
(800) 776-3449
www.prodigy.com

PAGERS, PERSONAL

Personal pagers are so ubiquitous now that it is estimated that one in eight Americans use one. One reason for their popularity is price—the price for personal pagers has tumbled to the point that for as little as $50, plus service charges of less than twenty-five cents a day, you could be on call. Personal pagers are basically FM receivers that decode radio signals into numbers and letters. Numeric pagers are the older stand-bys. The newer, fancier models come with alphanumeric technology, meaning they can receive words as well as numbers typed by an operator for transmission. Pagers work the same way whether they are numeric or alphanumeric. When someone dials your pager number, or types a message to be sent to that number, the pager vibrates or beeps on your belt or in your handbag. An LCD display shows you the number of the person who has called you, so you can call them back.

Choosing a Pager

Paging services are sold as a "bundle" that includes hardware (physical pager) plus the service (the entity that provides the radio waves and mechanism). A pager is activated when someone first dials your pager number then dials the number they want displayed. The service provider then broadcasts the message, which is picked up by the pager in a matter of seconds or minutes. The pager beeps or vibrates to alert you to the message now on its screen. Service providers operate at different frequencies so even similar pagers won't be able to pick up frequencies of other service providers without reconfiguration. Pagers and service are available from a variety of vendors, from office equipment retailers to the service providers themselves. The first thing to determine when shopping for a paging service is the type of coverage you need — local, regional, or national. Make sure each type is well-defined by studying the service provider's coverage maps.

Another factor to consider is volume—the number of pages, you expect to receive each month. Some bundles offer unlimited pages while others specify monthly limits, charging a per-page fee for any over. Alphanumeric pagers use two telephone numbers, one for numeric service, the other for text service, so the user is charged for each separately. Text messages can be costly when they go over the specified limit, sometimes as much as 50 cents per additional message.

Choosing a pager number requires more choices. Some service providers offer a local number and area code, others offer a toll-free number your callers must first dial before entering a PIN number specific to your pager. Some providers charge a one-time activation fee, insurance, and cancellation fees. Others require some payments in advance. There are currently two pager technologies. The older one, called POCSAG, an industry acronym, is the original. Flex, introduced in 1995 by Motorola, is a newer version. Flex systems are more efficient in their use of battery power, thus Flex pagers will last longer between battery replacement. A typical Flex pager will go for four or five months on a single battery, compared to one or two months with POCSAG. The other advantage of Flex pagers is that they will be able to carry new pager services such as voice and text services. Naturally, Flex pagers cost more than the older technology. Almost all the pagers sold today are made by Motorola, although many of them are marketed under different names. The listings below contain alphanumeric and numeric pagers, along with their overall ratings.

OVERALL RATINGS

Alphanumeric Models

Motorola Advisor Gold FLX	★ ★ ★ ★
Motorola Advisor Pro	★ ★ ★
Motorola Memo Express	★ ★ 1/2

Numeric Models

Motorola Express Xtras Flex	★ ★ ★ ★
Motorola Express Xtras	★ ★ ★ 1/2
Motorola Bravo FLX	★ ★ 1/2
Motorola Bravo Classic	★ ★
NEC Sport II	★

EXPLANATION OF RATINGS

Pagers were evaluated based on the following factors: the number and variety of features they offered. Factors could be given up to four stars, with one star being the lowest. The individual star ratings were then averaged to arrive at the overall rating. The features that were rated include:

Auto On/Off: This feature allows users to program the unit so it will power on and off at select times; convenient for those who forget to turn the pager off at bedtime.

Readable Display: Some pagers have LCDs that show letters so small one might have trouble reading it. Some alphanumeric models show a four-line, 80-character display while others show only a 15-character single line.

Out-of-Range Indicator: Displays a symbol to warn you when you've strayed out of the signal area of your service provider.

Battery Back-up: This feature retains clock settings and any messages stored in memory while batteries are being replaced.

Message Storage: This feature stores messages in memory. Most pagers can store at least eight messages, and some have a feature that prevents new messages from bumping old messages out of memory. Even others feature a duplicate message addition that lets you know when you've been beeped twice or more by the same caller.

Low Battery Warning: Displays prominently when battery is getting low and about to quit. All models have this feature.

Time/Date Stamp: Displays the time and date when a message was received by the pager.

ALPHABETICAL DESCRIPTIONS, *Alphanumeric Pagers*

Motorola Advisor Gold FLX
Price $160

Overall Rating ★★★★

This is Motorola's top of the line alphanumeric pager, and it is equipped with the new Flex technology. Features include an Optimax Holographic Display, a personal notebook function, a four-line text display screen and a 34-message memory. In addition, features such as Auto on/off, a date/time stamp, and an alarm clock function.

Motorola Advisor Pro
Price $120

Overall Rating ★★★

Another alphanumeric pager, the Motorola Advisor Pro uses the older POCSAG technology but features a two-line display screen that can hold up to 20 40-character messages. Includes features such as time/day stamp, selective and all-erase function, memory retention and battery back-up.

Motorola Memo Express
Price $90

Overall Rating ★★1/2

An alphanumeric pager with POCSAG technology, it features a one-line display screen, 15-message memory, and excellent sensitivity. The Memo Express features Auto on/off, time stamp, message lock, battery back-up and an alarm clock function.

ALPHABETICAL DESCRIPTIONS, *Numeric Pagers*

Motorola Bravo Classic
Price $50

Overall Rating ★★

The original numeric Motorola pager with POCSAG technology, it features 16-message memory, time stamp, message lock and memory retention. An excellent basic pager for those looking for bare-bones service at a reasonable cost.

Motorola Bravo FLX
Price $70

Overall Rating ★★1/2

The Bravo FLX is an updated version of the classic Bravo, using Flex technology. It includes the same features as the Classic. Added features include an alarm clock and an erase-all function.

Motorola Express Xtras
Price $70

Overall Rating ★★★1/2

The Express Xtras is Motorola's high-end numeric model with POCSAG technology, replacing their Ultra Express model. This is an excellent pager for the money, with 20-message memory, Auto on/off, message memory, selective erase, battery backup, and alarm clock function.

Motorola Express Xtras Flex
Price $90

Overall Rating ★★★★

The Flex version of the Express Xtras, it offers the same features but operates with the newer Flex technology, offering all its advantages.

NEC Sport II

Price $40

Overall Rating ★

A bare-bones numeric pager with POC-SAG technology, it features an eight-message memory but lacks such convenient features as message lock and date stamp.

CONTACT INFORMATION

Motorola
800-668-6765

NEC
800-CALL-NMI (225-5661)

SERVICE PROVIDERS

Below are three of the largest national paging service providers. For local service providers check the "Paging" listings in your Yellow Pages.

MobileComm
800-437-2337
www.mobilecomm.com

PageNet
800-217-5304

SkyTel
800-759-8355
www.skytel.com

TELEPHONE SYSTEMS

Probably nothing is taken more for granted in an office than the telephones. Workers expect that when they pick up the phone and dial a number they will be connected. The closet full of wires and switches that make such connections possible is usually kept out of sight; few people think about the company's phone system until it comes time to buy a new one to replace the existing system. Back when life was simpler, the phone system usually consisted of a receptionist or operator who would physically plug in lines to the appropriate socket. If she (and usually it was a she) made a mistake, she simply reconnected into the right socket. Today the job has been taken over by computer chips and electronics.

There are two types of phone systems. *Key Systems* are generally used by smaller businesses, those with less than 50 employees. *Private Branch Exchanges*, or PBXs, are made to handle heavier volumes. Key systems are much like multi-line phones. With the old key systems there was a "key" or button for each line, allowing one phone to access several phone lines. Now the "key" is electronic, but the system is basically the same. PBXs use switching equipment that is similar to that used by the phone companies. A switch reads the dialing sequence and automatically directs it to the appropriate line.

There used to be a marked distinction between the two systems, with a key system your basic, no-frills Volkswagen Beetle while a PBX represented the Cadillac, with all the extra features you could want. Now, however, there is little to distinguish between the two systems. Many key systems offer as many telephone lines and as many features as a PBX.

Both types of phone systems consist of the same components: a central cabinet housing a network of phone lines connected to individual telephones, called stations. Inside the cabinet are the brains of the system — circuit cards. Circuit cards contain the hardware for the system. If anything goes wrong, it usually requires replacement of a circuit card. At the other end of the system, the individual stations can be adapted to business needs. Most manufacturers offer different station types, from the basic desk station phone to the complex attendant station. The individual components of a phone system—the cabinet, phones, hardware, and software—are most often individualized for each company by the manufacturer. When choosing a phone system provider for your company, there are at least three factors to consider: the reliability of the manufacturer, the size and expansion capability of the system, and its compatibility with other phone services.

In choosing a manufacturer, it is important to make sure the company will be around to service and support your system in the long term. Therefore, a large, long-standing company with a proven track record would have the advantage over a newer company. Companies like Lucent, Nortel, Toshiba, Executone, and Inter-Tel are among industry leaders.

To determine the size of the phone system you need, take into account not only your present volume and needs, but the future as well. Buy a system that can be expanded to fit your needs for the foreseeable future because it is no easy task to install an entirely new system. The size of a phone system is defined by several criteria, but the most important is the number of phone lines and extensions. Key systems are usually defined by a combination of lines and extensions. The Telrad Key BX8/18, for example, will handle up to eight lines and 18 extensions. PBX systems are defined a bit differently, in terms of the maximum number of ports available. These ports can be any combination of lines and extensions. A system with a configuration of 150 ports, for example, can handle any combination of lines and extensions that add up to 150, whether it includes 100 extensions and 50 lines or 50 extensions and 100 lines, though some may have restrictions on the combinations.

Since phone systems never work entirely alone, they must be compatible with outside phone lines. Generally this isn't a problem, but if you expect to have your system handle fax machines and voice mail, or special telephone lines like T1 or ISDN, then it pays to make sure your system is compatible with these components.

Phone systems are sold either through direct sales forces from the manufacturer,
independent dealers, or telephone companies. Whichever source you buy from will customize your system for optimum performance. Phone systems contain many features, but not all the features are ones you will need.

We rated the phone systems below based on several criteria — the company's service and reliability, the system's compatibility with other phone features such as voice mail and fax/modem, and its expandability potential. The specific criteria are explicated in the "Explanation of Ratings" that follows the table.

Below are the systems rated in this chapter. They are categorized by size reflecting usage as follows.

OVERALL RATINGS

UNDER 50 LINES/EXTENSIONS

Nortel Norstar Plus Compact	★★★★
Telrad Digital Key BX8/18	★★★
Toshiba Strata DK16e	★★★
Lucent Partner II	★★
Samsung DCS Compact	★★
Iwatsu Omega Phone zt-S	★

OVER 50 LINES/EXTENSIONS

Lucent Merlin Legend	★★★★
Lucent Definity Prologix	★★★★
Nortel Meridian 1	★★★★
Panasonic DBS	★★★★
Mitel SX-200 ML	★★★
Samsung DCS	★★★

EXPLANATION OF RATINGS

The ratings above were based on evaluations of the following features, with the number of possible points in parentheses that the system could earn if it received high marks for that particular facet. In order to keep this somewhat complicated numerical rating system simple, once the total of category scores were determined, the telephone systems were then divided into four groups with the highest overall totals receiving a four-star overall rating, the next highest, three stars and so on. The lowest rating was one star. The individual reviews in the alphabetical descriptions that follow offer commentary on the various features listed below as they pertain to each system. If no mention of a feature is present, it means that that particular system does not have that feature.

Company (20 points): Since stability and reliability are neccessary to maintain a phone system, we weighed this factor accordingly. Only one company, Iwatsu, failed to make the maximum points, because it has experienced some financial difficulties recently.

Digital vs Analog (10 points): Communications between the central station, called the "cabinet" and its outlying phones can be either by digital or analog signals. Most of the newer systems use digital technology, which we gave the full 10 points.

Voice Mail (10 points): This feature indicates whether the system is connectible to a voice mail system, whether that system is provided by a third party or the manufacturer of the phone system. Such connectibility was worth 10 points.

ISDN (Integrated Services Digital Network) (10 points): Phone systems with this feature can connect to ISDN lines. ISDN can increase the data capacity of out-going calls. ISDN is generally supplied by the local phone company, and many businesses are using ISDN lines to connect with services such as Internet access. Therefore, if such usage is a possibility in the future, then ISDN capability is important in any new phone system installed. Such a feature was given 10 points.

DID (Direct Inward Dialing) (5 points): Direct inward dialing is a service provided by local telephone services. It allows users to dial directly to a number within the organization without having to go through an attendant. Phone systems with the capability to be hooked up with DID were awarded five points.

T-1 Lines (5 points): T-1 lines are leased from the local telephone company and can hold up to 24 simultaneous phone calls. Primarily used to link businesses with long distance companies, T-1 lines can be an important factor in a business's growth plans. T-1 support was worth five points.

Caller ID (10 points): A phone system's support of caller identification services, also known as ANI, was worth ten points. Caller ID allows the system to identify the originating number of the incoming call, and then either call up customer data or further route the call. Such support was worth ten points.

Fax/Modem (10 points): Phone systems should be equipped with analog ports for fax machines, modems, and other peripherals requiring analog connection. Such support was worth ten points.

OAI Conformity (10 points): This refers to whether the system conforms to the open architecture interface (OAI), which allows third-party software to be used with the phone system. There are two standards of OAI currently in use: Microsoft's TAPI and Novell/AT&T's TSAPI. Some phone systems conform to only one, some to both. Those conforming to both were awarded the full 10 points, those conforming to only one were awarded only five.

DNIS Compatibility (10 points): This feature, worth 10 points, refers to the compatibility between the phone system and dialed number identification service from the phone company. With DNIS, the phone system can detect the number dialed even when multiple phone numbers arrive at the same location, thus allowing the business to determine yield on special promotional efforts.

ALPHABETICAL DESCRIPTIONS

Iwatsu Omega-Phone ZT-S

Overall Rating ★

Iwatsu is a large manufacturer of key systems. Their Omega-Phone ZT-S is a small analog model that boasts few features but is adequate for small companies that will remain small and have only the most basic needs. The Omega-Phone has none of the more advanced features, but it does support a fax/modem extension, and can ac-

commodate up to 22 ports. The company does market a digital system it calls ADIX, which has many more features.

Lucent Definity Prologix

Overall Rating ★ ★ ★ ★

In contrast to the Partner system, the Definity system is geared for the high-end user. This system is recommended for companies with a high volume of calls needing more than 300 lines and extensions with the potential for further growth. The Definity Prologix features voice mail, supports ISDN, DID, T-1, Caller ID and fax/modem ports. It also conforms to the TAPI-type open architecture interface (OAI), and can accommodate up to 600 ports.

Lucent Merlin Legend

Overall Rating ★ ★ ★ ★

Lucent's Merlin Legend system is their mid-size model suitable for middle-volume businesses who want some high-end features. The Merlin Legend offers digital technology, voice mail, ISDN compatibility, and fax/modem ports. It also conforms to both types of open architecture interface (OAI) standards, Microsoft's TAPI and Novell/AT&T's TSAPI. The Merlin Legend can accommodate up to 255 ports.

Mitel SX-200 ML

Overall Rating ★ ★ ★

The Mitel company has become well-known for its sophisticated technology. Their SX-200 ML is their mid-size model with a maximum configuration of 96 ports and most of the features found on larger systems. It does lack connecting capability with ISDN, which would make it a poor choice for businesses planning to use such features. The company's SX-200 Light and SX-2000 Light are larger systems known for their use of fiber optic technology.

Lucent Partner II
Overall Rating ★★

Lucent Technologies is the manufacturing arm of AT&T, and is the largest supplier of key and PBX systems in the country. Their Partner models are marketed for low-volume users and are basic, no-frills phone systems. The Partner II offers digital technology, voice mail, Caller ID, fax/modem capability, and a maximum configuration of 24/48 lines/extensions, but not much else. It is suitable for a small business that doesn't plan on growing in the near future. Being the leading supplier of phone systems, Lucent has been known in the past for its slow support of small dealers, but is working to improve the problem.

Nortel Meridian 1
Overall Rating ★★★★

Northern Telecom is a strong second-runner to Lucent in the phone system market. The Meridian 1 is a top-of-the-line system with a maximum configuration up to 10,000 ports, enough for even the largest business. It features voice mail, fax/modem ports, Caller ID, DNIS capability, and it conforms to both open architecture interfaces. As one of the leaders in the field, Nortel systems are not inexpensive, but are available through the secondary market (see "Further Information" below).

Nortel Norstar Plus Compact
Overall Rating ★★★★

Nortel's Norstar Plus Compact is Nortel's prime offering for smaller businesses. Its maximum configuration of 8/24 lines/extensions makes it expandable, and it offers all the major features of the larger systems. One minor drawback may be that it is only compatible with the voice mail system provided by Nortel, not with any third party system.

Panasonic DBS
Overall Rating ★★★★

Panasonic is a well-known name in consumer electronics. Their DBS line of phone systems is expandable up to 192 ports, and offers a host of features. It is fully compatible with ISDN, compatible with both types of open architecture interfaces, and can accommodate voice mail, fax/modem ports, DID, T-1, and DNIS. A suitable choice for the budget conscious.

Samsung DCS Compact
Overall Rating ★★

Samsung is one of the newer players in the phone system field. Its DCS line is a digital system, and the DCS Compact is the smaller version with a maximum configuration of 10/32 lines/extensions. It features voice mail compatibility, Caller ID, fax/modem ports, and conforms to the open architecture interface. The DCS Compact is suitable for small businesses with no need for more advanced features.

Samsung DCS

Overall Rating ★★★

Samsung's DCS is the larger version of its digital line, with a maximum configuration of 192 ports. The DCS is suitable for larger businesses looking for a low-budget phone system. The DCS features open architecture interface support, voice mail, fax/modem ports, Caller ID, DNIS support, and both DID and T-1 support. What it doesn't have is ISDN compatibility.

Telrad Digital KeyBX 8/18

Overall Rating ★★★

Telrad has focused on the small business market. Its Digital KeyBX 8/18 is their smallest system, with a maximum configuration of 8/18 lines/extensions. But it is full of features for its size, including voice mail, fax/modem ports, and both types of open architecture interface support. In addition, it is one of the few small systems that offers DID (Direct Inward Dialing), a feature that enables employees on the road to access the system.

CONTACT INFORMATION

Iwatsu
(201) 935-8580

Lucent Technologies
(800) 247-7000

Mitel
(800) MITEL-SX (648-3578)

Northern Telecom
(800) 4-NORTEL (466-7835)

Panasonic
(800) 435-4327

Samsung
(305) 592-2900

Telrad
(516) 921-8300

VALUABLE RESOURCES

The secondary market for phone systems is growing rapidly. Since most companies buy new systems to replace old systems they have outgrown, there are plenty of phone systems that are fine except they are too small for the company that used them. These systems and their components such as telephones, switching equipment and cabinets, are remarketed by specialized dealers. Most of these dealers are small and local. Two of the larger ones are CIS Telecom-munications Group in Syracuse, NY, and D&S Communications of Elgin, IL CIS can be reached at (800) 343-5554; D&S at (800) 227-8403.

TELEPHONES, CELLULAR

OVERALL RATING

Sony CM-RX100	★ ★ ★ ★
Motorola StarTac	★ ★ ★ 1/2
Nokia 232	★ ★ ★
Audiovox MVX-406	★ ★ 1/2
Panasonic EB-H63S	★ ★ 1/2

Once a luxury, the cellular phone is now a necessity for business people and others. For those in the business world, cellular phones help you keep in touch with the office and clients. No matter where you are you can conduct business. Cellular companies are adding new services to attract customers, such as voice messaging, Caller ID, paging, digital technology, wider service areas, and competitive pricing. Pricing varies by retailer and using the retailer's phone service provider will dramatically reduce the cost of the phone. The list below shows the overall scores on a wide range of cellular phone models that were reviewed. Data on these phones was compiled from the vendor. Listed below are five popular cellular phones and their ratings.

Sony's CM-RX100, the top-rated cellular phone, has the best call reception and a 99-number alphanumeric memory.

EXPLANATION OF RATINGS

The phones were evaluated based on four aspects: battery life, memory, call quality, and options. Call quality was double-weighted, comprising 50% of the total rating. Each aspect could potentially earn up to four stars, with one star being the lowest rating. The ratings of these four aspects were then averaged, resulting in the overall rating.

The jargon associated with cellular phones can be confusing. To help simplify the explanations, the following list is a brief glossary of major terms.

Analog transmits voice signals by modulating radio signals. Most of the cellular phones on the market for the last few years are analog.

Digital transmission allows more data to be sent during calls because the data is sent as zeros and ones (bits). There are two standards: *TDMA* (time division multiple access) sends several calls at once; CDMA (code division multiple access) breaks calls into bits when sending them, then puts them back together on the receiving end.

Vox operation helps conserve battery life by allowing the phone to be switched off until it hears a voice.

ALPHABETICAL DESCRIPTIONS

Audiovox MVX-406

Price $269

Overall Rating ★★3/4

An important feature of a cellular phone is its ability to maintain a connection. The Audiovox MXV-406 has a tendency to "drop" calls because of weak signal strength. It also suffers from fair call quality. On the plus side, large buttons make it easy to dial and its memory can store up to 89 numbers. Other features include a battery life of 70 to 120 talk minutes and 12 to 24 hours on standby, three-number recall and call timer. There is also a modem port available for connecting to your notebook if you're on the road. Despite these features, if a phone does not have good call quality the rest of the bells and whistles do not matter.

Motorola Star TAC

Price $1,100

Overall Rating ★★★1/2

This phone gives you what you pay for. It's one of the most expensive phones reviewed and also one with a lot of features. Its size (3 3/4 x 2 x 3/4 inches) fits right into your hand and weighs only 3.1 ounces. Call quality and reception is very good. The phone's memory allows up to 99 numbers to be stored and you can recall the last 10 numbers dialed. Battery life gives you 60 to 70 minutes talk and 14 to 36 hours on standby. Modem connections are possible and you can choose from nine ring styles, audio or vibrating ring, and call timer; the phone also allows you to receive digital pages. The digital pages option depends on your service.

Nokia 232

Price $300 to $500

Overall Rating ★★★

This compact, well-built phone offers very good call quality with numerous features. It has a 99-memory storage for names and numbers. You can program the phone's four one-touch buttons to dial frequently called numbers. A modem port is included, allowing you to connect your notebook and receive e-mail or send faxes while on the road. Other features include five ring tones, memory scrolling, backlight adjustment, and key lock. There is also a continuous display of signal and battery strength and a five-number redial feature. Battery life gives you a whopping 110 to 150 minutes talk and 26 to 32 hours standby.

The Nokia 232 is lighter than the Nokia 2160 Digital model. Buttons on the Nokia 232 can be a little hard to press, but it has a curved face which makes it comfortable to use. If you need a phone with good call quality and a long battery life consider this one.

Panasonic EB-H63S

Price $269

Overall Rating ★★1/2

The best thing about this phone is its compact size (5 1/2 x 1 1/2 x 1 1/2). Memory is limited to 21 numbers, battery life gives you 90 to 150 minutes talk and 13 hours standby, and you can only redial the last number. The Panasonic call quality was only fair—static tended to drown out calls. Other features include two call timers, authentication capability and three ring volumes. If you're on a budget and desperately need a phone for very light use, you may find this a viable option, but the call quality should make you look elsewhere.

Sony CM-RX100

Price $499.99

Overall Rating ★★★★

The CM-RX100 has the best call reception of the products reviewed. It's a compact phone and could fit in your pocket. The phone controls are easy to use. The 99-number alphanumeric memory can be accessed through a small dial on the side of the phone. You can also use this dial to adjust the ring volume and view the call timer. Battery life gives you 90 minutes talk and 24 hours standby. Other features include Vox operation, redial of the last five numbers and a modem port. This phone is a top choice for those needing good call quality in a compact, easy-to-use phone.

CONTACT INFORMATION

Audiovox
800-229-1235
www.audiovox.com

Nokia
800-666-5553
www.nokia.com

Motorola
800-331-6456
www.motorola.com

Panasonic
800-447-4700
www.panasonic.com

Sony
800-222-7669
www.sony.com

TELEPHONES, DESK SETS

Wonder what Alexander Graham Bell would think of his invention today. Telephones now have more than a simple handset and dialing pad. They now come equipped with two-line access, speakerphones, LCD panels, address databases, clocks, calendars, audible reminders, conferencing capabilities and a host of other features. There are trade-offs when purchasing a phone for business. Selecting the right phone for you comes down to your work style and personal preferences. We took a look at a variety of telephones from desktop models to cordless phones. Each model was rated on the features it included. Two units tied for third-rank, therefore, there is no fourth-rated deskset.

RANKINGS AND OVERALL SCORES

1	Lucent Technologies 882	100
2	Panasonic KX-T3175	71
3	Southwestern Bell FM855	42
3	General Electric 2-9420	42
5	Sharp CL-355	75
6	Lucent Technologies 5860	88
7	Sony SPP-Q110	75

EXPLANATION OF RATINGS

Each model was rated on the number of features it included. We looked for these features: LCD screen, speakerphone, ad-dress storage, reminder features, distinctive rings, conferencing capability, and Caller ID. For cordless phones we looked also took into consideration its battery power. The more features the phone has the higher its score. This does not mean that phones with lower scores are of bad quality, it just indicates that its features are more basic.

ALPHABETICAL DESCRIPTIONS

General Electric 2-9420
Price $60

Rank 3 (tie)

The General Electric 2-9420 is a two-line phone that does not have as many features as other two-line models. This phone has good audio quality and can store up to 12 numbers in memory. There are three one-touch emergency numbers and 9 speed-dial stations. For each line there is a ringer control, line status lights, hold and pause and flash buttons. The phone can be placed on a desk or mounted on a wall and comes with a two-year limited warranty, a year more than in most models. This phone is good for a small office that needs two lines for occasional fax and modem use.

Lucent Technologies 882
Price $200

Rank 1

The Lucent 882 is a two-line speakerphone that has enough features to serve a small office. More than a telephone, it is billed as a Personal Information Center. It has an eight-line 24-character LCD display which shows the number dialed and Caller ID information. The address storage has an auto-dial feature; up to 200 names and contact information can be stored in its database. Data is entered on a typewrite style keyboard, which is hidden under a pull-down case. The reminder function provides audible and visual notes for appointments. The phone supports distinctive ring and three-way conferencing. One footnote—one of our editors bought this phone and the computerized brain blew out in a month. Customer service was very responsive to the problem. The telephone comes with a one-year warranty, so the service center fixed it with no problems. Also be aware that the phone needs batteries in addition to AC power. If you lose electrical power the phone will not operate.

Lucent Technologies 5860

Price $130

Rank 6

This 25-channel cordless phone offers sound quality found in corded telephones. It utilizes the federal governments expanded frequency range, which eliminates static and interference often found in ten-channel cordless phones. There's an LCD display in the handset that displays the number dialed and numbers stored in memory. Up to 20 numbers can be stored in the phone's memory. The Lucent 5860 has an intercom feature that acts as a pager or intercom, depending on the distance. Both the antenna and battery can be replaced. The phone comes with a one-year limited warranty.

Panasonic KX-T3175

Price $120

Rank 2

The Panasonic KX-T3175 offers a 12-digit LCD panel which displays a clock, number dialed, call duration and status. This two-line speakerphone can hold up to 24 numbers for one-touch auto-dialing for frequently called numbers. Each line has a separate ringer, hold button, and selector button. Three-way conferencing is available but there is no calendar or reminder feature nor Caller ID support. The warranty is for one year, parts and labor.

Sharp CL-355

Price $209

Rank 5

The Sharp CL-355 is a 25-channel cordless phone with dual speakerphones and keypads. This gives you your own intercom system with hands-free operation. The keypad is illuminated so you can dial in low light. You can store up to ten autodial numbers. The base unit can be mounted on a wall or placed on a desk while the handset can be placed vertically or down on the base unit. The battery has a 14-day standby life and charges in three hours. The warranty is for one year, parts and labor.

Sony SPP-Q110

Price $90

Rank 7

The Sony SPP-Q110 is a 25-channel cordless phone with a 21-day battery standby time. The battery strength indicator shows you when the battery is low and the signal strength indicator tells you when you're out of range from the base unit. This phone scans to find a clear channel and the noise reduction system automatically filters out background noise. A paging system is included but no intercom feature is available. The phone turns on by pressing any button. It includes 10-speed dialing locations and one-touch redial of the last number called. It can be placed on a desktop or wall and comes with a one year, parts and labor, warranty.

Southwestern Bell FM855

Price $35

Rank 3 (tie)

This one-line phone is a basic model with a minimal amount of features compared to the others. There is no LCD display panel but it does have a speakerphone with volume control for no-hands control. It's also hearing aid-compatible and can be placed on a desk or mounted on a wall. Up to 10 numbers can be stored and there are three speed dial settings. Other features include a last number redial, flash for call waiting, and a hold button that shuts off the microphone or mouthpiece temporarily. There

is no support for Caller ID, conferencing, distinctive ring, or reminder features. The Southwestern Bell FM855 has a one-year limited warranty.

CONTACT LIST

Lucent Technologies
(888) 584-6366
www.lucent.com

Southwestern Bell
(800) 331-0050
www.sbc.com

General Electric
(800) 626-2004
www.ge.com

Sharp USA
(800)-BE-SHARP
www.sharp-usa.com

Panasonic
(800) 338-0552
(201) 348-9090
www.panasonic.com

Sony
(888) 476-6972
www.sony.com

VIDEO-CONFERENCING SOFTWARE

If you have a computer and an Internet connection, you can set up your own videoconferencing system. Of course you'll have to add a few bits of hardware, including a camera, video capture board, and sound board. Most of the newer PCs come equipped with video conferencing capabilities (which includes a video capture board), but some older PC's do not. (If you have an older PC, refer to the chapter titled "Videophones.")

If you already have a video capture camera or plan to purchase one and also have a video capture board, there is software available that can give you video conferencing capabilities.

This chapter evaluates four software products priced under $100. All of these software products can be used with other video conferencing kits. The list below ranks these videoconference products.

RANK AND OVERALL SCORES

1	VDOPhone Internet	100
2	NetMeeting 2.0	96
3	CU-SeeMe 3.0	92
4	Intel Internet Video Phone 2.0	75

EXPLANATION OF RATINGS

Scores were computed in three categories: *Ease of Use*, which pertains to how easy the program is to setup and use; *Peformance*, which refers to image quality; and *Features*, which looks at the programs aspects such as chat options, whiteboard, and others. The highest possible score for each category is 100. The category scores were then averaged to obtain the overall score.

ALPHABETICAL DESCRIPTIONS

CU-SeeMe 3.0

Price $99	
Rank 3	
Ease of Use 100	
Performance 87.5	
Features 87.5	

CU-SeeMe started out as shareware before it became the popular standalone program it is today. Use CU-SeeMe on the Internet or any other TCP/IP network. This excellent package can be set up and put to use in minutes. After setup just wait for a call. The software does not have to be running to receive a call and you can screen the calls by the IP address before you answer. Video performance will vary between ISDN, Ethernet, and phone line connections. The phone line connection is usually the slowest. Features include a superb whiteboard utility and multipoint capability up to 100 conferees, file transfer utility, text-based chat, a Phone Book with graphical contact cards, and Caller ID. There is also an on-line directory of other CU-SeeMe users. To utilize this software you'll need to add a video camera, video capture board, and a modem. CU-SeeMe is an excellent package that would complete your videoconferencing setup. It works on both Windows-based PCs and Macintosh computers.

Intel Internet Video Phone 2.0

Price Free	
Rank 4	
Ease of Use 100	
Performance 75	
Features 50	

The Intel Internet Video Phone 2.0 is an easy program to use and it is H.323-compliant. The quality of the video is very good and connections are easy, you can just enter a person's IP address and be instantly connected. Audio is equally as good as the video. Volume controls include a mute option for private chats. Also you do not need to have a video capture card or camera to receive video images. If your system is limited to only a microphone and sound card you an still use the Internet Video Phone 2.0 to for audio-only calls. There is also directory support for directories such as BigFoot, Infospace, Four11, Switchboard and WhoWhere?, Microsoft's User Location Service, and Internet Address Finder. The best thing about this software is it's free.

NetMeeting 2.0

Price Free	
Rank 2	
Ease of Use 100	
Performance 87.5	
Features 100	

NetMeeting 2.0 is by Microsoft and is free, which makes it a good buy. Of course there is plenty more to like about this program. NetMeeting offers real-time communications between people in different locations. It's easy to set up and use and is also H.323 compliant. Overall performance is good. There are three communications modes you can connect in, personal, business, or adult-only. Features include a chat function, whiteboard application for collaborating on documents, a file transfer utility, and multiple conferencing capabilities. You can switch between conference participants easily. One bonus in this software is the ability to share documents with others even if the application program the document was created in does not reside on everyone's computer. Documents can be shared in two modes, View Only and Group Effort. View Only allows only the person who originated the call to edit the document while Group Effort lets all conference participants make changes. This software is not currently cross-platform compatible and can only be used to communicate with others on the Windows 95 platform.

VDOPhone Internet

Price $99	
Rank 1	
Ease of Use 100	
Performance 100	
Features 100	

If you already have a video camera and video capture board, then this package will put them to good use as a video conference system. VDOPhone Internet wins raves for its superb video quality. This software renders 320- by-240 resolutions. Video performance is also excellent. Using the program is simple with the uncluttered interface. You can connect to other users via analog telephone lines (POTS), digital lines (ISDN), or direct connections (LAN, etc.). To receive a call the program must be running. Calls can be screened before you answer. During a conference all controls are displayed on the screen along with information about transmission rates and lost packets. Also a chat window is displayed if you want to send text messages. VDOPhone Internet incorporates Microsoft NetMeeting, which offers numerous collaboration capabilities such as application sharing and whiteboard features. This is a great package and it can be found bundled in many videophone packages.

CONTACT INFORMATION

CU-SeeMe 3.0
White Pine Software
603-886-9050
www.cuseeme.com

Intel Internet Video Phone 2.0
Intel
800-628-8686
www.intel.com

NetMeeting
Microsoft Corp
800 426-9400
www.microsoft.com/netmeeting

VDOPhone
VDOnet Corporation
617-528-6000
www.vdo.net

VIDEO-CONFERENCING SYSTEMS,

ISDNs FOR DESKTOPS

This chapter concerns Integrated Services Digital Networks (ISDNs). A ISDN is a digital telephone service that requires a dedicated digital line—standard telephone lines are analog—which runs at two speeds: 128-Kbps basic-rate interface (BRI) and 1.54Mbps primary-rate interface (PRI). Such lines are obtained from your local telephone company. The cost, which will vary from phone company to phone company, is usually modest, around $50 per month, plus an installation fee of several hundred dollars. One "bonus" in having an ISDN line is that you can use it to surf the Internet as well, and do so at speeds many-fold that of standard telephone connections, providing you have a digital modem (they cost several hundred dollars).

This chapter takes a look at professional-quality videoconferencing using ISDNs on a desktop computer. The systems now offer better video quality and features at a reasonable price, at least more reasonable than renting time at a video conferencing site, which is the way videoconferencing has been traditionally done.

The top-rated ISDN, PictureTel's Live 200p, is designed for Windows 95, enabling you to conduct videoconferencing on a PC.

If you you wish to look into a less expensive alternative, there are the systems that can run on your computer over the Internet (See the chapter titled "Videoconferencing Software," and "Videophones"). However, if you want a first-class setup, the ISDN alternative is superior. ISDNs allow users on two systems, located in different areas, to visually communicate with one another, share applications, edit documents, transfer files, and conduct multipoint conferences with more than two people. There are a variety of systems that can give you this capability. These professional systems can either be set up in a conference room so that a number of people can attend the videoconference or can be at one's desk.

The list below evaluates some of the major videoconferencing systems on the market.

RANKINGS AND OVERALL SCORES

1 PictureTel Live 200p   92

2 Intel ProShare Conferencing
   Video System 200   88

3 CLI Desktop Video System 1000   58

4 VTEL Personal Collaborator   50

EXPLANATION OF RATINGS

Desktop videoconferencing systems were rated for the following facets: Setup, Picture Quality, and Conferencing Features. The highest possible rating for each category is 100. Scores for each were then averaged in order to compute the Overall Score.

ALPHABETICAL DESCRIPTIONS

CLI Desktop Video System 1000

Price $1,795

Rank 3

Setup 25

Picture Quality 100

Conferencing Features 50

The CLI Desktop Video System 1000 has high-quality video quality and a number of advanced features, but the setup and conferencing features are below par. The system requires a 100-MHz or higher Pentium with 16MB of RAM. This system includes a small Philips camera, a VCON-manufactured ISDN/Video board, and a earpiece. Before installing make sure your graphics accelerator works with the Desktop Video 1000. This system does not work with very many cards. The Desktop

Video 1000 produces great video quality and audio quality. The sound peripherals are superb. Video can be produced at 20 fps at FCIF resolution. Advanced features include JPEG still-image compression, PIP video (picture-in-picture), dual composite and digital video inputs and Twain scanner support for whiteboard input. Document-conferencing software is not included but the Intel ProShare Premier 1.9 document-conferencing software is available for $200. CLI has a 90-day parts and labor warranty and toll-free technical support for 24 hours, seven days a week.

Intel ProShare Conferencing Video System 200

Price $1,499

Rank 2

Setup 75

Picture Quality 87.5

Conferencing Features 100

The ProShare Conferencing Video System 200 offers standards-compatible videoconferencing over an ISDN line or LAN. For best results the system 200 should be used on an IntelDX2T or Pentium processor-based computer with a minimum of 16MB of RAM (20MB recommended) and 50MB hard disk space, plus 25MB extra for the installation's temp files. System 200 complies with the H.320 and T.120 ITU standards and supports ISDN speeds of 112 Kbps and 128Kbps. However, when connected to non-Intel H.320 systems, it does not have bi-directional support for 352-by-288 FCIF resolution video. Included with the System 200 is a multi-lingual conferencing software CD-ROM, an ISA bus

ISDN/audio board, a color video camera, an Intel Smart Video Recorder Pro motion video card, and a audio headset. Microphones and speakers are not included. The bundled Intel ProShare Premier 2.0 document-conferencing software has an updated icon-based interface, and tools that let you access Microsoft's NetMeeting tools. There is also support for mixed ISDN/LAN/POTS multipoint videoconferences with the right configuration of hardware and network management software. Conferencing tools include application sharing, which allows users on different systems to simultaneously use one application located on one of the systems; multipoint notebook, where files are imported for users to share or annotate; there is also an address book and auto dialer option and high-speed file transfer capabilities.

Video quality for the System 200 is sufficient with frame rates of 8 to 10 fps for a 100-MHz Pentium computer. This performance will vary depending on your system. The system's performance relies on your PC processor because video decompression is done in software. Installation is pretty straightforward. In addition to the excellent manual, Intel includes an online animated tutorial, and a video site you dial into where you can register and test your system's connections. Warranty covers one year parts and labor. Technical support is offered via the web and telephone but it's not toll free. Technical telephone support is available five days a week for 10 hours.

PictureTel Live200p

Price $1,495	
Rank 1	
Setup 100	
Picture Quality 87.5	
Conferencing Features 87.5	

As the top performer in this group, PictureTel Live 200p has superior performance, video quality, and document conferencing and is easy to set up and use. This system is built for Windows 95 computers, enabling them to conduct videoconferencing with any other H.320 system. It is also compatible with T.120 which allows users to share applications and documents in real-time with others in different locations. This makes working with remote team members easier. This system includes a PCI video/audio codec board with ISDN interface, Live200 CD-ROM videoconferencing software, a video camera, headset, speakers and microphone. An optional FlipCam is also available. There are no manual controls, but the software provides controls over contrast, color, brightness, and audio/video muting. Installation is effortless since the Live 200p is a true plug-and-play device. On-line documentation is available and includes a product guide, quick reference card, installation guide and on-line help. An optional hard copy of the documentation is available.

The video quality is superior with speeds from 10 to 15 fps. Sound quality is just as good with support for all H.320 audio codecs. Features include shared clipboard, application sharing, drag-and-drop file transfer, whiteboard with annotation tools, password-protected remote control, and phone book with on-screen dial pad. Advanced features include snapshot of local or remote video windows, far-end camera control, and dynamic bandwidth allocation. Warranty covers the hardware for one year and the software for 90 days. Toll-free technical support is available 12 hours daily, Monday through Friday.

VTEL Personal Collaborator

Price $2,495

Rank 4

Setup 25

Picture Quality 50

Conferencing Features 75

VTEL Personal Collaborator is not plug-and-play compatible and if there is a conflict during installation with the default I/O address you have to manually set the jumpers. Another drawback is this system can only be used with 15 graphics adapters. A graphics adapter, the Diamond Alpine Speedster Series, is included but it's not one of the best. The Feature connector limits color depths, screen resolutions, and refresh rates. Graphics mode can only display in 256 colors at 640-by-480, which effects video quality. Technical support is toll free, available nine hours a day, Monday through Friday. Support is also available via the web. Software in-

cludes the Intel ProShare 1.9a configured for Windows 95, and ObjectShare 120 for drag-and-drop slide presentations. The Personal Collaborator works with other H.320 conferencing systems and has features such as application sharing, document annotations, shared whiteboard, chat mode, remote pointer, remote control, picture-in-picture, phone book with auto-dialer, drag-and-drop file transfer, call blocking, Caller ID, and ISDN modem capability for high-speed access to the Internet, and online service for corporate networks. For the price of this product you need to get better performance.

CONTACT INFORMATION

Compression Labs Inc. (CLI)
800-538-7542
www.clix.com

Intel ProShare Conferencing Video System 200
Intel Corp.
800-538-3373
www.intel.com

PictureTel Corp
800-716-6000
www.picturetel.com

VTEL Corp.
800-299-8835
www.vtel.com

VIDEOPHONES, LOW-COST SOLUTIONS FOR VIDEO-CONFERENCING

This chapter concerns low-cost PC-based videoconferencing solutions. Using your computer, a regular phone line and the Internet, and a video capture card and software (See chapter "Videoconferencing Software"), you can set up a fairly good videoconference system. Several better, but more expensive, alternatives are videoconferencing systems using Integrated Services Digital Networks (ISDNs). A ISDN is a digital telephone service. (See the chapter titled "Videoconferencing Systems—ISDNs for Desktops"). Another, yet more expensive, way

3COM's number-one rated Bigpicture Video Kit, comes complete with a NTSC color camera with built-in microphone, video capture card (internal PCI card), an upgradeable V.80, a phone cord, 6-ft RJ11 connector, manual and Video Connections CD-ROM.

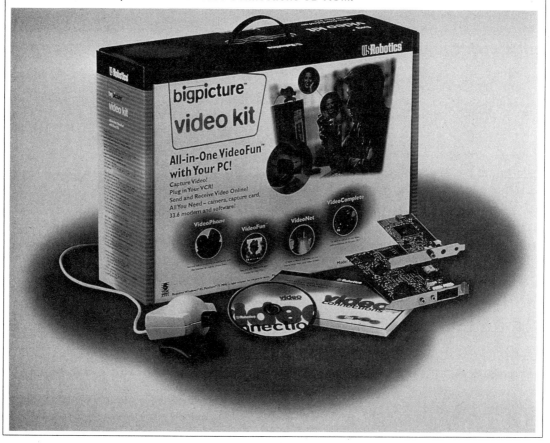

is to rent a videoconferencing room at companies that provide videoconferencing services. Just one seat in a video conference can cost over $1000.

Here we review lower-cost videoconferencing products priced under $500. These videoconferencing products can be used on older computers with no videoconferencing capabilities. All of these products include a small camera that is mounted on the computer monitor and attached to either the video capture card or through a parallel port. Performance will vary depending on how your camera is used. Cameras attached directly to the video capture card perform faster and produce better quality images. Cameras attached to the parallel port performs much slower.

The list below ranks some of the major videoconference products.

RANKINGS AND OVERALL SCORES

1 3COM Bigpicture Video
  Kit 1622   96

2 Diamond Supra Video
  Phone Kit 3000   92

3 Boca Video Phone Kit   63

4 SuiteVISIONS   58

EXPLANATION OF RATINGS

Scores were computed in three categories: *Installation*, which relates to how easy the program is to set up and use; *Performance*, which pertains to the ability to interface with other videophones, including the video's speed, color, brightness, and clarity; and *Features*, which refers to the included hardware, such as a modem and

software. Scores for each category were based on a scale of 0-100. The categories were then averaged and the result is the overall score.

ALPHABETICAL DESCRIPTIONS

3COM Bigpicture Video Kit 1622

Price $399

Score 96

Installation 100

Performance 87.5

Features 100

3COM's video conferencing product, the Bigpicture Video Kit, comes complete with a NTSC color camera with built-in microphone, video capture card (internal PCI card), an upgradeable V.80, a phone cord, 6-ft RJ11 connector, manual and Video Connections CD-ROM. This videophone package uses RapidComm Communications Suite, which has H.324 videophone, speakerphone as well as fax modem, messaging, and telephony features. Other software bundled with Bigpicture includes Asymetrix's Digital Video Producer 4.0, which is a video editing suite, a light version of Kai's Power Goo, and VDONet's VDOLive streaming Internet video player. The Bigpicture can work with other video conferencing products. The software's graphical interface is easy-to-use and offers sharp video quality. Images can be captures in 24-bit color at up to 30 frames per second. Video resolutions supported range from 160x120 pixels, 320x240 pixels to 640x480 pixels. It supports H.324 technology with V.80 support over regular phone lines. Image quality and audio are good. The modem from has DSP (Digital Signal Processing) built-ins which handles audio functions, thus making the sound good. There is a lower-priced version of this video kit that sells for $249, but it does not include a modem. Overall this is a good product which will only get better with time and technology upgrades.

Boca Video Phone Kit

Price $239

Score 63

Installation 62.5

Performance 62.5

Features 62.5

The Boca Video Phone Kit includes Sony's CCM-PC5 color camera, a built-in microphone with an RCA jack and Smith Micro's VideoLink 324 point-to-point video conferencing, software, and, for Internet conferencing, the VDOnet's VDO-Phone. To complete the package you'll need a V.80 modem and an adapter for the microphone. Performance is good and the Sony camera generates clear images. Videoconference speed can run up to 15 frames per second and the receiving party does not need to have a camera or video board to receive images. Display quality is SVGA at 16 bits. One drawback is that the Boca phone does not interface well with a lot of other cameras.

Diamond Supra Video Phone Kit 3000

Price $299

Score 92

Installation 100

Performance 100

Features 75

The Supra Video Phone Kit 300 is a plug and play product that includes everything you need to set up a basic videoconferencing system for use over standard phone lines or the Internet. Included in the kit is a Philips color PC video camera with built-in microphone, a Supra 33.6Kbps modem with the V.80 protocol, Diamond Crunch IT 1001 video capture card which includes a Super VHS port for a video camera, VDOPhone 2.0 Professional, video editing software, and Internet software. Since this kit is strictly plug and play, installation is a breeze. Image quality is excellent with resolutions up to 640x480 pixels and a range of 256 to 16 million colors. Performance is fast. This videophone can use any Internet phone software and is an excellent desktop videoconferencing solution.

SuiteVISIONS

Price $189

Score 58

Installation 75

Performance 50

Features 50

SuiteVISIONS offers an affordable videoconferencing package that includes the VisionCAM, a 24-bit, 16.7 million color, digital parallel port camera; Vision-Time Internet VideoPhone video conferencing software; ColorLink software for sending and receiving color documents; InternetFax fax software; Microsoft Internet Explorer; NetMeeting; and Net-Show. The Internet VideoPhone software includes a chat feature, interactive video-mail for sending video e-mail messages, a whiteboard application where you can collaborate, edit, and exchange documents, and video capture feature for capturing video images locally or remotely. There is a variety of other software such as ArcSoft PhotoImpression, a clip art CD-ROM, and a personal organizer. As far as performance is concerned, the proprietary software included is not H.23 compliant. Also since SuiteVISIONS uses a parallel camera, performance is not as good as with packages that use PCI cameras and capture cards.

CONTACT INFORMATION

3COM Bigpicture Video Kit
3COM (U.S. Robotics)
800-342-5877
www.3com.com

Diamond Supra Video Phone Kit 3000
Diamond Multimedia Systems
800-727-8772
www.diamondmm.com

SuiteVISIONS
Specom Technologies
www.specom.com

VOICE MAIL SYSTEMS

Voice mail systems are similar in function to answering machines — they record voice messages for people who are not available to answer their phones. Features often include the ability to call into the system to retrieve messages from another location, forwarding messages to other people, and broadcasting messages to groups or to everyone on the system. The callers either hear a standard greeting telling them how to leave their message or an individually recorded message that may include when the caller will reply or an alternative person who will be able to assist the caller.

One desirable feature is a "last resort" option, which involves speaking to a person instead of the system. People receive their calls by dialing into the system and using the touch-tone keypad to access their "mail-box," and then provide a password or key for security. A few systems are now capable of incorporating e-mail with voice messaging, which is called "unified messaging," letting you hear your e-mail when you are not able to access it directly from your computer.

Most voice mail systems today are standard personal computers with voice boards and software added. These work very well for small offices, but for larger companies or high-use environments, specialized proprietary systems developed explicitly for messaging may be needed. In choosing a system, you must first consider your current and future growth needs and select a system with sufficient capacity. Capacity means enough ports to handle callers without unreasonable delays and storage space for greetings and messages that have not been heard and deleted. Next, you must determine whether your current phone system will work with the voice mail system and, if not, how much it will cost to install a new phone system.

Other features that you may want in your system include caller-selectable routing options, the ability to replay or edit a message being left, the ability to get voice or fax responses from the system, or notification that a message is waiting. And if you want your system to collect information into a database or give the caller individual information, you should look for interactive voice response (IVR) capabilities. A common use of IVR is to give callers the status of their order or to take a new order, updating the database if needed.

If you have modest needs for 2 to 5 people and some computer expertise, you can purchase computer boards and software and do it yourself. You will need touch-tone phones and an inexpensive computer to dedicate to the system. Otherwise, it would be a good idea to contact several dealers and get proposals for the entire job including hardware, software, installation, mail-box setup, and training of the users. Sources for voice mail systems include retail outlets, value added resellers, and the manufacturer.

In this review we looked at voice mail systems that support from two to 500 mailboxes and that are not restricted to a particular type or brand of phone system. Data on these systems was obtained from the manufacturers. Prices indicated are the manufacturer's stated price when the system was reviewed.

The following are descriptions of features common to many voice mail systems:

Automated attendant projects a professional image for your company and routes calls to the appropriate department or person when the caller does not know the extension needed.

Audiotext helps you distribute information commonly requested from your company, such as directions, product information, business hours, and answers to frequently asked questions. It is sometimes called a "voice bulletin board" and can be spelled "audiotex."

Caller review generally includes the ability of a caller to review a message and optionally change or cancel it.

Fax-on-demand is the ability for a caller to select information from a menu or database for either immediate or delayed faxing back to the caller.

Interactive voice response (IVR) is a facility to interact with the system to select particular information or to record information digitally into the system. These are commonly used for applications like banking by phone, or checking order status.

Last name directory systems let you key in either the person's extension or enter the last name using the keypad to route you to the correct extension.

Personal greeting is a way of personalizing the system by letting each user record a message in their own voice for the callers. These can usually be easily updated such that a person can more precisely tell the caller when they will get a call back or that there is another person who can handle the call.

Replay speed control is usually similar to playing back an audio tape, with pause, rewind, and fast-forward options.

Return receipt is the ability to get a message from the system when a message has been delivered to another user of the system.

The following are terms you may encounter when evaluating voice mail systems:

Computer-Telephony Integration (CTI) is the technology that connects a telephone system to a computer.

Mail-boxes are queues of messages managed by each user. They can also be special mail-boxes to support audiotext fax-on-demand requests, or IVR.

Ports are the number of phone lines that can be connected to a voice mail system. In general, two ports should handle 25 users, four ports up to 100 users, and eight ports for around 300 users. But this can be impacted by heavy telephone usage by the users or by the system responding to audiotext or fax requests.

Voice storage is usually indicated in hours or in the amount of computer disk space required for a given number of hours of messages.

Below is a selection of voice mail systems that are currently on the market along with their overall ratings.

OVERALL RATINGS

Active Voice Replay 2.5	★★★ 3/4
AVT px100	★★★ 1/4
VoiceWorld SuiteTalker plus	★★★ 1/4
Octel Smooth Operator Ultra Lite	★★★
Talking Technology PowerVoice	★★★
Central Voice Express Lite	★★ 3/4
Key Voice Small Office	★★ 3/4
Cobotyx SOHO Secretary	★★ 1/4

EXPLANATION OF RATINGS

The voice mail systems were rated from one to four stars for Ease of Use, Recording Features, and Listening Features. The highest rating possible is four stars; the lowest, one. The star ratings were then averaged to arrive at the overall rating.

ALPHABETICAL DESCRIPTIONS

Active Voice Replay 2.5

Overall Rating ★★★ 3/4

Price $1,800 and up, including a 486 computer.

Ease of Use ★★★★

Calling Features ★★★★

Listening Features ★★★

This is their entry-level personal computer—based system with up to 100 mail-boxes and 45 hours of message storage.

They have other more expensive systems that can handle an unlimited number of mail-boxes and up to 85 hours of messages. Their "TeLANophy" products also allow e-mail, fax, and voice mail messages to be combined into one system. Setting up of mail-boxes can be done from any touch-tone phone or computer with a modem. Adding or changing users can be done without taking the system off-line. Employees can "enroll" using a self-guided tutorial, eliminating training. Users can record one personal greeting easily. The easy-to-use "one for yes, two for no" design can require a user to go through several levels of questions to complete an interaction. There is an option for traditional menu interaction. Calling features include automated attendant, last name directory, caller review and cancellation, and return receipt. Listening features include message pause, rewind and fast-forward, and message waiting notification including pagers. There are also basic fax functions to route an incoming fax to your fax machine, prompt the caller to leave a message, and notify you that a fax has been received by placing a message in your mail-box. Programmable "transaction boxes" can play audiotext, transfer calls, and play or take messages similar to IVR systems. Utilities are provided for message and system backup and system performance tuning.

AVT px100

Overall Rating ★★★ 1/4

Price $5,000, including a 486 personal computer

Ease of Use ★★★

Calling Features ★ ★ ★

Listening Features ★ ★ ★ ★

This is their basic four-port personal computer-based system that can handle up to 100 mail-boxes and store 20 hours of messages. A larger hard drive can be installed to increase the message storage. They offer higher-priced systems with more features and ports. Users can easily record up to two personal greetings. Caller features include caller review, automated attendant, and last name directory. Listening features include message pause, rewind, fast-forward and skip, forwarding to another phone or pager, message notification, and a saved message queue. Other features include forwarding messages to distribution lists, scheduling future delivery of messages, and standard reports.

Central Voice Express Lite

Overall Rating ★ ★ 3/4

Price $595 plus a 386DX or faster computer

Ease of Use ★ ★

Calling Features ★ ★ ★ 1/2

Listening Features ★ ★ ★

This is a two-port personal computer-based system that can be upgraded to 32 ports. There is no limit on the number of mail-boxes or message storage other than the capacity of your hard disk. They offer other systems that can be easily upgraded to for additional capacity or features. Users can record two personal greetings for "business" and "after hours" call handling. And they can set their own maximum message size and number of messages to accept. Ease of use may be impacted by having to take the system off-line to add mailboxes. And the user

cannot change greeting messages or other mail-box options from a remote location. Caller features include automated attendant, audiotext, fax on demand, and menu selection or routing. Listening features include call transfer, message forwarding to a phone or pager, and fax forwarding, Other features include IVR, using Special Questionnaire boxes.

Cobotyx SOHO Secretary

Overall Rating ★ ★ 1/4

Price $2,600

Ease of Use ★ ★ ★

Calling Features ★ ★

Listening Features ★ ★

This is a two-to-four port system that can handle up to 250 mail-boxes and 16 hours of messages. They offer higher priced systems with more ports and mail-boxes. Users can record only one personal greeting. Caller features include caller review and automated attendant. Listening features include message pause.

Key Voice Small Office

Overall Rating ★ ★ 3/4

Price $3,000 and up

Ease of Use ★ ★ ★

Calling Features ★ ★ ★ 1/2

Listening Features ★ ★

This is a two-to-four port system that can handle up to 100 mailboxes and and messages up to the limit of the storage you have available. It is upgradeable to their Corporate Office product, which was previously sold as the Verbatim Voice system. Users can record up to 10 personal greetings for different conditions. Caller features include caller review, automated attendant, last name directory, and return receipt. Listening features include message pause. There is a Visual Call Management option that lets users receive faxes and voice mail on a desktop computer and costs around $300 per computer.

Octel Smooth Operator Ultra Lite

Overall Rating ★★★

Price $3,000 including a computer.

Ease of Use ★★★

Calling Features ★★★ 3/4

Listening Features ★★

Octel has both proprietary systems appropriate for very large companies and a personal computer-based set of products, of which the Smooth Operator Lite is the least expensive. You can upgrade within the product line without disruption. It can handle from four-24 ports, 50 mailboxes, and more than 200 hours of messages depending on the amount of disk storage available. We included it because it has an entry configuration and price that is competitive. Users can have up to six personal greeting messages. Calling features include caller review, return receipt, audiotext, automated attendant, and last name directory. Listening features include message pause.

Talking Technology PowerVoice

Overall Rating ★★★

Price $695 plus a 386DX or faster computer

Ease of Use ★★★

Calling Features ★★ 1/2

Listening Features ★★★ 3/4

This is a two-port system that can handle any number of mail-boxes and hours of

messages, based on the hard drive space available. Users can record a personal greeting. Ease of use is supported by allowing remote access and mail-box customization by the users. Caller features include automated attendant, first and last name lookup, and menu selection or routing. Listening features include message notification by forwarding to a phone or pager, message forwarding including a personal message attachment, call transfer, and call screening. It will also place calls from a database, log completed calls and retry busy numbers. Add-on modules are available for fax-on-demand, Caller ID capture to a database, Btrieve database access, and other functions.

VoiceWorld SuiteTalker plus

Overall Rating ★★ ★ 1/4

Price $1,997 plus a 486 or faster computer

Ease of Use ★★★★

Calling Features ★★ 1/2

Listening Features ★★★

This is a two port system that can handle up to 50 extensions and an unlimited number of mail-boxes. It can be expanded gradually to as many as 12 phone lines and 1,500 extensions. Messages are stored on the computer's hard drive, with the limit on messages being a factor of the available disk space. It works with most phone systems, including PBXs. Users can easily record up to 99 greetings or other messages per mail-box. Ease of use features include being able to add mail-boxes without taking the system off-line, being able to transfer calls to any other number, and message notification via pager or phone by forwarding the message automatically when the person called is not answering. Caller features include out-of-time warning, menu selection or routing, and an optional fax-on-demand for another $500. Listening features include message pause, transfer to another mailbox, and conference calling. Other features include audiotext, IVR, and calculation of charges per unit, time, and date and usage for optionally billing mailbox owners.

CONTACT INFORMATION

Active Voice
206-441-4700
www.activevoice.com

Applied Voice Technology (AVT)
425-820-6000
www.appliedvoice.com

Central Technologies, Inc.
800-532-8053
www.centraltech.com

Cobotyx
800-288-6342
www.cobotyx.com

Key Voice Technologies
800-419-3800
www.keyvoice.com

Octel Communications Corporation
800-284-2869
www.octel.com

Talking Technology, Inc.
800-934-4884
www.tti.net

VoiceWorld
800-283-4759
www.voiceworld.com

Backup Tape Systems

In this chapter we review various backup tape systems, however, tape is not the only way to backup the data on your computer. Two other alternatives are discussed in this volume in the following chapters: "Removable Hard Drives" and "CRs" (CD-ROM Recordable and Rewritable Drives). Each method is unique and worth learning about, so it is suggested that you read all three chapters in order to determine which will work best to meet your needs.

"Your data is only as good as your last backup" is the mantra of computer gurus. In the corporate world, where data is viewed as an organization's most important asset, it should be your mantra too. In fact, anyone with a computer holding important programs or data should be doing backups — you never can tell when a hardware failure, theft, or fire will occur. So, why is backing up data so often overlooked? It is because it can be very time consuming and it only benefits you when there is a problem.

Before selecting a new backup system or upgrading an old one, you should review your data storage requirements and the available technologies to determine which

product best fits your backup strategy. Figure out how much data you need to put on a backup device in megabytes (millions of characters or MB) or gigabytes (billions of characters or GB) by looking at your applications carefully. Also decide whether you will backup all the programs as well as your data, or just the data. A backup strategy is simply what you will backup, how often you will do it, and how much time you have in which to complete the backup without disrupting your ability to use your computer. A common backup strategy, for example, is to backup your entire hard drive once per week and only backup changed data daily. Assuming a one GB hard disk and 100 MB changing per day, you need a tape backup system with a minimum of one GB capacity and four cartridges for a two-week cycle. The time to backup daily on the least expensive one GB tape drive we reviewed would be about 10-15 minutes with the weekly one GB backup taking almost two hours.

There are some terms and abbreviations you should be aware of when considering tape drives.

Client/Server is common computer industry terminology for workstations (clients) attached to a network server. There can be software drivers for client and/or server computers included with the hardware.

Interfaces come in serial, floppy, parallel, IDE, or SCSI ("scuzzy") types, which are actually ports on your computer. The slowest for backup speed is the floppy drive interface, then serial, parallel, and IDE ports respectively. The fastest is the

SCSI type, with designations of SCSI, SCSI-2 and Fast SCSI-2 where they are each progressively faster in backup data speed. Note, that most desktop computers do not come with a SCSI port, which can add about $200 to your purchase price.

MTBF stands for mean time between failures and is generally expressed as how many hours you can expect the tape drive to work before failing. 100K MTBF indicates approximately 100,000 hours of use between failures.

There are several tried-and-true tape hardware technologies available to meet your back up requirements. The technologies used in the tape systems in this chapter include the following:

QIC Format: This, designed for the smallest needs, are the minicartridge and quarter inch (QIC) tape drives. Their costs range from $649 to $1,295 and their specifications are: 17-32MB/minute backup and 2.5-4GB capacity.

Taravan Tape Drives: These have a larger cartridge and cost between $99 and $499. Their specifications are: 5-32MB/minute backup and 4-4GB capacity)

DAT Tape Drives: Its name is derived from Digital Audio Tape (DAT) and they come in three standards: *DAT DDS-1*: Their costs range from $729 to $1,295. Their specifications are: 12-33MB/minute backup and 1-2GB capacity. *DAT DDS-2*: Their costs range from $979 to $1,995. Their specifications are: 10-47MB/minute backup and 4GB capacity. *DAT-DDs*: Their costs range from $1,229

to $2,795. Their specifications are: 32-72MB/minute backup and 12GB capacity.

Below are the overall ratings of each of the tape backup systems in the various categories that are reviewed.

OVERALL RATINGS

QIC Format

Tandberg SLR5	★★ 1/4
Tecmar Wangtek 52000	★★
Valitek PST-TR4	★★

Travan Format

HP Colorado 5GB	★★★ 1/4
Seagate TapeStor 800	★★ 3/4
Seagate Hornet 8	★★ 3/4
HP Colorado SureStore T4i	★★ 1/2
Seagate TapeStor 8000	★★ 1/2
Iomega Ditto 2G	★★ 1/4
NCE Mountain Travan	★★

DAT DDS-1

Seagate Scorpion 4	★★ 3/4
HP SureStore 2000i	★★ 1/2
ValitekPST-DAT2+	★★ 1/2
Legacy DAT 4DX	★★ 1/2
NCE Mountain FileSafe	★★ 1/4

DAT DDS-2

Tecmar WangDAT 3800	★★ 3/4
HP SureStore DAT8i	★★ 3/4
Seagate Scorpion 8	★★ 3/4
Valitek PST-DAT4+	★★ 1/2

ADIC DATa 8008	★★ 1/2
TTi CTS-4410	★★ 1/2
NCE Emerald Systems GemStor	★★

DAT-DDS-3

Seagate Scorpion 24	★★★ 1/2
Tecmar WangDAT 3900	★★★ 1/4
HP SureStore DAT24i	★★★ 1/4
TTi CTS-4610	★★★
ADIC DATa 8024D	★★★
MicroNet SS-D24000	★★★
Valitek, PST-DAT12+	★★ 1/4

EXPLANATION OF RATINGS

Tape backup hardware devices were selected for review from currently available products that met the configuration types listed earlier. The overall rating was arrived at by giving individual scores form one to four stars for the following aspects of each tape system: Speed (backup and restore time per GB), Capacity (GB per dollar), Upgradeability (within the vendor line), and the Warranty. These scores were then averaged to arrive at the overall rating. The highest rating possible is four stars.

ALPHABETICAL DESCRIPTIONS

ADIC DATa 8008

Price $1,595
Overall Rating ★★ 1/2
Capacity Rating ★ 1/2
Speed Rating ★ 1/4
Upgradeability Rating ★★★★
Warranty Rating ★★★

This is a DAT-DDS-2 drive with a capacity of four GB and a speed of 22MB/minute with a Fast SCSI-2 interface. ADIC has a DDS-3 upgrade path. The warranty is one year. There is client-side OS support for Windows NT, OS/2, MacOS, and UNIX systems. It includes AppleShare, Netware 3.0/4.0, and Windows NT server side OS support.

ADIC DATa 8024D

Price $2,495
Overall Rating ★★★
Capacity Rating ★★
Speed Rating ★★★ 3/4
Upgradeability Rating ★★★
Warranty Rating ★★★

This is a DAT-DDS-3 drive with a capacity of 12 GB and a speed of 70MB/minute with a Fast SCSI-2 interface. There is no upgrade model available currently. The warranty is one year. There is client side OS support for DOS, Windows 3.x and up, OS/2, and UNIX. It includes AppleShare, Netware 3.0/4.0, and Windows NT server side OS support.

HP Colorado 5GB

Price $199 (internal), $249 (external)
Overall Rating ★★★ 1/4
Capacity Rating ★★★★
Speed Rating ★ 3/4
Upgradeability Rating ★★★★
Warranty Rating ★★★ 1/2

This is a Travan drive with a capacity of 2.5 GB and a speed of 32MB/minute with an IDE interface. There are models from HP that provide an upgrade path. The warranty is two years. There is client side OS support for DOS and Windows 3.x and up. It includes Lantastic, Windows for Workgroups, and Windows 95 server side OS support. Computer Associate's Colorado Backup software is included.

HP Colorado SureStore T4i

Price $499

Overall Rating ★★ 1/2

Capacity Rating ★★ 3/4

Speed Rating ★ 3/4

Upgradeability Rating ★★

Warranty Rating ★★★ 1/2

This is a Travan drive with a capacity of four GB and a speed of 30GB/minute with a SCSI-2 interface. There are no Travan models from HP that provide an upgrade path. The warranty is two years. There is client side OS support for DOS, Windows 3.x and up, and SCO UNIX. It includes Novell Netware 3.5-4.0 and Windows NT server side OS support. Computer Associate's Colorado Backup software is included.

HP SureStore DAT8i

Price $1,424

Overall Rating ★★★★

Capacity Rating ★ 1/2

Speed Rating ★ 3/4

Upgradeability Rating ★★★ 1/2

Warranty Rating ★★★★

This is a DAT DDS-2 drive with a capacity of four GB and a speed of 30MB/minute with a SCSI-2 interface. There is an upgrade to DDS-3 drives within the HP line. The warranty is three years. There is client side OS support for most available systems. It includes Novell Netware 3.5-4.0 and Windows NT server side OS sup-

port. Computer Associate's Colorado Backup software is included.

HP SureStore DAT24i

Price $2,101 and up

Overall Rating ★★★ 1/4

Capacity Rating ★★ 1/4

Speed Rating ★★★ 1/4

Upgradeability Rating ★★★

Warranty Rating ★★★★

This is a DAT DDS-3 drive with a capacity of 12 GB and a speed of 60MB/minute with a SCSI-2 interface. There are upgrades within the HP line. The warranty is three years. There is client side OS support for most available systems. It includes Novell Netware 3.5-4.0 and Windows NT server side OS support. Computer Associate's Colorado Backup software is included.

HP SureStore Tape 2000i

Price $904 and up

Overall Rating ★★ 1/2

Capacity Rating ★ 1/2

Speed Rating 3/4

Upgradeability Rating ★★★★

Warranty Rating ★★★★

This is a DAT DDS-1 drive with a capacity of two GB and a speed of 12MB/minute with a SCSI-2 interface. There are upgrades within the HP line. The warranty is three years. There is client side OS support for most available systems. It includes Novell Netware 3.5-4.0 and Windows NT server side OS support. Computer Associate's Colorado Backup software is included.

Iomega Ditto 2G

Price $149 (internal) $199 (external)	
Overall Rating ★ ★ 1/4	
Capacity Rating ★ ★ ★ 1/2	
Speed Rating 3/4	
Upgradeability Rating ★	
Warranty Rating ★ ★ ★ 1/2	

This is a Travan drive with a capacity of 1.6 GB and a speed of 12MB/minute with a floppy interface internal and parallel interface external. There are no upgrades within the Iomega line. The warranty is two years. There is client side OS support for most available systems. It is not intended for network backup usage. Ditto Tools backup software is included.

Legacy DAT 4DX

Price $1,000	
Overall Rating ★ ★ 1/2	
Capacity Rating ★ 1/4	
Speed Rating ★ 1/4	
Upgradeability Rating ★ ★ ★ ★	
Warranty Rating ★ ★ ★	

This is a DAT DDS-1 drive with a capacity of four GB and a speed of 24MB/minute with a SCSI-2 interface. There are upgrades within the Legacy line. The warranty is one year. There is client side OS support for most available systems. It includes Novell Netware 3.5-4.0 and Windows NT server side OS support.

MicroNet SS-D24000

Price $2,170	
Overall Rating ★ ★ ★	
Capacity Rating ★ ★ 1/4	
Speed Rating ★ ★ ★ 1/4	
Upgradeability Rating ★ ★ ★	
Warranty Rating ★ ★ ★	

This is a DAT DDS-3 drive with a capacity of 12 GB and a speed of 60MB/minute with a Fast SCSI-2 interface. There are upgrades within the MicroNet line. The warranty is one year. There is client side OS support for DOS, Windows 3.x and up, MacOS, and UNIX systems. It includes AppleShare, Netware and Windows NT server side OS support.

NCE Emerald GemStor

Overall Rating ★ ★	
Price $1,145	
Capacity Rating ★ 3/4	
Speed Rating 1/2	
Upgradeability Rating ★ ★ ★	
Warranty Rating ★ ★ ★	

This is a DAT DDS-2 drive with a capacity of four GB and a speed of 10MB/minute with a SCSI-2 interface. There are upgrades within the NCE line. The warranty is one year. There is client side OS support for most systems. Server OS support information was not available.

NCE Mountain FileSafe

Price $1,100	
Overall Rating ★ ★ 1/4	
Capacity Rating ★	
Speed Rating 3/4	
Upgradeability Rating ★ ★ ★ ★	
Warranty Rating ★ ★ ★	

This is a DAT DDS-1 drive with a capacity of one GB and a speed of 12MB/minute with a SCSI-2 interface. There are upgrades within the NCE line. The warranty is one year. There is client side OS support for most systems. At this low capacity, it is not suitable for server backups. Legato Data Backup Utility backup software is included.

NCE Mountain Travan

Price $350

Overall Rating ★★

Capacity Rating ★★

Speed Rating 3/4

Upgradeability Rating ★★

Warranty Rating ★★★ 1/2

This is a Travan drive with a capacity of 1.6 GB and a speed of 12MB/minute with a floppy interface internal or parallel interface external. There are no Travan upgrades within the NCE line. The warranty is two years. There is client side OS support for most systems. At this low capacity, it is not suitable for server backups. Seagate or Arcada backup software is included.

Seagate Hornet 8

Price $429

Overall Rating ★★ 3/4

Capacity Rating ★★★ 1/4

Speed Rating ★

Upgradeability Rating ★★★

Warranty Rating ★★★ 1/2

This is a Travan drive with a capacity of four GB and a speed of 18MB/minute with a SCSI interface. There are Travan upgrades within the Seagate line. The warranty is two years. There is client and server side OS support for most common systems.

Seagate TapeStor 800

Price $99 (internal) $129 (external)

Overall Rating ★★ 1/2

Capacity Rating ★ 3/4

Speed Rating 1/4

Upgradeability Rating ★★★★

Warranty Rating ★★★ 1/2

This is a Travan drive with a capacity of .4 GB and a speed of 5MB/minute with an internal floppy interface and an external parallel interface. While it is the slowest and has a small capacity, it is priced right. There are Travan upgrades within the Seagate line. The warranty is two years. There is client OS support for most common systems. The capacity and speed are not suitable for server backups. Seagate backup software is included.

Seagate TapeStor 8000

Price $369 (internal) $459 (external)

Overall Rating ★★ 3/4

Capacity Rating ★★★ 1/2

Speed Rating ★

Upgradeability Rating ★★★

Warranty Rating ★★★ 1/2

This is a Travan drive with a capacity of four GB and a speed of 18MB/minute with a SCSI interface. There are Travan upgrades within the Seagate line. The warranty is two years. There is client and server OS support for most common systems. Seagate backup software is included.

Seagate Scorpion 4

Price $729

Overall Rating ★★ 3/4

Capacity Rating ★ 1/2

Speed Rating ★ 3/4

Upgradeability Rating ★★★★

Warranty Rating ★★★ 1/2

This is a DAT DDS-1 drive with a capacity of two GB and a speed of 33MB/minute with a SCSI-2 interface. There are upgrades within the Seagate line. The warranty is two years. There is client and server OS support for most common systems. The capacity may not be suitable for server backups.

Seagate Scorpion 8

Price $979

Overall Rating ★ ★ 3/4

Capacity Rating ★ ★

Speed Rating ★ 3/4

Upgradeability Rating ★ ★ ★ 1/2

Warranty Rating ★ ★ ★ 1/2

This is a DAT DDS-2 drive with a capacity of four GB and a speed of 33MB/minute with a SCSI-2 interface. There are upgrades within the Seagate line. The warranty is two years. There is client and server OS support for most common systems.

Seagate Scorpion 24

Price $1,229

Overall Rating ★ ★ ★ 1/2

Capacity Rating ★ ★ ★ 1/4

Speed Rating ★ ★ ★ 3/4

Upgradeability Rating ★ ★ ★

Warranty Rating ★ ★ ★ 1/2

This is a DAT DDS-3 drive with a capacity of 12 GB and a speed of 66MB/minute with a SCSI-2 interface. This is among the fastest backup speeds of all tape systems reviewed in this chapter. There are upgrades within the Seagate line. The warranty is two years. There is client and server OS support for most common systems.

Tandberg SLR5

Price $649

Overall Rating ★ ★ 1/4

Capacity Rating ★ ★ 1/2

Speed Rating ★ 1/4

Upgradeability Rating ★

Warranty Rating ★ ★ ★ ★

This is a QIC drive with a capacity of four GB and a speed of 24MB/minute with a SCSI-2 interface. There are no upgrades within the Tandberg line. The warranty is three years. There is client and server OS support for most common systems.

Tecmar WangDAT 3800

Price $1,175

Overall Rating ★ ★ 3/4

Capacity Rating ★ 3/4

Speed Rating ★ ★ 1/2

Upgradeability Rating ★ ★ ★ 1/2

Warranty Rating ★ ★ ★ 1/2

This is a DAT DDS-2 drive with a capacity of four GB and a speed of 48MB/minute with a SCSI-2 interface. There are upgrades within the Tecmar line. The warranty is two years. There is client and server OS support for most common systems.

Tecmar WangDAT 3900

Price $1,625

Overall Rating ★ ★ ★ ★

Capacity Rating ★ ★ 3/4

Speed Rating ★ ★ ★ ★

Upgradeability Rating ★ ★ ★

Warranty Rating ★ ★ ★ 1/2

This is a DAT DDS-3 drive with a capacity of 12 GB and a speed of 72MB/minute with a SCSI-2 interface. This is the fastest drive of all tape systems reviewed in this chapter. There are upgrades within the Tecmar line. The warranty is two years. There is client and server OS support for most common systems.

Tecmar Wangtek 52000

Price $830

Overall Rating ★★

Capacity Rating ★ 1/2

Speed Rating ★

Upgradeability Rating ★★

Warranty Rating ★★★

This is a QIC drive with a capacity of 2.5 GB and a speed of 17MB/minute with a SCSI-2 interface. There are few upgrades within the Tecmar line. The warranty is one year. There is client and server OS support for most common systems.

TTi CTS-4410

Price $1,995

Overall Rating ★★ 1/2

Capacity Rating ★ 1/4

Speed Rating ★ 1/4

Upgradeability Rating ★★★ 1/2

Warranty Rating ★★★ 1/2

This is a DAT DDS-2 drive with a capacity of four GB and a speed of 22MB/minute with a SCSI-2 interface. There are upgrades within the TTi line. The warranty is two years. There is client and server OS support for most common systems.

TTi CTS-4610

Price $2,795

Overall Rating ★★★

Capacity Rating ★★

Speed Rating ★★★★

Upgradeability Rating ★★★

Warranty Rating ★★★ 1/2

This is a DAT DDS-3 drive with a capacity of 12 GB and a speed of 72MB/minute with a Fast SCSI-2 interface. This drive tied for the fastest of all tape systems reviewed in this chapter. The warranty is two years. There is client and server OS support for most common systems. There are upgrades within the TTi line.

Valitek PST-DAT2+

Price $1,295

Overall Rating ★★ 1/2

Capacity Rating ★ 1/4

Speed Rating ★ 3/4

Upgradeability Rating ★★★★

Warranty Rating ★★★

This is a DAT DDS-1 drive with a capacity of two GB and a speed of 32MB/minute with a SCSI-2 interface. There are upgrades within the Valitek line. The warranty is one year. There is client and server OS support for most common systems.

Valitek, PST-DAT4+

Price $1,599

Overall Rating ★★ 1/2

Capacity Rating ★ 1/2

Speed Rating ★ 3/4

Upgradeability Rating ★★★ 1/2

Warranty Rating ★★★

This is a DAT DDS-2 drive with a capacity of four GB and a speed of 32MB/minute with a SCSI-2 interface. There are upgrades within the Valitek line. The warranty is one year. There is client and server OS support for most common systems.

Valitek PST-DAT12+

Price $1,999

Overall Rating ★★ 1/2

Capacity Rating ★★ 1/4

Speed Rating ★ 3/4

Upgradeability Rating ★★★

Warranty Rating ★★★

This is a DAT DDS-3 drive with a capacity of 12 GB and a speed of 32MB/minute with a SCSI-2 interface. There are a few upgrades within the Valitek line. The warranty is one year. There is client and server OS support for most common systems.

Valitek PST-TR4

Price $1,295

Overall Rating ★★

Capacity Rating ★ 1/4

Speed Rating ★ 3/4

Upgradeability Rating ★★

Warranty Rating ★★★

This is a QIC drive with a capacity of 2.5 GB and a speed of 32MB/minute with a SCSI-2 interface. There are a no QIC upgrades within the Valitek line. The warranty is one year. There is client and server OS support for most common systems. The low capacity may rule it out for server backups.

CONTACT INFORMATION

Advanced Digital Information Corporation (ADIC)
800-336-1233
www.adic.com

Hewlett Packard (HP)
800-322-4772
www.hp.com

Iomega Corporation
888-4-IOMEGA
www.iomega.com

Legacy Storage Systems Corporation
800-966-6442
www.legacy.ca

MicroNet Technology, Inc.
714-453-6100
www.micronet.com

NCE Computer Group, Storage Solutions Division
800-767-2587
www.ncegroup.com

Seagate Technology, Inc.
408-438-8111
www.seagate.com

Tandberg Data, Inc.
800-826-3237
www.tandberg.com

Tecmar Technologies, Inc.
303-682-3700
www.tecmar.com

Transitional Technology, Inc. (TTi)
714-693-0225
www.ttech.com

Valitek Inc.
800-VALITEK
www.valitek.com

CD-Rs

CD-ROM RECORDABLE &

REWRITEABLE DRIVES

Today it seems hard to remember a time when PCs did not come with CD-ROM drives. They are so ubiquitous that even notebook computers are shipping them as standard equipment. It was only a matter of time until it became affordable for anyone to make their own CDs. That time is now reality, today you can buy a CD- Recordable (CD-R) drive for under $500. These CD-R drives allow you to create CDs for use as backups, to distribute programs that you create, or even create audio CDs. Most if not all of the drives looked at here are available at a discounted price via mail order, so it pays to do some comparison shopping.

CD-R drives fall into two categories, internal, which fit into an open drive bay in your PC, or external, which hook into your PC through a SCSI card or through the parallel port. You also have a choice on the speed of the drives. They fall into two categories, 2x6 and 4x4. No, this is not how many disks you can fit in, but an indication of how fast the drive can writes and reads CDs. For example, the 2x6 will write a CD at two times normal speed and read a CD at six times

normal speed. The 4x4s read and write at four times normal speed. New on the market and not very common are the real speed demons of the CD-Rs—the 4x6 drives.

CD-R technology is write-once, read-many (WORM), and you can neither erase nor reuse CD-R discs. Two new technologies, CD-Rewriteable (CD-RW), and Digital Versatile Disk (DVD) are now out and allow you to create CDs that can be rewritten and reused, almost in the manner of floppy disks. These two newcomers threaten CD-R with extinction.

There are several other facets you need to pay attention to when you go to buy a CD-R drive. The first is what operating system it works with. Some are supported for all versions of Windows, while others are specific to Windows 95 and Windows 3.x while ignoring Windows NT and Macintosh. Some support only Macintosh. The second item to look for is the software that comes with the drive. Believe it or not some CD-R drives come with no software whatsoever and you have to find some in order to create your disks. In any event you may want to upgrade the software if you find it does not fit your needs. The last item to be aware of is that you may need to buy an interface card and cables as not all drives come with all the hardware necessary. One last caveat, remember it is illegal to duplicate copyrighted software and audio.

OVERALL RATINGS

Smart and Friendly	★ ★ ★
Yamaha CRW4001	★ ★ ★

Philips EasyWriter CDD2600 ★★3/4

Pinnacle Micro RCD 4X4 ★★3/4

Pinnacle Micro RCDW226
Rewriteable CD Drive ★★3/4

HP SureStore CD-
Writer 6020es ★★1/2

Sony Spressa CDU-928E/H,
CDU-928E/K and
CDU-928E/C ★★1/2

OmniWriter CD-Rewriteable ★★ 1/2

Olympus CD-R2X6 ★★1/4

EXPLANATION OF RATINGS

The listings above rate the recordable CD-Rom drives according to data provided by the manufacturers. The scores look at several key areas, Write speed, read speed, hardware included and included software. The Overall Ratings were determined by assigning scores in each of the categories from one to four stars, the latter being the highest rating and then averaging them.

ALPHABETICAL DESCRIPTIONS

HP SureStore CD-Writer 6020es

Price $709

Overall Ratings ★★ 1/2

Read Speed ★★★

Write Speed ★★★

Hardware Included ★

Software Included ★★★

Hewlett-Packard's HP SureStore CD-Writer 6020 comes in at a price of $709. It is bundled with Easy-CD Pro software and an excellent advanced-replacement warranty and a SCSI cable. You must have a SCSI connector already installed in your PC as the HPs lack a SCSI controller. The SureStore CD-Writer 6020 is available in three formats: the 6020i for the internal model, 6020es for external SCSI, and 6020ep for external parallel port. All three are 6x 2x drives, which means that they read at 6x normal speed and write at 2x normal speed.

The HP comes with a decent bundle of software. The units come with Adaptec's Easy-CD Pro 2.0, IMR's Alchemy Personal Search 4.0 , and a multimedia tutorial. You will also find a single CD-R disk so you can make your first CD with no delay.

Olympus CD-R2X6

Price $499 (Internal); $649 (External)

Overall Rating ★★ 1/4

Read Speed ★★★

Write Speed ★★

Hardware Included ★

Software Included ★★★

No, the R2X6 from Olympus is not a droid from the new Star Wars movies, it is however one of the least expensive CD-R drives on the market. The CD-R2X6 reads at 6x speed and writes at 2x speed (a required SCSI card is not included). Both of the PC models include Adaptec's Easy-CD Pro 2.0 mastering software for recording audio, data, and multiformat CDs. The Mac version includes Adaptec's Toast Mastering software. The Olympus is available in three versions: an internal PC, an external PC, and an external Macintosh version. All have a one- year warranty.

Philips EasyWriter CDD2600

Price $499 (Internal) $599 (External)

Overall Rating ★★ 3/4

Read Speed ★★★

Write Speed ★★

Hardware Included ★★★

Software Included ★★★

For a price of around $600, the Philips EasyWriter CDD2600 is an outstanding choice for those new to CD-Rs. The Philips unit ships with an Adaptec ISA SCSI-2 adapter that is Plug and Play compatible, a SCSI cable, Adaptec's CD Creator software, Seagate Software's Backup Exec software and two blank discs for your recording pleasure. Philips provides documentation, and the installation should be a smooth process.

Unfortunately, the software can't make up for the 2x speed difference when stacked up against the 4x drives. Philips does provides a two-year parts-and-labor warranty which is better than the rest. But if you expect to record a lot of CDs, either audio or data, you will probably want to spend the extra money for the speed of a 4x writer.

OmniWriter CD-Rewriteable

Price $800

Overall Rating ★★ 1/2

Read Speed ★★★

Write Speed ★

Hardware Included ★★★

Software Included ★★★

Philips also has a new CD-RW drive that will allow you to record and re-record your CDs. The Philips OMNIwriter is available in three models: An external version OMNI/20 for the PC , OMNI/40 external for the Macintosh and the OMNI/12 internal IDE/ATAPI for the PC. All come with similar software to the Easywriter above. The OMNIwriter uses a SCSI connection that connects to your PC's parallel port. It does so with a parallel-to-SCSI adapter that is included. The OmniWriter reads at 6x speeds and writes and rewrites CDs at 2x speed.

Pinnacle Micro RCD 4X4

Price $877

Overall Rating ★★ 3/4

Read Speed ★★

Write Speed ★★★

Hardware Included ★★★

Software Included ★★★

Pinnacle Micro's RCD 4x4 is a bit expensive at $877 it is an external unit that comes with an Adaptec ISA SCSI-2 adapter and cables, Adaptec's Easy-CD Pro for Windows 3.1/Windows 95 (CD Burner for Mac), a backup program; Disk Archive 95 for Windows and a screensaver CD-ROM. Pinnacle Micro provides manuals for the SCSI card and all programs, a helpful touch. The RCD 4x4 is available in both internal and external configurations to accommodate PC, Mac and most Unix workstation environments. The Pinnacle Micro warranty is one year limited warranty on all parts and labor.

Pinnacle Micro RCDW226 Rewriteable CD Drive

Price $699 (External); $599 (Internal)

Overall Rating ★★ 3/4

Read Speed ★★★

Write Speed ★★

Hardware Included ★★★

Software Included ★ ★ ★

The RDCW226 comes in both internal and external versions. This drive will write and rewrite at 2x, and read at 6x. Both versions come with adapter cards so no worry there. The units ship with Easy-CD Pro for creating your CD-R media, Packet Writing Device Driver: Allows user to drag-and-drop or change files to CD-R media and drag-and-drop, change files, erase, and rewrite to CD-RW media. Disc Archive 97 is included for backups. The Macintosh version has Toast for Mac.

Smart and Friendly

Price $499 (External); $399 (Internal)
Overall Rating ★ ★ ★
Read Speed ★ ★ ★
Write Speed ★ ★
Hardware Included ★ ★ ★
Software Included ★ ★ ★ ★

Smart and Friendly probably has the largest line of CD-R and CD-RW drives with at least half a dozen units. These units range from a 2x read/2x write unit on the low end to a 4x write/6x read on the high end. Of course you will find the normal 2x4 and 4x4 units as well. You will find versions for the Mac, as well as internal and external PC versions. All units have similar software including Easy-CD Pro software for Windows 95 and Windows NT 4.0 and Toast for the Macintosh. Floppy-CD packet recording software, Backstage Designer Plus, MediaAgent for CDs, and Disc Inspector Pro are some other titles you will find. They even come with a SCSI 2 host adapter, Custom CD Label System and a blank CDR disc.

Sony Spressa CDU-928E/H, CDU-928E/K and CDU-928E/C

Price $339
Overall Rating ★ ★ 1/2
Read Speed ★ ★ ★ ★
Write Speed ★ ★
Hardware Included ★ ★
Software Included ★ ★

With 8x read/2x write speed and an ATAPI interface, Sony's latest Spressa CD-R drives ($339 street for all bundles) are the fastest reading CD-R drives around. The CDU-928E/K and CDU-928E/C come with Adaptec's Easy-CD Pro 2.1 software. The CDU-928E/H bundles Adaptec's DirectCD packet recording software.

Yamaha: CRW4001

Price $800 (Internal); $900 (External)
Overall Rating ★ ★ ★
Read Speed ★ ★ ★
Write Speed ★ ★ ★
Hardware Included ★ ★ ★
Software Included ★ ★ ★

Yamaha's CRW4001 ($800 street for the internal, $900 street for the external) is one of the pricier units to be had. They read at 6x speed, and write CD-R at 4x speed and CD-RW at 2x speed. Bundled with the drive are Easy-CD Pro and Direct CD. One nice feature of the Yamaha is a 2MB buffer. The large 2MB data buffer on the recorder virtually eliminates buffer underrun, thereby ensuring that writing data is sent in a constant stream and the drive won't have to wait for data. You have a choice of either SCSI or ATAPI (IDE) interfaces for connecting to the PC. Yamaha supports seven standard formats for recording, including: CD-ROM, CD-ROM/XA (both photo CD and Video CD), CD-I, CD-DIGITAL AUDIO, CD-EXTRA and CD+G. You can also get mastering software, from over twenty-three software companies for the Yamaha on all the major computer platforms, including IBM, Mac, UNIX, HP, SGI, SUN, and Novell.

Contact Information

Hewlett Packard
(408) 773-6200
http://www.hp.com

Olympus America
(800) 347-4027
(516)-844-5000

www.olympus.com

Philips Electronics
(800) 235-7373
www.pps.philips.com

Pinnacle Micro
(800) 553-7070
www.pinnaclemicro

Smart and Friendly
(800) 959-7001
www.smartandfriendly.com

Sony Computer
(800) 352-7669
www.sony.com/storagebysony

Yamaha Systems
(800) 543-7457
www.yamahayst.com

COMPUTERS, BUDGET DESKTOPS

Buying a computer is an important decision. You want a system that will give you power and flexibility and that is reliable. For the budget-minded consumer it's especially important that you get the best computer for your hard-earned dollars. And you do not want to fall too far behind in computing power because the newest software tends to demand more power and memory, larger hard drives, and better graphics cards just to keep up.

Processor speed is the first area you should consider when comparison shopping. If you are coming from a 486-type computer (or less powerful ones), you will want to get at least to the Intel Pentium 166mHZ or AMD K6/166 level. And if you have a 100 to 133 MHz Pentium, moving up to a 200 MHz that is upgradeable may be the best move. And MMX technology is a must if you are interested in multimedia applications or using the Internet extensively.

Buying a new computer is a daunting experience today. Retail stores have dozens of models with a variety of features, but at least you can see and touch these systems. Mail-order is another attractive option, if you know what you want to order. This source includes both warehouse-type resellers and direct manufacturer shipping. And now many manufacturers will let you configure and order a custom system by phone or directly on their Internet sites. But be sure you know what you are getting! The prices may include the monitor, a gigantic bundle of software, and various manufacturer or store-level service and support agreements.

To assist you in evaluating computers in the "budget" category, we reviewed several desktop computers ranging in price from $1,000 to $2,500 and speeds between 166 and 200 MHz.

The following list contains nine computers and their ratings.

OVERALL RATINGS

Micron Millennia MME 200	★★★ 3/4
Compaq Deskpro 2000 5200X/3200	★★★ 1/4
Quantex QP5/166 M1 MMX	★★★ 1/4
Midwest Micro MWO-200T	★★★ 1/4
CyberMax Power Max A5	★★★
IBM PC 350 6587KSX	★★★
Gateway 2000 G5-166 M	★★★
Dell Dimension M200A	★★★
Polywell Poly 500QX	★★ 1/2

EXPLANATION OF RATINGS

Budget desktop computers were selected for review from currently available PC-compatible products with a speed between 166 and 200 MHz. The overall rating was arrived at by giving individual scores on performance, features and support (including warranty). These three scores were then averaged to arrive at the overall rating, with one star being the lowest possible rating.

In addition to processor speed, there are a number of other factors you should consider when purchasing a new desktop system:

MMX Technology uses high-speed circuits to increase the processor's multimedia performance. This technology can be used to handle full-screen video and graphics, animation, videoconferencing, virtual reality, and 3-D graphics. It will produce a full-screen, full-resolution image that rivals that of a TV image. Having MMX technology already on your computer will eliminate the need for you to add a special board later if you need it for multimedia applications.

RAM system memory is critical. While many systems can come with 16MB (megabytes or millions of characters) or less, you should get at least 32MB if you plan to run Windows 95. If you have a choice between EDO and SDRAM type of RAM, get SDRAM because it is faster. Make sure the system's RAM is expandable to meet your needs.

Hard Drive Storage should be at least two gigabytes (billions of characters) in size. Video-intensive applications will want a sustained data rate of 5MB/second. SCSI drives are higher in price than the typical Enhanced IDE (ATA) but the performance they offer may be worth it. The computer should have space for adding at least one additional hard drive.

Removeable-media Drives are popular options for budget computers because you can get by with a smaller hard drive. And you can back up your precious data more quickly than using the more traditional tape drives or floppy disks. Examples are Iomega's 100MB Zip and one gigabyte Jaz drives and SyQuest's 230MB EZFlyer and 1.5 gigabyte SyJet drives.

Expandability means you really want a minitower or tower case rather than the desktop type case. You should have at least two open slots and bays to add in cards and features that you may need in the future. Desktop cases are less expensive if you do not plan any expansion.

Bundled Software varies widely, but you should get at least the operating system of your choice. If you do not need Windows 95, for example, it may take a lot of effort to replace it with another system. Many systens also include several high-quality programs or suites that you can use, but you can save some money by buying a system without these extras. Be sure to get the original CD-ROMs and the documentation in case you need to reinstall anything, .

Warranties are a must. A three-year parts-and-labor warranty with on-site service for the first year is good, and the opportunity to extend the warranty is a must.

Technical Support varies widely, but if you need 24-hour daily phone support, be sure to get a system that offers that level at a reasonable price. Per-call rates vary widely, and the wait time for service is also a consideration.

Other considerations, if you need them, include monitors, CD-ROM drives, modems, and graphics and sound boards, and other options. The newest multimedia option for high-end systems is called a DVD-ROM drive, which can play regular CDs as well as newer DVD formats for high-quality video playback; however, there is not a lot of software available for this drive at this time.

While this report reflects prices and features at the time it was written, the industry is changing quickly and competition is keen. Prices are dropping and standard features are growing. Getting prices, however, is becoming easy with many manufacturers listing up-to-date systems, prices, and features on their Internet sites.

ALPHABETICAL DESCRIPTIONS

Compaq Deskpro 2000 5200X/3200

Price $1,900

Overall Rating ★★★ 1/4

Performance   ★★★ 3/4

Features   ★★ 1/2

Support   ★★★ 1/2

This system is an economical Pentium 200 MHz minitower with MMX for multimedia with good performance. Features include 32MB of RAM expandable to 384MB, 256k secondary cache, 3.2 gigabyte hard drive, integrated graphics adapter with 1MB SDRAM for video, 15-inch V50 monitor, 16 X CD-ROM drive, a 56-kpbs modem, and sound card. Windows 95 comes pre-installed. Inside, the system can be accessed easily with big thumbscrews and I/O ports are color coded. Compaq's support is excellent and

is available 24 hours a day. They offer a three-year parts and labor warranty with the first year on-site.

CyberMax Power Max A5

Price $1,425

Overall Rating ★★★

Performance   ★★ 1/2

Features   ★★★ 1/4

Support   ★★★ 1/4

The CyberMax Power Max A5 is a tower computer that's economical, has solid multimedia performance and support policies. It uses the 166-MHz version of AMD's MMX-capable K6 processor. Its speed can match those of Pentium MMX-200 computers. Features include 32MB RAM upgradable to 384MB, 512k secondary cache, 3.2 gigabyte hard drive, STB Nitro 3D graphics adapter, 2MB EDO DRAM for video, 15-inch monitor, 16 X CD-ROM drive, K65flex modem, Ensoniq's Audio PCI Wavetable sound card and Altec Lansing ACS 45 speakers and subwoofer. Bundled software includes Windows 95, the Corel WordPerfect Suite 7, and a Max Business Pack. There's plenty of space for expansion. CyberMax backs the system with a one-year labor warranty and three-year parts. Support is available free on-site for the first year. Technical support is available 24 hours daily, or via the manufacturers' web site.

Dell Dimension M200A

Price $1,830

Overall Rating ★★★

Performance   ★★★ 1/2

Features   ★★ 1/2

Support   ★★★

Here's an excellent minitower computer with a Pentium 200 MHz processor and MX, 16MB RAM upgradeable to 64MB, a 512k secondary cache, and a 2.1GB hard disk. Additional features include an integrated graphics adapter, 2MB of DRAM video RAM, 15-inch monitor, a 24 X CD-ROM drive, and 56-kbps 3Com U.S.Robotics modem. Software includes Windows 95 and Microsoft Office 97 Small Business Edition. The Dimension M200A is easily upgradable. Dell offers a 30-day money back guarantee and backs their computers with a three-year parts and one-year labor warranty. Toll-free technical support is available seven days a week for 24 hours a day.

Gateway 2000 G5-166M

Price $1,900	
Overall Rating	★ ★ ★
Performance	★ ★ 3/4
Features	★ ★ ★
Support	★ ★ ★ 1/2

This minitower computer is solid but among the slower of those reviewed. It uses the Pentium 166 MHz MMX-capable processor. Features include 16MB RAM upgradable to 128MB, 512k secondary cache, 1.3 gigabyte hard drive, integrated graphics adapter, 2MB EDO DRAM for video. There is also a 17-inch monitor, 16 X CD-ROM drive, Teleflex 56-kbps modem, integrated sound card, and Altec Lansing ACS 45 speakers and subwoofer. Bundled software includes Windows 95, Encarta, MicroSoft Office 97 Small Business Edition, and Street Plus. Gateway backs the system with a three-year labor

and parts warranty. Technical support is excellent and it is available 24 hours daily.

IBM PC 350 6587KSX

Price $1,800	
Overall Rating	★ ★ ★
Performance	★ ★ ★
Features	★ ★ 1/2
Support	★ ★ ★ 3/4

The IBM PC desktop computer has a Pentium 166 MHz processor with MMX, 32MB of RAM expandable to 192MB, 256k secondary cache, and a 2.5 gigabyte hard drive. Other features include an integrated S3 Trio64V+ graphics adapter with 1MB EDO DRAM for video. No monitor, CD-ROM, modem, or sound board is included at this price as it is configured as a network workstation. Bundled software includes Windows NT 4.0, IBM PC Networking Tools, and the Lotus SmartSuite 97. There is a "Wake on-LAN" capability for administrators to upgrade and take inventories when no one is on the computer. IBM's warranty is three-year parts and labor with the first year on-site. Toll-free technical support is available 24 hours daily and there is an "Online Housecall" capability if you have a modem.

Micron Millennia MME 200

Price $2,250	
Overall Rating	★ ★ ★ 3/4
Performance	★ ★ ★ ★
Features	★ ★ ★ 1/2
Support	★ ★ ★ ★

This computer is geared toward small business use. System reliability and performance is good. The minitower contains a Pentium 200 MHz MMX processor,

48MB of SDRAM, 512K pipelin cache, and a four gigabyte hard drive. Additional features include a Diamond Stealth 3D 2000 graphics adapter, 4MB EDO DRAM for video, 17-inch monitor, 24-speed CD-ROM drive, 56-kbps modem, integrated sound board and standard speakers, and Iomega Zip drive. The computer itself is easy to open with the thumbscrews and has plenty of space for expansion. If you need help with your system, toll-free phone support is available 24 hours daily. The system comes with a 30-day money-back guarantee. The warranty covers the CPU and memory for five years and three years on the rest of the system. On-site service is available for the first year.

Midwest Micro MWO-200T

Price $2,280	
Overall Rating	★ ★ ★ 1/4
Performance	★ ★ ★ 3/4
Features	★ ★ ★ 1/2
Support	★ ★ 1/2

This Pentium-200 MHz equipped mini-tower has 32MB RAM expandable to 128MB, 512k secondary cache, 4.3 gigabyte hard drive, ATI 3D PC2TV graphics, 4MB SDRAM video memory, 17-inch monitor, 24 X CD-ROM drive, 56-kbps modem, Ensoniq Wavetable sound card and Altec Lansing Speakers. A Microsoft IntelliMouse is included, and the software is Windows 95 PLUS and the Microsoft Office 97 Small Business Edition bundle. Support is described at a "5/3 Year Blue Ribbon Warranty," with the five years being for labor.

Quantex QP5/166 M1 MMX

Price $1.930	
Overall Rating	★ ★ ★ 1/4
Performance	★ ★ ★
Features	★ ★ ★ ★
Support	★ ★ ★

This computer has a Pentium 166 MHz processor with MMX, which is quite affordable and has a lot of nice features. The system includes 32MB RAM expandable to 128MB, 512k secondary cache, 4 gigabyte hard drive, STB Nitro 3D graphics adapter, 4MB SGRAM for video, 17-inch monitor, 24-speed CD-ROM drive, 65-kbps modem, and Ensoniq PCI sound card. Expansion is possible as it comes in a minitower case. Toll-free technical support is available 24 hours daily. Quantex offers a three-year parts warranty.

Polywell Poly 500 QX

Price $1,395	
Overall Rating	★ ★ 1/2
Performance	★ ★
Features	★ ★ 3/4
Support	★ ★ 3/4

This "baby tower" comes with an AMD K5-166 MHz processor. Features include 32MB RAM upgradable to 128MB, 512k secondary cache, 2.5GB hard drive, Diamond Stealth 3D 2000 graphics board, 2MB/EDO DRAM for video, Crystal 16-bit sound card, Sound Force speakers, 15-inch monitor, 12 X CD-ROM drive, and GVC 33.6-kbps modem. Software includes Windows 95 and Microsoft's Encarta, Money, Works and more all on CDs. The Logitech mouse uses a serial port. General support by phone is 24 hours a day the first year. After a year free technical support is 12 hours a day weekdays and eight hours on Saturday. The warranty is five-years in-house labor and three-years parts. Polywell offers a 30-day money-back guarantee if you are not satisfied with the product.

CONTACT INFORMATION

Compaq Computer Corporation
800-888-5858
www.compaq.com

CyberMax Computer Inc.
800-349-8939
www.cybmax.com

Dell Computer Corporation
800-388-8542
www.dell.com

Gateway 2000 Inc.
800-846-2000
www.gw2k.com

IBM Corporation
800-426-2968
www.pc.ibm.com

Micro Express
603-894-5111
www.microexpress.com

Micron Electronics, Inc.
888-634-8799
www.micronpc.com

MidWest Micro
800-626-0544
www.mwmicro.com

Polywell Computers Inc.
800-999-1278
www.polywell.com

Quantex Microsystems
800-346-6685
www.quantex.com

COMPUTERS, BUDGET NOTEBOOKS

"Honey, I shrunk the desktop" is a good way to describe a notebook computer. These portable computers pack the same power as a desktop but in a smaller portable case. They combine a screen, hard drive, floppy disk drive, keyboard, and mouse or touchpad into one unit that covers about the same space as a piece of typing paper. Additional features can be included such as a CD-ROM drive, modem, and speakers—all of which can reside within the notebook case or swap with a removeable device in a bay designed for this modularity. Some features are add-ons to a base price, so make sure to see what features are included and which ones are extra. Notebook computers have made mobile computing easier with better screens, larger hard drives, and longer lasting batteries. You can now conduct business anywhere you can take your notebook. You can send faxes, send e-mail, cruise the Internet or connect to your desktop computer as long as you have a modem. Can you get a good notebook for less than 2,500? Yes, and without sacrificing features.

Buying a budget notebook computer is complicated by the variety of options and features available. Retail stores have inexpensive models with a variety of features, which would let you see the screen and try out the keyboard for comfort. Mail-order is an attractive option if you know what you want to order because many budget notebook computers are sold directly by their manufacturer. Warehouse-type resellers are another possibility. And now many manufacturers will let you configure and order a custom system by phone or directly on their Internet sites.

In this chapter the focus is on notebook computers under $2,500 with the following minimum configuration: 133 MHz MMX CPU or equivalent, 8MB of RAM, 12.1-inch color display, at least a one gigabyte hard disk, CD-ROM drive and sound. Note that a 150 MHz CPU is not a lot faster than the 133 MHz. Data on these models was compiled from the manufacturers. Prices indicated are approximate typical street prices when the systems were reviewed.

The following list contains 9 budget notebooks and their overall ratings.

OVERALL RATINGS

Dell Latitude LM M133ST	★★★ 1/2
NEC Versa 2650CDT	★★★ 1/2
Compaq Armada 1550 DMT	★★★ 1/4
Fujitsu LifeBook 435DX	★★★ 1/4
WinBook XP5 Pro	★★★ 1/4
AMS TravelPro 106 CT	★★★
CTX EzBook 750MS	★★★
Gateway Solo 2300 SE	★★★

IBM Thinkpad 365XD ★★ 3/4

EXPLANATION OF RATINGS

Budget notebooks were evaluated based on the following aspects: Performance, modularity, screen quality, mobility and support (including warranty). Each aspect could be given up to four stars, with one star being the lowest. The individual star ratings were than averaged, resulting in the overall rating.

In addition to processor speed, there are a number of other factors you should consider when purchasing a new notebook computer.

MMX Technology uses high-speed circuits to increase the processor's multimedia performance. This technology can be used to handle full-screen video and graphics, animation, videoconferencing, virtual reality, and 3-D graphics.

RAM system memory is critical. While many systems can come with 8MB (megabytes or millions of characters) or less, you should get at least 32MB if you plan to run Windows 95 or NT. If you have a choice between EDO and SDRAM type of RAM, get SDRAM because it is faster. Make sure the system's RAM is expandable to meet your needs.

Hard Drive Storage should be at least one gigabyte (billions of characters) in size and should be removeable or the computer should have an option for a second drive to be added. A SCSI port would let you add a faster drive, for example.

Screens on the budget notebooks are almost always dual-scan passive matrix displays. For a little more money you can get the brighter active matrix screen, if the quality of your screen output is critical to your decision. The differences are in size and brightness and in durability. You should get at least a 640 x 480 level of resolution with 64k (1k = 1024) colors.

Zoomed Video Ready is a new standard which allows imput from MPEG, TV tuner, or Video Capture Card to be sent directly to the display bypassing the computer's processor. This provides faster graphics performance and smooth video playback on notebooks with PC Card and Zoomed Video support. Few budget notebooks include this new option.

Modularity means that your notebook can grow to meet your needs for more power, RAM, disk space, and to add or change other options. Removeable devices like modems, hard drives, and CD-ROM drives should be included or extra ports for attaching additional devices should be included.

Mobility is increased if your battery will last longer and a charger is either built-in or included with the system. Overall size and weight are other factors to consider. Modem speed, and the recent addition of cellular phone ports, can make traveling and keeping in touch easier.

Bundled Software varies widely, but you should get at least the operating system of your choice. If you do not need Windows 95, for example, it may take a lot of effort to replace it with another system. Be sure to get the original CD-ROMs or diskettes in case you need to reinstall anything.

Warranties are a must. A three-year parts-and-labor warranty with either overnight courier or on-site service for the first year is good, and the opportunity to extend the warranty is a must. Warranties vary when it comes to replacing screens with bad pixels (dark spots on the screen), so be sure you look at this part of the warranty carefully.

Technical Support varies widely, but if you need 24-hour daily phone technical support, be sure to get a system that offers that level at a reasonable price. Per-call rates are becoming more common, and the wait time for service is also a consideration. Most large manufacturers are also putting support information and downloadable files on their Internet sites.

While this report reflects prices and features at the time it was written, the industry is changing quickly and competition is keen. Prices are dropping and standard features are growing. Getting prices, however, is becoming easy with many manufacturers listing up-to-date systems, prices, and features on their Internet sites.

ALPHABETICAL DESCRIPTIONS

AMS TravelPro 106 CT

Price	$2,300
Overall Rating	★★★
Performance	★★★★
Screen Quality	★★★★
Modularity	★★ 3/4
Mobility	★ 3/4
Support	★★★

This Pentium 166 MHz MMX computer includes 256k cache, 16 MB EDO RAM,

1.3 gigabyte hard drive, 88-key Windows 95 keyboard, and trackpad. It was the best performer in our review. The 12.1" active matrix screen supports 800 x 600 resolution and 64k colors. We added a 16X CD-ROM drive, which is the only size available as an option. Memory is upgradeable to 80 MB but there are no swappable bays for flexibility. The system is light at 6.9 pounds and the NiMH battery is rated at only two hours. No modem was included in this configuration. Software included is Windows 95 and some system accelerator utilities. Support is hurt by their annoying and sparse Internet site. The warranty is for three years parts and labor.

Compaq Armada 1550 DMT

Price	$2,500
Overall Rating	★★★ 1/4
Performance	★★★
Screen Quality	★★★ 1/2
Modularity	★★
Mobility	★★★ 1/4
Support	★★★★

This Pentium 133 MHz computer includes 256k cache, 16 MB EDO RAM, 1.4 gigabyte hard drive, 10X CD-ROM drive, an integrated 33.6 kbps modem, keyboard, and touchpad. A 12.2 CTFT screen supports 800 x 600 resolution and 64k colors. The system is average at 7.35 pounds and the battery is rated at about three hours. Software included is either Windows 95 or NT. Support is excellent with 24-hour toll-free phone support and a very informative and helpful Internet site. The warranty is for one year, but they guarantee two-day turnaround on repairs with only a few restrictions.

CTX EzBook 750MS

Price	$1,800
Overall Rating	★★★
Performance	★★ 3/4
Screen Quality	★★★ 1/2
Modularity	★★★ 1/2
Mobility	★★ 1/2
Support	★★★

This is one of the lowest-priced systems we reviewed. The Pentium 150 MHz MMX processor is good, but a slow 16 MB RAM, relatively slow 6X CD-ROM drive, and small one gigabyte hard drive could be better. Both the CD-ROM and hard drive are removeable and can be replaced with a floppy drive or another battery. The system can be expanded to only 40 MB RAM. The 12.1" dual-scan screen supports 64k colors and there is a keyboard and EzGlide touchpad conveniently located. There was no modem included. It is one of the lightest of the group at 6.6 pounds and has a battery rated at almost four hours. Software consists of only Windows 95. Support is nine hours daily but lots of helpful information is available from their Internet site. The warranty is one year parts and labor

Dell Latitude LM M133ST

Price	$2,500
Overall Rating	★★★ 1/2
Performance	★★★ 3/4
Screen Quality	★★★★
Modularity	★★★
Mobility	★★ 3/4
Support	★★★ 1/2

This contender has a Pentium 133 MMX processor, 16 MB EDO RAM, 256k cache, and a 1.6 gigabyte hard drive. Memory can be expanded to 72 MB. It has a brilliant 12.1" active matrix screen with 800 x 600 resolution and 64k colors. Other features are a 20X CD-ROM drive, Windows 95 keyboard, and a touchpad. A plus is the notebook's bay that allows you to swap the CD-ROM drive, floppy drive, or an optional battery. It weighs in at about seven pounds and the battery should last from three to five hours depending on what you are running. Software includes Windows 95, MS Office 97 Small Business Edition, and the Internet Explorer. Support by phone is available 24 hours daily and their Internet site is excellent. The warranty is for one year and is extendable.

Fujitsu LifeBook 435DX

Price	$1,800
Overall Rating	★★★ 1/4
Performance	★★ 3/4
Screen Quality	★★★
Modularity	★★★★
Mobility	★★★ 1/2
Support	★★★ 1/2

This LifeBook is one of the lowest-priced systems we reviewed. It excelled in modularity while it lagged in performance. The Pentium 133 MHz MMX processor is good, but a slow 16 MB RAM, relatively slow 10X CD-ROM drive, and small 1.3 gigabyte hard drive could be better. The system can be expanded to 80 MB RAM and the bay for the CD-ROM and floppy drive gives you hope that a faster CD-ROM could be installed in the future. The

12.1" dual-scan screen only supports 256 colors. And the 33.6 kbps modem is a PC Card type. It is the heaviest of the group at over nine pounds but has the longest-lasting battery at almost four hours. Software consists of only Windows 95. Support is not mentioned in their literature and their Internet site is slow and of limited value. The warranty is 1-year parts and labor and they provide a four-day turnaround on repairs.

Gateway 2000 Solo 2300SE

Price	$2,000
Overall Rating	★ ★ ★
Performance	★ ★ 3/4
Screen Quality	★ ★ ★ 1/2
Modularity	★ ★ 1/2
Mobility	★ ★
Support	★ ★ ★ ★

The Solo 2300SE has a 133MHz processor, 256K cache, and 16MB of SDRAM memory. Other features include a 1.3 gigabyte hard drive, 11X CD-ROM drive, 12.1" dual scan screen with a sharp picture, 85-key keyboard, the EZ Pad pointing device, and a carrying case. No modem was in this configuration, but could be added with a PC Card device. Since there are no swappable device bays, the system is not very upgradeable except for memory, with a maximum of 192 MB allowed. It is average in weight and has a NiMH battery for as estimated life of two to three hours. Software includes only Windows 95 and MS Works. Support is available by phone 24 hours a day and their web site is very helpful. The warranty is excellent at three years parts and labor.

IBM ThinkPad 365XD

Price	$2,100
Overall Rating	★ ★ 3/4
Performance	★ ★ 3/4
Screen Quality	★ ★ 1/2
Modularity	★ ★ 1/2
Mobility	★ ★ ★
Support	★ ★ ★ 1/2

This ThinkPad model offers 133MHz Pentium processor, 8 MB RAM, 1.35 gigabyte hard drive and 6X CD-ROM—which is why it is rated rather low in performance. Another disappointment is the 11.3" dual scan screen that supports only 256 colors. It does have an excellent keyboard and the famous TrackPoint III pointing device as well as a 33.6 kbps PC Card modem. It is a lightweight at only 6.2 pounds but the NiMH battery will only last about two hours. It does come with software including Windows 95, Lotus SmartSuite 97, and other packages to take advantage of the Internet. Support by phone is 24 hours daily, and their Internet site has a wealth of information and downloadable files. The warranty is only one year carry-in. The ThinkPad is still the prestige notebook to have because of its sleek design and the innovative TrackPoint, but this one is on the weak side of our reviewed systems.

NEC Versa 2650CDT

Price	$2,500
Overall Rating	★ ★ ★ 1/2
Performance	★ ★ ★ 1/2
Screen Quality	★ ★ ★ ★
Modularity	★ ★ ★
Mobility	★ ★ ★ ★
Support	★ ★ ★

The NEC Versa 2650CDT has a Pentium 150 MMX processor, 16 MB EDO RAM, 256k cache, and a 1.44 gigabyte hard drive. Memory can be expanded to 80 MB. It is one of the few at this price that has a brilliant 12.1 inch active matrix screen with 800 x 600 resolution and 64k colors. Other features are a 10X CD-ROM drive, 33.6kbps PC Card modem, 86 key Windows 95 keyboard, and their VersaGlide touchpad. One major plus is the notebook's two bays that allow you to have the CD-ROM drive and floppy drive installed at the same time, or you can use two batteries at the same time. The entire system weighs in at about seven pounds, includes a carrying case, and the battery should last from three to five hours depending on what you are running. Software includes an option for either Windows 95 or Windows for Workgroups, which you select the first time you turn on the computer. LapLink, virus protection, and several other useful CDs are also included. Support by phone is available 24 hours daily but their Internet site is not as helpful as the others. The warranty is for one year factory service.

WinBook XP5 Pro

Price	$2,100
Overall Rating	★ ★ ★ 1/4
Performance	★ ★ ★
Screen Quality	★ ★ ★ 1/2
Modularity	★ ★ ★ ★
Mobility	★ ★ ★
Support	★ ★ ★ 1/4

The WinBook XP5 Pro has a Pentium 150 MHz MMX processor and comes with 16 MB EDO RAM, 256k cache, a one gigabyte hard drive, an 8X CD-ROM drive, and a 12.1-inch dual-scan screen that can display 64k colors. Memory can be upgraded to 72 MB and the CD-ROM drive can be swapped with the floppy drive or with an optional second battery. There is a Windows 95 keyboard and a stick-like pointing device. We added a 28.8 kbps PC Card modem for $99. Weighing in at 6.4 pounds with its lithium-ion battery rated at two hours, it is easy to transport. Software is just Windows 95 and several Internet provider start-up packs. Support was rated lowest of the group because they have telephone support only 8 AM to 9 PM weekdays and a few hours on Saturday, but their Internet site has good support information. The warranty is for one year parts and labor, but you can extend it to three years plus overnight courier service for only $199.

CONTACT INFORMATION

AMS Tech
800-980-8889
www.amsnote.com

Compaq
800-345-1518
www.compaq.com

CTX
800-888-9052
www.ctxintl.com

Dell Computer Corp.
800-388-8542
www.dell.com

Fujitsu
800-8FUJITSU
www.fujitsu.com

Gateway
800-846-2000
www.gw2k.com

IBM Personal Computer Co.
800-426-2968
www.pc.ibm.com

NEC Computer Systems Division, Packard Bell
NEC, Inc.

888-863-2669
www.nec-computers.com

WinBook Computer Corporation
800-254-7806
www.winbook.com

COMPUTERS, POWER NOTEBOOKS

Notebook computers were once touted as supplements for your desktop computer for times you were away from the office. With the addition of more powerful processors, larger screens, better batteries, and multimedia options, the notebook computer has evolved into a computer that can be as powerful as a desktop. In some cases you could be very happy using a notebook as your only computer, if you don't mind the embedded numeric keypad keys and integrated pointing devices. While some notebooks provide places to attach external devices directly, some require an optional "docking station."

Buying a notebook computer is complicated by the seemingly endless options and features available. Retail stores have a few models with a variety of features, which would let you see the screen and try out the keyboard for comfort. Mail-order is an attractive option if you know what you want to order because most high-end notebook computers are sold directly by their manufacturer. Warehouse-type resellers are another possibility. And now many manufacturers will let you configure and order a custom system by phone or directly on their Internet sites.

In this review the focus is on high-powered notebook computers with the following minimum configuration: 166 MHz MMX CPU or equivalent, 32MB of RAM, 12.1-inch active matrix color display, a minimum of 256K of L2 cache, at least a 2.1 gigabyte hard disk, CD-ROM drive and sound. Note that a 233 MHz MMX CPU is about one-third faster than the 166 MHz.

The following list contains 14 power notebooks and their overall ratings.

OVERALL RATINGS

IBM ThinkPad 770 9549-1AU	★★★★
Dell Inspiron 3000 M233XT	★★★ 3/4
NEC Versa 6230	★★★ 3/4
Gateway 2000 Solo 9100XL	★★★ 1/2
Hitachi VisionBook Pro	★★★ 1/2
Quantex H-Series 1330	★★★ 1/2
Toshiba Tecra 750 CDT	★★★ 1/2
Apple PowerBook 3400c/240	★★★ 1/4
Gateway 2000 Solo 2300	★★★ 1/4
WinBook 233XL	★★★ 1/4
AMS TravelPro 2040	★★★
Compaq Armada 7750MT	★★★
Acer TravelMate 7063NT	★★ 3/4
Acer Extensa 670 CDT	★★ 3/4

EXPLANATION OF RATINGS

Power notebooks were evaluated based on the following aspects: performance, modularity, screen quality, mobility and support (including warranty). Each aspect could be given up to four stars, with one star being the lowest. The individual star ratings were then averaged to arrive at the overall rating.

In addition to processor speed, there are a number of other factors you should consider when purchasing a new notebook computer.

MMX Technology uses high-speed circuits to increase the processor's multimedia performance. This technology can be used to handle full-screen video and graphics, animation, videoconferencing, virtual reality, and 3-D graphics.

RAM system memory is critical. While many systems can come with 16MB (megabytes or millions of characters) or less, you should get at least 32MB if you plan to run Windows 95 or NT. If you have a choice between EDO and SDRAM type of RAM, get SDRAM because it is faster. Make sure the system's RAM is expandable to meet your needs.

Hard Drive Storage should be at least 2 gigabytes (billions of characters) in size and removeable, or the computer should have an option for a second drive to be added. A SCSI port would let you add a faster drive, for example.

Screens on the high-end notebooks are almost always active matrix displays. The differences are in size and brightness and in durability. You should get at least an 800 x 600 level of resolution with 64k (1k = 1024 bytes) colors. The alternative is "dual-scan" technology, which would save you some money if the quality of your screen output is not critical to your decision.

Zoomed Video Ready is a new standard that allows imput from MPEG, TV tuner, or Video Capture Card to be sent directly to the display, bypassing the computer's processor. This provides faster graphics performance and smooth video playback on notebooks with PC Card and Zoomed Video support.

Modularity means that your notebook can grow to meet your needs for more power, RAM, disk space, and to add or change other options. Removeable devices like modems, hard drives, and CD-ROM drives should be included or extra ports for attaching additional devices should be included.

Mobility is increased if your battery will last longer and a charger is either built-in or included with the system. Overall size and weight are other factors to consider. Modem speed, and the recent addition of cellular phone ports, can make traveling and keeping in touch easier.

Bundled software varies widely, but you should get at least the operating system of your choice. If you do not need Windows 95, for example, it may take a lot of effort to replace it with another system. Be sure to get the original CD-ROMs or diskettes and the documentation, in case you need to reinstall anything.

Warranties are a must. A three-year parts-and-labor warranty with either overnight courier or on-site service for the first year is good, and the opportunity to extend the warranty is a must. Warranties vary when it comes to replacing screens with bad pixels (dark spots on the screen), so be sure you look at this part of the warranty carefully.

Technical Support varies widely, but if you need 24-hour daily phone technical support, be sure to get a system that offers that level at a reasonable price. Per-call rates are becoming more common, and the wait time for service is also a consideration. Most large manufacturers are also putting support information and downloadable files on their Internet sites.

Other considerations include graphics and sound capabilities, speakers, microphones, infrared ports, keyboard and pointing devices. The newest multimedia option for high-end systems is a DVD-ROM drive, which can play regular CDs as well as newer DVD formats for high-quality video play-back; however, there is not a lot of software available for this drive at this time.

While this report reflects prices and features at the time it was written, the industry is changing quickly and competition is keen. Prices are dropping and standard features are growing. Getting prices, however, is becoming easy with many manufacturers listing up-to-date systems, prices, and features on their Internet sites.

ALPHABETICAL DESCRIPTIONS

Acer Extensa 670 CDT

Price $3,700	
Overall Rating	★ ★ 3/4
Performance	★ ★ 3/4
Screen Quality	★ ★ ★
Modularity	★ ★ 1/4
Mobility	★ ★ ★ 3/4
Support	★ ★ 1/2

This 166 MHz MMX computer with only a 256k L2 cache, is among the slower ones we reviewed. The 2.1 gigabyte hard drive is small. It comes with a 10X removeable CD-ROM, which is interchangable with a floppy drive. The 12.1" screen has 800 x 600 resolution and 64k colors, and you can view the display and external monitor simultaneously, which is good when making presentations. It comes with 32 MB EDO RAM, upgradeable to 80 MB. The 28.8-kbps modem is integrated and has a cellular port. There is an 84-key Windows 95 keyboard and a touchpad. The system supports the "zoomed video ready" standard with two Type II or one Type III PC Card slots. Its weight is light at 6.7 pounds and the battery will last three hours, which is good for mobility. Software provided is Windows 95 and a System Recovery CD. Support is available by phone 24 hours a day every day free for the first year, and they have an excellent Internet site. The warranty covers one-year parts and labor.

Acer TravelMate 7063NT

Price $4,800	
Overall Rating	★ ★ 3/4
Performance	★ ★ 1/2
Screen Quality	★ ★ ★
Modularity	★ ★ 1/4
Mobility	★ ★ ★ ★
Support	★ ★ 1/2

This 166 MHz MMX, computer with only a 256k L2 cache, is also one of the slower systems reviewed. The 3 gigabyte hard drive is adequate. It comes with a 10X removeable CD-ROM which is swappa-

ble with the floppy disk drive. The 12.1" screen is at 800 x 600 resolution and 64k colors, and you can view the display and external monitor simultaneously. The systems starts at 32 MB EDO RAM, upgradeable to 64 MB. The 33.6-kbps modem is integrated. There is a comfortable 88-key Windows 95 keyboard and a touchpad. The battery will last almost seven hours and can be recharged in two hours, which is the best we reviewed, and its weight is about average at 7.5 pounds. Windows NT Workstation 4.0 software and infrared, file transfer and sleep manager programs are included. Support is available by phone 24 hours a day every day free for the first year, and they have an excellent Internet site. There is a three-year Limited Warranty.

AMS TravelPro 2040

Price $5,000	
Overall Rating ★★★	
Performance ★★★ 3/4	
Screen Quality ★★★	
Modularity ★★ 1/2	
Mobility ★★★ 3/4	
Support ★★ 1/2	

This 233 MHz MMX computer weights only 6.3 pounds with the 20X CD-ROM and battery installed. For mobility, two batteries, an AC adapter, and carrying case are included. Its performance is excellent due to the 512k L2 cache, high amount of RAM and fast CD-ROM drive. The 3.1 gigabyte hard drive is small, but removeable, and swaps with the floppy drive. The 13.3" screen has 1024 x 768 resolution with 65k colors. It comes with

a 20X CD-ROM drive, and 80 MB EDO RAM minimum, but no additional RAM can be added. The 33.6-kbps modem and Trackpad pointing device are integrated, and a Windows 95 keyboard has 88 keys. The system supports the "zoomed video ready" standard with one Type III PC Card slot. Software includes Windows 95, Internet utilities and system accelerator utilities. Support is available by phone 12 hours a day weekdays and on the Internet, but the interface on the Internet is slow and difficult to use. Warranties include a 30 day money back guarantee and three-year parts and labor.

Apple PowerBook 3400c/240

Price $5,700	
Overall Rating ★★★ 1/4	
Performance ★★★ 1/2	
Screen Quality ★★★	
Modularity ★★★	
Mobility ★★★ 1/4	
Support ★★★ 1/2	

The only non-Pentium notebook in our review is the PowerPC 240 MHz Apple PowerBook. It is a 7.4-pound notebook, which is about average weight for these systems. It comes with 16 MB RAM minimum, which is upgradeable to 144 MB and has a 12X CD-ROM, which resulted in a lower rating in the performance area. Also included is a 3 gigabyte hard drive, 12.1" screen that will operate at 800 x 600 resolution, and 33.6 kbps integrated modem. The keyboard has an integrated numeric keypad and a trackpad pointer is conveniently located at the front of the unit. There is an expansion bay on the right side that can contain either the CD-ROM or a floppy disk drive or optional storage and backup modules, such as an additional hard drive or Zip drive. The battery lasts from two to four hours. The system supports the "zoomed video ready" standard with two Type II or one Type III PC Card slots. Software includes the Mac OS 7.6 and other Internet and office packages. Addition of the Insignia Solutions' SoftWindows software lets you run MS-DOS 6.2 and Windows 3.1. Support by phone is free for 90 days after purchase with fee services available after that time. The warranty is one year limited hardware coverage.

Compaq Armada 7750MT

Price $5,000	
Overall Rating	★★★
Performance	★★
Screen Quality	★★★
Modularity	★★★ 3/4
Mobility	★★★
Support	★★★ 3/4

This 166 MHz MMX computer also suffers in performance areas due to the 256k cache and slow CD-ROM. The 8X CD-ROM is removeable from the MultiBay, which can also hold the floppy drive, a second hard drive, or a second battery. It comes with a small 2.1 gigabyte hard drive, a 12.1" screen at 1024 x 768 resolution with 64k colors, and 32 MB EDO RAM upgradeable to 144 MB. The 33.6-kbps modem with a cellular port and an "eraser head" style pointing stick are integrated and there are few ports to attach other devices. A full-size 101-key key-

board makes it an easy computer to use. It weighs in at 7.8 pounds because the re-charging power supply is built-in. The battery will last about 2 1/4 hours. The system supports the "zoomed video ready" standard with two Type II or one Type III PC Card slots. Software is sparse —just Windows 95 or NT and a communications program for faxing and connecting to the Internet. Support is available by phone 24 hours a day every day and they provide a lot of information and drivers on the Internet. The warranty covers three years parts and labor.

Dell Inspiron 3000 M233XT

Price $4,650	
Overall Rating	★★★ 3/4
Performance	★★★★
Screen Quality	★★★ 1/2
Modularity	★★★ 1/2
Mobility	★★★★
Support	★★★ 1/2

This 233 MHz MMX computer has excellent performance due to the fast 4 gigabyte hard drive (removeable), 512k L2 cache, and SDRAM memory. A modular bay can contain the CD-ROM, floppy disk drive, or a second battery. It comes with a 20X CD-ROM, a 13.3" screen at 1024 x 768 resolution and 64k colors, and 32 MB RAM upgradeable to 144 MB. The 56-kbps PCMCIA X-Jack modem is very convenient and fast. The keyboard includes Windows 95 keys and a touchpad is convenient. It weighs in just under seven pounds and the battery will last about 2 1/2 hours. The system supports the "zoomed video ready" standard with two

Type II or one Type III PC Card slots. Software includes Windows 95 and the Microsoft Office 97 Small Business Edition package. Support is available by phone 24 hours a day every day and they have an excellent Internet site. The warranty covers three-years parts and labor and is called their "Rapid Response" option.

Gateway 2000 Solo 2300

Price $4,150	
Overall Rating ★ ★ ★ 1/4	
Performance ★ ★ 3/4	
Screen Quality ★ ★ ★	
Modularity ★ ★ ★ 1/4	
Mobility ★ ★ ★ ★	
Support ★ ★ 3/4	

This 233 MHz MMX computer is lightweight at 6.5 pounds. The 2.2 gigabyte hard drive is on the small side and only has 256k L2 cache. It comes with a 10X CD-ROM (swappable with the floppy drive), a 12.1" screen at 1024 x 768 resolution and 64k colors, and 32 MB SDRAM upgradeable to 192 MB. The 33.6-kbps PCMCIA Telepath modem is very convenient. There is an 85-key keyboard and a EZ Pad touchpad. The battery will last over five hours, which is among the best we reviewed. The system supports the "zoomed video ready" standard with two Type II or one Type III PC Card slots. Software included is Windows 95 and the Microsoft Office 97 Small Office Edition package plus other titles. Support is available by phone 24 hours a day every day and they have an excellent Internet site. The warranty covers one-year parts

and labor and is extendable for two more years for only $99.

Gateway 2000 Solo 9100XL

Price $5,600	
Overall Rating ★ ★ ★ 1/2	
Performance ★ ★ ★ 3/4	
Screen Quality ★ ★ ★ 1/2	
Modularity ★ ★ ★ 1/2	
Mobility ★ ★ ★ 3/4	
Support ★ ★ 3/4	

This 233 MHz MMX computer is the heaviest we reviewed at 11 pounds. The 5 gigabyte hard drive is among the largest we saw and is removeable. It comes with a 10X removeable CD-ROM, a 13.3" screen at 1024 x 768 resolution and 64k colors, and 64 MB SDRAM upgradeable to 192 MB. The large standard RAM coupled with 512k L2 cache make it among the fastest we reviewed. The 33.6-kbps PCMCIA Telepath modem is very convenient. There is an 88-key Windows 95 keyboard and a EZ Pad touchpad. The battery will last about four hours, which is among the best we reviewed and there is a battery charger included. The system supports the "zoomed video ready" standard with two Type II or one Type III PC Card slots. A carrying case and mini-docking station, which adds a lot of flexibility, are also included in the price above. Software included is Windows 95 and Microsoft Office 97 Small Business Edition and Encarta 97. Support is available by phone 24 hours a day every day and there is an excellent Internet site. The warranty covers one-year parts and labor

and it is extendable for two more years for only $99.

Hitachi VisionBook Pro

Price $4,800
Overall Rating ★★★ 1/2
Performance ★★★
Screen Quality ★★★ 1/2
Modularity ★★★ 3/4
Mobility ★★★ 3/4
Support ★★★★

This 166 MHz MMX computer weighs in at 7.9 pounds. Performance is not as good as others reviewed, as it has only 256k L2 cache, 10X CD-ROM, and EDO memory. It comes with a 13.3" screen at 1024 x 768 resolution and 64k colors, and 32 MB RAM upgradeable to 144 MB. The floppy drive swaps with the CD-ROM when needed. The 56-kbps integrated modem includes a cellular phone port. The keyboard includes Windows 95 keys and an Alps GlidePoint touchpad is excellent. The battery will last about three hours. The system supports the "zoomed video ready" standard with two Type II or one Type III PC Card slots. Software includes Windows 95, LapLink, Netscape Navigator, and other titles. Support is available by phone 24 hours a day every day and they have an excellent Internet site. The warranty covers three-years parts and labor and can be extended for two more years. They guarantee a 24-hour turnaround on repairs with some restrictions.

IBM ThinkPad 770 9549-1AU

Price $8,200
Overall Rating ★★★★
Performance ★★★★
Screen Quality ★★★★
Modularity ★★★★
Mobility ★★★★
Support ★★★★

This 233 MHz MMX is the fastest system we reviewed. The 5 gigabyte hard drive is among the largest available and is removeable. It comes with a 20X removeable CD-ROM in the UltraBay, which can optionally hold a second 5.1 gigabyte hard drive, second battery, floppy disk drive, Zip drive, or a DVD-ROM drive. The system has the largest available screen at 14.1" at 1024 x 768 resolution with 64k colors. There is also a 512k L2 cache and 32 MB SDRAM upgradeable to 256 MB. The 33.6-kbps integrated modem is upgradeable to 56-kbps with planned software. There is a Windows 95 keyboard and the famous Trackpoint III pointing device that has been enhanced to let you click the mouse by simply tapping the Trackpoint. Another unique feature is a button for scrolling and zooming the image on your screen. The computer is on the heavy side at 7.8 pounds and the battery will last about 3.5 hours, which is good considering the power and features included. The system supports the "zoomed video ready" standard with two Type II or one Type III PC Card slots. Software included is Windows 95, but you can order it with Windows NT or OS/2 Warp, and other packages depending on the operating system you choose. Support is available by phone 24 hours a day every day and they have an excellent Internet site. The warranty covers three-years parts and labor, it is extendable, and it includes a free courier service to and from a repair center.

NEC Versa 6230

Price $5,750	
Overall Rating	★ ★ ★ 3/4
Performance	★ ★ ★ ★
Screen Quality	★ ★ ★ 3/4
Modularity	★ ★ ★ 1/4
Mobility	★ ★ ★ ★
Support	★ ★ ★ 1/4

This 233 MHz MMX computer is light in weight and very fast due to the large standard RAM and 512k L2 cache. The 5.4 gigabyte hard drive is among the largest available. It comes with a 20X removeable CD-ROM in the Versa Bay, or you can put in the floppy disk drive or an optional extra battery, optional second hard drive, or an Iomega Zip drive option. The display is NEC's brilliant 13.3" high resolution screen. It comes with 64 MB SDRAM upgradeable to 128 MB. The 33.6-kbps modem is integrated. There is a full-size keyboard and a small touchpad. The battery will last about three hours. The system supports the "zoomed video ready" standard with two Type II or one Type III PC Card slots. Windows 95 is included. Support is available by phone 24 hours a day every day and they have some information on their Internet site. The warranty covers three-year parts and labor with the first year including UltraCare courier service with a one-day turnaround time for repairs. NEC will replace screens that have six or more bad pixels while it is under warranty

Quantex H-Series 1330

Price $3,900	
Overall Rating	★ ★ ★ 1/2
Performance	★ ★ ★ 3/4
Screen Quality	★ ★ ★
Modularity	★ ★ ★ ★
Mobility	★ ★ ★ 3/4
Support	★ ★ ★

This 233 MHz MMX computer is among the fastest systems we reviewed and it is upgradeable when faster options become available! The 3 gigabyte hard drive is adequate. It comes with a 20X removeable CD-ROM (swappable with the floppy drive or an optional second battery), a 13.3" screen at 1024 x 768 resolution and 64k colors, 512k L2 cache, and 32 MB SDRAM upgradeable to 144 MB. The 33.6-kbps PCMCIA modem is convenient. There is an 88-key keyboard and touchpad pointing device. The weight is average at seven pounds, and the battery will last about three hours, which is good. The system supports the "zoomed video ready" standard with two Type II or one Type III PC Card slots. Windows 95 is included. Support is available by phone 24 hours a day every day and they have an excellent Internet site. The warranty covers one-years part and labor and three years for the processor and memory.

Toshiba Tecra 750 CDT

Price $6,800	
Overall Rating	★ ★ ★ 1/2
Performance	★ ★ ★ ★
Screen Quality	★ ★ ★ 1/2
Modularity	★ ★ ★ 1/2
Mobility	★ ★ ★ 1/2
Support	★ ★ 3/4

This 233 MHz MMX computer is heavy at 9 pounds for travel. It is also one of the fastest notebooks due to its 512k L2 cache, fast hard drive and CD-ROM drive, and SDRAM memory. The 4.7 gigabyte hard drive is among the larger ones we saw and is removeable. The SelectBay, which can contain the floppy disk drive or 20X CD-ROM drive, can also hold an optional DVD-ROM drive, second hard drive, or second battery. It comes with a 13.3" screen at 1024 x 768 resolution and 16 million colors, and 32 MB SDRAM upgradeable to 160 MB. The K56 flex integrated modem includes a cellular port, is upgradeable, and very convenient. There is an 84-key keyboard and an AccuPoint pointing stick. The battery will last about 3.5 hours, which is good. The system supports the "zoomed video ready" standard with two Type II or one Type III PC Card slots. Software includes Windows 95, plus Internet access and utility packages, or optionally Windows NT or Windows for Workgroups. Support is available by phone 24 hours a day every day and they have an excellent Internet site. The warranty covers three-years parts and labor.

WinBook 233XL

Price $4,300	
Overall Rating	★★★ 1/4
Performance	★★★ 1/4
Screen Quality	★★★ 1/2
Modularity	★★ 1/2
Mobility	★★ 3/4
Support	★★★ 3/4

This 233 MHz MMX computer is on the heavy side at 7.8 pounds, but it is also among the faster systems we reviewed. The 3 gigabyte hard drive is adequate. It comes with a 20X CD-ROM, floppy disk drive, a 13.3" screen, 256k L2 cache, and 32 MB RAM upgradeable to 128 MB. There is an full-size keyboard and an integrated touchpad. The battery should last about three hours. Windows 95 is preinstalled. Support is available by phone 8 AM to 9 PM weekdays and 7 hours on Saturday. They have an informative Internet site. The warranty covers three-years parts and labor, and it includes a free overnight pickup service for repair.

CONTACT INFORMATION

Acer America Corporation
800-767-0334
www.acer.com

AMS Tech
800-980-8889
www.amsnote.com

Apple Computer Inc.
800-538-9696
www.powerbook.apple.com

Compaq Computer Corp.
800-888-5858
www.compaq.com

Dell Computer Corp.
800-388-8542
www.dell.com

Gateway 2000 Inc.
800-846-2000
www.gw2k.com

Hitachi PC Corporation
800-HITACHI
www.hitachipc.com

IBM Personal Computer Co.
800-426-2968
www.pc.ibm.com/thinkpad

NEC Computer Systems Division, Packard Bell
NEC, Inc.
888-863-2669
www.nec-computers.com

Quantex Microsystems
800-346-6685
www.quantex.com

Toshiba America Information Systems Inc.
800-457-7777
www.computers.toshiba.com

WinBook Computer Corporation
800-254-7806
www.winbook.com

COMPUTERS, POWER DESKTOPS

Computer technology changes so fast at times it's hard to keep up. The computer bought a few years ago is now considered a dinosaur compared to the faster models available now.

If you're looking for a more powerful computer you're probably looking to buy a Pentium computer. But as you'll find out, there are different types of Pentium computers. Intel, the microprocessor manufacturer, has released several types of Pentium processors: basic Pentium processors, Pentium Pro processors, Pentium processors with MMX technology, and Pentium II processors, which are the combination of the Pentium Pro processors with MMX technology. Cyrix has also developed the 6x86MX, which offers Pentium II power at Pentium prices. And AMD offers its K6 that operates at Pentium levels. With all this new technology on the market today, choosing the best computer for your needs can be confusing.

Buying a new computer is a daunting experience. Retail stores have dozens of models with a variety of features, but at least you can see and touch these systems. But you will not see all the options because many of the "power" manufacturers do not offer their products at retail. Mail-order is another attractive option, if you know what you want to order. This source includes both warehouse-type resellers and direct manufacturer shipping. And now many manufacturers will let you configure and order a custom system by phone or directly on their Internet sites. But be sure you know what you are getting! The prices may include the monitor, a gigantic bundle of software, and various manufacturer or store-level service and support agreements.

To help you understand the marketplace, we reviewed several Pentium desktop computers ranging in price from $2,000 to $4,000 and with a minimum speed of 233 MHz. Data on these models was compiled from the manufacturers. Prices indicated are approximate typical street prices when the systems were reviewed. The following list contains 11 desktop computers and their overall ratings.

OVERALL RATINGS

Micron Millenia XKU 300	★★★★
Gateway G6-300XL	★★★ 3/4
Gateway 2000 G6-266	★★★ 1/2
Hewlett Packard Vectra VL/266	★★★ 1/2
Dell Dimension XPS H266	★★★ 1/4
Gateway 2000 G6-233 M	★★★
Gateway 2000 GP5-233	★★★
Dell OptiPlex Gn 233	★★★
Quantex QP6/233 SM-3	★★ 3/4

Dell Dimension XPS M233S ★★ 3/4

CyberMax SuperMax P3 ★★ 3/4

EXPLANATION OF RATINGS

Power desktop computers were selected for review from currently available PC-compatible products with a 233 MHz Pentium processor or its equivalent as the minimum speed. The overall rating was arrived at by giving individual scores on performance, features, and support (including warranty) and then averaging the three scores and rounding to the nearest 1/4. The maximum overall rating a computer could receive was four stars.

In addition to processor speed, there are a number of other factors you should consider when purchasing a new power desktop system.

MMX Technology uses high-speed circuits to increase the processor's multimedia performance. This technology can be used to handle full-screen video and graphics, animation, videoconferencing, virtual reality, and 3-D graphics. It will produce a full-screen, full-resolution image that rivals that of a TV image. Having MMX technology already on your computer will eliminate the need for you to add a special board later for multimedia applications.

RAM system memory is critical. While many systems can come with 16MB (megabytes or millions of characters) standard, you should get at least 32MB if you plan to run Windows 95 or 64MB for Windows NT. If you have a choice between EDO and SDRAM type of RAM, get SDRAM because it is faster. Make sure the system's RAM is expandable to meet your needs.

Hard Drive Storage should be at least 3 gigabytes (billions of characters) in size and have an access time of 12 milliseconds or less. Video-intensive applications will want a sustained data rate of 5MB/second. SCSI drives are higher in price than the typical Enhanced IDE (ATA) but the performance they offer may be worth it. The computer should have space for adding at least one additional hard drive.

Removeable-media Drives are popular options for high-end computers because you can back up your precious data more quickly than using the more traditional tape drives or floppy disks. Examples are Iomega's 100MB Zip and one gigabyte Jaz drives and SyQuest's 230MB EZFlyer and 1.5 gigabyte SyJet drives.

Expandability means you really want a minitower or tower case rather than the desktop type case. You should have at least two open slots and bays to add in cards and features that you may need in the future.

Bundled Software varies widely, but you should get at least the operating system and several high-quality programs or suites that you can use. Be sure to get the original CD-ROMs and the documentation in case you need to reinstall anything,

Warranties are a must. A three-year parts-and-labor warranty with on-site service for the first year is good, and the opportunity to extend the warranty is a must.

Technical support varies widely, but if you need 24-hour daily phone support, be sure to get a system that offers that level at a reasonable price. Per-call rates vary widely, and the wait time for service is also a consideration.

Other considerations, if you need them, include monitors, CD-ROM drives, modems, and graphic and sound boards. The newest multimedia option is called a DVD-ROM drive, which can play regular CDs as well as newer DVD formats for high-quality video play-back; however, there is not a lot of software available for this drive at this time.

While this report reflects prices and features at the time it was written, the industry is changing quickly and competition is keen. Prices are dropping and standard features are growing. Getting prices, however, is becoming easy with the manufacturers listing up-to-date systems, prices, and features on their Internet sites, and some even have the ability to compute a price based on selected options.

ALPHABETICAL DESCRIPTIONS

CyberMax SuperMax P3

Price $2,000	
Overall Rating ★★ 3/4	
Performance ★★★	
Features ★★ 1/4	
Support ★★★	

This computer is a bargain with a Pentium II-233 MHz MMX processor. It comes fully loaded with 32MB SDRAM expandable to only 64MB, 512k cache, a 3.2 gigabyte hard drive, a 56-kbps modem, a graphics card with 4MB of video memory,

an Ensoniq wavetable sound card, Altec Lansing ACS 90 speakers with subwoofers, a 17-inch monitor, and a 24 speed CD-ROM drive. Software includes Windows 95 with the Corel Office Suite 7. Technical support is available 24-hours a day and the computer is covered by a one-year labor and three-year parts warranty with one year on-site service.

Dell Dimension XPS H266

Price $2,890	
Overall Rating ★★★1/4	
Performance ★★★ 1/2	
Features ★★★	
Support ★★★	

This computer is a strong performer with good features and a Pentium II-266 MHz processor. It comes fully loaded with 32MB SDRAM expandable to 256MB, 512 cache, a 8.4 gigabyte hard drive, a Matrox Millennium II graphics card with 8MB of video memory, a wavetable Yamaha sound card, Altec Lansing ACS 90 speakers with subwoofers, a 17-inch monitor, 24 speed CD-ROM drive, a 56-kbps modem with x2 technology, and Windows 95 with the Microsoft Office 97 for Small Business Edition software. One hindrance is the system's case, which is difficult to get off. Technical support is available 24 hours a day. The Dell Dimension line is covered by a one-year labor and three-year parts warranty.

Dell Dimension XPS M233S

Price $2,320	
Overall Rating ★★ 3/4	
Performance ★★ 3/4	
Features ★★ 1/2	

Support ★★★

This computer comes with a 233-MHz Pentium MMX processor, 32MB of SDRAM expandable to 64MB, 512K cache, 4.3 gigabyte hard drive, 24X CD-ROM drive, Matrox Millennium II with 8MB video memory, a 17-inch Trinitron monitor which produces vibrant color, an integrated sound board, Altec Lansing ACS290 speakers with subwoofers and a internal 3Com U.S. Robotics Sportster x2 56-kbps modem. The RAM maximum of 64MB makes upgrading this system a problem if you plan to keep it for a long time. Also included is a Microsoft Intelli-Mouse. Software includes Windows 95 and the Microsoft Office 97 Small Business Edition software, Publisher, and Photo Editor. Technical support is available 24 hours a day. The system is covered by Dell's 1-year labor and 3-year parts warranty.

Dell OptiPlex Gn 233

Price $3,280	
Overall Rating ★★★	
Performance ★★★	
Features ★★ 3/4	
Support ★★★	

This computer has a 233MHz Pentium II MMX processor, Features include 32MB of RAM expandable to 256MB, 256k secondary cache, 3.2 gigabyte hard drive, Matrox Millenium graphics adapter with 4MB VRAM, 17-inch monitor, 24 X CD-ROM drive, and Creative Labs Sound Blaster AWE 32 PnP sound board. A 56-kbps modem is included. If you wish to expand your system you are restricted to three free slots and two available drive

bays. Technical support is available 24 hours a day. The system is covered by Dell's 1-year labor and 3-year parts warranty.

Gateway 2000 GP5-233

Price $2,175	
Overall Rating ★★★	
Performance ★★ 3/4	
Features ★★★	
Support ★★★ 1/2	

This fully loaded multimedia computer is a Pentium MMX 233 MHz-based mini-tower computer that's almost as fast as the Pentium II-233 systems. It comes loaded with 32MB of RAM expandable to 256MB, 512k cache, four gigabyte hard drive, STB Virge 4MB 3D PCI graphics adapter, 4MB of video RAM, 24 speed CD-ROM drive, a 56-kbps x2 modem, Ensoniq Audio PCI wavetable sound board, and a 17-inch monitor. Software includes Windows 95, and the Microsoft Office 97 Small Business Edition.

Gateway has excellent 24-hour phone support, free on-site service for one year, and a three-year parts and labor warranty.

Gateway 2000 G6-233 M

Price $2,400	
Overall Rating ★★★	
Performance ★★ 1/2	
Features ★★★ 1/4	
Support ★★★ 1/2	

Both business and home users will find this computer a superb multimedia mini-tower system with a 233 MHz Pentium II processor. The system includes 64MB of EDO RAM expandable to 384MB, a 4 gigabyte Ultra-DMA hard drive, a 16-bit

Ensoniq Audio PCI wavetable sound card, Altec Lansing speakers with sub-woofer, a 56-kbps modem with U.S. Robotics x2 technology, a 24-speed CD-ROM drive, and a STB Virge 4MB 3D PCI graphics card. You can access the inside of the system easily with big thumbscrews and I/O ports are color coded; however, you may have a hard time accessing the drive bays. Gateway's support is excellent and is available 24 hours a day. Gateway offers free on-site service for one year and a three-year parts and labor warranty.

Gateway 2000 G6-266

Price $2,800	
Overall Rating ★ ★ ★ 1/2	
Performance ★ ★ ★ 1/2	
Features ★ ★ ★ 3/4	
Support ★ ★ ★ 1/2	

This computer has a Pentium II-266 MHz processor that offers excellent speed and performance in a sturdy tower case. It includes 64MB of RAM expandable to 384MB, an 8.4 gigabyte hard drive, a STB Virge 3D PCI graphics adapter with 4MB of VRAM, MicroMedia speakers, a 56-kbps modem, a 21-inch Trinitron monitor, and a 24-speed CD-ROM drive. Software includes Windows 95 and home-related titles. Gateway technical support is available toll-free 24 hours daily. The Gateway warranty is the same for all their machines, free on-site service for one year and a three-year parts and labor warranty.

Gateway 2000 G6-300XL

Price $3,800	
Overall Rating ★ ★ ★ 3/4	

Performance ★ ★ ★ ★	
Features ★ ★ ★ 3/4	
Support ★ ★ ★ 1/2	

This computer has a Pentium II-300 MHz processor that offers outstanding speed. It includes 64MB of RAM expandable to 384MB, an 8.4 gigabyte hard drive, a STB Virge 3D PCI graphics adapter with 4MB of VRAM, speakers, a 56-kbps modem, a 19-inch monitor, and a DVD (9 speed or CDs) ROM drive. Software includes Windows 95 and home-related titles. Technical support is available toll-free 24 hours daily. Their warranty includes free on-site service for one year and a three-year parts and labor warranty.

Hewlett-Packard Vectra VL/266

Price $3,500	
Overall Rating ★ ★ ★ 1/2	
Performance ★ ★ ★ 1/2	
Features ★ ★ ★ 1/2	
Support ★ ★ ★ 1/2	

This computer has a Pentium II 266 MHZ processor and comes with 64MB RAM expandable to 192MB. It also has a 512k cache, 4 gigabyte hard drive, Matrox Millenium II 4MB video card, integrated Sound Blaster audio, speakers, and a 17-inch monitor. Software can be Windows NT or 95 with Microsoft Office 97. Support is available 24 hours a day. The warranty includes one-year on-site service and three years parts and labor coverage.

Micron Millennia XKU 300

Price $3,900	
Overall Rating ★ ★ ★ ★	
Performance ★ ★ ★ ★	
Features ★ ★ ★ ★	

Support ★★★★

This very powerful computer has a 300 MHz Pentium II MMX processor with outstanding performance, a great design and good system reliability. It comes standard with 128MB of SDRAM expandable to 384MB, 512 cache, 8.4 gigabyte Ultra ATA fast hard drive, Diamond Viper V330 AGP 128-bit video card with 4MB SGRAM and MPEG, 17-inch monitor, 24-speed CD-ROM drive, 56-kbps modem, and 32-voice wavetable audio with Advent 009 speakers and subwoofer. Software includes Windows 95 and the Microsoft Office 97 Small Business Edition. You can also choose from a variety of Micron Software Solutions Paks with one free and others for a small additional charge. Support is excellent with 24-hour availability. Micron offers a five-year limited warranty on the microprocessor and main memory components with a three-year limited warranty on the rest of the system.

Quantex QP6/233 SM-3

Price $2,500

Overall Rating ★★ 3/4

Performance ★★ 1/2

Features ★★ 3/4

Support ★★★

The Quantex Pentium II 233 MHz computer holds its own in this group with its low cost and good features. However, some users view the Quantex's system reliability as only fair. It includes 32MB of RAM expand-able to 128MB, 512k cache, a 4 gigabyte hard drive, an Matrox Millenium graphics adapter with 4MB VRAM, a 17-inch monitor, a 16-speed CD-ROM drive, a 33.6 kbps modem, and a Yamaha OPL3-SA X sound board with Altec Lansing AC45 speakers and subwoofers. Included software is aimed at home users, but includes the Corel WordPerfect Suite seven and Windows 95. The warranty covers parts for three-years and labor for one-year. There is free on-site support for one-year and 24-hour technical support.

CONTACT INFORMATION

CyberMax Computer, Inc.
800-345-8939
www.cybmax.com

Dell Computer Corporation
800-388-8542
www.dell.com

Gateway 2000 Inc.
800-846-2000
www.gw2k.com

Hewlett-Packard Corporation
800-752-0900
www.hewlett-packard.com

Micron Electronics, Inc.
888-634-8799
www.micronpc.com

Quantex Microsystems
800-346-6685
www.quantex.com

COMPUTERS, ENTERPRISE SERVERS

As companies move more of their data into enterprise-wide databases, the need for storing those databases and making them available to the entire company has become a priority. Over the past decade the fileserver has become more than just a PC that a department connects to in order to store files for group access/backups.

These days a file server has to be able to store multi-gigabyte databases that may be accessed from around the globe as well as possibly pull duty as a web server. Servers have to be up 24 hours a day, seven days a week. Moreover, they must be fast and powerful. These servers can support an entire company, hence they are called "Enterprise Servers" or "Enterprise-level Servers." These two terms are interchangeable.

In this section we will look at some of the more popular Pentium Pro-based servers. We are not looking at Sun or DEC Alpha-based servers because they are in another category of their own. Almost all of the servers looked at here are quad Pentium Pros running at either 166 MHz or 200

The number-one rated server, the Compaq Proliant 5000, is feature-packed, has good performance, and good reliability. It has two large fans to keep the system cool.

MHz. You probably won't find these servers at your local CompUSA or Computer City. You'll most likely have to order them from the companies directly. Furthermore, this kind of power doesn't come cheap. The minimum price for these servers is around $15,000 and goes up to a high of over $60,000. The prices will vary somewhat depending on the actual number of processors, amount of memory, the size and number of hard drives, and any other accessories you may request.

Server technology is changing and advancing on an almost daily basis. This rapid change makes many managers nervous about making a decision concerning what server to get. All of the servers in the round up will serve an enterprise well. Some better than others, but you will not be disappointed with any of them. Of course, servers are not the whole picture in a network. You will have to deal with hubs, routers, network cards, and cables. One caveat, the prices for all of the reviewed systems will vary based on the exact configuration you purchase.

Following is a list of 11 enterprise servers and their overall ratings.

OVERALL RATINGS

Compaq Proliant 5000	★★★3/4
SAG Electronics STF Quad RAID File Server	★★★1/4
ALR Revolution Quad 6	★★★
Data General Aviion AV-4900	★★★
Data General Aviion AV-3600	★★3/4
Netserver LX Pro 6/166	★★3/4
Netserver LX Pro 6/200 SMP	★★3/4
Netserver 5/166 LS4	★★3/4
Tangent EP6Q-X2-S	★★3/4
Acer Altos 19000	★★1/4

EXPLANATION OF RATINGS

The enterprise servers were evaluated based on the following three aspects: configuration, which covers items such as the number and type of processors, the base amount of memory, and the amount of space for expansion; reliability features, such as redundant power supplies, the ability to swap hard drives and other components without having to shut down the server, and alarms to notify you when there are problems; and software/diagnostics.

Each aspect could potentially earn up to four stars, with one star being the lowest rating. The ratings were then averaged, resulting in the overall rating.

ALPHABETICAL DESCRIPTIONS

Acer Altos 19000

Price $22,000	
Overall Rating	★★1/4
Configuration	★★
Reliability	★★★
Software/Diagnostics	★★

The Acer Altos is one of the larger systems available, it has room for 14 hot-pluggable drives and room for an additional 4 standard drives. You can install up to 3 redundant power supplies to help ensure that your system stays up and running. If the system does go down, the Acer has a well designed alarm system to alert you of any problems. The major down side of this server is its inability to accept more than 2 processors. This puts it behind the curve in relation to the other systems here. The Acer also has half the level 2 cache of the other systems. At $22,000, you may want to hold out for a system that can use 4 processors.

ALR Revolution Quad 6

Price $32,999	
Overall Rating	★★★
Configuration	★★★
Reliability	★★★
Software/Diagnostics	★★★

With the ALR you have a choice of 4 166 MHz Pentium pro processors to power it or 200 MHz CPUs. Your choice of processor will have an effect on the system's performance. This is another very large-sized system. It can hold up to 9 hot pluggable disk drives, and 7 others for a total of 16 drive bays. The unit's LCD display is a great place to get information about the system status, internal temperature, and other system information. The Quad 6 comes with a 575-watt power supply that can be made redundant. The $32,999 system has six cooling fans to make sure your system does not overheat.

Compaq Proliant 5000

Price $25,288	
Overall Rating	★★★3/4
Configuration	★★★★
Reliability	★★★★
Software/Diagnostics	★★★

Both *Network World* and *PCWeek* thought the Compaq Proliant 5000 as a best buy for the money. It is featured packed, has good performance, and good reliability. The Proliant has two large fans to keep the system cool. The price of $25,228 is middle of the road. The system comes with some very good installation and management software. The documentation is reasonable.

Data General Aviion AV-4900 File Server

Price $63,148	
Overall Rating	★★★
Configuration	★★★
Reliability	★★★
Software/Diagnostics	★★★

Based on 4 200 MHz Pentium Pro processors the Data General AV-4900 is one of the best performing systems evaluated. It has many redundant systems such as three hot-swappable power supplies, and disk drives. It comes with HP Openview software to allow you to manage the server and more. It runs a expensive $63,148 as tested by Network World, but is one of the best values if you have a need for 7/24 operations.

Data General Aviion AV-3600 File Server

Price $31,663	
Overall Rating	★★3/4
Configuration	★★
Reliability	★★★
Software/Diagnostics	★★★

Unlike the AV-4900, the AV-3600 offers less performance for its price. It does, however, offer similar reliability, software and components. The 3600 has a remote diagnostic board that allows you to troubleshoot the system even if there is no power. Some of the components, such as memory, are a little tough to get to.

Hewlett Packard Netserver LX Pro 6/166

Price $29,450

Overall Rating ★★3/4

Configuration ★★★

Reliability ★★1/2

Software/Diagnostics ★★★

The LX Pro 6/166 and the LX Pro 6/200 SMP are virtually identical. The only real differences between these are the CPUs. The 6/166 has four 166-MHz Pentium Pros while the 200 has four 200 MHz chips. The LX pro chassis hold up to 12 swappable drives and six other types of drives. The cost of the LX pro 200 was $32,124.

Netserver LX Pro 6/200 SMP

Price $32,124

Overall Rating ★★3/4

Configuration ★★★

Reliability ★★1/2

Software/Diagnostics ★★★

Hewlett Packard had three entries in the enterprise server category. The 6/166 has four 166-MHz Pentium Pros while the 200 has four 200 MHz chips. The LX pro chassis hold up to 12 swappable drives and six other types of drives. The cost for the 166 MHz version is $29,950. All of the systems come with HP's OpenView management software, which is used in servers from other manufacturers as well.

Netserver 5/166 LS4

Price $29,950

Overall Rating ★★★3/4

Configuration ★★★

Reliability ★★★★

Software/Diagnostics ★★★★

The LS4 is a bit smaller. This version holds up to six swappable drives and had four 166 MHz Pentium Pros for power. All came with good support and service but the LX Pros had better documentation. The LS4 came in at $29,450 for the server. For $3,000 more, the 200 LX pro is the best deal.

SAG Electronics STF Quad RAID File Server

Price $19,999

Overall Rating ★★★1/4

Configuration ★★★★

Reliability ★★★

Software/Diagnostics ★★★

The specs of the STF Quad are a promising start. They include four 200MHz Pentium Pro for power, dual processing capability, 512K of Level 2 cache, a welcome 12 gigabyte DAT tape drive, three Seagate Cheetah Disk drives, and plenty of room for expansion and cooling. The server comes with LANDesk Pro for remote access to the server when it can't be accessed over the network. All of the documentation was from the OEM vendors and was sufficient.

Tangent EP6Q-X2-S

Price $24,507

Overall Rating ★★3/4

Configuration ★★

Reliability ★★★

Software/Diagnostics ★★★

The base Tangent system comes with two Pentium Pro processors running at 200 MHz. It also comes with a base 64 megabytes of ram. But not to worry, as the tangent can handle up to four processors and 2 Gigabytes of memory, making for a powerful system. It includes room for 12 hot-swappable drives and comes with 2 redundant power supplies with an option for a third. Configured with four 200 MHz CPUs and a 9.1 GB SCSI drive and a 9 GB RAID drive array, 128 MB of Ram and a host of other niceties the system beat the Compaq Proliant on price. As there are a lot of OEM components, your performance will not be as good as the Compaq, which is engineered from the ground up. But, barring any component failures, this could turn out to be a steal.

CONTACT INFORMATION

Acer America Corporation
408-432-6200
800-SEE-ACER

Advanced Logic Research, Inc.
800-444-4ALR
http://www.alr.com

Compaq Computer Corporation
281-370-0670
http://www.compaq.com

Data General Corp.
508-898-5000
http://www.dg.com

Hewlett Packard
408-773-6200
http://www.hp.com

SAG Electronics
800-989-3475; 508-683-0339
http://www.sagelec.com

Tangent Computer
800-342-9388
http://www.tangent.com

COMPUTERS, HANDHELD

Handheld computers give you the power of a desktop and the portability of a notebook combined into a device that fits in your hand. Also known as Handheld Personal Computers (HPC) and Personal Digital Assistants (PDA), these devices offer organization tools such as to-do lists, note taking, calendar, address database, e-mail, fax, and data synchronization with your desktop or notebook computer.

Some models even have web browsers for surfing the Internet.

Handheld computers are for convenience, to keep track of appointments and schedules, send off a quick fax, or take notes. These devices are convenient because they are small and can easily fit in your pocket, purse, or briefcase. Another great feature is the ability to synchronize data on your handheld with your main computer. You can make changes in your schedule on your handheld then transfer the data to your desktop or notebook computer without having to key in the data again. The operating system for most of these units is Windows CE, which is a

The Phillips Velo 1, the number-one rated handheld, comes with a 15-hour battery and an integrated 19.2 kbps modem with fax software. There is also a voice recorder that can record up to 16 minutes per megabyte of memory, which is great for verbal note taking.

watered-down version of Microsoft's Windows.

Data is input through a keyboard or by writing directly on the screen with a stylus. All of these models run on two AA batteries, have an LCD screen, and come with 2MB of RAM and 4MB of ROM. Since these devices do not have hard drives, memory is important. Applications for these devices are stored in ROM, the Read-Only Memory of the device. RAM (Random Access Memory) is where all the processing is done, so the more RAM you have the better.

Another feature to check is the screen resolution. It's small anyway, so make sure you have sufficient resolution for scrolling and viewing. Most of these units had insufficient backlighting and the text was tiny, but check for yourself and see what you can live with.

Modems are usually extra. These devices are not suitable for surfing the net, but some do have browsers. They also have fax and e-mail capabilities. This review takes a look at eight handheld style computers. Information was gathered from the manufacturer's web sites and opinions of our editors. Results are in the chart below.

OVERALL RATINGS

Phillips Velo 1	★★★★
Compaq PC Companion	★★★
Psion Series 3C	★★★
U.S. Robotics Pilot	★★★
Casio Cassiopeia	★★★
Sharp Zaurus ZR-3000	★★★

NEC MobilePro	★★1/2
Apple Newton MessagePad 2000	★★1/2

EXPLANATION OF RATINGS

Each device is rated in five categories: ease of use, speed, computer connection, web connection, and software. The highest score possible is four stars, the lowest, one. The overall rating represents the average rating of the five categories.

ALPHABETICAL DESCRIPTIONS

Apple Newton MessagePad 2000

Price $899
Rating ★★1/2
Ease of Use ★★
Speed ★★★
Computer Connection ★
Web Connection ★★★1/2
Software ★★★

The MessagePad 2000 pen-based interface and productivity applications are touted as an alternative to a notebook. About the size of a normal book (1.1 by 4.7 by 8.3 inches) it weighs a whopping 1.4 pounds, heavier than other handheld models. It uses the Newton OS, has a 160-MHz Strong Arm CPU, and 16 grayscale screen with better backlighting than other Windows CE devices. All input is done via the touch screen. This model uses handwriting recognition for note taking. This is a slow process and not very accurate. However an optional keyboard is available. Productivity applications included are a word processor, spreadsheet, a web browser, and e-mail package. Modems are extra. Other features include two

PCMCIA-card clots, infrared, LocalTalk-compatible serial port. The $900 price tag is too high for this device for it not to have a modem and better handwriting recognition technology included .

Casio Cassiopeia

Price $499 (Model A-10 2MB); $599(Model A-11 4MB)

Rating ★★★

Ease of Use ★★

Speed ★★1/2

Computer Connection ★★★★

Web Connection ★★★

Software ★★★1/2

The Cassiopeia weighs 13.4 ounces and measures 1 by 6.8 by 3.6 inches. This Windows CE device comes with 2MB or four MB of RAM and 4MB of ROM, supports four grayscales with a 480 by 240 pixel resolution. The screen has poor backlighting, making it hard to read. Viewing documents can be tedious because you have to constantly scroll to view long documents. The Cassiopeia is about average in performance. You can be notified of appointments while the device is off through its programmable LED light. Sound WAV files can be played, but the quality is very poor. Other features include a PCMCIA-card slot, a serial port, infrared port, and speakers. This device runs on two AA alkaline batteries or the lithium backup battery which holds about 20 hours of charge. Rechargeable NIMH battery packs, docking cradle, and AC adapter are available at an extra charge.

Compaq PC Companion

Price $499 (Model C120 2MB); $599 (Model C140 4MB)

Rating ★★★

Ease of Use ★★

Speed ★★1/2

Computer Connection ★★★★

Web Connection ★★★

Software ★★★★

Compaq took the Casio Cassiopeia model, placed the Compaq name on it and resold it as the PC Companion. No other changes to the model was made. It is being marketed towards the corporate customers along with bundled software for data synchronization, e-mail, handwriting recognition, and other wireless programs for this device. Some of the extras, like an AC adapter or device cradle, may be priced lower. Overall it's an average performer, like its clone, the Casio Casiopeia.

NEC MobilePro

Price $399 (MobilePro 200 2MB); $649 (MobilePro 400 4MB)

Rating ★★1/2

Ease of Use ★

Speed ★

Computer Connection ★★★★

Web Connection ★★★

Software ★★★1/2

MobilePro is a Windows CE device with a standard 8MB of ROM, 2MB or 4MB of RAM, an infrared, Type II PCMCIA-card slot, speakers and lithium-ion backup battery. Like other CE devices it runs on two AA batteries. There are separate ports for serial cable and AC adapter. It measures 1 inch by 6.9 inches by 3.7 inches and weighs 8 ounces. Despite the fact that the device's design is sleek, its performance is poor. The touch screen works well with the stylus but there is no backlighting, which means it's hard on the eyes. Loading documents and scrolling through files can be a very long process. The speaker's sound quality is terrible. Overall, the performance leaves a lot to be desired.

Phillips Velo 1

Price $599 (2MB); $699 (4MB)

Rating ★★★★

Ease of Use ★★★1/2

Speed ★★★★

Computer Connection ★★★★

Web Connection
★★★★

Software ★★★★

Velo1 is a fast performer with a R3910 RISC processor. It's a Windows CE device, weighing in at 13.2 ounces and measuring 1.25 by 6.75 by 3.75 inches. It comes with the standard 2MB of RAM which is upgradeable to 4MB, 8MB of ROM, infrared, serial port,

The convenient size and light weight of Phillips' Velo 1 is demonstrated above.

but there is no PCM-CIA-card slot. However there is a connector for an add-on PCMCIA-card module. The battery gives you 15 hours of power. It features an integrated 19.2 kbps v.32bis modem with fax software. There is also a voice recorder that can record up to 16 minutes per megabyte of memory, which is great for verbal note taking.

Psion Series 3C

Price $599

Rating ★★★

Ease of Use ★★★1/2

Speed ★★★

Computer Connection ★★★

Web Connection ★★★

Software ★★★★

Psion Series 3C is not a Windows CE device. It uses its own proprietary operating system. It does not have a touch screen. All input is done by keyboard and arrows are used for navigation. Features include a word processor, spreadsheet, address book, and calendar. You can write your custom applications with Psion's OPL programming language which is built-in. It weighs 9.7 ounces and measures 0.87 by 6.5 by 3.35 inches, comes with 2MB of RAM. There are also two memory-only PCMCIA-card slot, a RS232 serial port and infrared. A PCMCIA-card slot add-on is available. What is not included will cost you a lot extra. Serial cable and PC-connectivity software cost $100 extra. If you want a 14.4 modem that's another $199 and web browser and e-mail software is $49.95. To synchronize data you'll have to use the Psion Manager software and convert files. The Psion is compatible with software other than Microsoft applications. You want a handheld PC to work easily with your desktop or notebook computer. This one doesn't do that without a lot of work and money.

Sharp Zaurus ZR-3000

Price $399

Rating ★★3/4

Ease of Use ★★★

Speed ★★★

Computer Connection ★★★1/2

Web Connection ★

Software ★★★

The Zaurus does not run Windows CE, opting instead to use their own proprietary Synergy OS. Weighing in at 10.9 ounces it measures 0.9 by 6.3 by 3.6 inches. The screen is 320 by 240 pixel resolution with no backlighting. It's keyboard driven and comes with a bundle of software, including a spreadsheet, word processor, note taker, and personal information manager. The Zaurus is easy to use. For data synchronization, you can drag and drop files from the Zaurus to your computer using the Sharp Application Partner. Zaurus files can also be converted to Word and Excel files with the file translation software you install on your main computer. There is no web browser, modem, or PCMCIA-card slot included with this device. But you can add a modem to the serial port.

U.S. Robotics Pilot

Price $249 (Pilot 1000, 128 K); $299 (Pilot 5000, 512 K)

Rating ★★★

Ease of Use ★★★1/2

Speed ★★★

Computer Connection ★★★★

Web Connection ★

Software ★★★

The Pilot fits neatly in your hand, measuring 0.7 by 3.2 by 4.7 inches and weighing only 5.7 ounces. It is entirely pen-based with all major functions accessed through six buttons displayed on the screen. Features include notepad, calendar, calculator, to-do list, and address book. To use this device you use a stylus to select a feature or write on the screen in a specialized shorthand called Graffiti. The shorthand technique requires you to write in a box, switching modes for upper- and lower-case letters and numbers. It's easy to learn and you should get the hang of it after a while.

For your desktop or notebook you get a Personal Information Manager, connectivity software, and cradle. To synchronize data from your Pilot to your PC, place the Pilot in the cradle and the data is synchronized from the Pilot to your desktop and vice versa. This process is very quick. It uses the Intellisync software from Puma Technology which transfers data from the Pilot to any PIM program. You can also connect to a Macintosh as well as a PC.

This device is not for surfing the Internet or e-mail. Its main function is storing information such as schedules, notes, etc. and then synchronizing this data with your desktop computer or notebook. The drawbacks are the small type on the screen and having to learn the Graffiti method of printing.

CONTACT INFORMATION

Apple Computer
(800) 776-2333
www.apple.com

Casio
(800) 962-2746
www.casio.com

Compaq Corporation
Houston Texas
(800) 345-1518
www.compaq.com

NEC
(800) 632-8377
www.nec.com

Philips
(888) 367-8356
www.philips.com

Sharp
(800) 237-4377
www.sharp.com

U.S. Robotics
(800) 881-7256
www.usrobotics.com

Psion
(800) 997-7466
www.psion.com

GRAPHICS ACCELERATOR BOARDS

In order for your monitor to display text and graphics, the computer must have a video adapter. Some computers—particularly lower-end ones—have this circuitry integrated into the motherboard. This is not a good solution today, because the main computer processor is used for graphics, which degrades overall system performance. A better solution is to have a *graphics accelerator board* installed in your computer. By offloading most of the graphics processing tasks from the main processor this way, you can improve the overall performance of your system as well as improve your graphics capabilities.

Why would you want to upgrade your graphics board? If your needs are to run standard business applications like word processors or spreadsheets, just about any graphics card will be adequate to offload your main processor. But first check to see if your computer already has a separate board because you will get very little additional performance by replacing it. If you are getting into fancier business

The STB Velocity 128, which tied for the number-one board, is excellent for standard business applications, with resolution up to 1600x1200. 3D performance is among the best of those reviewed.

graphics—especially multimedia applications—with higher resolution, more colors, animation, or motion video, you may find your current graphics card is inadequate. And, if you are into the latest in 3D animation or computer games, you will definitely want one of the newest three-dimensional (3D) graphics boards.

Graphics boards can be purchased from computer outlets or by mail-order, but there are no places to shop and actually see the board in action before you buy one. This makes the ability to try it and return it if not satisfied a very important consideration. And some retail stores will install the board in your computer for a nominal fee, which can be an advantage if you are not experienced in the installation of boards and driver software.

The following are some terms you will need to know about when evaluating graphics boards. Learning them will also bring to light to what a good graphics board can do that an ordinary video adapter on your motherboard cannot do.

2D/3D stands for two-dimensional or three-dimensional graphics. 2D is adequate for most business uses, but many new games require 3D to make their images more realistic.

3D Software uses an application program interface to control the graphics card. *Direct3D* is Microsoft's standard, but some game makers are writing their own drivers specific to certain boards to improve game performance. OpenGL is another standard used in computer-aided design (CAD) software.

Alpha Blending is a way of blending two textures in a 3D image. The classic example is seeing a laser beam against a wall with blending of the laser and wall color to make it more realistic.

AVI Video is the term used for full-motion video support. Speed is expressed as "frames-per-second," with 30 being equal in quality to a television image.

Color Depth indicates the maximum number of colors that can be displayed at one time: 8-bit = 256 colors, 16-bit = 65,536 (64k) colors, and 24-bit shows over 16 million colors. Images recorded at the higher bit level are degraded by displaying them at lower levels.

DPI stands for dots-per-inch and is the standard way that image resolution is described. The lowest resolution on a PC is 640x480, and it increases upward to 800x600, 1024x768, and 1280x1024.

Dual-ported Memory is faster than regular memory on a graphics board. It is listed as VRAM, WRAM, or a faster EDO VRAM.

Filtering eliminates blockiness in 3D images.

Fogging makes an object look like it is appearing or disappearing into fog or darkness.

MIP Mapping keeps the edges of a tectured object from flickering.

MPEG is a set of motion video compression standards.

Perspective Correct makes 3D objects appear better at various angles and distances.

RAMDAC is a RAM digital-to-analog converter. Fast RAMDAC improves your refresh rate.

Refresh Rate indicates the number of times per second your screen is redrawn. Rates below 75MHz will flicker.

Synchronous Memory works at the same rate as your system bus, which may mean your graphics speed is doubled. It is listed as SDRAM or DGRAM, with the latter having additional features to enhance graphics images.

System Bus is the connection from your graphics board to the main processor. ISA and EISA buses run at 8MHz, a PCI bus runs faster, but the best is called a local bus. Check your computer to see what type of bus it has before shopping!

Texture Mapping makes 3D objects look more realistic by mapping a texture on the object's surface.

Video Interpolation smooths out the edges of video windows when you resize them. Good cards interpolate on both the X and Y axes.

VRML is short for the "Virtual Reality Modeling Language," which is used by game producers to create a 3D space on your screen.

Below are boards with 3D capability costing under $300 with the following minimum configuration: 4 MB RAM, with support for 800 x 600 DPI resolution graphics. Data on these boards was compiled from the manufacturers. Some of the boards that we rated highly were also rated highly by *PC World* magazine and *Family PC* magazines, both excellent sources you might wish to consult if feel you need additional information.

OVERALL RATINGS

Diamond Fire GL 1000 Pro	★ ★ ★ 3/4
Hercules Stingray 128/3D	★ ★ ★ 3/4
STB Velocity 128	★ ★ ★ 3/4
Diamond Viper V330	★ ★ ★ 1/2
VideoLogic Apocolypse 3D	★ ★ ★ 1/2
ATI 3D Pro Turbo PC2TV	★ ★ ★ 1/4
Creative Labs 3D Blaster PCI	★ ★ ★ 1/4
STB Velocity128	★ ★ ★ 3/4
Orchid Righteous 3D	★ ★ ★
Matrox Millennium II	★ ★ 3/4
VideoLogic GrafixStar 750	★ ★ 3/4
Number Nine Imagine 128 Series 2-E	★ ★ 1/2
STB Nitro 3D	★ ★ 1/2

EXPLANATION OF RATINGS

Graphics boards were selected for review from currently available products that met the configuration minimums listed earlier in this chapter. The overall rating was arrived at by giving individual scores on 3D Performance, Features, and Support (including warranty). The highest rating possible for each category is four stars; the lowest is one. The 3D performance score was doubled, as that is the most important selection criterion, and then the scores were averaged to arrive at the overall rating.

ALPHABETICAL DESCRIPTIONS

ATI 3D Pro Turbo PC2TV

Price $219

Overall Rating ★ ★ ★ 1/4

3D Performance ★ ★ ★ 1/2

Features ★ ★ ★ ★

Support ★ 1/2

This board does an outstanding job at 2D, but if that is all you need, there are less expensive alternatives. For the serious graphics pro, this is an excellent choice due to its fast 3D performance. However, if you are including video, its AVI speed is about 1/3 as fast as needed for smooth viewing. Filtering, shading, and perspective correction are included. Resolution is supported up to 1600x1024 DPI at a 75 MHz refresh rate. Drivers are provided for Windows 95, DirectX, Windows for Workgroups, Windows NT, X-Windows, and OS/2 systems. Connection to your computer is via a PCI local bus V 2.1. Features include the ATI Rage II chip, 8MB SGRAM, 220 MHz RAMDAC, and television connectivity. Bundled software includes utilities to adjust graphics settings and programs for graphics modeling, animation, rendering, photo editing, and adding 3D objects to documents. Vream's WIRL, an interactive virtual web browser, is also included. Support by phone involves a toll call. The warranty is for five years, either by repair or replacement for the hardware only.

Creative Labs 3D Blaster PCI

Price $200

Overall Rating ★ ★ ★ 1/4

3D Performance ★ ★ ★ 1/4

Features ★ ★ ★ 1/2

Support ★ ★ ★

2D performance is good; however, there are less expensive boards if this is all you need. And it requires a Pentium 90 or faster computer with a free PCI 2.0 bus

slot to use it and a CD-ROM to install it. The maximum resolution is 1280x1024 DPI with 24-bit true color for 16.7 million colors. 3D performance is excellent due to the use of Rendition's Verite chip, which has a high-speed processor designed to run 3D games at full speed. They use MIP mapping, texture mapping, filtering, and anti-aliasing to improve the images. Video playback is not as good as others reviewed. Drivers are available for DirectX, CGL, and Rendition Speedy3D applications and for Windows 95, Windows 3.1, and DOS. Features include 4 MB EDO RAM and 175 MHz RAMDAC. Software includes 3D games, an MPEG-1 player, and Blaster Control utilities.

Support by phone is available daily for 16 hours a day via toll call. They have a special support web site at www.creative-help.com and there is a Video WebPhone option weekdays. The warranty is for three years.

Diamond Fire GL 1000 Pro

Price $250

Overall Rating ★ ★ ★ 3/4

3D Performance ★ ★ ★ 3/4

Features ★ ★ ★ ★

Support ★ ★ ★

2D performance is excellent, and should be at this price. Resolution ranges from 640x480 to 1920x1080 DPI. This board is based on the 3Dlabs Permedia 2 graphics chip and rendering engine, which offers outstanding 3D performance on Windows NT or Windows 95 systems. There are hardware accelerators for rasterization, texture mapping, and buffering. Note that it requires a Pentium computer with a PCI v2.1 bus or AGP adapter to install it. Features include 8 MB SGRAM, 230 MHz RAMDAC, and an integrated Stereo Graphics-compatible connector to connect external 3D-shutter glasses for three-dimensional stereo viewing. Software includes the COSMO Player 2.0, Caligari Truespace3 SE, Crystal Graphics' 3D Impact for fonts and animation, and Diamond's AutoCad 2D and 3D utilities. Support by phone is available daily for 16 hours a day via toll call. They have a special support web site at www.creative-help.com and there is a Video WebPhone option weekdays. The warranty is for three years.

Diamond Viper V330

Price $200

Overall Rating ★ ★ ★ 1/2

3D Performance ★ ★ ★

Features ★ ★ ★ ★

Support ★ ★ ★ 3/4

2D performance is outstanding, as you would expect in this high-performance board. 3D is outstanding with nVidia's Riva 128 integrated controller that accelerates most software as well as Direct3D, Internet VRML, and OpenGL. This means that games and other software using these technologies will run at full speed smoothly. Video playback is excellent. Requires a Pentium system with a PCI v2.1 bus or AGP adapter, CD-ROM, and either Windows 95 or Windows NT. Features include 4 MB 100 MHz SGRAM with a 230 MHz RAMDAC, television output at 640x480 DPI, and 11 software titles including games, a photo suite, 3D and VRML browsers, MPEG player, and

utilities. Support by phone is available six days per week. Their Internet site offers a tech support "Wizard" and driver updates. The warranty is for five years.

Hercules Stingray 128/3D

Price $299

Overall Rating ★ ★ ★ 3/4

3D Performance ★ ★ ★ ★

Features ★ ★ ★ 1/2

Support ★ ★ ★ 1/2

This board is clearly designed for 3D game playing and high-end business users doing multimedia presentations on large television monitors. Resolution ranges from 640x480 to 1600x1200 with a high refresh rate for flicker-free viewing. But you will need another board for 2D operations. In addition to Pentium computers, this board will work with Cyrix 6x86 and the AMD K6. 3D performance is the best of the group due to the 128-bit Alliance ProMotion 2D processor coupled with the 3Dfx Voodoo Rush 3D Arcade chipset on one PCI board. And they have implemented in hardware most of the better image quality options, like filtering, MIP mapping, anti-aliasing, texturing, and shading, which many board makers put in their software drivers. Features include 8 MB EDO RAM and 180 MHz RAMDAC. Software includes drivers, image management utilities, the "Hercules Entertainment Center" for control of sound and video playback, and three popular 3D games. Support by phone is toll-free weekdays and there is a lot of information and downloadable files at their Internet site.

Matrox Millennium II

Price $219

Overall Rating ★ ★ 3/4

3D Performance ★ ★ 3/4

Features ★ ★ ★ ★

Support ★ 1/2

2D performance is outstanding, with resolution up to 1920x1200 DPI with 65,000 colors on Windows NT, Windows 95, Windows for Workgroups, and OS/2. 3D performance is fast with their MGA-2164W chip, but looks blocky because they do not do hardware filtering. They do provide perspective correction, texture mapping, and shading. Video plays at full speed. Features include 4 MB dual-ported WRAM upgradeable to 16 MB and 220 MHz RAMDAC. Software includes Micrografx Picture Publisher and Simply 3D, Kai's Power Tools, CompCore's MPEG player, Sonnetech Colorific calibration, Vreal WIRL 3D web browser and Netscape Navigator. Support by phone is available by toll call weekdays and their Internet site has information and updated drivers for download. The warranty is for three years on parts only.

Number Nine Imagine 128 Series 2-E

Price $299

Overall Rating ★ ★ 1/2

3D Performance ★ ★ ★

Features ★ ★ 1/2

Support ★

This board is designed for the high-end desktop user or CAD designer. 2D performance is excellent on Windows for Workgroups, Windows 95, and Windows NT; there are drivers for DirextX, Auto-CAD, and MicroStation. True Color is supported at resolutions up to 1124x768. The board requires a PCI local bus to install it. 3D performance for multimedia is good due to the S3D ViRGE VX processor and 3D rendering capability using shading, texture mapping, perspective correction, and more. It is not the best choice for realistic gaming. Full-screen digital video playback is not very good. Features included are 4 MB dual-ported VRAM and 220 MHz RAMDAC. Software include Cirrus Logic 3D games and the Hawkeye graphics adjustment utility. Support requires a toll call, with no weekend support.

Orchid Righteous 3D

Price $299

Overall Rating ★ ★ ★

3D Performance ★ ★ ★ 3/4

Features ★ ★ ★ 1/2

Support ★

This board includes arcade-like action for games, but you will need to keep your other graphics card for 2D operations. 3D is supported by the 3Dfx Interactive Voodoo Graphics processor, which is the fastest of 3D chip sets. Hardware acceleration is provided for shading and fogging. It requires a PCI v2.0 or 2.1 bus on a Pentium 90 or faster system with a CD-ROM drive. Features include 4MB of EDO DRAM, software drivers, and four 3D games with demo copies of other games. Support is available by phone and from their Internet site. The warranty is for two years.

STB Nitro 3D

Price $99	
Overall Rating ★★ 1/2	
3D Performance ★ 3/4	
Features ★★	
Support ★★★★	

The STB Nitro 3D offers superb business graphics, AVI and MPEG video playback, and swift 2D performance. It has a 120-HZ refresh rate at 1024 by 768 DPI. 3D performance is OK, but it is not designed for serious game playing. Video playback is excellent. It uses the S3 Virge/GX chip. Features include four MB of EDO DRAM, 170 MHz RAMDAC, Active Movie MPEG player, and a optional television tuner. Software includes the Active Movie, MPEG and video player, and DirectX support, which must be installed manually. Support by phone is toll-free and their Internet site has information, trouble-shooting tips, and drivers for downloading. They offer a limited lifetime warranty.

STB Velocity 128

Price $149	
Overall Rating ★★★ 3/4	
3D Performance ★★★★	
Features ★★★1/2	
Support ★★★★	

2D performance is excellent for standard business applications with resolution up to 1600x1200. 3D performance is among the best of those reviewed, and it is very smooth due to the new nVidia Reva 128 processor. Texturing, filtering, perspective correction, MIP mapping, and shading are all included in the hardware. However, video playback is less than one-third the needed speed on slower computers, but it can be improved on very fast Pentium computers. It will connect to either a PCI or AGP bus. Features include 4 MB SGRAM and 230 MHz RAMDAC. Software includes 32-bit drivers for Windows 95 and Windows NT, 3D imaging software and games. Support by phone is toll free and their Internet site has information, trouble-shooting tips, and drivers for downloading. The board comes with a limited lifetime warranty.

VideoLogic Apocolypse 3D

Price $199	
Overall Rating ★★★ 1/2	
3D Performance ★★★ 3/4	
Features ★★★ 1/2	
Support ★★★ 1/4	

2D performance is provided by your existing graphics card. 3D performance supports arcade-type games on a Pentium 100 or faster computer using PowerVR technology and a NEC PCX1 processor. Hardware supports perspective correction, anti-aliasing, textures, fog, and shading for excellent and realistic 3D images. A Pentium 100 processor with a PCI local bus and a CD-ROM is required. Features include 4 MB SDRAM, software drivers, and PowerVR games. Support is via technical hotlines and their Internet site has a special technical support request form you can send in as well as downloadable drivers. The warranty is for five years on the hardware.

VideoLogic GrafixStar 750

Price $299	
Overall Rating ★★ 3/4	

3D Performance ★ ★ ★

Features ★ ★

Support ★ ★ ★

2D performance is fast with a 64-bit S3 ViRGE/VX processor. It supports a 120-MHz refresh rate at 1024 by 768 DPI and a maximum resolution of 1800x1440 DPI. Video playback is not very fast. There is 3D acceleration for shading, perspective correction, MIP mapping, filtering, and fogging. AVI video playback is excellent. Features include 4 MB VRAM upgradable to 8 MB and 220 MHz RAMDAC. Software includes the Prolab multimedia suite for image and video editing and photo editing. Documentation and utilities are excellent. Support is via technical hotlines and their Internet site has a special technical support request form you can send in as well as downloadable drivers. They offer a five year warranty.

CONTACT INFORMATION

ATI Technologies Inc.
905-882-2600
www.aitech.ca

Creative Labs, Inc.
800-998-1000
www.creativelabs.com

Diamond Multimedia Systems Inc.
800-468-5846
www.diamondmm.com

Hercules Computer Technology, Inc.
800-532-0600 or 510-623-7449
www.hercules.com

Matrox Graphics Inc..
800-361-1408
www.matrox.com

Number Nine Visual Technology, Inc.
800-GET-NINE
www.nine.com

Orchid Technology
800-577-0977
www.orchid.com

STB Systems Inc.
888-234-8750
www.stb.com

VideoLogic Inc.
800-578-5644
www.videologic.com

KEYBOARDS

Keyboards are peripheral input devices that enter text and commands into your computer. So a keyboard is a keyboard...right? Not really. Since you will be using this peripheral constantly, you should use one that is easy on your hands and increases your productivity.

The majority of personal computers purchased today come with a keyboard. Most include a 101-key standard layout which includes a typewriter-like keyboard area in the middle, function keys across the top, navigation keys to the right of the typewriter-like area, and a numeric keypad at the far right side. For IBM-compatible computers, the industry is beginning to ship a newer 104-key Windows 95 keyboard, which adds several keys specific to Windows 95 operation.

Keyboards can and do wear out or break and there are replacement no-frill models available. Most computer manufacturers offer replacement keyboards, if the one that came with the computer is not satisfactory. New to the marketplace are enhanced keyboards with additional features that address health, comfort, and productivity issues as described below.

The ergonomic layout of the Acer Future, the number-one rated keyboard, arranges keys in two angled sections with large spacebars and a centrally located integrated touchpad. A third detachable section contains the numeric keypad.

Ergonomic Keyboards are designed for comfort and to avoid injuries to the wrists and hands that can occur with heavy use. The key layout surface is wavy and it slopes gently back-to-front to reflect a normal position of hands typing.

Some have a split design into two or even three sections of key groupings set at angles or detachable so that they can be placed wherever the user feels most comfortable.

Imbedded Pointing Device Keyboards for desktop computers include track balls or touch-sensitive pads with buttons much like those included on laptop and portable computers to replace the mouse device. These keyboards reduce arm movement and can be more comfortably placed— perhaps on your lap—since mouse functions are conveniently provided right under your hands.

Programmable Keyboards include software to remap the keyboard to better suit its usage by replacing commonly used word commands and multiple-key commands with "hotkeys" you can define. This type of keyboard can be tailored to speed up use of a favorite word processing program or launch programs, for example.

Wireless Keyboards enable operation of the computer without being tied to it by a cable, by using either infrared or radio signals. Conference room computers used for presentations and meetings are an example of where this type is most useful in an office environment.

When purchasing any new keyboard, there are some basic things to consider.

Look for products that are built to the internationally recognized ISO 9000 manufacturing quality standards. The warranty should be for at least two years. The keyboard should be adjustable in tilt, feel strong and durable, have non-skid pads underneath, and either be spill-proof or spill-resistant. If it has a cable, the cable should be at least six feet long and the plug must match the computer's socket.

Durability of the keys is another consideration if heavy use of the keyboard is expected. Mechanical keys are sturdier and will last longer because each key uses a mechanical switch which provides the user with a better feel and an audible click, like a 'typewriter. Membrane-switch keys have a softer feel and are quieter, but they will wear out faster than the mechanical ones. About 85% of all keyboards sold are membrane-switch units, because they are cheaper to make.

For situations where moisture is inevitable, such as a fast-food counter, membrane keyboards are available that do not have individual keys — just images of keys printed on top of a plastic-coated printed circuit board. These keyboards were not included in this review.

The final choice is a combination of personal preference and how the computer keyboard is to be used. Try out any keyboard before you buy it, or at least make sure you can return it for a full refund. Make sure all the keys are large enough and that important heavy-use keys, like the Enter and spacebar keys, are easy to use.

Below are keyboards that are currently on the market that have new or advanced features. Those with designs that would require re-learning how to type were not included.

OVERALL RATINGS

Acer Future Keyboard	★ ★ ★ ★
Alps GlidePoint Wave Keyboard	★ ★ ★ 3/4
Cirque Input Center	★ ★ ★ 3/4
Sejin Wireless Freeboard Beamer	★ ★ ★ 1/2
Kinesis Professional Keyboard	★ ★ ★ 1/4
Key Tronic Lifetime Wireless Trackball Keyboard	★ ★ ★ 1/4
Microsoft Natural Keyboard	★ ★ ★
Wireless Computing Wireless Surfboard	★ ★ 1/2
Darwin LaunchBoard	★ ★ 1/2
Janesway Folding Keyboard	★ ★ 1/4
NMB RT-8200W	★ ★

EXPLANATION OF RATINGS

Keyboards were scored on Comfort, Features, and Price. The price factor in the ratings relates to "bang for the buck"; that is, how much you really get relative to what an average keyboard offers. The maximum rating for each of these three categories is four stars; the lowest is one star. The overall rating was achieved by averaging the ratings pertaining to the three aforementioned categories.

ALPHABETICAL DESCRIPTIONS

Acer Future Keyboard

Price $99

Overall Rating ★ ★ ★ ★

Comfort ★ ★ ★ ★

Features ★ ★ ★ ★

Price ★ ★ ★ ★

The ergonomic layout arranges keys in two angled sections with large spacebars and a centrally located integrated touchpad. A third detachable section contains the numeric keypad. Built-in wrist pads help you place you hands into a typing position that is easy on your hands and wrists. Typing response is average due to the membrane-keyswitch design. The circular touchpad is a comfort to use, with arrow keys encircling the pad to let you position the cursor easily. Setup is easy, just plug the keyboard and serial mouse into the correct computer ports. A keyboard connector adapter is included.

Alps GlidePoint Wave Keyboard

Price $89.95

Overall Rating ★ ★ ★ 3/4

Comfort ★ ★ ★ 1/2

Features ★ ★ ★ 1/2

Price ★ ★ ★ ★

The ergonomic layout arranges 109 keys in two angled sections with an extra mouse button, Tab, and Backspace key between the sections. A rectangular touchpad is located at the right side under the arrow keys, which may be a problem for left-handed users. A built-in adjustable wrist rest makes typing comfortable. Typing response is average due to the membrane-keyswitch design. "Enhanced

Windows control panel software" is included to program the two mouse buttons. A full range of adapters is included to make setup easy. A five-year warranty is included.

Cirque Input Center

Price $129.95	
Overall Rating ★★★ 3/4	
Comfort ★★★ 1/2	
Features ★★★★	
Price ★★★ 1/2	

A 104-key keyboard that incorporates Cirque's GlidePoint Cursor-control device, which can be operated with your finger or a metal stylus. This makes it possible to trace your signature on the trackpad and then paste it into your documents. The trackpad is located on the right side of the palm rest, which may be a problem for left-handed users. Typing response is excellent. Software lets you adjust cursor tracking and other features of the Input Center. A full range of adapters is included.

Darwin LaunchBoard

Price $69.95	
Overall Rating ★★ 1/2	
Comfort ★	
Features ★★ 1/2	
Price ★★★★	

This Windows 95 keyboard has no ergonomic features and no pointing device included. It comes preprogrammed with a set of eight "Launch Keys" that take you quickly to popular web sites such as Yahoo!, Pathfinder, and E!. A toggle switch doubles the use of the 15 function keys across the top of the keyboard. It comes with a key-pulling tool and some blank keys, labels, and software for creating your own "Launch Keys" and accessing the web. The keyboard is sturdy, but typing response is average, and since the software comes separate for $39.95, you may want to just re-program your current keyboard.

Janesway Folding Keyboard

Price $69.95	
Overall Rating ★★ 1/4	
Comfort ★ 1/2	
Features ★	
Price ★★★★	

This is a full-sized 101-key keyboard with no pointing device included. It has hinges in the middle that allow it to fold up and lock in the closed position. This makes it easy to take with you if you want to use it with a notebook or store it when it is not being used. A safety mechanism prevents it from working unless it is completely unfolded, but you can't lock it open. So, if you like to work with your keyboard on your lap, you could have some mishaps when typing. The keyboard connects to a standard connector. There is an optional monitor stand for $24.95 with space underneath for storing the keyboard..

Key Tronic Lifetime Wireless Trackball Keyboard

Price $169.99	
Overall Rating ★★★ 1/4	
Comfort ★★	
Features ★★★★	
Price ★★★ 1/2	

This Windows 95 keyboard has an integrated two-button track ball that is located conveniently under the large space bar. It is connected to your computer through an infrared receiver, letting you use it on your desktop or from distances up to 50 feet away. This is handy for making presentations or just getting away from your monitor. Other features included AT and serial port adapters, software, and batteries. Typing response is average as there is no click or resistance. To set up the keyboard, install the batteries, connect the infrared receiver into the keyboard and mouse ports, then start your computer. The infrared receiver has five LED lights that show you if your cap lock, num lock or scroll lock is on, battery level and the infrared activity status. Lifetime guarantee.

Kinesis Professional Keyboard

Price $355	
Overall Rating ★ ★ ★ 1/4	
Comfort ★ ★ ★ 1/2	
Features ★ ★ ★	
Price ★ ★ ★	

This ergonomic keyboard is unique in its clustering of sets of keys in "concave wells" at opposite ends of the keyboard. Editing keys are under the thumb positions and the numeric keypad is embedded, where it can be activated with a foot switch. Padded palm supports make it comfortable to use. Mechanical keyswitches make typing response excellent. A pointing device is not included, but there is room to mount a touchpad or track ball in the middle of the keyboard. Using on-board memory, the keyboard is highly programmable. Kinesis Keyware lets you remap your keyboard to match various tasks and store multiple keyboard layouts

on disk. There is an optional second foot switch. It comes with a 60-day money-back return policy and a limited lifetime warranty.

Microsoft Natural Keyboard

Price $74.95	
Overall Rating ★ ★ ★	
Comfort ★ ★ ★	
Features ★ ★	
Price ★ ★ ★ ★	

This ergonomic keyboard splits the keys into two angled sections with a built-in adjustable wrist leveler and palm rests, which makes it a very comfortable keyboard. Mouse action is provided from the numeric keypad with cursor control software, which may not help a left-handed user and it is less convenient than having an integrated pointing device. Additional "Intellitype" software improves control over Windows 95 operation. Typing response is excellent. Setup is easy as adapters are included.

NMB RT-8200W

Price $49.95	
Overall Rating ★ ★	
Comfort 1/2	
Features ★ 1/2	
Price ★ ★ ★ ★	

This Windows 95 keyboard has a thumb-activated Backspace Key and a rather small spacebar in an otherwise standard layout. Typing response is excellent due to its mechanical key-switch design, which also provides sturdiness under heavy usage. Setup is easy for a standard keyboard port, but additional adapters are optional. The keyboard has a three-year warranty.

Sejin Wireless Freeboard Beamer

Price $99.50	
Overall Rating ★ ★ ★ 1/2	
Comfort ★ ★ ★	
Features ★ ★ ★	
Price ★ ★ ★ ★	

This 86-key compact keyboard has an embedded numeric keypad for 104-key functionality. The integrated track ball is on the right side while the mouse keys are on the left side of the keyboard area. Infrared transmission to the computer makes this wireless keyboard work from as far as 16.4 feet from the receiver. Typing response is average due to the tactile rubber membrane key-switches. Setup is easy with included adapters and batteries. It comes with a one-year warranty.

Wireless Computing Wireless Surfboard

Price $399.00	
Overall Rating ★ ★ 1/2	
Comfort ★ ★	
Features ★ ★ ★ 1/2	
Price ★ ★	

This 83-key compact keyboard has an embedded numeric keypad for 101-key functionality. The integrated touchpad is located to the right of the key area, which may be a problem for left-handed users. Radio frequency technology makes this keyboard wireless, and it can operate from up to 50 feet away from the receiver, which is useful if doing presentations to large audiences. Typing response is average. Setup is easy as all adapters and batteries are included.

CONTACT INFORMATION

Acer America Corp.
(800) SEE-ACER
www.acer.com

Alps Electric USA
(800) 950-ALPS
www.alpsusa.com

Cirque Corp.
(800) GLIDE-75
www.glidepoint.com

Darwin Keyboards Ltd.
(415) 621-1151
www.darwinkeyboards.com

Key Tronic Corp.
(800) 262-6006
www.keytronic.com

Kinesis
(206) 402-8100
www.kinesis-ergo.com

Janesway Electronics Corp.
(800) 431-1348
www.janesway.com

Microsoft Corp.
(800) 426-9400
www.microsoft.som

NMB
(800) 662-8321
www.nmbtech.com

Sejin America
(408) 980-7550
www.sejin.com

Wireless Computing, Inc.
(512) 263-8204
www.wireless_computing.com

Modems, 33K External

Modems are an integral part of today's telecommunications. These devices are used to send e-mail, faxes, and files, connect to online services, bulletin board systems, the Internet, and other remote computers. Modems can not only transmit data but voice as well, all of which is done over conventional telephone connections. Features such as a speakerphone, voice mail and Caller ID can turn your modem into a call management system. Speed of modems is getting faster even as you read this. Right now there are several speeds of modem on the market, 28.8 kilobytes per seconds (Kbps), 33.6 Kbps and 56Kbps. The faster the modem, the less time it takes to transmit data. Modems can either be external, housed in a separate case and attached to your computer via a cable, or internal, placed inside of your desktop or notebook computer. The list below ranks 33.6 kbps external modems. Data on these modems were compiled from the manufacturers. To the right of each modem is its overall score. The higher the score the better. Because of a tie for second place, there is no third ranked modem.

RANKINGS AND OVERALL SCORES

1	U.S. Robotics Courier V. Everything /V.34	97
2	Zoom Fax/Modem V.34X Plus	94
2	Motorola VoiceSURFR 33.6	94
4	Hayes Accura 336 Office Communications Manager	91
5	Diamond Multimedia Supra-Sonic 33.6V+	88
6	Best Data Smart One 336 FLX	83

EXPLANATION OF RATINGS

Modems were scored on their speed, price, and options. Speed comprised 50% of the overall score. Don't be fooled into believing that all 33.6 Kbps modems operate at the same speed. Overall speed is not just a function of transmitting kilobytes of data per second; it also is related to data compression. Some 33.6Kbps units compress data faster than others, therefore they can operate faster. Overall speed is also related to the error correction speed. In sum, speed is a function of several factors and the ratings used to determine the speeds below take all of them into account.

The price factor in the ratings relates to "bang for the buck;" that is, how much you really get relative to what an average-priced modem offers. External modems are a bit more expensive than the internal modems. Some advantages to external modems are that they can be moved from computer to computer and they are easier to install. Also you can hear and see what your modem is doing. Most modems have a built-in speaker and a LCD panel with lights so you can see when transmissions are being made. The premium modems can display transmission speed and status.

Many modems include a FlashROM feature that lets you upgrade your modem when the manufacturer adds new features. Upgrading is as easy as downloading software onto the modem's flash ROM chip. This feature lets you keep your modem current and can save you from buying another model when features change.

Most modems can handle basic tasks like faxing, but if you plan on sending a lot of faxing make sure your modem can handle both Class 1 and Class 2 transmissions. Also your fax software program should be full-featured so it will have the capacity to handle heavy faxing. Other advanced features that can be useful are distinctive rings, which can distinguish a fax call from a phone call, and Caller ID, which reads out contact information when you get a call. For those who need to use their modem with a cellular telephone, make sure it supports the MNP-10 protocol. This will give you better error correction over cellular circuit.

ALPHABETICAL DESCRIPTIONS

Best Data Smart One 336 FLX

Price $159	
Rank 6	
Speed 30	
Price 37.5	
Options 15.63	

The Data Smart One 336 FLX is a tiny fax/data modem (4x56x1 inches) that offers good performance. It supports V.17 Group III fax at 14,400 bps and MNP 5

data compression and MNP 2-4 error correction for error throughput to 115,200 bps. Features include Caller ID (but extra software is needed to use this feature) and distinctive ring which allows your modem to distinguish between a fax and voice call. Also included are Smith Micro's QuickLink II fax/modem software, America Online, CompuServe, and other online and Internet software.

Diamond Multimedia Supra-Sonic 33.6V+

Price $249	
Rank 5	
Speed 43.75	
Options 25	

The SupraSonic offers above average performance and a bundle of features. This tiny modem packs a lot into its 6.5x3.8x1 inch box. Besides its English-language LCD display and voice mail capabilities, you get a hands-free headset with a microphone and earphones and a high-speed serial cable. Other features include FlashROM, Caller ID, distinctive ring, Class 1 and Class 2 fax support and MNP-10 cellular error correcting support. Bundled software includes COMit voice/fax/data software, and America Online, CompuServe, Netcom, Global Network Navigator, and Supra VoiceMail. The SupraSonic comes with a five-year warranty and 14-hour per day support.

Hayes Accura 336 Office Communications Manager

Price $169	
Rank 4	
Speed 28.75	

Price 37.5

Options 25

Hayes is an old familiar name in the modem industry and they're still producing high-speed top-quality modems. The Acura 336 Communications Manager automates all of your communications such as e-mail and voice mail. Features include data through-put up to 115,200 bps with compression, voice mail capability with up to 1,000 secure voice mail boxes, fax on demand, and support for all type of fax machines . Also included are full versions of Hayes' Smartcom Message Center, Quarterdeck WEBTalk, InternetSuite 2 and CYBERsitter plus Hayes Bonus Bundle with online software. Warranty covers replacement of malfunctioning modem within three business days.

Motorola VoiceSURFR 33.6

Price $179

Rank 2 (tie)

Speed 37.5

Price 37.5

Options 18.75

The Motorola VoiceSURFR offers solid performance along with a variety of voice and data capabilities. Features include answering machine and voice mail capabilities, phone number directory for storing up to four numbers, alphanumeric paging, Caller ID, and fax on demand. The VoiceSURFR can be turned into a full-duplex speaker phone with the addition of an external microphone and speakers.

Other features include Class 1 and Group III fax support, ITU V.42/V.42bis and MNP 2-5 error correction and data com-

pression support. Bundled software, includes an Internet kit, Smith Micro's QuickLink fax/data/voice software and other game demos. This modem can be mounted with the wall-mount slots that are on the bottom of the modem. This modem is covered by a five year warranty.

U.S. Robotics Courier V.Everything/V.34

Price $395

Rank 1

Speed 50

Price 31.25

Options 15.63

The Courier V.Everything offers high-speed data transmission and superior performance. It handles basic data and fax functions with lightning speed. It supports Class 1, Class 2 and Group III faxes. Other features include FlashROM for easy upgrades, Caller ID, and distinctive ring. Bundled software includes QuickLink II and Relay Gold, a remote access software package. However, this model does not have voice capabilities or fax-back software. If you're more concerned with speed and performance than voice capabilities and don't mind the high price tag, then this modem is the best choice.

Zoom Fax/Modem V.34X Plus

Price $189

Rank 2 (tie)

Speed 37.5

Price 37.5

Options 15.63

The Zoom Fax/Modem V.34X offers basic 33.6 Kbps data and 14.4 Kbps fax communications in a small device. Fax quality from this modem is as good the quality of those sent using a fax machine. Features include Class 1, Class 2 and Group III fax support, MNP-10 error control, distinctive ring, storage of multiple profiles, modem speed sensing up to 115,200 bps and COMit software and DOS/WinFax Lite fax/data software. This is a basic modem that lacks password protection and communications capabilities such as voice mail and speakerphone; however, you do get a distinctive ring, which can determine a phone call from a fax call. Also Included is WinFax Lite, a popular fax management software program, and a seven-year warranty.

CONTACT INFORMATION

3COM (U.S. Robotics)
800-877-2677
www.3com.com

Best Data
www.bestdata.com

Diamond Multimedia
800-727-8772
www.diamondmm.com

Hayes
770-840-9200
www.hayes.com

Zoom Telephonics
800-631-3166
www.zoomtel.com

Modems, 56K, External

With businesses and people communicating via the Internet and using computers from remote locations, modems are speeding up to handle communications more efficiently. The new 56K modem boasts a faster speed, 56 kilobytes per second (kbps), than previous models. However there are two standards for this modem, 3COM's (U.S. Robotics) x2 and Rockwell/Lucent's 56flex. This will change when a global ITU-T 56K standard is set (sometime in 1998).

For now users will find many modems to choose from. If you already own a 33.6 kbps modem, no need to worry. Many of the major model brands are upgradeable to the new 56K technology. In this review we rate four 56K external modems to give you a flavor of things to come. Most of these modems are capable of 56 Kbps downloads, but there are factors such as FCC restrictions, line conditions, and other outside influences that can limit download speeds to under 56 kbps. The models reviewed can reach top speeds over 40 kbps. Internal models of these modems are also available. The following

U.S. Robotics' Courier V.Everything is the fastest one reviewed and handles analog and digital connections with equal ease.

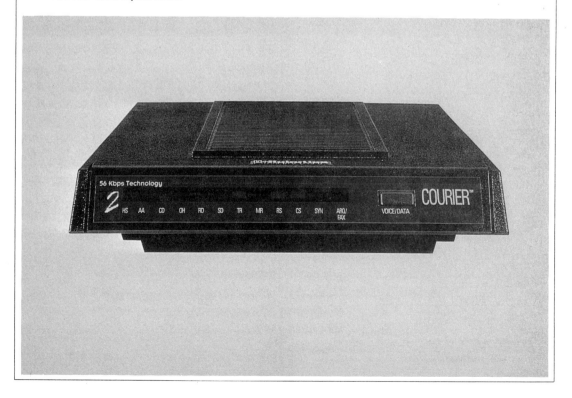

list contains four external modems, their rankings and overall scores.

RANKINGS AND OVERALL SCORES

1 U.S. Robotics Courier
   V.Everything 56k   93

2 Zoom FaxModem 56Kx   89

3 Diamond Supra
   Express 56e   87

4 Hayes Accura 56K Data/
   Fax Modem   86

EXPLANATION OF RATINGS

Modems were evaluated based on the following criteria: speed and options including Caller ID, distinctive ring, voice mail etc. Speed counted for 75% of the total score.

ALPHABETICAL DESCRIPTIONS

Diamond SupraExpress 56e

Price $140	
Rank 3	
Overall Score 87	
Speed 71	
Options 16	

Diamond SupraExpress offers reliability and great performance. This modem uses Rockwell's K56flex technology and is upgradable to the 56k standard when it becomes available. This reasonably priced modem can hold its own in the speed department with speeds comparable to other top 56K modems. The SupraExpress is a tiny modem and easily connects to the serial port of your computer. However to connect the computer you may need a 9-to-25 pin adapter for the included 25-pin female cable. Features include support for V.80 Video Phone, hardware based compression, supports ITU V.34, upgradable memory and Class one and Group II fax support. Bundled software includes online software for America Online, CSI (CompuServe) and NetCom; Microsoft Internet Explorer; Though Communications' FaxTalk Plus and COMit; and VDOnet's VDOLive Player videoconferencing program. To use the videoconferencing program you need a video-capture card and video camera. The help manual is available only in digital format on a CD-ROM.

Hayes Accura 56K Data/ Fax Modem

Price $189	
Rank 4	
Overall Score 86	
Speed 71	
Options 15	

The Hayes Accura 56K Data/Fax modem is K56flex compatible device with middle-of-the-road performance. This plug and play modem installs easily to the serial port and can handle line distortions with little problems. Like all the other new 56K modems FlashROM is included for easy upgrading to future 56k standards. Bundled software includes the Hayes Smartcom data/fax program and online services CD-ROM from CompuServe (CSI) Prodigy and America online.

U.S. Robotics Courier V. Everything 56k

Price $275	
Rank 1	

Speed 80

Options 13

The Courier V.Everything is one of the highest-speed 56K modems around. This modem is the fastest of the ones reviewed here. A solid performer this modem handles analog and digital connections with equal ease. This modem is strictly plug and play. Windows 95 easily detects the modem on startup, which makes installation simple. A bundled CD-ROM contains all necessary modem drivers. Features include: FlashRom, distinctive ring, manual volume control, password, Caller ID and callback security, remote configuration and carrier loss redial. Bundled software includes Stampede Remote Office Gold, a remote control package and RapidComm Win/DOS fax/data software. To complete this great package is an excellent manual, cross-ship replacement and toll- free support. One feature missing is voice capabilities. Overall, if you're looking for speed and can do without voice, then the Courier V.Everything is what you want.

Zoom FaxModem 56Kx

Price $200

Rank 2

Speed 77

Options 12

The Zoom FaxModem 56Kx offers "zooming" speed, an affordable price and exceptional performance. It uses Rockwell's K56flex technology and as far as speed goes it ranks right up there with other top high-speed modems such as the U.S. Robotics Courier V. Everything (which is faster). The 12 LEDs can indicate at what rate the modem is transmitting data. This modem can handle line distortions with no problem. FlashROM is included so you can upgrade the modem with new standards. Bundled software includes Delrina's WinFax, online services software from CompuServe (CSI), Prodigy, and America Online.

CONTACT INFORMATION

3COM (U.S. Robotics)
800-877-2677
www.3com.com

Diamond Multimedia
800-727 8772
www.diamondmm.com

Hayes
770-840-9200
www.haycs.com

Zoom Telephonics Inc.
800-631-3166
www.zoomtel.com

Motorola Inc.
205-430-8000
www.motorola.com

Modems, 33K Internal

Modems are faster and more powerful than ever. Though the ones in this portion operate at only 33.6 Kbps (kilobytes per second), the newest ones operate at 56 Kpbs. Even so, a 33 K modem allows you to efficiently connect to online services, cruise the Internet, send and receive e-mail, faxes and files, as well as to control computers in remote locations. Not only can data be sent via a modem, but voice as well. With extra features like Caller ID, speakerphones and voice mail, your modem can turn your PC into a call management center. The list below ranks internal modems for your desktop computer. Data were compiled from the manufacturer. To the right of each modem is its overall score. Two modems tied for third place; therefore, there is no fourth ranked modem.

RANKING AND OVERALL SCORES

1 U.S. Robotics Courier
   V.Everything   92

2 Hayes Optima 336B
   Internal Business Modem   87

3 Motorola VoiceSURFR
   33.6 Data/Fax Modem   79

3 Zoom FaxModem
   V.341 Plus   79

5 Particle Peripherals
   Practical 33.6 Voice/
   Data/Fax   60

EXPLANATION OF RATINGS

Overall score is the sum of the individual scores for *Speed*, *Options* and *Price*. The three categories could potentially score up to 100 points when totaled.

Speed could potentially score up to 75 points. Overall speed is not just a function of transmitting kilobytes of data per second; it also is related to data compression. Some modems compress data faster than others, therefore they can operate faster. Overall speed is also related to the error correction speed. In sum, overall speed is a function of several factors and the speeds used to determine the ratings below takes all of them into account.

Price relates to "bang for the buck;" that is, how much you really get relative to what an average priced modem offers. Price could potentially score up to 10 points.

Options relates to various features and could potentially score up to 15 points.

ALPHABETICAL DESCRIPTIONS

Hayes Optima 336B Internal Business Modem

Price $249	
Ranking 2	
Speed 67	
Price 5	
Options 15	

The Optima 336B's lightning-fast speed and great extras make this analog modem a highly suitable for businesses. Features include: a 16-bit card, Caller ID, voice mail, distinctive ring, FlashROM and SmartCom Message Center LE fax/data software. If you already have a microphone and speakers, you can plug them into their respective jacks, located on the ISA card's metal mounting bracket, and your computer then takes the place of the telephone or Web phone. This modem, which can be configured remotely, is convenient for traveling in that settings can be changed from afar. Among the drawbacks are the long 8.5 inch card that may conflict with other ISA cards and cables in your computer. Also, tech support is available only 10 hours a day, but not on weekends.

Motorola VoiceSURFR 33.6 Data/Fax Modem

Price	$179
Ranking	3
Speed	56
Price	8
Options	15

The internal version of the Motorola VoiceSURFR has the same solid performance as the external version. It's easy to install and comes backed with many useful features. Features include answering machine, voice mail capabilities, phone number directory for storing up to four numbers, alphanumeric paging, Caller ID (however, you need Caller ID service to use this feature), and fax on demand. The VoiceSURFR can be turned into a full-duplex speaker phone with the addition of an external microphone and speakers.

Other features include Class 1 and Group III fax support, ITU V.42/V.42bis and MNP 2-5 error correction and data com-

pression support. Bundled software includes an Internet kit, Smith Micro's QuickLink fax/data/voice software and other game demos. There is a five year warranty on the product.

Practical Peripherals Practical 33.6 Voice/Data/Fax

Price	$119
Ranking	5
Speed	38
Price	8
Options	15

Though performance is not the top-rated in its class, it has a good mix of features, a moderate price tag and good support policies, but it's not too speedy. Features include: Caller ID, distinctive ring, full-duplex speakerphone, microphone, QuickLink II, McAfee's VirusScan, MindQ Internet Online Edition, Quarterdeck's Webtalk and Practical Message Center LE fax/data voice software. The manual provides the basics for installation, but if you need more help there's tech support available seven days a week, though there is no toll-free number.

U.S. Robotics Courier V.Everything

Price	$215
Ranking	1
Speed	75
Price	6
Options	11

The U.S. Robotics Courier V.Everything is a plug and play modem that's easy to install and upgrade. Features include: FlashRom, 8-bit card, distinctive ring, Caller ID and QuickLink II fax/data software and Remote Office Gold software. The manual is well written and user friendly. This modem is fairly fast, similar to its external version. If you're a telecommuter, you'll find the Remote Office Gold software, which comes with the unit, to be useful. It's most effective at accessing remote computers from the road or anywhere. Toll-free technical support is available weekdays only. It is covered by a five-year warranty.

Zoom FaxModem V.341 Plus

Price	*$89*
Ranking	*3*
Speed	*56*
Price	*8*
Options	*15*

The Zoom FaxModem V.34I Plus is a no frills modem that is fast, easy to install and includes a nice bundle of software. Features include: 8-bit card, distinctive ring, MNP10 and MNP10EC cellular protocols, Comit and WinFax Lite fax/data software. This modem lacks FlashRom so it's not upgradeable. Also missing are fea-

tures like password protection, Caller ID, voice mail and speakerphone. The bundled software, WinFax Lite, is a good package for faxing from your modem. This is not a plug-and-play modem, but installation is straightforward. Technical support is available seven days a week. It is covered by a seven-year warranty.

CONTACT INFORMATION

Diamond Multimedia
800-727 8772
www.diamondmm.com

Hayes
800-441-1617
www.hayes.com

Practical Peripherals
770-840-9966
www.practinet.com

3COM (U.S. Robotics)
800-877-2677
www.usr.com

Zoom Telephonics
800-631-3166
www.zoomtel.com

Modems, PC Cards

PC Card modems are used primarily for notebook computers. PC Card modems connect to a PCMCIA slot, in a notebook computer. Modems are now faster and more powerful with speeds ranging from 28.8 Kbps (kilobytes per second), 33.6 Kbps, and 56 Kbps. The faster the modem, the less time it takes to transfer data over telephone lines. In the list below are four PC Card modems that are commonly found on the market.

Many modems include a FlashROM feature that lets you upgrade your modem when the manufacturer adds new features. Upgrading is as easy as downloading software onto the modem's Flash ROM chip. This feature lets you keep your modem current and can save you from buying another model when features change. Most modems can handle basic tasks like faxing, but if you plan on sending a lot of faxing make sure your modem can handle both Class 1 and Class 2 transmissions. Also, your fax software program should be full-featured so it will have the capacity to handle heavy faxing. Other advanced features that can be useful are distinctive rings, which can detect a fax call from a phone call, and Caller ID, which displays callers' information when a call comes in. For those who need to use their modem with a cellular telephone make sure it supports the MNP-10 protocol. This will give you better error correction over cellular circuits.

RANKINGS WITH OVERALL SCORES

1	Megahertz XJ 1336	90
2	Motorola Montana 33.6	88
3	Practical Peripherals ProClass 336 V.34 Data/Fax PC Card with EZ-Port	82
4	Zoom/PC-Card Fax-Modem V.34C	76

EXPLANATION OF RATINGS

Scores were derived from a combination of factors pertaining to: speed, price, and options.

Speed, which is weighted as 75% of the overall score, is not just a function of transmitting kilobytes of data per second; it also is related to data compression. Some 33K units compress data faster than others, therefore they can operate faster. Overall speed is also related to the error correction speed. In sum, speed is a function of several factors and the speeds used to determine the ratings below take all of them into account.

The price factor in the ratings relates to "bang for the buck"; that is, how much you really get relative to what an average priced PC card costs.

Numerical scores were assigned to each of the aforementioned factors, then computed with, as previously stated, speed, accounting for 75% of the overall score.

ALPHABETICAL DESCRIPTIONS

Practical Peripherals ProClass 336 V.34 Data/Fax PC Card with EZ-Port

Price $159

Overall Score 82

Speed 66

Price 5

Options 11.25

Practical Peripherals ProClass 336 V.34 is fast, inexpensive and, feature-filled. One nice feature is the EZ-port, a built-in phone jack. Features include FlashROM, 230.4-kbps modem-to-PC speed, distinctive ring, password protection, call-back, Caller ID, and QuickLink II fax/data software. If you need assistance help is available Sunday though Saturday. The ProClass has a good price and and offers cross-shipment of a new modem if yours goes on the blink. Overall, the speed, price and features give this modem a thumbs up.

Motorola Montana 33.6

Price $199

Score 88

Speed 69

Price 7.5

Options 11.25

The Motorola Montana 33.6 is pretty speedy. Features include: digital line protection with alert, FlashROM, data throughout up to 115,200 bits, direct cellular connect, and QuickLink Mobile fax/data software. If you plug into a digital line, this modem will sound an alert before any damage can be done to your modem. For you road warriors this modem offers direct cellular connections along with the bundled QuickLink Mobile fax/data software for managing your communications. There is toll-free support, but not on the weekends.

Megahertz XJ 1336

Price $239

Score 90

Speed 75

Price 3.75

Options 11.25

The Megahertz XJ 1336 from 3COM (U.S. Robotics) is a fast-performing 33.6kbps modem, but a little on the expensive side. Features include FlashROM, data throughput to 230.4-kbps, digital line-voltage protection, built-in XJAACK connector phone jack and FaxWorks fax/data software. The XJ 1336 is X2 upgrabeable. Connection is easy with the built-in phone jack and digital line-voltage protection which safeguards your system if you plug into a digital phone line.

Support is available toll-free only from Monday through Friday. If your modem does malfunction there is no cross-ship replacement or money-back guarantee. The XJ 1336 is covered by a five-year warranty.

Zoom/PC-Card Fax-Modem V.34C

Price $199

Score 76

Speed 56

Price 5

Options 15

The Zoom/PC-Card Fax-Modem V.34C is a 33.6k fax modem that offers both cellular capabilities along with solid performance over standard telephone lines. This fax modem card can be used in a variety of computers, desktop, notebooks, palmtops or PDA with a compatible PCMCIA slot. To use the cellular function you have to purchase an cellular phone activation kit for your cellular phone. This kit can be ordered directly from Zoom at (800) 877-2624. Features include Flash memory for upgrading, built-in DAA phone-line interface, distinctive ring, PC CardGuard for protection from digital PBX phone systems, MNP 10EC Enhanced Cellular error correction, support for Class 1 and 2 fax machines, and ZoomGuard for surge protection.

Bundled software includes WinFax Lite, DOSFax, and COMit data communica-tions and a memory-saving enabler and card and socket services software. Zoom covers this modem with a two-year warranty and overnight replacement for malfunctioning modems. Support is available Monday through Friday.

CONTACT INFORMATION

Practical Peripherals
770-840-9966
www.practinet.com

Motorola
800-427-2624
www.mot.com/pccards

Megahertz US Robotics
800-527-8677
www.usr.com/mobileusr

Monitors

Monitors vary in size and screen resolution, which is measured in dot pitches; that is, the size of the smallest dot that a monitor can display. Inexpensive monitors have dot pitches as high as 0.32 mm. Better monitors have dot pitches of 0.28 mm or less. The following list contains six 17-inch monitors, their rankings and overall scores. Due to a tie for fourth-place, there is no fifth rank.

RANKINGS AND OVERALL SCORES

1	Mag InnoVision DJ707	91
2	Mitsubishi Diamond Pro 87XTM	81
3	Sony CPD-220VS	78
4	Samsung SyncMaster 700b	75
4	NEC MultiSync A700	75
6	ViewSonic PT775	69

EXPLANATION OF RATINGS

Overall scores were calculated on display quality and price. Display quality inlcuded the monitor's viewable area, refresh rate, dot pitch, and screen resolution. The highest possible score was 100 points.

Though ranked number-two overall, the Mitsubishi Diamond Pro 87XTM has the sharpest display quality, making it the choice for users who require high-detail.

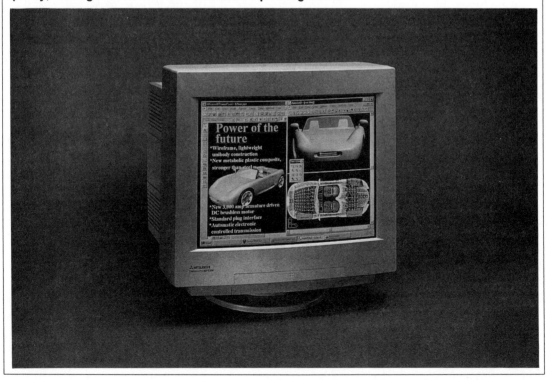

The majority of these monitors have a 85-Hz refresh rate. The refresh rate is the speed at which the monitor passes the electron guns of a cathode ray tube (CRT) from the top of the monitor's display to the bottom. The refresh rate determines how much a display will flicker. The refresh rate is measured in Hertz (Hz). If a monitor has a resolution of 1280 pixels by 1024 lines, a refresh rate of 72 Hz or more will eliminate visible flicker. Check to make sure your computer's graphics card can handle your monitor. Look in the back of your graphics card to see what it supports.

ALPHABETICAL DESCRIPTIONS

Mag InnoVision DJ707

Price $599

Rank 1

The Mag InnoVision DJ707 uses an Invar shadow mask tube and offers great image quality and a bright display. The monitor's viewable area is a spacious 16.1 inches and has a .26-mm dot pitch. Refresh rates are easy on the eyes at 110 Hz at 800 by 600 and 85 Hz at 1,024 by 768. The monitor's Jag Control Knob makes image adjustment easy. Push the knob in to access the on-screen display of icons. The icons are placed in a circle, so you only have to rotate the control knob to pick an icon you want to change, then push and turn the knob to make the corrections. The three-year warranty covers parts, labor and the CRT. The 24-hour toll-free support is available seven days a week..

Mitsubishi Diamond Pro 87XTM

Price $749

Rank 2

The Mitsubishi Diamond Pro 87XTM has stellar display quality. The screen has a 15.7-inch viewable area, .25mm Diamondtron tube and a 107-Hz refresh rate at 1,024 by 768. Text and graphics are displayed equally sharp and clear. This monitor's images are sharply focused, from small text to photographic details like sweat or dew. Image-adjusting software is included that enables you to adjust your screen and advanced controls are included to demagnetize your display and shape images. Toll-free support is available Monday through Friday for 12 hours. There is a three-year warranty.

NEC MultiSync A700

Price $649

Rank 4 (tie)

The NEC MultiSync A700 has a small viewable image size of 15.6 inches. It has a maximum refresh rate of 85 Hz at 1,024 by 768 and 109 Hz T 800 by 600. The MultiSync tube uses an Invar shadow mask with a .288mm dot pitch. Its display quality is adequate. There are on-screen controls and a free adapter to connect the monitor to a Macintosh computer. NEC covers the MultiSync with a three-year parts, labor and CRT warranty. Technical support is available Monday through Friday from 8am-8pm EST.

Samsung SyncMaster 700b

Price $699

Score 4 (tie)

The Samsung SyncMaster 700b features a 15.7-inch viewable area, a .28 mm dot, pitch tube and a 85-Hz refresh rate at

1,024 by 768. Designed for small business, the SyncMaster display is sharp and clear on all type of images from plain text to graphics. On-screen controls are easily accessible with one-button adjustment for contrast and brightness. Samsung offers a three-year warranty and 24-hour toll-free support.

Sony CPD-220VS

Price $899

Rank 3

The Sony CPD-220VS is a multimedia monitor with speakers, subwoofer, microphone, USB ports, sharp display quality and a high price tag. The screen has a 16-inch viewable area, .25mm Trinitron tube and a 85-Hz refresh rate at 1,024 by 768. This monitor also has two very light lines across the screen. The speakers are shielded and built into the sides of the screen with the subwoofer at the bottom. Volume controls are located on the left of the monitor. The sound from these speakers is good and the screen won't quiver if your bass isn't booming too loud. On-screen controls are easily accessible from the monitor's front 12 buttons. When you activate a control, numbered gauges display the screen's current adjustment levels. Support is available 24 hours daily. Sony only offers a one-year warranty on this monitor.

ViewSonic PT775

Price $849

Rank 6

If you work with photographs or need to be able to view images in great detail, the ViewSonic PT775 is a monitor you should consider, if you don't mind the high price tag. The display is very good for both graphics and text. The screen has a 15.9-inch viewable area, a .25mm Diamondtron tube and up to 119-Hz refresh rate at 1,024 by 768, but only a few controls. This monitor can display images in great detail, from true-to-life flesh tones to 8-point text. There is a three-year warranty and toll-free support available 11-hours on weekdays.

CONTACT INFORMATION

Mag InnoVision
800-827-3998
www.maginnovision.com

Mitsubishi
800-843-2515
www.mitsubishi.display.com

NEC Technologies
800-632-4636
www.nec.com

ViewSonic
800-888-8583
www.viewsonic.com

Samsung SyncMaster
800-747-6249
www.sosimple.com

Sony
800-476-6972
www.ita.sel.sony.com

MOUSES

Mouses are peripheral input devices that are used to navigate a pointer that appears on the computer monitor, which is a necessity when using Microsoft's Windows or a Mac. The mouse is used to "point and click" to select objects, open menus or lists, and scroll data that is too large for the current window size, for example.

The majority of personal computers purchased today come with a mouse. Most of these are small two-button devices attached to the computer with a cord and connected to the PS/2 port or a serial port. Movement of the device across a pad rolls a small ball underneath, and that movement is translated by software into motion of the pointer on the monitor.

Replacement basic mouse devices are available for under $25, but the industry is beginning to add features beyond the basics and to make them more durable and accurate. Some have additional buttons or scrolling mechanisms to increase productivity when scrolling the screen or using the Internet. Many are ergonomically designed for comfort with raised buttons and sculptured support for the fingers and wrist. And, for the person who wants mobility, radio frequency controlled cordless models are available. For durability and accuracy, new-technology has improved the tracking ball mechanisms by replacing the basic mechanical type with optical-mechanical and optical mechanisms. Accuracy is measured in "dots-per-inch" with higher numbers indicating greater pointer control.

When purchasing any new mouse device, there are many things to consider. Do you really need the higher priced cordless model for making presentations or freedom from your desk? Are you going to use the features that are exclusive to Windows 95- or Microsoft Office 97-compatible products? Are you going to be using the mouse in an environment where the traditional tracking ball can get dirty or wet? Do you really need the programmable functions or extra buttons and keypads?

If it has a cable, it should be at least six feet long and the plug must match your computer's mouse socket or attach to a serial port. For the cordless models, consider the size of the room you will be using it in. The distance from the computer within which they will accurately work varies widely.

Try out any mouse before you buy it, or at least make sure you can return it for a full refund. Make sure the mouse keys are large enough and located in a comfortable position for your hand.

The following list contains eight mouses and their overall ratings.

OVERALL RATINGS

iXMicro GyroPoint Pro Cordless Mouse	★★★ 3/4
Alps Adjustable Mouse	★★★ 1/2

Logitech Cordless
  MouseMan   ★ ★ ★ 1/4

Microsoft IntelliMouse   ★ ★ ★ 1/4

Key Tronic Lifetime Mouse   ★ ★ ★ 1/4

Contour Mouse   ★ ★ ★

Vector UNIA Mouse   ★ ★ 3/4

Genius NetMouse   ★ ★ 1/2

EXPLANATION OF RATINGS

Mouse devices were selected for review from current products that are moved by the user and have new or advanced features. The mouses were evaluated based on the following aspects: features, comfort, and durability. Each aspect could potentially earn up to four stars, with one star being the lowest rating. The individual ratings were then averaged for the overall rating.

ALPHABETICAL DESCRIPTIONS

Alps Adjustable Mouse

Price $39.95	
Overall Rating	★ ★ ★ 1/2
Features	★ ★ ★
Comfort	★ ★ ★ 1/2
Durabilit	★ ★ ★ 3/4

This three-button mouse is programmable with included software to control mouse behavior and button assignments. The adjustable shell height will fit small, medium, and large hands, making it comfortable to the fingers and the wrist. Tracking is at 400 dots-per-inch and comes with a lifetime warranty. Installation is by connecting a cable to a PS/2-type of port, or to a serial port with an included adapter on PC-compatible com-

puters. The Macintosh version connects to an ADB port.

Contour Mouse

Price $85.95	
Overall Rating	★ ★ ★
Features	★ ★ ★
Comfort	★ ★ ★ ★
Durability	★ ★ 1/4

This three-button mouse is contoured to fit the fingers. A thumb rest encourages you to hold your hand at a natural angle. It takes very little effort to move with the palm of the hand instead of the fingers. Software is included to adjust the mouse action and assign macros or shortcuts, including many options to improve accuracy in applications where it is critical. It comes in five sizes based on the length of your fingers and two left-handed sizes at the higher price listed above. Installation is by connecting a cable to a serial port or a PS/2 type port with an included adapter for PC-compatible systems. Macintosh and Sun versions are also available.

Genius Netmouse

Price $39.95	
Overall Rating	★ ★ 1 / 2
Features	★ ★ ★ 1/4
Comfort	★ ★ 1/2
Durability	★ 1/2

This mouse has two standard buttons with a scrolling button in the middle that lets you scroll the screen without moving the mouse. Software is included for programmable functions. Tracking is at 400 dots-per-inch. Durability is average. Installation is by connecting a cable to a

PS/2-type port on PC-compatible systems.

iXMicro GyroPoint Pro Cordless Mouse

Price $169.99	
Overall Rating ★★★3/4	
Features ★★★ 1/2	
Comfort ★★★ 1/2	
Durability ★★★★	

This two-button mouse has no tracking ball and almost no moving parts. It is operated by a gyroscope that interprets your hand and arm motion to glide the mouse pointer across the screen. No special software drivers are required, but it comes with GyroTools software to add special effects to your application. Installation is by connecting a radio frequency transmitter to your computer's serial or mouse port. The mouse can be operated up to 75 feet from the computer. Two AA lithium batteries and a 20-foot cable are included. PC compatible, Macintosh, and Philips CD-i versions are available.

Key Tronic Lifetime Mouse

Price $49.99	
Overall Rating ★★★ 1/4	
Features ★★★ 1/4	
Comfort ★★ 1/2	
Durability ★★★★	

This mouse has two buttons standard, but it can be ordered with two other optional configurations. Unique motion-detection feet replace the tracking ball, with the advantage that it is sealed to prevent skipping or slipping. No mouse pad is required as it can be run across any surface—even upside down. The mouse can be con-

nected by a cable to a nine-pin serial port or a PS/2-type port (buy the version you need) on a PC-compatible system

Logitech Cordless MouseMan

Price $79.95	
Overall Rating ★★★ 1/4	
Features ★★★★	
Comfort ★★★	
Durability ★★ 1/2	

This mouse has two standard buttons on top and a third button on the left side, which could be a problem for left-handed users. The case is cordless, sculptured and tilted for comfortable use. The mouse can be operated up to 6 feet from the computer in any direction. Software is included to customize the mouse functions. There is a new "Hyperjump" feature for Windows 95 operation. Durability is average. Installation is by connecting a radio frequency transmitter to a PS/2 or nine-pin serial port on a PC-compatible system. A Macintosh version is also available.

Microsoft IntelliMouse

Price $84.95	
Overall Rating ★★★ 1/4	
Features ★★★ 3/4	
Comfort ★★★ 1/4	
Durability ★★ 1/2	

The standard two buttons have a wheel/button between them for zooming, scrolling, or jumping to commonly used icons on the screen without moving the mouse. These features work only in software compatible with Microsoft Office 97 applications. It is a very comfortable mouse to use due to its sculptured case and size. Software is included to customize the cursor and wheel functions. Durability is average. Installation is by connecting a cable to a PS/2 type port on a PC-compatible system.

Vector UNIA Mouse

Price $69.95

Overall Rating ★ ★ ★ 3/4

Features ★ ★ ★ ★

Comfort ★ ★ 1/2

Durability ★ ★

This oversized mouse has three buttons for standard mouse functions and an 18-key keypad for increased productivity—especially when doing numeric data entry. Four modes can be selected: regular mouse, numeric keypad (default), 15-function keypad, and character keypad for entering symbols. The large case feels cumbersome at first, but it is easy to move and use. A cover is provided for the keypad. Durability is average . Installation is by connecting a cable to a nine-pin serial port on a PC-compatible system. The PS/2 port version costs a little more.

CONTACT INFORMATION

Alps Electric USA
800-825-2577
www.alpsusa.com

Contour Design, Inc.
800-462-6678
www.contourdes.com

Genius-KYE International
626-369-0427
www.genius-kye.com

iXMicro
888-467-8282
www.ixmicro.com

Key Tronic Corp.
800-262-6006
www.keytronic.com

Logitech Inc.
(800) 231-7717
www.logitech.com

Microsoft Corp.
800-426-9400
www.microsoft.com

Vector Research Group
408-323-8642
www.vrg.net

MULTIFUNCTION PERIPHERALS

Equipping an office with a printer, copier, fax, and scanner can be costly. If you're watching the bottom line, a multifunction peripheral (also known as a multifunction printer or MFP) could be a wise choice. MFPs combine four machines into one compact standalone unit, sometimes for less than $1,000. Average list prices are closer to $600.

Not all MFPs are created equal. While they perform the same basic functions of printing, scanning, copying, and faxing, it is how well they perform these functions that distinguish the machines from one another. Selecting the right MFP for your business depends on a combination of factors. Before investing in an MFP, evaluate your business' document handling needs. You should consider the following before shopping:

Printing: This is the most important function of a MFP, therefore you should evaluate the print quality you need. Most MFPs have inkjet printers, a few support color printing, and some have laser printers. Laser jets typically produce better quality output, however some inkjets' resolutions are now on par with lasers.

The Hewlett-Packard OfficeJet Pro 1150C, which tied as the top-rated unit, does everything in color— printing, scanning, and copying. Its flatbed design allows you to copy bound materials such as magazines and books. Copies can be reduced to 50% or enlarged to 400%.

The type of printer your MFP has dictates the quality of your printed output. Check the print resolution of the MFP. A print resolution of 300 x 300 dpi (dots per inch) produces acceptable printed documents. This may work if you are only printing out general business correspondence or homework. Higher resolutions produce better-quality documents. Print resolutions of 600 x 600 dpi will produce cleaner and sharper text and graphics. For high-volume printing and printing of complex graphics a higher resolution is needed to do the job right. Keep in mind that printing speed for MFPs are relatively slow. Most units print at speeds of three to six ppm (pages per minute).

Copying: Determine the original sizes of documents to be copied. MFPs are different than conventional copiers. The original to be copied is fed from a paper tray rather than being placed on a flatbed. Bound materials cannot be copied unless you take them apart first. Check to see if the unit offers enlargement and reduction of copies. If you need copies in colors there are only a few MFPs that offer color copying. MFPs normally copy in monochrome only.

Faxing: Consider the number of faxes sent and received, their length and complexity. Check the fax memory of the unit. The manufacturer measures fax memory in pages. When sending a fax the MFP uses its memory to store the fax until it can send it. Some MFPs store the fax while performing redials if the receiving fax machine is busy. The ability to store incoming faxes is essential. This keeps the phone line from being tied up while the fax is being printed. Fax memory will store faxes if the unit runs out of paper or ink. The pages indicated as the fax memory can be reduced if you receive faxes that contain complex graphics.

Also take into consideration if the MFP will be used on a voice phone line. If it will, check whether the unit is equipped with a distinctive ring for voice/fax. This feature routes an incoming call to either the MFP's fax or answering machine.

Scanning: Determine what will be scanned. Will the unit be used for only text scanning or will color photographs and graphics be scanned. MFP scanners, like copiers, only accept sheet-fed input. This makes them less versatile than a stand-alone flatbed scanner. MFPs scan only in grayscale but there are a few new MFPs coming to the market that scan in color. (These color scanning units lack the fax option.) For the best scanned image make sure the MFP scans with the highest shades of gray. For most graphics, 64 shades of gray should suffice.

Check to make sure the MFP is TWAIN compatible. When using image editing software, TWAIN compatibility is important in scanning photographs and images. The TWAIN function ensures proper communication between the computer and the MFP. Check the optical resolution of the scanner. For text, 300 dpi will suffice, but for graphics and photos a higher resolution is needed.

Additional Options: Check out the warranties and telephone functions of the MFPs. Remember to read the terms of the warranty and the availability of customer service, including repair terms and the hours of their support hotline.

Most MFPs have jacks for answering machines and options for programming frequently used phone numbers. Check if the answering device is built in or if you have to add your own. Also look into how the MFP stores phone numbers.

The list below rates six multifunction peripherals. Data were gathered from the manufacturers and combined with our observations.

OVERALL RATINGS

Brother MFC-4550 ★ ★ ★ ★

Hewlett-Packard OfficeJet Pro 1150C ★ ★ ★ ★

Hewlett-Packard Office Jet 570 ★ ★ ★ 1/2

Canon MultiPass C2500 ★ ★ ★

Sharp F-2700M ★ ★ 1/2

Xerox Document Work-Center 250 ★ ★

EXPLANATION OF RATINGS

Scores were computed on how well the key tasks of printing, scanning, copying, and faxing were performed. Two other factors were evaluated: Software, that is, the bundle that comes with the machine and "Usability," which pertains to the general ease of use, pertaining to things such as paper handling, page storage and front-panel operations. MFPs that were more difficult to operate in these areas received a lower rating in usability. Print-

ing was weighted as 50% of the overall rating. Each of the foregoing categories was rated one to four stars, the more stars, the higher the rating. The various categories were averaged, resulting in the overall rating.

ALPHABETICAL DESCRIPTIONS

Brother MFC-4550

Price $799

Overall Rating ★ ★ ★ ★

Printing ★ ★ ★ ★

Copying ★ ★ ★ ★

Scanning ★ ★ ★ ★

Faxing ★

Software ★ ★ ★ ★

Usability ★ ★ ★

Powered by a laser engine, the Brother MFC-4550 speeds through printing, copying, and scanning, but slows to a crawl when faxing. It produces high-quality printed output at 600-by-600 dpi. This resolution produces clear, detailed text

The Brother MFC-4550 ties with the Hewlett-Packard OfficeJet 1150 C as the number-one unit.

and images. This unit is tops in print quality. The copier can be adjusted to three settings: photo, fine, and superfine. Copies can be reduced to 50 percent or enlarged up to 200 percent, but there is no collating function. Scanning can be done at True Gray and Error diffusion. The standard memory for the Brother MFC-4550 is 512K. Where memory is concerned more is better. Memory upgrades are available in 1MB ($200 list) or 2MB ($300 list) configurations. This unit's weak spot is its slow faxing and its confusing design. Its front panel design is confusing making it hard to use. The software that comes with the unit offers many options, but finding your way around the different applications may be difficult. Despite these two drawbacks, if speed and print quality is your primary concern this MFP makes the grade.

Brother also makes a new MFP with all of the features of the MFC- 4500.

The Brother MFC-6550mc has the same features and performance as the Brother MFC-4550 except it includes an answering machine with voice/fax mailboxes.

Canon MultiPass C2500

Price $599
Overall Rating ★★★
Printing ★★★
Copying ★★
Scanning ★★★
Faxing ★★★★
Software ★★★
Usability ★★★★.

MultiPass C2500 offers four-color printing and fast faxing. It also has the highest resolution of all the MFPs on this group, with a 720-by-360 dpi setting. Print quality is good, but the color quality is lacking. Simple graphics and text came out nicely in color, but photos produced ugly results. Scanning and copying can only be done in monochrome. Multiple copies can be made but there are no enlargement or reduction options. Faxing is fast but not straight forward. The fax has to be scanned first then faxed with the software. The unit's software is easy to use and controls all functions, but no OCR software is included.

HP OfficeJet Model 570

Price $599
Rating ★★★1/2
Printing ★★★★
Copying ★★★★
Scanning ★★★
Faxing ★★★★
Software ★★★★
Usability ★★★★.

The OfficeJet 570 is one in the 500 series of MFPs from Hewlett Packard. This model can print in both black and white and color. Black-and-white printing resolutions are up to 600dpi and color is 600 x 300dpi. Print speeds are four ppm for black and white and one ppm for color. This device has a 14,400bps fax modem and can hold 150 sheets in the paper tray and up to 20 sheets in the document feeder.

One unique feature is the ability to fax hard copy documents and documents on your computer at the same time. You can scan at a resolution of 300 dpi and OCR software is included for converting scanned text into an editable format for use in your favorite word processor. Another advantage is that you don't have to switch cartridges, both the black-and- white and color cartridges remain in the device.

HP OfficeJet Pro 1150C

Price $1,000
Rating ★★★★
Printing ★★★★
Copying ★★★★
Scanning ★★★★
Faxing NA
Software ★★★★
Usability ★★★★.

If you can spend a bit more and have more desk space this MFP is quite a deal. It does everything in color; printing, scanning, and copying. The OfficeJet Pro 1150C is larger then the usual MFP and has a flat-bed design, but it works so well.

You can copy bound materials, magazines, photos and more. Copies can be reduced to 50% or enlarged to 400%. Whether you reduce, enlarge, or just copy straight, the copy quality is top-notch. Black-and-white printing has a resolution of 600 x 600 dpi, color resolution is 600 x 300. Print speeds are eight ppm for black and white and four ppm for color. Print quality is excellent.

Scans can be done in either grayscale or 24 bit color up to 1200 dpi enhanced (300 dpi optical). Also included is Caere OmniPage LE OCR for converting scanned text into an editable format and Adobe PhotoDeluxe Image Editor for enhancing photographs.

The only thing missing here is fax capability through the device. However if your PC already has a fax modem you can scan a document, save it to your hard drive, then fax it through your PC.

Sharp F-2700M

Price $1,249
Rating ★★
Printing ★★★
Copying ★★
Scanning ★
Faxing ★
Software ★★
Usability ★★

In reality the Sharp F-2700M is a stand-alone fax machine, copier, and four-page-per-minute, 300-dot-per-inch Windows laser printer. It has a telephone handset where you can make voice calls, but its interaction with the computer are limited. Standard features include a 9,600-bps modem, 512K of memory, and a 20-page document feeder.

You cannot scan a document and save it on your computer, or send and receive faxes from your computer, but you can print from Windows. The Windows Printing system controls the F-2700M. If the device is faxing, a dialog box displays on screen and the computer tells you "Fax in Use." Faxes take priority to other functions. If a document is printing when a fax is received, printing will be suspended until the fax transmission is completed. Also, copying occasionally produced crooked copies even if the paper was fed through straight. Overall the F-270M is efficient and simple to use. Printed output is sharper than other inkjet models.

Xerox Document Work-Center 250

Price: $549

Rating: ★★

Printing ★★

Copying ★★★

Scanning ★★

Faxing ★★

Software ★★

Usability ★★.

Xerox is known for its photocopiers so it's no surprise that this unit has great copying capabilities; however, the other functions are lacking. The WorkCenter's control panel and software are difficult to use. Scan quality is low and scanning process speed is slow. Printing speed and quality lagged behind other units. When it comes to copying, the WorkCenter offers speed, enlargement and reductions, collation, and contrast adjustments. The WorkCenter's excellent copying capabilities are not enough to overcome its poor printing, scanning, and faxing performance.

CONTACT INFORMATION

Xerox Corp.
(800) 832-6979
www.xerox.com

Brother Industries, Ltd.
(800) 276-7746, 714/859-9700
www.brother.com

Canon U.S.A., Inc.
(800) 848-4123, 714/438-3000
www.canon.com

Hewlett-Packard Co.
(800) 752-0900
www.hp.com

Okidata
(800) OKI-TEAM extension 9
www.okidata.com

Sharp Electronics Company
(800) 237-4277
http://www.sharp-usa.com.

POWER SUPPLIES, UNINTERRUPTIBLE

Beyond what standard power supplies or surge protectors sold at hardware stores do, an Uninterruptible Power Supply (UPS) protects your computer from power outages, lightning and surges, brownouts, and overvoltages. This device can keep your computer from being fried by a power surge and keeps it up and running during a power outage. If there is a power outage, the UPS keeps your computer on until you can save your data and shut down your system. A Uninterruptible Power Supply can be a lifesaver for your computer and your data.

Following are the ratings for five UPS models. Most of them have a load capacity from 400 to 450 VA. Each manufacturer offers other models with more load capacity for larger computer systems and power desktops. We picked midrange UPSs that are well-suited for stand-alone computers. Though the ratings are very close for the UPSs, some are better suited than others for various situations that you will read about in the alphabetical reviews.

The APC Back-UPS 450, the top-rated unit, features four surge-protected outlets, swappable replaceable batteries, an interface port for automatic shutdowns, a test switch, site diagnostics, and an audible on-battery/low-battery alarm.

OVERALL RATINGS

APC Back-UPS 450	★★★★
Deltec PowerRite Max	★★★ 1/2
Tripp Lite Internet Standby UPS 450 I	★★★ 1/2
Best Power Patriot 420VA	★★★ 1/4
Opti-UPS 420E	★★★ 1/4
Liebert PowerSure 400VA	★★★

EXPLANATION OF RATINGS

UPS models were scored on Load Capacity, Features (which included the number of outlets and shutdown capabilities), and Price. The highest rating is four stars; the lowest is one. The overall rating was achieved by averaging the category scores, with with load capacity accounting for 50% of the overall rating.

ALPHABETICAL DESCRIPTIONS

APC Back-UPS 450

Price $199

Overall Rating ★★★★

Load Capacity ★★★★

Features ★★★★

Price ★★★★

The APC Back-UPS 450 has a 450VA carrying capacity and is designed for standalone computers with peripherals or 486 network workstations. Features include four surge-protected outlets, swappable replaceable batteries, an interface port for automatic shutdowns, a test switch and site diagnostics, and an audible on-battery/low-battery alarm. The Back-UPS 450 is covered by a two-year warranty and a $25,000 Lifetime Equipment Protection Policy that covers all computer equipment connected to the APC in case of damage due to surges or lightning.

Best Power Patriot 420VA

Price $199

Overall Rating ★★★1/4

Load Capacity ★★★

Features ★★★

Price ★★★★

The Patriot 420VA has a carrying capacity of 420VA and can provide adequate protection for PCs; however, it only has two outlets, which would make it a less than optimal choice for computers with a lot of peripherals. There is a battery management system which gives you a back-up time of five to 15 minutes if there is a power fluctuation or outage. Indicators for battery charging, battery replacement time, power and overload are included. Automatic shutdown is available on this UPS, but special software is needed, but not included. Software and cables for automatic shutdown can be obtained by sending in a coupon. Patriot is covered by a two-year warranty.

Deltec PowerRite Max

Price $339

Overall Rating ★★★ 1/2

Load Capacity ★★★★

Features ★★★★

Price ★★

The PowerRite Max is the highest-priced UPS in this group. It has a 450VA carrying capacity and four backed-up outlets. Installation is easy since the PowerRite Max is a plug-and-play device. To take advantage of ''Plug and Play'' you will have to order the cable from Deltec Electronics for $39.95 for overnight air freight or $24.95 for ground shipment. The price includes shipping and handling. Indicator lights are located on the front panel and show you the unit relative load levels. Batteries can be changed without shutting down the system. This is a good feature for networks. Bundled with this UPS is the FailSafe III software for automated shutdowns of your standalone systems or LanSafe III software for use on networks during a power loss. The software has an animated control module that displays your system's load and status. The PowerRite Max has great features, and good load capacity, which afford it a high rating, but it is a little high-priced.

Liebert PowerSure 400VA

Price $258	
Overall Rating ★★★	
Load Capacity ★★3/4	
Features ★★1/2	
Price ★★★★	

The PowerSure 400VA is a lightweight, microprocessor-based UPS system. Its load capacity is 400VA and has fouroutlets. Battery backup ranges from five to 45 minutes depending on the load. Features include a built-in EasySwap battery for quick replacements, automatic battery testing, communications ports for LAN connections and Black-start capabilities, which let you start your computer and UPS from the battery. There are also audible and visual alarms for low battery, battery test failure, charger overload/short circuit, and overvoltage. Additional options include the SiteNet 1 shutdown management kit, which monitors UPS activity, informing you of remaining power and performing automatic shutdowns when the battery reaches a certain level.

Opti-UPS 420E

Price $ 199	
Overall Rating ★★★1/4	
Load Capacity ★★★	
Features ★★★	
Price ★★★★	

Viewsonic's Opti-UPS 420E offers great software and a great price, but only has two battery-backed outlets. Its carrying capacity is 420VA and it can handle automated shutdowns. The Opti-Safe+ software gives you plug-and-play installation. The software also features on-screen controls that display status information about the unit. If there is an alarm the system can send e-mail or paging messages about the alarm. If you use the Opti-UPS on a network, system shutdowns can be done in the order you choose. The Opti-UPS would be an excellent choice if not for the lack of outlets. The Opti-UPS is covered by a three-year limited warranty and a $25,000 life insurance coverage on computers connected to the Opti-UPS.

Tripp Lite Internet Standby UPS 450 I

Price $199	
Overall Rating ★★★1/2	
Load Capacity ★★★★	
Features ★★	
Price ★★★★	

The Internet Standby UPS 450 I is good for those on a budget. This not only protects your computer from power outages, but it also protects you while you are connected to the Internet. Modem surge protection is provided with the built-in fax-modem jacks. If you experience a power outage or fluctuation while online, this system's battery backup will kick in and protect you. It has three surge-protected outlets, plus three battery-backed outlets. Other options include a low battery indicator, power and backup mode, and a test-mute alarm switch. One drawback is that there is no automatic shutdown.

CONTACT INFORMATION

American Power Conversion (APC)
800-877-4080
www.apcc.com

Best Power Uninterruptible Power Systems
800-356-5794
www.bestpower.com

Deltec
800-335-8321
www.deltecpower.com

Liebert Corporation
www.liebert.com

Viewsonic Corporation
800-843-6784
www.opti-ups.com

Tripp Lite
312-755-5400
www.tripplite.com

PRINTERS, COLOR LASERS

Once a luxury, the cost of high-quality networkable color printers has dropped sharply in the last couple of years.

Most color printers are based on a CMYK color model — they print in four basic colors: cyan (blue), magenta (red), yellow, and black. Combinations of these colors either near or on top of each other can simulate most other colors in the spectrum. Other types of color printers use either different technologies or are somewhat different. They may be found elsewhere in this portion of your book. (See "Printers, Dye Sublimation" and "Printers, Ink Jet,")

Color printer quality varies with the printing method used and how the colors are blended on the output. The best quality is called "continuous-tone" where each dot on the page can contain a mixture of colors. Bi-level printers print different dots for each color . In between these two is "Contone," which provides more shades per dot than bi-level printers but less than the continuous-tone. These various technologies are noted in the alphabetical descriptions that follow, but only if they dictate what you can reasonably expect from the printers; often they mean little due to the fact that other facets of the printer's technology determine its quality on a practical level.

Another consideration is speed — how many pages-per-minute will come out of the printer at high quality. In networked office environments, 8 to 14 pages-per-minute monochrome and two to five pages-per-minute in color is the norm. In effect you are sacrificing some speed on monochrome output to get the color option.

Yet another aspect of a printer to consider is the input and output trays. How many pages of paper or envelopes can be ready for printing at one time? Must you feed envelopes manually? Will the output be stacked in collated sequence? Is the paper path pretty straight to avoid damaging the paper or jamming the printer?

Once you have some ideas as to your color printer needs, contact the manufacturers and they will send you samples and literature and direct you to places where their printers can be purchased. Mail order houses may also have these types of printers available to ship. Most popular computer retail outlets will not have these types of printers on display, but may be able to order them for you. And finally, there are outlets on the Internet where you can get information and place an order.

In this review the focus is on color printers costing under $7,500 with the following minimum configuration: 600x600 DPI resolution, and 8 pages-per-minute monochrome with three pages-per- minute in color. Data on these models was compiled from the manufacturers. Recent reviews of workgroup printers in PC World and Lan Times magazines included some of the printers we included below. Prices indicated are approximate "typical street prices" when the printers were reviewed.

OVERALL RATINGS

Tektronix Phaser 550 ★★★★

Tektronix Phaser 560 Deluxe ★★★ 3/4

HP Color LaserJet 5M ★★★ 1/2

Xerox DocuPrint C55mp ★★★ 1/2

IBM Network Color Printer ★★★ 1/2

Minolta Color Pageworks
  Printer ★★★ 1/4

EXPLANATION OF RATINGS

Color printers were selected for review from currently available products that met the configuration minimums listed earlier in this review. The overall rating was arrived at by giving individual scores on print quality, performance, features, and support (including warranty). These scores were then averaged to arrive at the overall rating. The highest rating possible is four stars; the lowest, one.

Other factors to consider when purchasing a laser printer include the following:

Cost of operation can vary greatly and may over several years be more than the initial purchase price of your printer! Many manufacturers will state a "cents-per-page" amount, which should range from about five cents to a dollar in this printer range for color output. If this is not available, find out how much the consumables will be and how often they will need to be replaced. Usually the toner cartridge and internal drum are sold separately and last different numbers of pages,

but be careful if the toner and drum are combined to make sure the cost is not exorbitant.

Overall size is often much larger than the stated "footprint." Input and output trays must be accessible, and in some cases unfold when in use.

Upgradeablility may be important if your printing needs are growing. Additional input trays, more RAM memory, and font cartridges will extend the printer's use, but they are not able to print any faster than their rated pages-per-minute speed.

Durability is expressed as a "monthly duty cycle," or the number of pages the manufacturer expects you to print in one month. If your needs exceed this level, your printer is more likely to break down early in its lifetime.

Software can range from simply including the printer drivers to elaborate suites of programs for printing. And sometimes the software is just "demonstration" level and not able to be used. Today's hot software is "Internet-related" and may not even be of interest to you.

ALPHABETICAL DESCRIPTIONS

HP Color LaserJet 5M

Price $4,999

Overall Rating ★★★ 1/2

Quality ★★★★

Speed ★★★

Features ★★★★

Support ★★★ 1/2

The HP ColorLaserJet 5M is the highest quality printer in this group at 1,200 DPI resolution and continuous tone color output with a powerful set of ColorSmart drivers for Windows, OS/2, DOS, and Macintosh computers. Black-and-white output is sharp, colors printed are bright and unlimited in range, and photorealistic images can be produced. Printing is direct-to-drum using four toner colors to achieve pages-per-minute ratings of 10 black-and-white, two-to-three color, and one on transparencies. Although the printer has the most expensive price of those we reviewed, the estimated cost of operation is very low with a per-page estimate of 1.8 cents for black-and-white and only five cents for color. Features include a standard 36 MB of RAM expandable to 76 MB, HP JetDirect card for Ethernet and Local Talk environments, and one 250-sheet input tray. The only option for growth is an additional 250 sheet input unit. HP JetAdmin printer-management software makes network management of the printer easy to do. The duty cycle rating for this printer is 12,000 pages per month. Support is available by phone weekdays. The warranty is for one year and includes next-day on-site service, with an optional extension to three years. HP's Internet site is among the best for technical support information.

IBM Network Color Printer

Price $4,999	
Overall Rating ★★★ 1/2	
Quality ★★★ 3/4	
Speed ★★★ 1/2	
Features ★★★ 1/4	
Support ★★★★	

Another excellent laser printer, IBM's only color model produces excellent color output at 600 DPI continuous-tone and three pages-per-minute. Black-and-white printing is crisp and fast at 12 pages-per-minute. Features included are 16 MB RAM expandable to 48 MB, a network card that supports Novell NetWare, Ether-Talk, and TCP/IP protocols, a 341 MB SCSI hard disk for spooling output or storing fonts, two input trays totaling 350 sheets, and a 100-sheet output capability. The only option is a 250-sheet input tray. A comprehensive set of network printing utilities and drivers for Windows, Apple, OS/2, and IBM AIX are included. Support is IBM's strong point with toll-free 24-hour seven-day a week phone coverage. The warranty is for one year on-site. IBM's Internet site provides comprehensive technical information, guides, and downloadable drivers.

Minolta Color Pageworks Printer

Price $3,495	
Overall Rating ★★★ 1/4	
Quality ★★ 1/4	
Speed ★★★ 1/2	
Features ★★★ 3/4	
Support ★★★ 1/4	

This gem, the least expensive color laser, holds its own in output speed for pages-per-minute at 12 black-and-white and three in color at 600 DPI resolution. It comes with only 4 MB RAM expandable to 48 MB, which they state is enough due to their Memory Reduction Technology data compression scheme, but complex graphics output will surely require more than 4 MB. Other features include 400 sheet input capacity in two trays, a 250-sheet collated output tray, and Local Talk capability. An additional 250-sheet input tray can be added, and interfaces to Ethernet or Token-Ring networks are optional. The duty cycle rating for this printer is 30,000 pages per month. The only software mentioned is an "Improve Your Image" CD with an array of templates to improve your documents. There is one year of toll-free 24-hour, seven day phone support and a one-year warranty with on-site service. Their Internet site could be more helpful and informative.

Tektronix Phaser 550

Price	*See text immediately following*
Overall Rating	★ ★ ★ ★
Quality	★ ★ ★ ★
Speed	★ ★ ★ ★
Features	★ ★ ★ 3/4
Support	★ ★ ★ 3/4

This color laser gives you both speed and extraordinary color image quality. Unfortunately it was discontinued just before press time; however, you may find 550 the model for sale at the dealer level anyway. If not, Tektronix sells reconditioned models and, at far less that the original street price of about $6,000.

The Phaser 550 B1 model offers full color photorealistic continuous-tone printing on any type of paper (including labels!) at five pages-per-minute and 1200 DPI resolution. Black-and-white is a fast 14 pages-per-minute and as sharp as any regular laser printer. The printer come standard with 8 MB of RAM expandable to 72 MB, but Tektronix's proprietary RAM must be used for upgrading and it is expensive at around $1,195 for a 16MB SIMM. Other features include a 250 sheet input tray, large output tray, and Ethernet support for

Novell, EtherTalk, and TCP/IP. In addition to paper tray options, you can turn your printer into a color copier for only $1,695 (list price for the Copystation hardware add-on)! Software includes the PhaserShare printer administration tools and drivers, and new PhaserLink software lets you check printer status, change settings and use the Internet to access on-line documentation. Support is available by phone toll-free, and the warranty is one year on-site with extensions available. They have an excellent technical support capability at their Internet site.

Tektronix Phaser 560 Deluxe

Price	*$5,495*
Overall Rating	★ ★ ★ 3/4
Quality	★ ★ ★ 1/2
Speed	★ ★ ★ ★
Features	★ ★ ★ ★
Support	★ ★ ★ 3/4

This color laser printer gives you the option of fast printing at lower quality or slower printing at comparable quality to the 500 B1 model. Fast Color mode runs at 5 pages-per-minute but only 600 DPI, Standard mode runs at 14 black-and-white or 3.5 color pages per minute at 600 DPI, and Premium mode provides 7 black-and-white or 1.8 color pages-per-minute at 1200 DPI. In addition to regular paper and labels, this printer can print on fabric transfer sheets and card stock. Included in this price are 40 MB RAM, two input trays totaling 350 sheets, large output tray, and an Ethernet network card for use with Windows, DOS, NT, OS/2, Macintosh, and UNIX computers. Duplex printing is provided by the two input trays. There is an option for another 500 sheet input in two more trays. Software, support, warranty, and the Internet site are the same as for the 500 B1 printer.

Xerox DocuPrint C55mp

Price $4,500

Overall Rating ★ ★ ★ 1/2

Quality ★ ★ ★ 1/2

Speed ★ ★ ★ 1/2

Features ★ ★ ★ 1/2

Support ★ ★ ★ 3/4

The Xerox DocuPrint C55mp offers good image quality using Contone at 600 DPI and good speed at page-per-minute rates of 12 for black-and-white and three for color. It also has a "fast blue" option at six pages-per-minute. Features include standard 30 MB RAM expandable to 70 MB, a 250-sheet input tray, 150-sheet collated output tray, and an Ethernet network card for Novell NetWare, Windows, OS/2, UNIX, and Macintosh computers. Options include a 250-sheet input feeder and various network cards, an 810 MB hard drive called a "Media Server" to hold print files for reprinting multiple copies without resending them over the network multiple times. Software includes drivers and network administration using CentreWare DP and CentreWare Internet Services. The duty cycle is stated to be 20,000 prints per month. Support by phone is available as well as on their Internet site, but it is very slow. The warranty is for three years replacement with the Xerox Total Satisfaction Guarantee.

CONTACT INFORMATION

Hewlett-Packard Corporation
800-752-0900
www.hp.com

IBM Printing Systems Company
800-358-6661
www.printers.ibm.com

Minolta Co., Ltd.
888-2MINOLTA
www.minoltaprinters.com

Tektronix, Inc.
800-835-6100
www.tek.com

Xerox Corporation
800-34-XEROX
www.xerox.com

PRINTERS, DYE SUBLIMATION

Dye sublimation printers are designed for use by pre-press workgroups, graphics artists, designers, and the scientific and engineering community. It is for those whose output requirements include brilliant colors, sharp edges, and the ability to capture fine detail and continuous shading. Sublimation is the scientific term for converting a solid to a gas without going through an intervening liquid phase. These printers use thermal dye technology, which uses film or ribbon that contains consecutive panels of cyan, magenta, yellow and black dye that passes over a transfer roll. As the transfer roll crosses the thermal printhead, thousands of heating elements heat the dye until it vaporizes and diffuses onto the paper's surface. By controlling the temperature of each element on the printhead, you can control the amount of dye that is applied. The process requires special paper that is designed to absorb the vaporous dye on contact.

Continuous-tone output implies the use of 16.7 million colors. The capability to produce this many colors ensures smooth and subtle gradients, and eliminates any dithering problems that are associated with other color printer technologies (such as laser, inkjet, and thermal wax transfer).

The transfer of dye to the printed page is mechanically similar to thermal wax transfer technology. Several of the printers reviewed here take full advantage of this mechanical similarity by offering offer dual mode printers. Dual-mode operation allows you to choose printing using either thermal wax technology or dye sublimation technology. While thermal wax printers exhibit obvious dithering patterns, you could potentially save thousands of dollars per year (depending on volume) and time by using thermal wax mode for previewing output prior to producing final pre-press output using dye sublimation mode because of the cost per page differential.

Before selecting a printer, you should identify your output requirements and find the printer that best fits your business needs and budget. This report contains representative models from the major manufacturers. Each manufacturer offers several other related models that may match your specific business requirements more closely. Typically, other models use the same print engine and technology. As a rule of thumb, printers that support tabloid size (Type B) output cost approximately twice as much the printers that are limited to letter size (Type A) output.

The following list contains eight dye sublimation printers and their overall ratings.

OVERALL RATINGS

Seiko Color Point 835 PS	★★★3/4
Tektronix Phasar 480X	★★★1/4
Agfa DuoProof Ultra	★★★1/4
Shinko ColorStream	★★★1/4

Kodak Digital Science 8650 PS	★ ★ ★
Mitsubishi S6600-40U	★ ★ ★
Fargo PrimeraPro	★ ★
Spectra Star DS	★ ★

EXPLANATION OF RATINGS

The printers were evaluated based on their output quality, performance and feature set. Each feature was judged on a four-star rating, with one star being the lowest. The individual star ratings were then averaged to arrive at the overall rating.

Output quality considerations included tonal variation, detail, sharp edges and registration for both photographic and graphic images.

Also, cost was not considered in determining quality. All the printers in this evaluation produced satisfactory quality. It is unreasonable to expect a $1,500 printer to produce the same quality as one costing 10 times as much, thus lower- priced printers generally produced lower (but not poor) quality output.

Performance considered speed and reliability. The score for this feature was derived from the following features: amount of memory; hard disk size; Type A (letter and legal) or Type B (tabloid) output; ease of setup; full-bleed capabilities; type of network support included; and other special categories such as design, plug-and-play technology, and support of specialty paper capabilities.

Prices range from a pedestrian $1,500 to $16,000 for the well-heeled. Prices cited in this review reflect the manufacturer's sug-gested retail price. Typically, the street price is 10 to 20% lower than the MSRP, so it pays to shop around. Cost was not considered in the evaluation on the belief that budget constraints control this factor.

ALPHABETICAL DESCRIPTIONS

Agfa DuoProof Ultra

Overall Rating ★ ★ ★ 1/4	
Quality ★ ★ ★	
Performance ★ ★ ★	
Feature Set ★ ★ ★ ★	

Agfa advertises its printer as a pre-proof and pre-press "system." This means it supports dual-mode operation and Agfa's own color management technology dubbed FotoTune. In thermal wax mode, it offers the ability to proof traps and overprints, In pre-press mode, it produces photographic quality images. Agfa claims that the color management system maintains color integrity with final printing processes and inks.

An Ethernet card that supports plug-and-play network connectivity is included. 28 MB of RAM and a 250 MB SCSI hard drive provide adequate memory and queuing capabilities.

Fargo PrimeraPro

Price $1,895	
Overall Rating ★ ★	
Quality ★ ★	
Performance ★ ★	
Feature Set ★ ★	

Fargo has a reputation as an innovator in providing pre-press photographic quality printing capabilities to the financially challenged. The PrimeraPro is by far the lowest-priced entry at $1,895. Fargo ac-complishes this by using the host computer's CPU for processing, rather than including a separate print engine in the printer. Additionally, no hard drive is provided, necessitating that you have approximately 200 MB of free disk space on your host if you want to queue print jobs. Of course, you cannot use your computer while the print job is in process, so plan your lunch breaks accordingly. Setup requires a significant amount of technological sophistication. Another expensive inconvenience is the lack of warning when a ribbon runs out of ink. This leads to costly misfeeds.

On the plus side of the ledger is the price and dual-mode operation. The PrimeraPro offers letter and legal size only. Relatively speaking, the output is good.

Kodak Digital Science 8650 PS

Price $10,795

Overall Rating ★ ★ ★

Quality ★ ★ ★

Performance ★ ★ ★

Feature Set ★ ★ ★

Setup of the hardware and software is easy. It produces excellent output in both the photographic and graphics categories. It produces photo quality images with fine detail and smooth shading. The graphics output produces brilliant colors and crisp edges. This printer has the fastest print speed of any of the printers included in this review. It handles letter and legal size paper at a moderate cost. On the negative side, some tests reported registration that was slightly askew.

Mitsubishi S6600-40U

Price $14,995

Overall Rating ★ ★ ★

Quality ★ ★ ★

Performance ★ ★ ★ ★

Feature Set ★ ★

The Mitsubishi S6600-40U is marketed to pre-press and scientific communities. Setup was straight forward except for the installation of the ribbons which was confusing. The documentation offered little assistance. Both graphics and photo quality output were excellent.

The S6600-40U printer supports plug and play technology. They also offered the only system that protected the paper from dust through out the printing process. Network support is offered for an additional $900.

Seiko ColorPoint 835 PS

Price $16,499

Overall Rating ★ ★ ★3/4

Quality ★ ★ ★ ★

Performance ★ ★ ★1/2

Feature Set ★ ★ ★ ★

This printer won *PC Magazine's* Editor's Choice for 1996. It produces photographic quality that frequently surpassed the quality achieved by professional pre-press machines that cost twice as much. It supports dual-mode operation which can save thousands of dollars based on the difference between its cost per page. This printer was the slowest printer in the group. It was also the most expensive. However, the superior quality of output more than justifies the expense in dollars and time.

Shinko ColorStream IIDPL

Price $15,990

Overall Score ★ ★ ★1/4

Quality ★ ★ ★ 1/2

Performance ★ ★ ★

Feature Set ★ ★ ★

The Shinko family of printers was introduced in 1996. They are designed to meet the requirements of the pre-press and digital photographic reproduction crowd. The ColorStream IIDPL offers the largest full-bleed image size of any of the printers reviewed. Its color management system includes Agfa's FotoTune, Apple ColorSync, and ColorBlind software. The ColorStream boasts of superior continuous tone printing and super tight registration. The unit contains 16 MB of memory and 543 MB hard drive. Network connectivity is supported, but costs extra.

SpectraStar DSx

Price $6,295

Overall Rating ★ ★

Quality ★ ★

Performance ★ ★

Feature Set ★ ★

The SpectraiStar DSx is a stripped-down printer for the budget conscious. It offers many features as options that other printers include as standard, most noticeable of which is a 120 MB hard disk. Using this printer without the supplemental hard disk leads to excessive print times and a lack of queuing capability. The SpectraStar DSx supports letter size (Type A) output only. It does include color matching capabilities.

Tektronix Phasar 480X

Price $14,995

Overall Score ★ ★ ★ 1/4

Quality ★ ★ ★ 1/2

Performance ★ ★ ★

Feature Set ★ ★ ★

Setup is easy. and the output quality and feature set have improved. The 480X model supports standard and tabloid size pages and produces excellent quality at a competitive price. The speed performance of the 480X was mid-range, but an optional 64 MB memory upgrade is available and designed to improve performance. Network for Local Talk is standard, but support for Ethernet protocols is additional.

CONTACT INFORMATION

Agfa Inc.
800-227-2780
www.agfahome.com

Eastman Kodak Company
800-235-6325
www.kodak.com

Fargo Electronics, Inc.
800-327-4622
www.fargo.com

Mitsubishi Electronics America, Inc.
800-842-2515
www.mitsubishi-imaging.com

Seiko Instruments USA, Inc.
800-888-0817
www.cgg.seiko.com

Shinko Intl.
520-441-1175
www.shinkotech.com

Tally Printer Corp.
510-524-3950
www.tally.com

Tektronix,Inc.
800-835-6100
www.tek.com/color_printers/

PRINTERS, MONOTONE LASERS

Lasers printers are high-resolution printers that create printed output by fusing text and graphics images to paper. Once a luxury, laser printers are now priced for every budget. Listed below are five personal laser printers, their rankings and overall scores.

RANKINGS AND OVERALL SCORES

1	Brother HL-720	77
2	NEC SuperScript 660plus	73
3	HP LaserJet 5L Xtra	70
4	Panasonic KX-P6500	50
5	NEC SuperScript 860	42

EXPLANATION OF RATINGS

Laser printers were evaluated based on output quality and speed. The highest score for each category is 100. The overall

The Brother HL-720, the number-one rated printer, comes standard with 512K of RAM, print resolution of 600-by-600-dpi, a 200-sheet input tray, and Surf n' Print software.

score was achieved by averaging the scores for each category with output quality double-weighted.

ALPHABETICAL DESCRIPTIONS

Brother HL-720

Price $350

Rank 1

The Brother HL-720 is fast, inexpensive and has good print quality. It comes standard with 512K of RAM, print resolution of 600-by-600-dpi, a 200-sheet input tray, and Surf n' Print software. The printer is not a plug and play model, but installation was not a hassle. The Brother HL-720 prints 6 pages per minute (ppm) and approximately 2.5 ppm for graphics. Print quality of text is good, however graphics look lifeless because of the Brother's limited grayscale capacity. But for its price range the print quality is fine. The bundled software Surf n' Print can be used to print documents and Web pages as booklets. Technical support is available Monday through Friday. The printer is covered by a one-year warranty.

HP LaserJet 5L Xtra

Price $399

Rank 3

The HP LaserJet 5L Xtra may be a slow-poke but it can't be beat when it comes to print quality. At press time the company discontinued this model and replaced it with the 6L SE Model which is basically the same as the 5L, however the newer machine prints two pages more per minute, hence slowness is no longer a factor. Features on both the newer and older version include 1MB of RAM, 600-by-600dpi maximum resolution, a 100-sheet input tray, and a CD-ROM of software applications. On-screen controls are simple and easy to use; however, the icons on the printer aren't easily identified. To find out what these icons mean, open the printer and you'll find their meanings...not very intuitive is it? Print quality is excellent from tiny text to large graphics. The LaserJet 5L is well designed and includes a curved paper path for envelopes and other sized media, plus a manual feed slot. Support is not toll-free and the printer carries a one-year warranty.

NEC SuperScript 660plus

Price $349

Rank 3

For its price, the NEC SuperScript 660plus has adequate text and graphics. The printer comes standard with 256K of RAM, 600-by-600-dpi maximum resolution, 150-sheet input tray and a parallel cable. This printer is stated to print at 6 pages per minute (ppm), and approximately 2.5 ppm for graphics. The printer is on the slow side and graphics tend to be banded. The toner cartridge comes in two pieces and is not easily put in place. The bundled software program can be used for printing business cards, envelopes and stationary; however, other similar software offers more professional templates. On-screen controls allow you to print watermarks, to print double-sided and print multiple reduced pages on one page. The electronic manual is in Adobe Acrobat format, which makes it easy to search through. Support is available via the web and telephone during the week. The 660 is covered by a two-year warranty.

NEC SuperScript 860

Price $449

Rank 5

The NEC SuperScript 860 is one of the fastest 600-dpi printers in this group; however, the print quality is only satisfactory. It comes standard with 1MB of RAM and a 200-sheet input tray. Also included is software for creating watermarks and booklets. For text printing, the 860 is quick but the print quality was not quite as good as the lower-priced SuperScript 660plus. Gray-scale images were blotchy and some line art suffered from the "jaggies." Another hitch is that output will collate in reverse order, unlike the other laser printers that collate output in order. Support is available via the web and by phone during the week. The printer is covered by a two-year warranty.

Panasonic KX-P6500

Price $449

Rank 4

The Panasonic KX-P6500 has great text and graphics quality and a space-saving design, but is rather high-priced. The printer comes with 512K of RAM, 2400-by-600-dpi maximum resolution and a 100-sheet input tray. The printer speed is 6 pages per minute (ppm) per the manufacturer but tests show it closer to 5.6 ppm for text and 2.3 ppm for graphics, which is a decent speed. The KX-P6500 print quality is second only to the HP LaserJet 5L Xtra. Its design makes it ideal for those who lack space. The on-screen controls can walk you through double-sided printing and lets you print multiple reduced documents on one page. Support is available by phone on weekdays only.

CONTACT INFORMATION

Brother
800-827-6843
www.brother.com

Hewlett-Packard
800-752-0900
www.hp.com

NEC
800-632-4636
www.nec.com

Panasonic
800-742-8086
www.panasonic.com

PRINTERS, MONOCHROMES

FOR WORKGROUPS

Workgroup printers are laser printers that are designed to work on a network, either attached to one computer or directly by cable to the network. These printers create high-resolution black-and-white output using a laser beam to produce an image of a page on an internal drum. A type of black ink called "toner" is then transferred to the drum and fused with heat and pressure onto the paper. They are quiet in operation due to the nonimpact nature of the mechanisms involved. These printers tend to cost more than personal laser printers but they are more economical than getting a laser printer for each person's desk.

An important thing to know about a laser printer is the resolution, or how many dots per inch (DPI) of toner is applied to print your page. Some printers can range from 300 DPI at the low end to 1,200 DPI at the high end, or print at various levels in-beween to print economically in draft mode. High-resolution graphics will also require a lot of printer memory (RAM). A full-page graphic at 600 DPI may require 4MB of RAM to function correctly; however, some printers overcome this with internal software.

Another consideration is speed, or how many pages-per-minute will come out of the printer at high quality. In three-five person networked office environments, 12 pages-per-minute is adequate, but if you have a larger network and need faster printing, higher-priced models are available.

Also find out about the input and output capacity and paper handling options. What size paper will it handle? How many pages of paper or envelopes can be ready for printing at one time? Are there multiple input trays for different paper sizes? Are these sources selected automatically or manually? Must you feed envelopes manually? Will the output be stacked in collated sequence? Is the paper path pretty straight to avoid damaging the paper or jamming the printer? Is there an automatic sensor on the paper input and output trays to tell you when they are empty or full?

Make sure the printer will work with your computers and network. What operating systems are supported with printer drivers? Does the interface card match the network you have installed? Must it be attached to the network server or can it stand alone on the network? Is there network management software or must you go to the printer to see what is happening?

Once you have some ideas as to your printer needs, there are several places to shop. Retail outlets will have printers you can try. Call the manufacturers and they will send you samples and literature and direct you to places where their printers can be purchased. For the higher-priced models, you can get a salesperson to come to your office. Mail-order houses also have these types of printers available to ship. Finally, there are outlets on the Internet where you can get information and place an order.

In this chapter, the focus is on laser printers costing under $4,000 with the following minimum configuration: 600 x 600 DPI resolution, 12 pages-per-minute or more, and a 250-page input tray with support for letter- to legal-sized paper. Data on these models was compiled from the manufacturers. Prices indicated are approximate "typical street prices" when the printers were reviewed.

The following list contains nine workgroup printers and their overall ratings.

OVERALL RATINGS

Lexmark Optra S 2450N	★ ★ ★ ★
Lexmark Optra N 245	★ ★ ★ ★
Xerox DocuPrint N24	★ ★ ★ 3/4
IBM Network Printer 24	★ ★ ★ 1/2
Okidata Okipage 16n	★ ★ ★ 1/4
Brother HL-1660N	★ ★ ★
HP LaserJet 4V	★ ★ ★
IBM Network Printer 12	★ ★ ★
NEC SuperScript 1260N	★ ★ 3/4

EXPLANATION OF RATINGS

Laser printers were selected for review from currently available products that met the configuration minimums listed earlier in this review. The overall rating was arrived at by giving individual scores on print quality, performance, features, and support (including warranty). These scores were then averaged to arrive at the overall rating. The highest rating possible is four stars.

Other factors to consider when purchasing a network laser printer include the following:

Cost of Operation can vary greatly and may over several years be more than the initial purchase price of your printer! Many manufacturers will state a "cents-per-page" amount, which should range from about two to five cents in this printer range. If this is not available, find out how much the consumables will be and how often they will need to be replaced. Usually the toner cartridge and internal drum are sold separately and last different numbers of pages, but be careful if the toner and drum are combined to make sure the cost is not exorbitant.

Overall Size is often much larger than the stated "footprint." Input and output trays must be accessible, and in some cases unfold when in use.

Upgradeability may be important if your printing needs are growing. Additional input trays, more RAM memory, and font cartridges will extend the printer's use, but they are not able to print any faster than their rated pages-per-minute speed. Also in this category of printers you can find options for offline multiple copies, automatic duplex printing, collating, stapling, offsetting of print jobs in the output tray, and even multiple output destination "mail boxes"! Network printing can be enhanced with optional hard drives to contain fonts and software.

Durability is expressed as a "monthly duty cycle," or the number of pages the manufacturer expects you to print in one month. Printers in this group should be rated for 10,000 to 100,000 pages per month. If your needs exceed the printer's level, your printer is more likely to break down early in its lifetime.

Software can range from simply including the printer drivers to elaborate suites of programs for printing. Network management software is important to let remote users check on their output status and alert the users to printer errors or paper-out conditions. And sometimes the software is just "demonstration" level and not able to be used. Today's hot software is "Internet-related" and may not even be of interest to you.

ALPHABETICAL DESCRIPTIONS

Brother HL-1660N

Price	$ 1,525
Overall Rating	★★★
Quality	★★★★
Speed	★★★ 1/2
Features	★★ 1/2
Support	★★

The Brother HL-1660N has excellent print quality with up to 1200x600 DPI true graphics resolution and up to 256 shades of grey. It also has a very straight paper path that reduces the curl for paper and "scrunching" of envelopes, and also reduces the frequency of paper jams. This printer is rated at 16 pages-per-minute with 4 MB RAM expandable to 66 MB with standard SIMMs. Features include both 500- and 150-sheet input trays with

options to a total of 1,150 sheets on-line, a 250-sheet output tray, 6,000-page toner cartridge, and modes to save toner and "tile" pages two or four to a physical page. An optional IC Card slot accepts Flash Memory cards or hard drives. Networking is supported by both 10BaseT and 10Base2 connections and simultaneous multple LAN protocol support for IPX/SPX with NDS, TCP/IP, and EtherTalk Phase II. Network operating systems supported include Novell (2.x, 3.x, and 4.x), Unix, Windows NT, OS/2 Warp Connect, Apple Macintosh AppleShare, SCO Xenix, and others through TCP/IP. Workstations can be attached with Windows (3.x, 95, NT) and Apple Macintosh through Network OS Client Support or TCP/IP applications. Software includes drivers and network management with NIManage. Support is available by phone on weekdays only and the warranty is for one- year. Their Internet site has useful information and drivers available for download.

HP LaserJet 4V

Price	$1,750
Overall Rating	★★★
Quality	★★★ 1/4
Speed	★★★ 1/2
Features	★★ 1/2
Support	★★ 3/4

The HP LaserJet 4V has good print quality for text but only has 120 levels of grey, which lowers the quality of graphics output. It is rated at 16 pages-per-minute and comes standard with 4MB of RAM expandable to 68MB with standard SIMMs. Features include a 250-sheet input tray with two cassettes for different paper sizes, a 100-sheet multipurpose tray, and a 250-collated output sheet tray, a toner cartridge, and an economy mode to save toner. Paper capacity maxes out at 850 sheets on-line with an optional 500-sheet tray. An MIO slot can have either the HP JetDirect network interface card or other third-party connections. Software includes drivers and HP network management utilities. Support is available by phone on 6 AM to 10 PM weekdays and 9 AM to 4 PM Saturdays (Mountain time). The warranty is for one year. Their Internet site has useful information and drivers available for download.

IBM Network Printer 12

Price $1,300	
Overall Rating	★ ★ ★
Quality	★ ★ ★ 1/2
Speed	★ ★ ★
Features	★ ★ 1/2
Support	★ ★ 3/4

The IBM Network Printer 12 has very good output quality. It is rated at 12-pages-per-minute and comes standard with 4MB of RAM expandable to 66MB. Accessories include a 250 sheet input tray and 80-sheet multipurpose tray, a 250 sheet output tray collated, and a toner cartridge for 6,000 pages. Options include a 500-sheet paper tray and a drawer for envelopes, flash memory for fonts, an 810MB hard drive, a duplexing unit, and various network cards. Network support is provided for both PC and Macintosh computers with Ethernet, Token-Ring, Coax or Twinax interface cards. Software includes drivers for Windows (3.x, 95, and NT), OS/2, and AIX, and a network printer manager. Support is available by phone 24 hours a day every day. The warranty is for one year with customer mail-in or drop off, upgradeable to on-site service. Their Internet site has a lot of useful information and drivers available for download

IBM Network Printer 24

Price $3,000	
Overall Rating	★ ★ ★ 1/2
Quality	★ ★ ★ 3/4
Speed	★ ★ ★ 3/4
Features	★ ★ ★ 1/2
Support	★ ★ ★ 1/4

The IBM Network Printer 24 also has very good output quality. It is rated at 24 pages-per-minute and comes standard with 4MB of RAM expandable to 68MB. Accessories include two 500-sheet input trays and a 100-sheet multipurpose tray, a 500 sheet output tray collated, and a toner cartridge for 15,000 pages. Options include a 2,000-sheet paper tray and a feeder for 100 envelopes, a three-bin 2,000 sheet stacker with stapler, flash memory for fonts, an 810MB hard drive, a duplexing unit, and various network cards. Network support is provided for both PC and Macintosh computers with two slots for Ethernet, Token-Ring, Coax or Twinax interface cards. Software includes drivers for Windows (3.x, 95, and NT), OS/2, and AIX, and a network printer manager. Support is available by phone 24 hours a day every day. The warranty is for one year on-site service. Their Internet site has a lot of useful information and drivers available for download

Lexmark Optra N 245

Price $4,000	
Overall Rating	★★★★
Quality	★★★ 3/4
Speed	★★★★
Features	★★★★
Support	★★★★

The Lexmark line of printers are solid, well-designed printers with great print quality. This printer is rated at 24 pages per minute (13 ppm on large paper) and comes with 16MB of RAM expandable to 64MB. Features include two 500-sheet input trays, a 100-sheet multipurpose tray, and a 500-sheet output tray collated, and a 15,000 page toner cartridge. Options include a 2,000-sheet input drawer, 100-envelope feeder, duplexer, flash memory for fonts, and hard drives. Networking is supported by a standard Ethernet 10BaseT/10Base2 interface and supports all major client and network operating systems. Software includes drivers for Windows (3.x,95,NT), OS/2, and AIX, and a remarkable network manager called MarkVision which is the most comprehensive network management tool we found. Support is available by phone 24 hours a day every day. The warranty is for one year "LexOnSite" on-site service. Their Internet site has much useful information and drivers available for download and an "Assistant" question-and-answer troubleshooting tool.

Lexmark Optra S 2450N

Price $4,000	
Overall Rating	★★★★
Quality	★★★★
Speed	★★★★
Features	★★★★
Support	★★★★

The Lexmark Optra S 2450N is one of the best. This printer is rated at 24 pages per minute (12 ppm at 1200x1200 DPI) and comes with 12MB of RAM expandable to 132MB. Features include two 500-sheet input trays, a 250-sheet multipurpose tray, and a 500 sheet output tray collated, and a 17,600-page toner cartridge. Options include a 2,000 sheet input capacity, up to three 500-sheet output stackers, a high-capacity mailbox/finisher with ten 200-sheet mailboxes and a 500-sheet bin, 85 envelope feeder, duplexer, flash memory for fonts, and hard drives. Networking is supported by a standard Ethernet 100BaseT/10BaseT/10Base2 interface and supports all major client and network operating systems. Software includes drivers for Windows (3.x, 95, and NT), OS/2, and AIX, and MarkVision, which is the most comprehensive network management tool we found.. Support is available by phone 24 hours a day every day. The warranty is for one year "LexOnSite" on-site service, which can be expanded to four years. Their Internet site has much useful information and drivers available for download and an "Assistant" question-and-answer troubleshooting tool.

NEC SuperScript 1260N

Price $1,050	
Overall Rating	★★ 3/4
Quality	★★★
Speed	★★★
Features	★★ 1/4
Support	★★ 1/2

The NEC SuperScript 1260N has good text printing quality but graphics are impacted by limit of 124 grey shades. It is rated at 12 pages per minute and comes with 2MB RAM expandable to 16MB with standard SIMMs. Features include a 250-sheet input tray, an 80-sheet multi-purpose tray, a 250-page output tray collated, and a toner cartridge for 6,000 pages. Special printing features include watermarks, two-sided manual, proof-sheet tiling, booklet, poster, and photo-copy-ready printing. Options include a 500-sheet input tray, 50-envelope cassette, and various other cassettes for different paper sizes. It comes network ready with a network interface card for Ethernet 10BaseT. Software includes drivers for Windows (3.x, 95, and NT) and Mac OS, a Solutions CD with drivers, a status monitor, and other packages from Adove. Support is available by phone 12 hours a day weekdays. The warranty is for one year which can be extended. Their Internet site has information and drivers available for download but it is difficult to find what you want.

Okidata Okipage 16n

Price $1,000	
Overall Rating	★ ★ ★ 1/4
Quality	★ ★ ★
Speed	★ ★ ★ 1/4
Features	★ ★ ★ 1/4
Support	★ ★ ★ 1/4

The Okidata Okipage 16n has an LED print engine instead of a laser and it is rated at 16 pages per minute. It is the least expensive of the printers we reviewed in the initial purchase price, but it may cost more to operate than others with higher capacity. The printer comes standard with 2MB of RAM expandable to 66MB. Features include a 500-sheet input tray, 250-sheet output tray collated, a 100 sheet output tray for uncollated output, and a 5,000-page toner cartridge. Networking is supported with an OKI HSP interface with OKILAN Ethernet or Token-Ring card. Software includes the OkiView Network Software monitor and drivers for Windows (3.x, 95, and NT). Support is available weekdays by phone and the warranty is for one year on-site for the unit and five years on the LED printhead. Their Internet site contains information and drivers, but it is not as comprehensive as others we reviewed.

Xerox DocuPrint N24

Price $2,800	
Overall Rating	★ ★ ★ 3/4
Quality	★ ★ ★ 1/2
Speed	★ ★ ★ ★
Features	★ ★ ★ ★
Support	★ ★ ★ 1/2

The Xerox DocuPrint N24 came in second overall to the printers from Lexmark with lower ratings in quality and support, but very much lower. And the price is less, so it deserves a good look. It is rated at 24 pages per minute and comes with 12MB RAM upgradeable to 128MB. Features include two 500-sheet input trays, a 50-sheet bypass feeder for envelopes and other page sizes, a 500-sheet output tray collated, 200-page output tray face-up, and a 23,000 page toner cartridge. Options include a 2,500-sheet feeder, 100 envelope feeder, 2,000-sheet output finisher/stapler with three bins, a 10-bin mailbox with 100 sheets per bin, and a duplexing unit. Network support is Ethernet 10Base2 and 10BaseT built into the printer and other options with interface cards. Network protocols include IPX/SPX, TCP/IP, DLC/LLC, NetBEUI, and AppleTalk. Software drivers are provided for Novell Netware, Windows (3.11, 95, and NT), OS/2, UNIX, and System 6 and 7 for the Mac. Extensive network and printer management software is included. Support is available by phone every day. The "Xerox Total Satisfaction Guarantee" warranty is for three years—they will replace the printer if you are not totally satisfied. We found their Internet site disappointingly slow and hard to use.

CONTACT INFORMATION

Brother Industries Ltd.
800-827-6843
www.brother.com

Hewlett-Packard Corporation
800-752-0900
www.hp.com

IBM Printing Systems Company
800-358-6661
www.printers.ibm.com

Lexmark International, Inc.
800-LEXMARK
www.lexmark.com

NEC USA, Inc.
800-632-4636
www.nec.com

Okidata, Division of Oki America, Inc.
800-654-3282
www.okidata.com

Xerox Corporation
800-34-XEROX
www.xerox.com

PRINTERS, INKJETS

If you're looking to add color to your documents without spending thousands of dollars, consider buying an inkjet printer. These non-impact printers are a low-cost alternative to laser printers. Images are created by spraying ink from a matrix of tiny jets. The output can sometimes be as good as laser output. Inkjets vary in their resolution, and their print quality. There are two types of inkjets: Three-color—CMY (cyan, magenta, and yellow)— and four color—CMYK (cyan, magenta, yellow, and black). Three-color inkjets costs less and come with a color cartridge and a black cartridge which are switched when you are printing black only or color only. In color documents the three-color printer combines these colors to produce black. Print quality for these printers are not the best. Four-color printers have one black cartridge that remains in the printer for both monochrome and color documents. Four-color printers cost a bit more, but produce better quality color and monochrome documents. The resolution of an inkjet printer affects its output. The higher the resolution the better quality image it produces. Inkjets have resolutions that

The Epson Stylus Color 800, the top-rated inkjet, offers photorealistic output at 1,400 dpi and prints seven pages per minute.

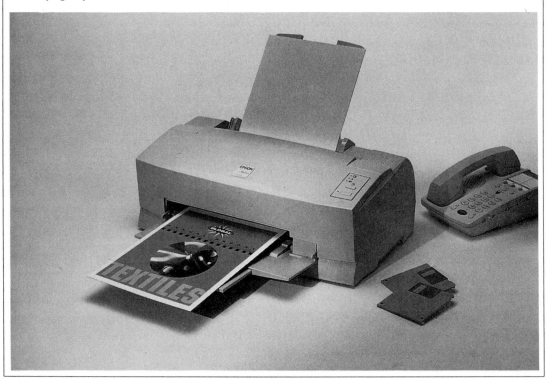

range from 300 by 300 dots per inch (dpi) to 1,400 by 720 dpi.

Following are several four-color inkjet printers with resolutions over 300 dpi. Specifications for each printer were compiled from the manufacturer. Below is the overall rating for each inkjet printer.

OVERALL RATINGS

Epson Stylus Color 800	★★★★
Lexmark 7000 Color Jetprinter	★★★
Epson Stylus Color 600	★★★
HP DeskJet 870 Cse	★★★
Canon BJC 4550	★★★
HP DeskJet 694C	★★★
Canon BJC 620	★★ 1/2
Lexmark 2055 Color Jetprinter	★★1/2
OKIJET 2010	★★

EXPLANATION OF RATINGS

Each printer is rated for Print Quality, which accounts for 50% of the overall score; Speed, 25%; Printing Costs, 15%; Bundled Software that comes with the unit, 5%; and cost to operate, 5%. The highest rating for each category is four stars, the lowest, one.

Canon BJC 620

Price $399	
Overall Rating ★★1/2	
Printing Costs ★★★	
Price ★★★	
Print Quality ★★★ 1/2	
Speed ★	

Bundled Software ★★★★

The Canon BJC-620 produces photographic color output at a resolution of 720 x 720 dpi. This printer is specially designed for Windows and it's easy to setup and use. Even though the BJC-620 produces top-notch color output it only prints in color at 1.7 pages per minute. Black and white is faster at a speed of three pages per minute. The built-in sheet feeder holds up to 100 sheets of paper. An inkjet cartridge can produce 600 monochrome pages but only 53 color pages. Monochrome ink cartridges cost around $12, single-color ink cartridges costs $8. The cost per page for monochrome is two cents and color pages seven cents. All printer functions are controlled through the Microsoft Windows Printing system. This system allows you to control print jobs and find out how long a document will take to print. An added plus for this printer is the free Canon Creative 2 CD which includes programs that can help you enhance and color correct images and design professional quality business documents. Also included is a collection of hundreds of fonts, images, borders, and clip art. The CD also has programs to help you with printer operations and troubleshooting; The Visual Guide is an on-screen reference tool and Super Solver is an interactive printer troubleshooting program.

Canon BJC 4550

Price $499	
Overall Rating ★★★	
Printing Costs ★★	
Price ★★★	
Print Quality ★★★ 1/2	

Speed ★★ 1/2

Bundled Software ★★★★

This is a two-cartridge printer with a dual interface for either a Windows or Macintosh computer. It produces crisp documents with a resolution of 720 by 360dpi. Near photo-realistic color images can be produced with the printer's optional Photo Kit. It can print paper up to 11 x 17 inches and optional Neon Ink cartridges and Adobe Postscript Level 2 software can be used to create more dramatic documents. Even though print quality is high, the printer's performance is basically low because of its slow printing speed. Black text is printed at a rate of five pages per minute while color clocks in at one page per minute. You can produce 900 pages per ink unit for monochrome and 200 for color. Cartridges cost approximately $35 for black and white and $50 for a multiple color cartridge. Cost of printing varies with monochrome costing around four cents per page and color 14 cents per page. A few minor drawbacks are the output tray is not long enough to hold paper, status of print jobs are not displayed, and the system does not warn you when the ink cartridges are empty. It comes with a bundle of software on the Canon Creative CD-ROM, full technical support and an InstantExchange warranty.

Epson Stylus Color 600

Price $299

Overall Rating ★★★

Printing Costs ★★★

Price ★★★★

Print Quality ★★★★

Speed ★★

Bundled Software ★★★★

Compatible for both Macintosh and Windows computers, this dual-cartridge printer produces high-resolution color documents at 1,440 by 720 dpi. Special paper is required for this resolution and printing time is slow, but the results are top-notch. Photo Quality color printing is built in so no add-on is needed. Print speed is more dependent on the speed of your computer is. The manufacturers specified speeds are four pages per minute for monochrome while color prints at three pages per minute. Setup is quick and easy with the Quick Setup Guide and the well thought-out users manual. The LED panel on the front of the printer tells you when the ink cartridge is low. Ink cartridges cost $24 for black and white and $29 for color. Ink cartridges can produces 540 monochrome pages and 300 color pages. Cost per page is six cents for monochrome and eight cents for color. Bundled software includes the Look Your Best Color Pak which features software from Adobe, Sierra On-Line, high resolution photos, fonts, paper and more.

Epson Stylus Color 800

Overall Rating ★★★★

Price $499

Printing Costs ★★★★

Price ★★★

Print Quality ★★★★

Speed ★★★★

Bundled Software ★★★★

This printer offers photorealistic output at 1,400 dpi at a rate of seven pages per minute. It features a Micro Piezo print technology that produces finely detailed output. For best results special paper is needed for printing. Its dual interface makes it compatible for both Windows and Macintosh computers and can support both Ethernet and LocalTalk networks. Easy to set up and use, the LED panel tells you when your ink cartridges are low on ink. This is a dual-cartridge printer that holds both black and color cartridges, but the black cartridge is smaller and will run out of ink quickly. The driver software lets you monitor and control your print jobs easily. Printing speeds are eight papers per minute for monochrome with 7 pages per minute for color. Number of pages printed per ink unit are 900 for monochrome and 150 for color. Cost per page for monochrome is three cents and four cents per page for color. Each ink cartridge costs $29 for both black and color. Bundled software includes the Look Your Best Color Pak which features software, fonts, paper, and more. This printer cost a bit more than others but the quality of printed documents is first-class.

HP DeskJet 694C

Price $299	
Overall Rating ★★★	
Printing Costs ★★★	
Price ★★★★	
Print Quality ★★★	
Speed ★★1/2	
Bundled Software ★★★★	

The HP DeskJet 694C is a photo-quality printer capable of producing high-quality but expensive documents. The printer uses six colors instead of four which makes document better looking. The HP snap-in Photo Cartridge is included along

with HP's Photo Project CD. The Photo cartridge works with the color cartridge to produce photo-quality images. It prints at a resolution of 600 x 600 dpi for monochrome and up to 600 x 300 dpi for color. Print speeds range from five pages per minute for color and up to 1.7 pages per minute for color. Ink cartridges can produce 650 monochrome pages and 157 color pages. Cost per page for monochrome is four cents and six cents for color. Cartridges cost $32 for black and $34 for color. It prints on all types of paper and has a continuous feed for banner printing. The bundled software along with a sample paper pack can help you create colorful brochures, labels, greeting cards and other documents that you may want to add a photograph to.

HP DeskJet 870Cse

Price $599	
Overall Rating ★★★	
Printing Costs ★★★	
Price ★★	
Print Quality ★★★	
Speed ★★★1/2	
Bundled Software ★★★★	

This is one of HP's Professional Series Printers. It offers a high-performance color printer designed for small businesses. Its dual interface makes it compatible with standalone DOS, Macintosh, and Windows computers or a workgroup. It prints at a resolution of 600 by 600 dpi for black text documents and 600 x 300 dpi for color. Using a 20-MHZ RISC processor it prints at a speed of eight pagers per minute for monochrome and four pages per minute for color. Ink cartridges cost

$32 for black and $35 for color. Ink cartridges can produce 650 monochrome pages and 350 color pages. Cost per page translates to approximately four cents for monochrome and six cents for color. As with other HP printers, installation and use is simple. It comes bundled with a variety of fonts and includes HP's From Start to Business Print Kit that includes business templates, a how-to guide, and a HP sample paper pack.

Lexmark 7000 Color Jetprinter

Price $499
Overall Rating ★★★
Printing Costs ★★
Price ★★★
Print Quality ★★★★
Speed ★★★1/2
Bundled Software ★

This is a solid printer which outputs a 1200 x 1200 dpi page for both black and color. It prints at speeds up to three pages per minute for color draft and eight pages per minute for black draft. The input tray can hold up to 150 sheets of paper or 50 labels or transparencies. There is an automatic envelope feeder. The printer accepts all type of papers including card stock, labels, envelopes, letter, legal, A4, and B5. The high-resolution ink cartridges cost $32.95 for black and $38.95 for color. There are standard ink cartridges that cost $31.99 for black and $36.99 for color. Monochrome cartridges have a nominal yield of 600 pages; color cartridges yield 200 pages. Cost per page for monochrome is three cents and cost per page for color is 19 cents. This price is based on the price of the standard ink cartridges. As with

other Lexmark products, this printer has a one-year next business day exchange warranty.

Lexmark 2055

Price $239
Overall Rating ★★1/2
Printing Costs ★★
Price ★★★★
Print Quality ★★★
Speed ★★
Bundled Software ★

The Lexmark 2055 offers laser quality performance at an inkjet price. It delivers clean and crisp black text and vibrant colors. This is a thermal inkjet with 600 x 600 dpi for both black and color. It prints at a speed of up to four pages per minute for black and one page per minute for color. The printer can handle all types of paper and has a 150 sheet input tray, 50-sheet label or transparency capacity, and manual envelope feeder. There are a variety of ink cartridges available for this printer. The Super Sharp Waterproof black ink cartridge costs $35.95; standard ink cartridges cost $34.95 for black, $37.95 for color. Cost per page for monochrome is three cents and color cost per page is 16 cents. These prices are based on the price for the standard ink cartridges. The unit is geared towards business and includes the Lexmark Workshop Deluxe CD-ROM for business. Among the many programs are: Peachtree First Accounting; Inc. Magazine BusinessPlan Pro; MarketingPlan Pro, Inc.; Business Resources; Sharkware Professional, which is a business development tool; Monotype Business FontPak; and EarthLink Network for Internet access. The printer comes with a one-year next business day and exchange warranty.

OKIJET 2010

Price $499

Overall Rating ★★

Printing Costs ★

Price ★

Print Quality ★★★

Speed ★

Bundled Software ★

The OKIJET 2010 is a dual-head, thermal inkjet printer. It prints at a resolution of 600 x 300 dpi in monochrome and black. Print-speed time clocks in at three pages per minute in black text and .025 pages per minute for color. One ink cartridge can produce 1,000 monochrome and 100 color pages. Ink cartridges cost $33 for black and $38 for color. Cost per page ranges from three cents for monochrome to an expensive 39 cents for color. The input tray holds up to 150 sheets and up to 15 envelopes. The printer comes with a standard two-year warranty. If you're planning to print mostly text documents this printer is a good bet, but if you need color capabilities on a regular basis it would not be cost-effective.

CONTACT LIST

Canon Corp.
(800) OK-CANON
www.canon.com

Epson
(800) GO-EPSON
www.epson.com

Hewlett-Packard
(800) 752-0900
415 857-1501
www.hp.com

Lexmark
(800) 539-6275
www.lexmark.com

Okidata
(800) OKI-Team extension 9
www.okidata.com

REMOVABLE STORAGE DEVICES

Removable storage lets you expand your storage capacity with add-on drives for your computer. These drives can be used to backup and store data. Removable storage hardware uses cartridges that are rewritable. These rewritable cartridges come in various sizes, from 100MB on up, and have differing formats which include zip disks, magneto-optical disks (MO), Winchester cartridges, and phase change rewritable.

Even though computers today come with large-capacity hard drives, the 1.44 MB floppy drive is still small in comparison. The need for large-capacity backup and storage capability is greater now because the computer's floppy drive capacity has not kept pace with the growth of hard drives. Also, today's software applications take up a lot of hard disk space; if you're into multimedia, graphics, sound, and video take up a lot of hard disk space.

What's the right removable storage drive for you? Selecting the right removable storage device really depends on your needs. It used to be this type of peripheral hardware was only used in certain professions like the graphic arts, but now almost everyone that uses a computer may find themselves needing one of these drives.

There are various technologies used in today's removable storage devices. The alphabetical reviews will discuss which ones are used in the devices reviewed here. Following is a brief summary of the technologies. A separate chapter in this volume, "CR-Rs," discusses and reviews CD-ROM recordable and rewritable drives which are close cousins to "PCRs," which are summarized below.

Zip Disks hold up to 100MB of information on a thin, film-like material. They're about 1/4 inch wider than a floppy disk and thicker and can hold 70 times more information than a floppy. Zip disks are rapidly becoming a standard. These disks offer good performance but are prone to damage due to dust particles.

Winchester Cartridges are essentially removable hard drives. They are not as speedy or inexpensive as hard drives but they offer portability, unlimited capacity, and better performance than other removable storage.

LS-120 Disks look like a 3.5-inch floppy disk but has 83 times the capacity and backward compatibility. However its performance is slow.

OR Technology a:drive indicates it has a 120MB capacity and can read and write 1.44MB floppy disks. It does not perform as well as other removable storage devices.

Magneto-optical Disks (MO) write data to an optical disk using both lasers and magnets. A laser heats a specific spot on the disk, then a magnetic head charges this spot, making it susceptible to its magnetic orientation changed by the read/write head. MO cartridges come in CD-ROM size 5 1/4-inch disks, which can store up to 2.6GB or 3.5-inch disks which store up to 640MB of data.

Phase Change Rewritable Disks (PCR) look like a CD-ROM in a caddy and has a 650MB data capacity. It utilizes lasers that heat spots on the disk in two states, amorphous (non-reflective) and crystalline (reflective), which in turn get interpreted by the PD drive as either one or zero binary information. This makes it immune to magnetic glitches. Phase change drives (PD) can read regular CD-ROMs and audio CDs at 4x speeds, but can't write on CD-Rs. The Phase Change rewritable disks can't be read by standard CD-ROM drives but are compatible with DVD technology. These disks are rugged and less susceptible to dust particles and their surfaces can be wiped off. One major drawback is the slow speed of these drives.

Below are various removable storage devices on the market. Information on these products was gathered from the manufacturers. The list below gives the overall ratings.

OVERALL RATINGS

Fujitsu DynaMo 640	★★★1/2
SyQuest SyJet	★★★1/2
Iomega Jaz Drive	★★★
Iomega Zip Drive	★★★
Olympus Sys.230	★★★
Pinnacle Micro Tahoe 640 MB	★★★
Pinnacle Micro Apex 4.6 GB	★★★
Nomai 540 MCD	★★1/2

Panasonic PD CD-ROM Drive	★★1/2
SyQuest EZFlyer 230MB	★★1/2

EXPLANATION OF RATINGS

Each device was rated on these features; Storage Capacity, Cost per MB, Speed, and Compatibility. Each category was given a one- to four-star rating. The overall rating was achieved by averaging the ratings in the four categories.

ALPHABETICAL DESCRIPTIONS

Fujitsu DynaMo 640

Price $659	
Rating ★★★1/2	
Capacity ★★★	
Cost per MB ★★★★	
Speed ★★★★	
Compatibility ★★★	

The Fujitsu DynaMo 640 is an external 640 magneto-optical (MO) drive, which uses LIMDOW (Light Intensity Modulation Direct Overwrite) technology. This technology overwrites at full speed in a single pass, instead of the two-pass method which is slower. The DynaMo uses 3.5 inch LIMDOW MO cartridges which sell for $45, or non-LIMDOW cartridges which cost $35 This converts to just below one cent per MB, which is a good price. You should use LIMDOW cartridges to take full advantage of this technology. Cartridges are not included with the drive. The DynaMo 640 is compatible with other 128MB, 230MB, and 540MB MO cartridges.

The DynaMo connects via a 50-pin Centronics SCSI-2 connection. An Adaptec AHA-2940UW SCSI adapter is needed to attach the drive to the computer. This adapter is additional. The data transfer rate is between 2.3 MB/sec and 3.9MB/sec. Seek time is 35ms and the buffer is 2 MB. Installation is simple. The DynaMo comes with a 50-pin-Centronics-to- 50-pin-Centronics SCSI cable, the FormatterOne Pro software for formatting cartridges for the Macintosh, Data Saver, a backup program for Windows 95, Windows 3.1, and Macintosh systems, and a one-year warranty.

Iomega Jaz Drive

Price $499 external version; $399 internal version

Rating ★ ★ ★

Capacity ★ ★ ★ ★

Cost per MB ★ ★ ★ ★

Speed ★ ★ ★ 1/2

Compatibility ★

The Jaz Drive offers fast performance and a large 1GB capacity. The 3.5-inch 1GB disks cost around $99, which give you a cost of around 10 cents per megabyte. The drive comes with installation software and Iomega Jaz Tools software on a 1GB Jaz disk, an external power supply, 50-pin high-density SCSI connector, a SCSI pass-through connector, a SCSI address switch, and a terminator resistor switch on the back. No blank cartridges are provided.

Installation is easy and the documentation is written in understandable English. Included with the installation software is the Guest 95 utility, which recognizes all Iomega SCSI products. Once installed you'll find the Jaz drive is an excellent performer averaging an overall through-

put of 872K/sec with write and read times transfer rates well over 1MB/sec and 2MB/sec. One drawback with this drive is it's only compatible with its own media and does not have a battery pack for portability. If you have large-capacity data needs, one of these drives will be worth the cost in the long run.

Iomega Zip

Price $199

Rating ★ ★ ★

Capacity ★ ★ ★

Cost per MB ★ ★ ★

Speed ★ ★ 1/2

Compatibility ★ ★ ★

For a more affordable removable storage option, the Iomega is fast becoming a standard that is vying to take the place of the standard 1.44MB floppy disk drive. Internal Zip drives are now being installed in new computers. The Zip drive disks are a little larger and thicker than the 1.44MB floppy and can hold up to 100MB of data, nearly 70 times more then the 1.44MB floppy. Each Zip disk costs around $19.95. This translates to a cost of 20 cents per megabyte which is a bit higher than other removable storage devices, but the overall price tag is lower. Each drive includes installation software, the Iomega Zip Tools, a 25-pin-D-sub-to-25-pin-D-sub cable and external power supply. No blank cartridges are included. The Zip drive is available in SCSI-2 or parallel port external versions. The SCSI card is not included with the Zip drive. Installation is easy, just plug it in, run the installation software, and you're up and running. The drive is designed to be stacked with other Zip drives or Jaz drives. The Zip drive is marketed as a floppy disk replacement and it does an admirable job in storing your data. If you do not require large-capacity storage the Zip drive offers solid performance.

Nomai 540MCD

Price $299 Mac; $299 (PC internal, SCSI); $359 (PC external, SCSI or parallel)

Rating ★★1/2

Capacity ★★★

Cost per MB ★★

Speed ★★★

Compatibility ★★

The Nomai 540MCD uses 540MB MCD (Multimedia Cartridge Drives) which cost $59 each, which translates to 11 cents per megabyte of storage. Nomai is based on the Winchester hard drive technology. This drive is bundled with a 50-pin, high-density-SCSI-to-50-pin Centronics cable, installation software, and a Adaptec AHA-1502B ISA SCSI board. It also includes a preformatted cartridge with an online MCD user manual, Adobe Acrobat reader, and Adaptec's EZ SCSI 4.0 Lite SCSI utilities. The power supply is built in. The external SCSI Nomai includes the SCSI card and cable. Installation is made simple with the manual's series of illustrations and, once installed, Windows 95 will recognize the drive so no software is needed. The 540MCD outperforms any CD- ROM drive. It has a verify-on-write feature that cannot be disabled. The 540MCD is an excellent performer with throughput times averaging 860K/sec. The drive can read and write on 3.5-inch 270MB disks and comes with a two-year warranty.

Olympus Sys.230

Price $299

Rating ★★★

Capacity ★★★

Cost per MB ★★★★

Speed ★★★

Compatibility ★

The Olympus Sys.230 is a magneto-optical drive which holds 230 MB of data. Each 230MB cartridge costs $10 bring the cost per MB to less than one cent. This is a fast magneto-optical device but it does not run as fast as a hard drive. The Sys.230 transfers data at a rate 27 percent faster than the Zip drive. Also, because it is an optical device, your data is a bit safer from those dust particles that can wreak havoc on a disk. One drawback is its compatibility. It is not as popular as the Zip drive and if you're planning to exchange data you may have a hard time if you use this format. However, if you don't have to be compatible with other users than the Sys.230 is a good choice.

Panasonic PD/CD-ROM Drive

Price $499.95 internal; $599.95 internal with SCSI card; $649.95 external

Rating ★★1/2

Capacity ★★★

Cost per MB ★★

Speed ★★

Compatibility ★★★

This device is both a four-speed CD-ROM as well as a phase change drive that can read and write to 650MB optical disks. The internal drive sells for $499.95, a drive with a 16-bit SCSI drive sells for $599.95, and an external drive costs

$649.95. The 650MB optical cartridges cost around $50, giving you eight cents per megabyte. These optical disks are very durable and not as susceptible to dust and other debris. Cartridges the Panasonic PD writes can only be read by other PD drives, not CD-ROM drives. They are also compatible with DVD drives. Applications can be run directly from these disks because it uses the same hard-drive style random access. It's one of the fastest PDs with an average write rate of 426K/sec, but other media types, especially Winchester cartridges, are faster.

Pinnacle Micro Tahoe 640 MB

Price $699 internal; $799 external

Rating ★★★

Capacity ★★★

Cost per MB ★★

Speed ★★★

Compatibility ★★★

The Pinnacle Micro Tahoe 640 is a magneto-optical drive with a capacity of 640MB. Cartridges cost around $50, which gives you a cost of eight cents per megabyte. The device comes with a 28-inch, 50-pin SCSI cable, Disc Archive 95, a Windows 95 and NT backup utility and a one-year parts and labor warranty. You have to buy a SCSI card.

Pinnacle claims faster speed time than a real-world test showed. The manufacturer states that maximum read data transfer rates are 3.07MB per second and write rates are 1.07MB per second. The Tahoe's cartridges are backward compatible with 128MB and 230MB MO media.

Pinnacle Micro Apex 4.6GB

Price $1,895 internal; 1,995 external

Rating ★★★

Capacity ★★★★

Cost per MB ★★★

Speed ★★

Compatibility ★★★

For those of us who are hard-disk hogs and are always looking for more space, look no further. The Apex 4.6GB is a magneto-optical drive that can fulfill your large-capacity storage needs, but not at a low price. For the cost of an average computer this drive can store up to 4.6GB of data. All of this space is not accessed at once. Each side of the optical disks has 2.3GB of storage on it. You'll have to flip the disk to obtain data stored on each side. The drive uses proprietary 4.6GB optical disks but is backward compatible with 2.6GB MO disks. These disks cost around $169, giving you a low 3.76 cents per megabyte. The Apex has a fast read data rate of 5.5MB/second and write rate of 445K/second. This device is more for the user who has massive data to store and backup. If you want fast and efficient storage and backups, this optical disk technology can deliver it—if you can afford it.

SyQuest EZFlyer 230MB

Price $294

Rating ★★1/2

Capacity ★★★

Cost per MB ★★

Speed ★★★

Compatibility ★★

The EZFlyer uses 230MB cartridges and can read, write, and format SyQuest's 135MB cartridges. Storage costs around 14 cents per megabyte, with each cartridge costing around $32. The EZFlyer is similar to the Iomega Zip drive in design but its performance is not up to par with Iomega's Jaz mechanisms. The EZFlyer 230 comes in three flavors, all for the same price: parallel-port and SCSI versions with either a small SCSI-2 connector or 25-pin connector, which can be used with both PCs and Macs.

The drive comes bundled with a SCSI cable, power supply, installation software, and bonus software. The bonus software includes SyQuest utilities for controlling, formatting, and write-protecting cartridges; SyBack for compressed hard-drive backups and restores; the Triazzle puzzle; and Zip Zap, an online guide for finding Zip and area codes. The EZFlyer is not in the same performance class as the SyJet or Jaz drive, but it is speedier than the Zip drive.

SyQuest SyJet

Price $500 external SCSI; 530 external parallel

Rating ★ ★ ★ 1/2

Capacity ★ ★ ★

Cost per MB ★ ★

Speed ★ ★ ★

Compatibility ★ ★

The SyJet drive is targeted toward professionals in the design and publishing business. The SyJet offers storage of 1.5 GB with cartridges costing $125, which makes the price per megabyte around eight cents. It comes in an external SCSI versions and a parallel port version for $30 more.

The SyJet offers 50 percent more capacity than the Jaz drive and has similar performance. The device comes with cables, installation software, SyQuest utilities, SyBack backup program, and bonus software that includes Alta Vista Technology's Howdy!, which can create multimedia postcards; Zip Zap, a city guide; and Triazzle, a brain teaser. It has a minimum 3.7MB/sec transfer rate and 512k cache, which gives it optimal performance with multimedia applications.

CONTACT INFORMATION

Fujitsu Computer Products of America
(800) 626-4686
(408) 432-6333
www.fujitsu.com

Iomega Corp.
(800) 697-8833
(801) 778-1000
www.iomega.com

Nomai USA
(800) 556-6624
(561) 367-1216
www.nomai.com

Olympus
(800) 347-4027
(516) 844-5000
www.olympus.com

Panasonic Communications and Systems Co.
(800) 742-8086
(210) 348-7000
www.panasonic.com

Pinnacle Micro
(800) 553-7070
(714) 789-3000
www.pinnacle.com

SyQuest Technology
(800) 245-2278
(510) 226-4000
www.syquest.com

SCANNERS, COLOR FLATBEDS

Scanners were once only used by people in specialized fields such as graphic arts or for converting paper documents into digital files. Now, scanners are more a necessary computer peripheral rather than a luxury, giving the user the ability to capture full-color images for use on a web page, desktop publishing application, or multimedia project. This review took a look at color flatbed scanners that are capable of outputting files at high resolutions, ranging from 1,200 to 9,600 dpi (dots per inch).

It should be noted that the scanners reviewed here actually scan at either 300 dpi or 600 dpi; however, due to "interpolation," which is simply a built-in software application, they can simulate higher resolutions when they output files. Unless it's noted otherwise, when the dpi is quoted as a single figure (i.e. 600 dpi), it means the machine scans 600 x 600 dpi (the former figure pertains to horizontal width; the latter to vertical depth). Some more expensive machines scan at 600 dpi horizontally and 1,200 dpi vertically, which is

The Microtek ScanMaker E6, the top-rated flatbed scanner, is a 30-bit single-pass flatbed, with a resolution of 600 by 1,200. Its optimized color palette has 1.07 billion colors.

explained below. On these machines, a full-length (8 1/2" x 11") document scans the full 600 x 1,200 dpi and some of these units interpolate to as high as 9,600 dpi. The less-expensive units scan at only 300 x 300 dpi, and can interpolate to only 1,200 dpi. In sum, what this means is a 300 dpi scanner can give you reasonably high output resolution due to the miracle of interpolation; however, if you're scanning a large document, the output will not result in a high resolution image. On the other hand, a more expensive unit that scans at 600 x 600 dpi or 600 x 1,200 dpi and can interpolate to between 4,800 to 9,600 dpi, will therefore provide a higher resolution output of a large document.

What should you look for in a good scanner? Of course, image quality would be the number-one consideration, along with speed and price. Scanners perform in either a single-pass or three-pass scan. A single-pass scanner works more quickly than a three-pass and will suffice for most jobs. Consider the scanner's color depth, optical resolution. Scanner's color depths vary from 24-bit color (true color) to 36-bit color. For higher-resolution images such as transparency and photos, a resolution higher than 600 dpi should be used. A scanner with 24-bit color will suffice for most tasks. A 30- to 36-bit color is only necessary if you are scanning slides or transparencies or producing output for a graphics house. The alphabetical reviews discuss which scanners have these various specifications.

RANKINGS AND OVERALL SCORES

1	Microtek ScanMaker E6	93.8
2	Epson Expression 636 Pro	87.5
3	UMAX Vista-S12	81.3
4	Nikon Scantouch 210	81.2
5	PacificImage Electronics ScanAce III	78.2
6	HP ScanJet 4c	78.1
7	Plustek OpticPro 4800P	72.5
8	Ricoh FS2	75.0
9	Info Peripherals Image-Reader FB	73.5
10	Mustek Paragon 600 II sp	72.5

EXPLANATION OF RATINGS

These products were rated on Image Quality, Price, and Features. Image quality counted for 50% of the total score. The price factor in the ratings relates to "bang for the buck"; that is, how much you really get relative to what an average scanner offers. This is why some 300 dpi scanners rated higher than a few 600 dpi ones.

ALPHABETICAL DESCRIPTIONS

Epson Expression 636 Pro

Price $1,800

Rank 2

Image Quality 50

Price 12.5

Features 25

The Epson Expression 636 Pro offers 36-bit color scanning with a resolution of 600 x 1,200 dpi with interpolation up to 4,800.

A transparency adapter is included along with a SCSI cable. OCR software packages included are TextBridge Pro, Presto!, PageManager LE, and e.Paper Document Management and Archival Suite. Other bundled software includes Adobe Photoshop, Claris Home Page, Kai's Power Tools, and EPSON scanning utilities. Image resolution is good. The Expressions Twain driver limits image adjustment to the master RGB channel instead of the individual RGB channels like other Twain drivers do. Epson offers this scanner in three models, the $900 Executive Model, the $1,300 Artists Model, and the model reviewed here which is the Professional Model. The difference between the three is the depth of the bundled software packages and the optional transparency adapter, which is included only with the Professional Model.

HP ScanJet 4c

Price $900	
Rank 6	
Image Quality 50	
Price 15.6	
Features 12.5	

The HP ScanJet 4C is a higher-end flatbed scanner for business users. It has a 30-bit color depth with a 600 dpi optical resolution, interpolated to 2,400 dpi. The scanner can accept documents up to 8.5 x 14 inches. Additional options include a $759 transparency adapter and a $559 fifty-sheet document feeder. Software includes Corel Photo-Paint Select, OmniPage LE, and PaperPort. Image quality is very good; this scanner is good for scanning line-art and OCR tasks. The 4c is ex-

tremely easy to use and adjustments are made automatically. Hewlett Packard offers a one-year parts and labor warranty, but support is not toll free, and waiting time can be considerable.

Info Peripherals Image-Reader FB

Price $330	
Rank 9	
Image Quality 36	
Price 25	
Features 12.5	

The Info Peripherals ImageReader FB is a light-duty flatbed scanner that's good for light photo scanning, line art scans, OCR tasks, copying, or faxing. Resolution for this 300 dpi scanner was better than the other similar models. The ImageReader FB has a 30-bit color depth with a 300 dpi resolution interpolated to 2,400 dpi. Additional options include a $199 transparency adapter and a $349 fifty-sheet document feeder. Bundled software includes Image Pals 2 Go! image editing software plus OCR software Info-Center and Recognita 3.5. Warranty is for two years, parts and labor. Toll-free technical support is available Monday through Friday.

Microtek ScanMaker E6

Price $559; Standard version $299	
Rank 1	
Image Quality 50	
Price 25	
Features 18.8	

The Microtek ScanMaker E6 is a 30-bit single-pass flatbed scanner, with a resolution of 600 by 1,200. Its optimized color palette has 1.07 billion colors optimized to 16.7 million colors and 1,024 shades of gray optimized to 256 shades. This scanner is available in a Pro or standard package. Features in the E6 Pro package include Adobe Photoshop full version; Xerox TextBridge Pro; Adobe Acrobat Reader; and Microtek ScanWizard.

Features in the standard package include Ulead PhotoImpact full version; Ulead ImagePals 2 Go!; Caere OmniPage Limited Edition; Adobe Acrobat Reader, and Microtek ScanWizard. Add-on options include a transparency adapter for $299 and a $400 fifty-sheet document feeder. The ScanMaker E6 is good for OCR because of its excellent resolution quality. Color-image quality is tops. There are also verions of this scanner for the Macintosh. Warranty covers parts and labor for one year. Technical support is not toll free and is available only Monday through Friday.

Mustek Paragon 600 II sp

Price $300	
Rank 9	
Image Quality 35	
Price 25	
Features 12.5	

The Mustek Paragon 600 II sp is a light-duty scanner for the SOHO market. This 24-bit color has a 300 dpi color depth, interpolated to 4,800 dpi. Image quality is adequate. Bundled software includes Micrografx Picture Publisher 5.0 and 6.0 and OCR software TextBridge. Options include a $199 transparency adapter and a $199 twenty-five-sheet document feeder. This low-cost scanner is lacking in some areas. It only has one zoom level so if you use the Twain driver to scan just a part of an image it is difficult to correctly select the portion you want to scan. Settings are also not remembered when zooming in and out. Also, adjusting interpolation resolutions is bothersome. Color scans were good. Mustek offers a two-year parts and labor warranty but support is not toll free. Support is available Monday through Friday.

Nikon Scantouch 210

Price $730	
Rank 4	
Image Quality 50	
Price 15.6	
Features 15.6	

The Nikon Scantouch 210 is a single-pass higher-end scanner with 24-bit color and a 600 dpi resolution, interpolated to 9,600 dpi. The Scantouch 210 is great for line art and OCR because its resolution quality is excellent—one of the best in the group. Image quality was about average with good color saturation and accuracy. Software includes Adobe Photoshop LE and OmniPage LE. Additional options are a $499 transparency adapter and a $595 fifty-sheet document feeder. The scanner is covered by a one-year parts and labor warranty. Support is available Monday through Friday but it's not toll free.

PacificImage Electronics ScanAce III

Price $900	
Rank 5	
Image Quality 43.8	
Price 15.6	
Features 18.8	

The PacificImage ScanAce III is designed to compete with the HP ScanJet 4c. This single-pass scanner has a 36-bit color depth with a 600-dpi resolution, interpolated to 9,600. Resolution quality was good. The scanner bed can accept documents up to 8.5 x 14 inches. Options include a $379 transparency adapter and a 50-sheet document feeder for $329. Software includes Adobe Photoshop, Image Pals 2 GO!, and Textbridge. Installation and use are simple. The scanner's bundled software, CyberView, lets you scan different areas of an image in only one scan. Zoom levels are unlimited and you can preview scans or portions of scans. It's covered by a two-year parts and labor warranty. Toll-free technical support is available Monday though Friday.

Plustek OpticPro 4800P

Price $299	
Rank 9	
Image Quality 35	
Price 25	
Features 12.5	

The Plustek OpticPro 4800P is a low-priced, 24-bit color scanner with a 300-dpi optical resolution, interpolated to 4,800. No transparency adapter or document sheet feeder is available for this model. Software includes Image-in for image editing, Recognita for OCR, and Action Manager. There are no zoom levels so selecting portions of scans will be difficult. Documents up to 8.5 x 11.7 inches can be scanned. This scanner does not use a SCSI card, but connects right into the computer's EPP parallel port, which makes setup a breeze. Color-image qual-

ity is average. There are other low-cost scanners that can give you better image quality than the OpticPro. The one-year warranty covers parts and labor. Technical support is toll free from Monday through Friday.

Ricoh FS2

Price $2,500	
Rank 7	
Image Quality 37.5	
Price 12.5	
Features 25	

The Ricoh F2 is the most expensive scanner in this group. Though this heavy-duty scanner does not interpolate (unless you purchase separate software and run the application on your computer), its combination of a 600 x 1,200 dpi scan and 30-bit color depth, produces a very high resolution image and interpolation might not be necessary, as it would be in a unit that does not have these high-end specifications. A transparency adapter and 30-sheet document feeder are included. The scanner can accept documents up to 8.5 x 14 inches. You can choose other software bundled from Adobe Acrobat Capture or Omni-Page Professional, Recollect Gold or and Laser Fiche, which are document management programs, Teleform, a forms processor, and the ImageBASIC Electronic File Cabinet. Picture Publisher also is included along with 16-bit and 32-bit Twain drives and Isis drivers (for document management programs). The Ricoh FS2 is good for heavy-duty OCR and document management tasks, as well as color image scanning. The manufacturer states that the Ricoh FS2 can produce 250,000 scans.

Installation is straightforward and poses no difficulty. Color-image quality is very good, though the scan can come out darker than the original. The Ricoh FS2 is rather expensive, but remember the transparency adapter and document feeder are included, which drives up the price. If your primary scanning tasks are document management you should take a second look at this scanner. Warranty is one-year parts and labor. Support is toll free from Monday through Friday.

UMAX Vista-S12

Price $500

Rank 3

Image Quality 43.8

Price 25

Features 12.5

The Vista-S12 is a good all-purpose scanner, with an affordable price and excellent performance. The UMAX Vista-S12 is a single-pass, 24-bit color depth scanner with 600-dpi optical resolution, interpolated to 9,600. Documents up to 8.5 x 11.7 inches can be scanned. Options include a $395 transparency adapter and a $495 fifty-sheet document feeder. Bundled software includes PhotoDeluxe and OCR software Presto! PageManager and ASAP. Additional software is available at an extra cost; $100 more for Adobe Photoshop LE and $200 extra for a full version of Photoshop. The Twain driver is high-powered enough for professionals yet easy for beginners to use. It is the only Twain driver with an HSB (hue-saturation-brightness) adjustment and it can scan in RGB or CYMK color mode

through an RGB-CMYK conversion. Color-image quality and resolution is excellent. The one-year warranty covers parts and labor. Toll-free technical support is available Monday through Friday.

CONTACT INFORMATION

Epson America Inc.
800-463-7766
www.epson.com

Hewlett-Packard Co.
800-722-6538
www.hp.com

InfoPeripherals
800-777-3208
www.infoconnection.com

Microtek Lab Inc.
800-654-4160
www.microtekusa.com

Mustek Inc.
800-468-7835
www.mustek.com

Nikon Inc.
Electronic Imaging Dept.
800-526-4566
www.nikonusa.com

PacificImage Electronics Co.
800-909-9996
www.scanace.com

Plustek USA Inc.
800-685-8088
www.plustekusa.com

Ricoh Corp.
800-955-3453
www.ricoh.com

UMAX Technologies Inc.
800-562-0311
www.umax.com

SCANNERS, SHEETFED

Are you surrounded by piles of paper? Sheetfeed scanners (sometimes called personal scanners) are designed mainly to convert documents to digital files. Most produce only monotone images, but a few reviewed here produce color as well. Whichever you prefer, they can help you manage your paper clutter.

These devices take up a small amount of space and one in the following review is even built right into the keyboard. The purpose of a personal scanner is document management. You can convert business cards, photos, magazine articles, reports, memos, receipts, or any other type of paper into electronic documents. Once converted you can organize, file, fax, copy, edit, or e-mail your documents electronically.

Before you buy a personal scanner, determine your paper handling needs. Keep in mind the size and type of documents you will be scanning, and what you'll be doing with these documents once you get them into your computer. Remember, your needs today may change over time, so it would be a good idea to buy with the future in mind.

When getting ready to make a purchase, consider the following information. A scanner is only as good as the images it produces. For better quality scans look for scanners that can render 256 shades of gray with at least a resolution of 300 dpi. This is preferred for photos or images with graduated tones. Some scanners can interpolate the resolutions up to 800 dpi or higher. (Interpolation is just a technique used to improve scanner output by means of a software algorithm.)

To check for scan quality, take a magazine photo with you to the retailer and make a test scan. Check for streaks, blurred contrasts, bands of lines along the scan and other imperfections. Test several machines and compare the scans to each other to see which is best. Also see if you can select lower resolutions to speed-up scanning; it will help when scanning text documents.

Besides photographs, scanners can be used to convert paper-based documents into digital text via Optical Character Recognition (OCR). OCR is a process that converts scanned text into editable text. OCR software is usually included with the scanner. To test a scanner's OCR performance, scan a document with multiple columns of text. Look at the output and check if column formatting was retained and for the number of mistakes. One misread letter per every three words is about average. Take into consideration whether the scanner is a parallel or SCSI model. If you buy a parallel scanner it should have a pass-through option which is an additional connection for your printer. Keep in mind that SCSI scanners can be difficult to install if you're not technically inclined.

Another feature to look for in a scanner is its software. The scanner's software acts as a control center for scanning operations. Look for software that gives you a drag-and-drop filing utility that can organize scans in folders searchable by keywords; annotation tools that can add emphasis to documents using sticky notes, text comments, and freehand drawings; and image editing tools for cleaning up faxes and images. The following is a list of six of the more popular personal scanners and their ratings.

OVERALL RATINGS

Visioneer PaperPort Vx for Windows	★★★★
Logitech PageScan Color	★★★1/4
Hewlett-Packard ScanJet 4s	★★3/4
Umax PageOffice for Windows	★★3/4
Microtek PageWiz	★★3/4
Plustek PageReader Portable	★★

EXPLANATION OF RATINGS

The following four factors were rated: setup and use, image quality, document management capabilities and bundled software. A four-star rating was used, with one star being the lowest rating. The ratings of these four factors were then averaged, resulting in the overall rating.

ALPHABETICAL DESCRIPTIONS

Hewlett-Packard ScanJet 4s

Price $299

Overall Rating ★★3/4

Setup and Use ★★★

Image Quality ★★1/2

Bundled Software ★★★

Document Management ★★1/2

Hewlett-Packard's ScanJet 4s is a compact and fast scanner, similar in design to the Visioneer PaperPort. It's a serial device but there is no parallel adapter. HP has even licensed the PaperPort software for use with its scanners. However, the capabilities of these scanners are not necessarily the same.

Document management is weak. The ScanJet uses version 3.0 of Visioneer PaperPort so it does not have the same document management capabilities as the PaperPort models. Scans can't be stored by headings, rather you attach sticky notes to scans, organize multiple scans by stacks of images, or highlight parts of an image. There is also a links feature that allows you to fax or e-mail your scanned documents through a fax or e-mail program of your choice.

Scans are limited to 16 shades of gray with resolutions only to 200 dpi (interpolated up to 400 dpi). Better scanners have 256 gray-scale capabilities. Photos and more complex images will lose detail. If you will be scanning a lot of photos or complex images, this scanner isn't up to the job. However, for text and simple line drawings this scanner is fine.

Logitech PageScan Color

Price $399

Overall Rating ★★★1/4

Setup and Use ★★★★

Image Quality ★★★

Bundled Software ★★★

Document Management ★★★

The Logitech PageScan Color scanner offers speed, 24-bit color, document management, and flexibility in a compact size. Installation is painless—the scanner plugs right into the parallel port with a pass-through option so your printer can operate on the same port. PageScan Control Center software is as simple as point and click. Just insert a document into the scanner and then select an icon to archive, convert to text, print, or fax your document. To fax a scan you do need a fax modem attached to your computer.

PageScan's flexibility sets it apart from other scanners. Its 10-page automatic document feeder accepts paper from the front or rear. Detach the scanner from its base and it becomes a handheld scanner. This enables you to scan books, catalogs, magazines, and other bound materials.

Scan quality is adequate. The optical resolution of this scanner is 200- by 400-dpi, which is slightly lower than other personal scanners. Color images are scanned at 200 dpi; black-and-white images have resolutions up to 400 dpi.

PageScan costs a bit more than other scanners, but you do get the luxury of a color handheld scanner which makes it worth the price.

Microtek PageWiz

Price $112
Overall Rating ★★3/4
Setup and Use ★★★
Image Quality ★★
Bundled Software ★★★
Document Management ★★★

If you took the PageSuite software bundled with this scanner and coupled it with a better scanner you might have a pretty good product. This scanner can render 300 by 300 resolutions but only in 16 shades of gray. At this resolution, detail on photographs is lost.

The PageSuite software bundled with the scanner gets good marks. Its well-integrated interface lets you switch scanning speeds, resolutions, and scanning views. Scans can be viewed in full-page, half-page, or thumbnail. Document management allows you to attach keywords and long file names to scans, which can be stacked. There is a nice array of annotation tools, fax options and e-mail through Microsoft Mail.

For optimal scanner performance, a scanner should render images in at least a 256 gray-scale. Any scanner with resolutions less than that is not worth the money.

Plustek PageReader Portable

Price $196
Overall Rating ★★
Setup and Use ★★★
Image Quality ★★
Software ★
Document Management ★★

Personal scanners are primarily used for document management, and that function is conspicuously absent from the Plustek PageReader Portable. This affordable scanner is easy to set up and use. Its Action Manager software lets you setup buttons for OCR, printing, and faxing, but that's it. No filing utility for storing images in folders or keyword searches is available.

The scan quality is poor, which affects the OCR quality. The OCR software Recognita Plus regularly ignores the last lines of text on a page, adds extra spaces, and jumbles italicized words. Multicolumn documents cannot be converted to editable text.

Umax PageOffice for Windows

Price $349

Overall Rating ★★3/4

Setup and Use ★★

Image Quality ★★★

Software ★★★

Document Management ★★★

Umax PageOffice for Windows is a SCSI device which offers you speed but lots of hassles in installation. However, once it's all set up, performance is good.

PageOffice is extremely easy to use. Document management is basic. Place up to 10 pages in the sheet feeder and scan documents to your desktop, a fax module or any other application on the programs button bar.

Scan quality is adequate. The image editing program has a wide array of filters which can smooth, emboss, or sharpen an image or adjust the contrast and brightness. JPEG compression is also available.

A downside of this scanner is the OCR program. OCR quality and speed is dismal. Formatting gets lost and converted documents need a lot of cleaning up to be of any use. If you want to convert documents to editable text, this scanner doesn't cut it. You can buy a parallel scanner for less and get more.

Links are provided to other applications allowing you to drag-and-drop scans to other programs. Multiple desktops can be created for document folders, pages can be stacked and searched. Annotation tools include the usual sticky notes, text comments, and simple line drawings.

Visioneer PaperPort Vx for Windows

Price $299

Overall Rating ★★★★

Setup and Use ★★★★

Image Quality ★★★★

Software ★★★★

Document Management ★★★★

Managing your piles of paper is now easier with the Visioneer PaperPort Vx. Installation and setup is a breeze—just plug it in, install the software, and let the PaperPort do the rest. This device almost works by itself. When you place a document into its feeder it automatically turns on, scans the document, then displays the scanned document on screen. PaperPort's drag-and-drop interface easily lets you fax, file, e-mail, or copy your scanned documents. PaperPort Vx is a serial device which frees up your parallel port for your printer. You can scan almost anything: business cards, newspaper clippings, receipts. PaperPort Vx can accept paper up to 8.5 inches wide by 30 inches long.

Scan quality is excellent. Blotches and dim contrasts are automatically corrected with PaperPort's SharpPage technology. This proprietary technology makes faxes sharper and is especially useful for clearly scanning documents with colored text on a dark background. Photos can be scanned up to 256 shades of gray. Scanning speed isn't too bad either.

Organizing your documents is a snap. You can search for stored scans by name, date stamp, note, or keyword. It also manages business cards by creating a contact database from your scanned business cards. Documents can also be scanned as text with the included OCR software, thus eliminating the need to re-type data. Standard annotation can be done with sticky notes, highlighting, or text inserts.

What does this program not have? An image editing program. If you need to edit images you have to use your own software. However, PaperPort does provide links to many popular image-editing programs. Overall, PaperPort Vx's performance, scan quality, and reliability makes for a top-notch document management system.

CONTACT INFORMATION

Hewlett-Packard ScanJet 4s
Hewlett-Packard Co.
800-722-6538, 208-396-2551
www.hp.com/

Logitech PageScan Color
Logitech Inc.
510-795-8500
www.logitech.com/

Microtek PageWiz
Microtek Lab, Inc
800-654-4160, 310-297-5000
www.mteklab.com/

Plustek PageReader Portable
Plustek USA
800-685-8088, 408-745-7111
www.plustek.com/

Umax PageOffice for Windows
Umax Technologies, Inc
800-562-0311, 510-651-4000
www.umax.com

Visioneer PaperPort Vx for Windows
Visioneer, Inc
800-787-7007, 415-812-6400
www.visioneer.com/

SPEAKERS, MULTIMEDIA FOR PCs

Is there a business application for good speakers? If you are among those who use computer applications to make presentations there is. Or if you use computer sound in anyway to communicate to more than any one individual in the office, you may need good sound quality to do so well. Many perfectly acceptable computers—especially low-priced ones—come with speakers with poor sound quality and volume. You may wish to upgrade for various reasons.

Sound was once used mainly in computer games, but is now being used in Web sites, e-mail, help files, and tutorials to name a few. Today's computers can now play music CDs and, with the right speakers, you can get sound quality that equals that of your stereo. You may be wondering why you would need another set of speakers if your PC came bundled with a set of speakers. Unless you purchased your

BOSE's Acoustimass Multimedia System, which offer the top-rated PC speakers, is a miniature three-component system.

computer system with specialized speakers, the speakers that came with your system are generic, offering sound comparable to an AM radio broadcast. To truly get the benefit of the multimedia experience, upgrading to multimedia speakers may be a necessary move.

Before purchasing your new speakers there are a few technical tidbits you need to know. First, to get any sound out of your computer you need a sound card. Most of today's computers come with a sound card installed. If you don't have one, you can purchase a 16-bit sound card at any computer retailer.

Next, your speakers should be shielded. Multimedia speaker systems are made up of two or three components. Some speaker systems only have the two speakers, but there are those that have two satellite speakers and a subwoofer. A subwoofer handles the bass or low-frequency sounds. If you have a three-component speaker system, a logic circuit sends the bass signals directly to the subwoofer while the other sounds are routed to the satellite speakers. These satellite and subwoofer speakers contain magnets that manipulate a speaker's cone, making it vibrate to create sound. Multimedia PC speakers are shielded so they will not wreak havoc with your computer's data or monitor's color display. If the speaker is not shielded it cannot be safely used with your computer. One part of the three-component speaker system, the subwoofer, is not shielded, so keep this part of the speaker system at least 18 inches from your computer system.

Another important aspect of your speaker system is how easily integrated the speakers are with your current computer system. Check the design of the speakers before buying. Will they fit on your desktop? Do they attach on your monitor or do they stand alone? Remember these types of speakers will be close to your face so make sure you have enough room to accommodate them. Speaker controls should be easy to reach and it's best if they're located on the satellite speakers. Some speakers do have software-based controls that allow you to make adjustments right from your computer without leaving your desk.

Sound quality is the most important aspect of a good speaker system. Some speakers come with 3D sound which surrounds the listener in aural pleasure. This is also called surround sound.

Listed below are nine speaker systems and their ratings. Due to a tie for sixth place, there is no seventh ranked system.

RANKINGS AND OVERALL SCORES

1	Bose Acoustimass Multimedia	85
2	AKS Acoustics Pump Pro Combo	83
3	Cambridge SoundWorks SWK1	81
4	Atlantic Technology M105/M110	75
5	JBL Media4	65
6	Altec Lansing ACS55	62
6	Sony SRS-PC71/SRS-PC3DW	62
8	Yamaha System 45	59
9	Labtec LCS-2612	50

EXPLANATION OF RATINGS

Speaker systems were evaluated on the following criteria: sound quality, speaker controls, and setup. Sound quality comprised 75% of the score.

ALPHABETICAL DESCRIPTIONS

Altec Lansing ACS55

Price $199	
Rank 6	
Overall Score 62	
Setup 5	
Speaker Controls 12	
Sound Quality 45	

The Altec Lansing ACS55 offers an impressive surround sound experience with the aid of Dolby Multimedia Surround technology. The speakers have good high and low-range sound but mid-range sounds lacked depth and the subwoofer rattled with bass-intensive music. You can easily place the speakers on your desk without being mounted, but make sure there is ample space around the satellite speakers. The speaker controls are placed on the right speaker's base. An external audio source can be attached to the speakers' dual input. Bundled with the speakers is WaveCube software for customizing MIDI songs. These speakers offer realistic surround sound and can just as adequately handle music in non-surround mode.

AKS Acoustics Pump Pro Combo

Price $279	
Rank 2	
Overall Score 83	
Setup 2	
Speaker Controls 6	

Sound Quality 75

You may not be able to pump up the volume with this speaker system, but you will get high-quality sound. The AKS is a three-component speaker system that uses SRS 3D technology, which make these speakers really stand out. This 3D technology helps with the middle and upper frequencies by compensating for loss of tone. The system's subwoofer handled bass adequately even with bass-intensive music. Even though the sound was clean and crisp it was not the loudest. One drawback is the way the speakers are set up. They use a signal splitter to transmit signals to the satellite's speakers and the subwoofer. Setup is not straightforward. A wire from the sound card is attached to the subwoofer. This wire has a dial that controls the subwoofer's volume so the wire should be placed in an easily accessible manner if possible. The right satellite speaker controls the treble and bass controls, but not the bass on the subwoofer. If you're a techie or have someone to help you set up these speakers you'll get excellent sound for all your multimedia needs.

Atlantic Technology M105/M110

Price $249	
Rank 4	
Overall Score 75	
Setup 3	
Speaker Controls 12	
Sound Quality 60	

The Atlantic Technology M105/M110s are good multipurpose speakers that have great midrange and upper frequency sound. This is a three-component speaker system that can easily fit on your desktop.

For an extra $20 you can purchase speaker stands. Speaker controls are on the right satellite speaker while the subwoofer has a level control and a crossover control. The subwoofer's frequency can be set at 100 Hz or 120Hz. The subwoofer was able to handle low-frequency, but vibrating sounds can be heard with bass-intensive music. These speakers are lacking good treble of higher-end systems, but its mid-range and volume make it an all-purpose system.

Bose Acoustimass Multimedia

Price $699

Rank 1

Overall Score 85

Setup 4

Speaker Controls 6

Sound Quality 75

Bose is a well-recognized name in speaker systems and you won't be disappointed with the sound of these PC speakers. The BOSE Acoustimass Multimedia speakers offer you excellent sound with no crackle or distortions, just high-quality sound. The speakers are a miniature three-component system. They can be placed anywhere, but if you want to mount them you have to provide the mounting hardware. Unlike other speakers, the controls are inconveniently placed on the subwoofer so placement of this component would hinge on your ability to reach it easily. There is a mechanism that will shut down the speakers when not in use. The price tag for this speaker system is high, but if you want the very best and money is no object, go for it.

Cambridge SoundWorks SWK1

Price $219.99

Rank 3

Overall Score 81

Setup 6

Speaker Controls 15

Sound Quality 60

The sound really pumps out of these three-inch speakers and subwoofer. The Cambridge SoundWorks SWK1 can be placed on stands, attached to your monitor, or to the wall. Mounting hardware is included. Speaker controls are placed on a separate unit so they can be mounted on your monitor. The sound is very good, but there are no 3D effects here. These speakers can handle loud volumes without cracking, but midrange is lacking a bit at the higher volumes. If you're short on space but want high-fidelity sound, the SWK1 will work.

JBL Media4

Price $249.95

Rank 5

Overall Score 65

Setup 5

Speaker Controls 15

Sound Quality 45

The JBL Media4 is a two-component speaker that does not include a subwoofer. You can add a subwoofer for an extra $199.95. The speaker gives you good sound and can adequately handle most music. If you don't add the subwoofer, the bass will not be as intense as with it. The speakers can be placed on your desktop. The controls are located on the back of the right speaker, but the only control is volume. The speakers will automatically be put into sleep mode when not in use.

These speakers do an adequate job of handling sound even though the highs aren't all that high.

Labtec LCS-2612

Price $119	
Rank 9	
Overall Score 50	
Setup 5	
Speaker Controls 15	
Sound Quality 30	

The Labtec LCS-2612 is a nicely designed three-component speaker system. The satellite speakers hang on your monitor with Labtec's mounting hardware and the magnetically shielded subwoofer can sit on your desk. The speaker controls are on the subwoofer along with the Spatializer switch. Headphones and microphone jacks are included on the speakers. While the design is great, the sound is not. The LCS- 2612 is known as a ''gaming system,'' good for PC games but inadequate for playing music.

Sony SRS-PC71/SRS-PC3DW

Price $299.90	
Rank 6	
Overall Score 62	
Setup 5	
Speaker Controls 12	
Sound Quality 45	

This Sony speaker system is a three-component set that can also be purchased as a two-component system for $149.95. The speakers' triangular design fits conveniently on your desk, but they can be knocked over rather easily. The subwoofer is magnetically shielded and the speaker controls are on the left satellite speaker. There is an input jack for headphones and a mix control on the satellite. The sound is clear and crisp, but bass-intensive music made the subwoofer to rattle. Without the subwoofer, the speakers responded just as well. So you could get a bargain here by trimming the speaker system to just the two satellite speakers.

Yamaha System 45

Price $199	
Rank 8	
Overall Score 59	
Setup 5	
Speaker Controls 9	
Sound Quality 45	

The Yamaha System 45 is a three-piece system that offers little to make it stand out among others in its price range. It's easy enough to set up. The satellite volume controls can be used for the entire system, and the tone dial can cut or add treble while the High Cut switch steers high frequencies away from the subwoofer. The Yamaha's sound is good but the upper midranges produced shrill sounds. The subwoofer was a bit better than others in its price range but high volumes could overdrive it. The price is a good value but the sound quality could be better.

CONTACT INFORMATION

Altec Lansing Technologies, Inc.
800-648-6663
www.altec.com

AKS Acoustics
800-213-5119
www.aks.com

Atlantic Technology
800-648-6663
www.atlantic.com

Bose
800-444-2673
www.bose.com
Cambridge SoundWorks
800-367-4434
www.cambridge.com

JBL Inc.
800-336-4525
www.jbl.com

Koss Corp.
800-872-5677
www.koss.com

Labtec Enterprises Inc.
360-896-2020
www.labtec.com

Sony Electronics
800-352-7669
www.sony.com

Yamaha
800-823-6414
www.yamaha.com

DIGITAL CAMERAS

Just about any business that needs instant photographs—especially those that will be part of a computer document—will find a digital camera useful, particularly companies that frequently update their web pages, multimedia presentations and other applications.

Digital cameras take photographs that can be instantly viewed on your computer. These cameras don't use films like conventional cameras so you don't have to wait for your photographs to be processed. The images are stored digitally in the camera's memory until they are transferred to your computer.

In this chapter we look at digital cameras that cost from $500 to just over $1,000. All of them are upgradeable—more features may be added, that is—and if fully loaded can cost as much as $2,500. The prices shown in the descriptions are, in most cases, for the base model. The camera that have been selected for review are geared more toward small businesses or bigger corporations that don't want to invest in expensive alternatives such as professional photo shoots or high-end digital

Tied for number one with the Kodak DC50, the Cannon PowerShot 600 (below) comes with a rechargeable battery pack, computer docking station, neck strap and software including Power-Shot TWAIN driver v.1.0, Ulead's PhotoImpact 3.0 and ImagePals 2.0.

cameras that can cost up to $15,000, and are mainly used by professional photographers.

The cameras that follow can be used with Windows and Macintosh computers. Two cameras tied for the number one spot.

RANKINGS AND OVERALL RATINGS

1	Canon PowerShot 600	95
1	Kodak DC50	95
3	Ricoh RDC-1	80
4	Olympus D-200L	73
5	Epson PhotoPC 500	70
6	Apple QuickTake 150	68
7	Chinon ES-3000	63
8	Dycam 10-C	57

EXPLANATION OF RATINGS

Cameras were reviewed on their image quality, software, and ease of use. Image quality counted for 50% of the overall score, therefore the highest scoring models will usually give you the best quality image. This is the most important thing to consider when buying a digital camera. It's partly a function of the camera's resolution. Average image resolution varies from 320 by 240 to 640 by 480. Better cameras will have resolutions higher than these. Picture quality is also affected by the camera's compressions, which reduce the image size so that they fit into its memory. If images are uncompressed (let's say a 24-bit image at 640 by 480) then that image can take up a megabyte of memory. Speaking of memory, your camera should have enough of it, the more the

better. Since images are held in the camera's memory, make sure your unit has a sufficient amount. Another key factor is the software that comes with the camera. This software should be able to manipulate images and save files in a variety of formats.

ALPHABETICAL DESCRIPTIONS

Apple QuickTake 150

Price $639

Rank 6

Apple QuickTake 150 captures color images at a resolution of 640 by 480 pixels in 24-bit color (more than 16 million colors) It can store 32 standard-quality images or 16 high-quality images. It has a built-in automatic flash and a LCD control panel that allows you to switch between standard or high-quality. The QuickTake 150 weighs about a pound including its lithium battery. The battery has enough juice to capture over 200 images (100 with flash, 100 no flash), download and erase all images. The accompanying software helps transfer your images from the camera and offers several image-editing tools to enhance photographs. Once on your computer you can view thumbnails of your images and manipulate them to your liking. Images can be saved in BMP, PCX, JPEG, TIFF and QuickTake formats. The software PhotoNow can be used with any TWAIN-compliant Windows application for use within many popular software applications. QuickTake 150 can be used on a Windows-based computer with an optional connection kit or the Macintosh. Image quality is acceptable but check out the other cameras and compare. You'll probably find one with better image quality.

Canon PowerShot 600

Price $950

Rank 1

Business professionals can get great results from this high-quality digital camera. The Canon PowerShot 600 has superior resolution of 832 by 680. Image quality is on par with photos that are scanned with a 24-bit scanner. The sharpness of the Power-Shot 600 images is due to its ability to save uncompressed files and its fixed-focal-length 7.5-mm lens (equivalent to 50 mm on a 35-mm camera). Images are saved to a standard PC Card memory card. Its 1MB internal memory can store up to 18 images

The Canon PowerShot 600 has a built-in microphone to provide voice annotations.

and with the optional 4MB compact flash memory PC Card it can store up to 72 images. There is an optional 170MB hard disk drive PC Card that can store up to 900 photos at 832 by 608 resolution. The camera has an automatic exposure and has an equivalent ISO speed of 100, with shutter speeds of 1/30 to 1/500 second. The Nicad battery has a life for 200-300 images, which may vary if you use flash.

Included with the PowerShot is a parallel interface docking station that easily transfers images to portable or desktop computers. Software includes PowerShot TWAIN driver, Ulead PhotoImpact and Ulead ImagePals 2.0.

Another impressive option is the attach-voice annotation, which adds sound to an image file. You can also select JPEG image compression (fine, normal, or economy) to enhance transmission speed and image storage. The downside is the proprietary lens mount is limiting. Canon does have an adapter that is the equivalent of a 28-mm lens.

Chinon ES-3000

Price $999

Rank 7

This digital camera looks more like a camcorder, but it's easy to use with auto focus, a built-in flash and 3x power zoom. The ES-3000 captures images in three modes: standard (320 by 240 with maximum compression), fine (640 by 480 with medium compression), and superfine (640 by 480 with minimal compression). The camera's built-in 1MB of memory can hold 40 standard images, 10 fine images, and five superfine images. More memory is available in 2MB to 16MB PC cards. Images are transferred via the included serial cable. Image editing software and a TWAIN drive is also included. The software is basic and the image-editing tools lack sophisticated features. Image-quality is average but for this price you can get a lot more.

Dycam 10-C

Price $499

Rank 8

The Dycam 10-C is a clone of the Chinon ES-3000. They share design and their performance is almost similar. It can capture images in three modes: standard (329 by 240), fine (640 by 480) and superfine(640 by 480). Image quality is not that good, but it can be improved a bit with its image enhancement tools. The 1MB of built-in memory holds up to 40 standard images, 10 fine images, or five superfine images. This camera also has a lens ring for attaching different filter and adapters. But once again image quality is the deciding factor and the poor image quality of the Dycam 10-C will make you decide against it.

Epson PhotoPC 500

Price $599

Rank 5

The Epson PhotoPC 500 offers features that are found in higher-priced models. It captures images in 24 bit color at a resolution of 640 by 480. This unit can store up to 30 high-resolution images and 60 standard-resolution images. Memory can be expanded to 2MB or 4MB with a memory module. The PhotoPC is compact, easy to hold, and fits in your pocket. The built-in flash can take indoor pictures from a distance of 20 to 30 feet. The standard viewfinder makes images appear less lit then they really are and tends to flare. The PhotoPC 500 images were of average quality but were better than Epson's previous PhotoPC model. The PhotoPC 500 connects to your computer via a serial cable. The included software helps download and enhance images. The software includes EasyPhoto by Storm which has basic tools for image-editing and retouching. The camera runs on four standard AA batteries but battery life is short. For longer life get the longer-lasting lithium batteries. An adapter is not standard, you have to buy one for around $49.

Kodak DC50

Price $499

Rank 2

Eastman Kodak has several digital cameras on the market and its Digital Science DC 50 is one their most versatile entry-level products. Looking more like a small camcorder (similar to the Dycam 10-C) it captures images in 24-bit color at a resolution of 768 by 504 pixels, which is better than VGA. The DC50 has a motor-driven 3x zoom lens, auto-focus, built-in flash, and a self timer. Its 1MB of internal memory can store up to seven low-compression images. Images can also be stored on removable PC Cards, which could increase storage to 35 shots on a 4MB card. The optional card costs $230. The software included with the camera offers full-featured image processing tools. You can convert images to grayscale or black and white and change color depth. The program's By Example feature allows you to control exposure, brightness, contrast and color balance. It also has 45 automatic enhancement options making it easy to adjust images visually rather than numerically. The DC50's top-notch image quality, sophisticated software, and easy use make it a good investment.

Olympus D-200L

Price: $600

Rank 4

The Olympus D-200L comes standard with an optical viewfinder, built-in flash and a LCD screen for previewing images. This camera needs lots of battery power. It runs on four standard AA batteries and comes with a set of alkaline cells. An AC adapter is extra for about $40. The D-200L is compact and can fit easily in your pocket. It's easy to hold and offers good pictures too. Images are taken at a resolution of 640 by 480. Up to 20 high-quality images can be stored at the high resolution and

The Kodak DC50, tied for the number-one rank, has a motor-driven 3x zoom lens, auto-focus, built-in flash, and a self timer.

up to 80 images can be stored in standard mode at 320 by 240 pixels. The camera has excellent exposure and color control, especially in natural light. The viewfinder or LCD screen is used to preview images, frame shots, browse stored images at up to nine at a time in a 3-by-3 thumbnail array. The software includes a TWAIN driver and Adobe PhotoDeluxe which has full-featured image-editing tools and supports Photoshop effects filters. With this program you can't batch download images or open more than one image at a time. However the TWAIN driver supports batch downloads. One other drawback is the software is a memory hog requiring 16MB free RAM. The D-200L is a nicely designed camera that can produce good quality images for use in your business applications without breaking the bank.

Ricoh RDC-1

Price $1,159

Rank 3

The Ricoh RDC-1 comes standard with the RDP-1 playback adapter, remote control, wrist strap and PC and Mac utility software. However, to get the most out of this camera you need additional add-ons. Ricoh bundles the camera with the add-ons in three packages: System package 3 sells for $1,399 and includes the camera, AK-1 Accessory Kit, and RDT-1 Communications/Serial Adapter; System package 2 sells for $1,939 and includes everything in package 3 plus a DM-1 monitor; System package 1 sells for $2,399 and includes everything in package 2 plus an 8MB memory card. Additional memory is available in 2MB ($299), 8MB ($459), and 24MB ($1,699) reusable memory cards.

The Ricoh RDC-1 is one of the most versatile cameras. Image quality is quite good, with a resolution of 768 by 576 pixels and 24-bit color. It comes with a 3x zoom lens, a real viewfinder, automatic white-balance exposure control, and frame-by-frame, forward and reverse slow-motion and playback controls. The optional 2.5-inch LCD monitor lets you view your images as you capture them. The RDC-1 also has the ability to record motion and sound. The camera's memory can hold up to 10 seconds of video with still images, five seconds of video, and up to 100 minutes of audio with the 24MB memory card. An 8MB PCMCIA memory card can store up to 81 images in standard mode or 162 in economy mode. It can also hold up to 20 seconds of video or 100 minutes of audio. Images can be transferred to a PC or Mac but connecting the camera to a Mac can be complicated. The camera's software lacks editing tools, only rotates images, and has two specialized filters for removing artifacts. Images can be saved as PICT, JPEG, TIFF, or bit-mapped files. RDC-1's image quality is first rate but, with all the extras adding to the price, you'd better be a high-volume user to get your money's worth.

CONTACT INFORMATION

Apple Computer, Inc.
(800) 538-9696
www.apple.com

Chinon America, Inc.
(800) 441-0222
www.chinon.com

Canon Computer Systems, Inc.
(800) 848-4123
714 438-3000
www.canon.com

Dycam
(800) 883-9226
(818) 407-3960
www.dycam.com

Epson America
(800) 289-3776
www.epson.com

Eastman Kodak Cp.
(800) 235-6325
www.kodak.com

Olympus America Inc.
(800) 622-6372
(516) 844-5000
www.olympus.com/digital

Ricoh Corp.
(800) 255-1899
www.ricoh.com

LCDs,

OVERVIEW OF PANELS AND PROJECTORS

Not too many years ago a good business presentation was a box full of slides, a tray of acetates, a slide projector, and an overhead projector. Now technology has developed two new weapons in the quest for the perfect presentation—LCD panels and projectors. These enable you to take presentations directly from your computer and project them to a room full of people without needing a room full of computer screens. They can also be equipped to project video images from a VCR.

Both panels and projectors use the same LCD (Liquid Crystal Display) technology found in computer notebooks and other devices. The LCD panel is a translucent screen within a plastic frame. To use it you place the panel on an overhead projector and connect it to a computer. The light shines through the panel and projects an image of the computer screen onto the projection screen. With an LCD projector you don't need the overhead projector; a built-in projector beams a powerful image from a computer onto a screen or wall.

LCD screens are of two types: active and passive matrix. Active matrix screens individually power each LCD cell, which results in brighter colors and faster response times. But active matrix costs more. Passive matrix panels, though cheaper, produce duller colors and rapidly moving images which become distorted. Most of the new LCD panels and projectors use the active matrix, which is rapidly becoming the industry standard.

As good as LCD technology is now, there is something new on the horizon: Digital Light Processing, or DLP. LCD technology works by shining light through a transparent panel of LCD cells, each cell controlled by a tiny transistor, which changes the cell's polarity to produce the image. Unfortunately, these transistors block out some of the light, which becomes a problem when projecting high-resolution images.

With DLP, the images are projected by reflecting light against a set of mirrors. Each mirror represents a pixel and is powered by electronics that adjust the angle of the mirror according to the color displayed. The electronics are located under the mirror, so they do not cut down on the light, the result being brighter images. The technology was developed by Texas Instruments and several LCD manufacturers have begun producing models featuring the new technology.

Creating a presentation using the new LCD technology has several advantages over slides and transparencies. First, computer presentations can include sound and video, making them much more alive and interesting than static slides. They are also more flexible, allowing you to make last minute changes with a keystroke on the computer. Finally, although LCD panels and projectors are expensive, over the long run they may be cheaper since there are no ongoing costs. Slides and transparencies cost money every time you create or change them.

The major difference between a panel and projector, besides the technology, is cost. Projectors are quite a bit more expensive. But a panel is much more portable, since some of the projectors can weigh over 50 pounds. A panel is about the size of a hardcover book. The image a panel can produce depends on the power of its light source, the overhead projector. So if you know there will be a high-quality overhead projector wherever you make your presentations, then a panel would serve well. If getting a panel will require an investment in a high-quality projector, then the better choice would be a projector.

FEATURES

The most important quality of LCD panels and projectors is the quality of the image projected. This includes such features as brightness, resolution and color. The brightness of an LCD image is measured in standardized ANSI lumens. Most projectors on the market range from 100 to 400 lumens, the higher the number the brighter the image. Resolution refers to the number of dots of light appearing on the screen or projection. Higher resolutions allow more information to be dis-

played on a specific area. Most systems on the market project a 640 by 480 image, about what a 14-inch video monitor displays. Some systems project images at a resolution as high as 1024 by 768, detailed enough for computer- aided design work. Like most computer monitors, LCD panels and projectors can show varying numbers of colors. The number of colors ranges from several thousand to 16.7 million. However, a panel or projector that is able to show so many colors may be hindered by a computer that can't.

Other important features include video and audio capability, remote control, zoom, and screen markup capability. Video and audio capability refers to whether the system can support video or audio hookups to enhance presentations. Some systems, for example, have built-in speakers, others only have jacks for hooking up external speakers. Remote control refers to whether or not remote control is a possibility, allowing the presenter to roam about at will while still controlling the presentation. A zoom feature allows the presenter to enlarge a portion of the screen for detailed viewing. Screen markup refers to the capability of drawing digitally on a screen to focus points of interest.

CONTACT INFORMATION

ASK
(800) ASK-LCD1
(800-275-5231)

Buhl Industries
(201) 423-2800 x3115

Dukane Corp.
(800) 676-2485

Eiki
(800) 242-3454

Epson America
(800) 289-3776

In Focus Systems
(800) 294-6400

NEC
(800) NEC-INFO (800-632-4636)

nView Corp.
(800) 775-7575

Proxima Corp.
(800) 447-7692
'Sharp Electronics
(800) 237-4277

LCD
PANELS

Before reading this portion please refer to the preceding chapter, "LCDs, Panels and Projectors, Overview." The following list contains 10 LCD Panels, their rankings and overall scores.

RANKINGS AND OVERALL SCORES

1	Proxima Ovation +842	86.2
2	ASK Impact WSK	85.0
3	ASK Impact 400	82.8
4	Dukane MagnaView 488B	81.2
5	Sharp QA-2500	80.0
6	InFocus PanelBook 550e	76.2
7	nView Z250	72.8
8	Sharp QA-1500B	67.2
9	Buhl 5020	62.5
10	nView Z110	62.0

EXPLANATION OF RATINGS

LCD panels are simple in design and are usually lower in price and more portable than LCD projectors. The technology is such that most systems, regardless of manufacturer, are basically trouble-free, except when abused or misused by the user. The panels rated above were evaluated using the following criteria:

Company (40 points): Companies were judged on the basis of their willingness to service and support their products and their warranty policies. Two of the companies—InFocus and Proxima—stand out for their progressive warranties and exceptionally responsive service, while Sharp reportedly is slow to respond to consumer problems. The highest possible score was 40 points.

Number of Colors (10 points): Refers to the number of colors or shades of gray that can be projected per image. The best in this category can project 16.7 million colors, worth the full 10 points.

Zoom Option (10 points): Refers to whether the system has the capability of enlarging a portion of the projected image, worth 10 points.

Audio (10 points): Refers to whether the system offers sound as a standard or optional feature, worth 10 pts.

Video (10 points): Refers to whether the system can be used with video inputs, worth 10 points.

Remote (10 points): Refers to whether the system offers a standard or optional remote control, enabling the presenter to leave the panel and still control the presentation. Such an option was worth 10 points.

Projected Resolution (10 points): Refers to the number of dots of light, called pixels, that appear in the projected image. The best in this category can project an image of 1024 by 768 pixels, worth the full 10 points.

ALPHABETICAL DESCRIPTIONS

ASK Impact 400

Price $6,295

Ranking 3

The ASK LCD is a member of a Norwegian-based group of high-technology companies. They manufacture LCD panels, projectors and flat-screen monitors for sale in the North American market. One unique feature of the company is that all of their models are available with an infrared remote device with built-in mouse. The Impact 400 can project 800 by 600 resolution images while weighing less than five pounds, and still offer zoom and video options. ASK LCD is one of the newer competitors in the market, so their products may not be as well promoted by dealers with longer-standing relationships with other manufacturers. This may result in their being one of the better values in the industry.

ASK Impact WSX

Price $9,495

Ranking 3

The ASK Impact WSX is about the same model as the 400 but projects images at the higher resolution of 1024 by 768. Otherwise, it offers the same features as the Impact 400, including zoom and video options. One feature with both ASK models is that they can accept images from a higher-resolution computer and project them at the lower resolution listed, which is a handy feature when making up presentations on high-end computers.

Buhl 5020

Price $5,485

Ranking 9

Although they've been manufacturing audio-visual equipment for over 40 years, Buhl Industries is relatively new in the LCD market. The 5020 is a relatively bare-bones model offering 2.1 million colors at 640 by 480 resolution. It features audio capability and can be upgraded to video for an extra charge. The 5020 can accept images at a higher resolution than it can project.

Dukane MagniView 488B

Price $4,995

Ranking 4

Dukane Corporation of Saint Charles, Illinois, has recently entered the LCD market after many years in the overhead projector industry. The company makes both panels and projectors. The MagniView 488B is the high end of the 480 series, offering 16.7 million colors, video capabilities, and remote control. For users not needing all the colors, the 486 and 487 models are available at about $1,000 less.

In Focus PanelBook 550e

Price $5,799

Ranking 6

In Focus Systems has become the largest player in the LCD field, and has acquired a strong reputation for well-regarded service and support. In Focus has an agreement with the 3M Company which offers In Focus LCD panels under the 3M label. The Panel-Book models all feature active matrix technology and accept images at higher resolution than they can project. The 550e offers the full spectrum of 16.7 million colors, with a standard video capability and remote control.

nView Z110

Price $2,995

Ranking 10

fnView Corporation was founded in 1987 and already has a diverse lineup of LCD systems. The Z100 series of panels are noted for their durability and low prices. The Z110 features 640 by 480 resolution and 1.4 million colors with standard audio and optional video capability. Its low price makes it a suitable choice for budget-minded users who don't need high resolution or the full color spectrum.

nView Z250

Price $5,495

Ranking 7

The nView Z250 is among the newer Z200 series which offers higher resolution and color capabilities. The Z250 features 800 by 600 resolution and the full 16.7 million colors. Standard audio capability and optional video capability add to the plus side, but lack of remote control takes away some points.

Proxima Ovation+842

Price $4,495

Ranking 1

fThe Proxima Corporation is one of the leading manufacturers of color and monochrome projection panels, LCD projectors, and other presentation systems. The company stands out as a leader in technical support and service, and is highly regarded by their dealers. The Ovation+ series is designed for high-volume users. The 842 is similar to the 840 but has the video option as a standard feature and comes recommended for high-volume users

who need video. Other stand-out features are the 16.7 million colors and the optional audio capability.

Sharp QA-1500B

Price $4,695

Ranking 8

Since Sharp Electronics Corporation manufactures a large percentage of LCD screens used in notebook computers, it seems natural they would compete in the LCD panel and projector markets. Unfortunately, Sharp's products are considered to be stronger than their support and service. Being a large corporation, it sometimes is difficult to get through to the right person for support. The QA-1500B has a unique feature: a built-in memory card slot which allows the presenter to store and play back presentations without a computer. The QA-1500B comes with video and audio standard.

Sharp QA-2500

Price $9,995

Ranking 5

The Sharp QA-2500 is a top-of-the-line model LCD panel with a high resolution of 1024 by 768 and a full 16.7 million colors. It can accept images of even higher resolution, while audio and video capabilities are standard.

CONTACT INFORMATION

Refer to the end of the chapter titled "LCDs, Overview of Panels and Projectors," where a list of manufacturers and their telephone numbers is provided.

LCD PROJECTORS

For general information on LCD Projectors and Panels, readers should first consult the chapter "LCDs, Overview of Panels and Projectors," which preceeds this chapter.

LCD projectors combine the functions of an LCD panel and an overhead projector into one machine. The LCD projector sits on a table and projects the computer screen image on a wall or large screen for group viewing. They weigh more and are thus less portable than LCD panels, but there is an advantage to not having to depend on an overhead projector. LCD projectors use two different lamps for their light source: halogen and the newer metal, halide. Halogen lamps project a lower color temperature, so there is some yellow distortion to lighter images, but they are inexpensive to replace. The newer halide lamps are much brighter than halogen and last much longer, but cost about 20-times what their halogen counterparts cost.

The following list contains 10 projectors, their rankings and overall scores.

RANKINGS AND OVERALL SCORES

1	Epson ELP-3000	90.9
2	Eiki LC-6000	86.2
3	Sharp XV-H37UP	77.8
4	In Focus LitePro 570	77.5
5	ASK Impression 960	75.7
6	NEC Multisync MT	74.5
7	Proxima 2810	73.3
8	Dukane ImagePro 8010	69.5
9	nView Luminator L115	66.8
10	In Focus LitePro 560	61.3

EXPLANATION OF RATINGS

Projectors in this section were evaluated on several criteria:

Company (40 points): Companies were judged on the basis of their willingness to service and support their products and their warranty policies. Three of the companies—InFocus, Epson and Proxima—stand out for their progressive warranties and exceptionally responsive service, while Sharp reportedly is slow to respond to consumer problems. The highest possible score was 40 points.

Number of Colors (5 points): Refers to the number of colors or shades of gray that can be projected per image. The best in this category can project 16.7 million colors, worth the full five points.

Zoom Option (10 points): Refers to whether the system has the capability of enlarging a portion of the projected image, worth 10 points.

Audio (10 points): Refers to whether the system offers sound as a standard or optional feature, worth 10 pts.

Video (10 points): Refers to whether the system can be used with video inputs, worth 10 points.

Projected Resolution (10 points): Refers to the number of dots of light, called pixels, that appear in the projected image. The best in this category can project an image of 1024 by 768 pixels, worth the full 10 points.

Image Size (10 points): Refers to the maximum size of the projected image, measured diagonally. The best in this category measured 450 inches, worth the entire 10 points.

Brightness (5 points): Refers to the brightness of the projected image, measured in ANSI lumens, with the brightest in this category having a brightness of 400 lumens, worth five points.

ALPHABETICAL DESCRIPTIONS

ASK Impression 960

Price $16,995

Ranking 5

The ASK Impression 960 is the only model reviewed that has both high resolution at 1024 by 768, and 16.7 million colors. It can present images from computers, videos, and work stations, and is able to project images from higher resolution sources. ASK is one of the newer competitors in the North American market, so their products may not be as well promoted by dealers with longer-standing relationships with other manufacturers.

This may result in their being one of the better values in the industry.

Dukane ImagePro 8010

Price $8,995

Ranking 8

The Dukane ImagePro 8010 is a hefty machine whose weight (27 pounds) could make it a better choice in situations where its installation would be permanent. With 300 ANSI lumens and a metal halide lamp, it's one of the brighter projectors on the market, but with 2.1 million colors as compared with 16.7, it falls behind in that category. A unique feature of the Dukane ImagePro line is that they come with standard lamp life meters that tell you when to replace the metal halide bulb.

Eiki LC-6000

Price $9,995

Ranking 2

The Eiki LC-6000 has some strong points that make up for the company's weak reputation for service and support. The model projects the largest image size of those reviewed, at 450 inches, and also the brightest image at 400 ANSI lumens. Unfortunately, the unit weighs over 50 pounds, so it is not a good choice for those needing portability. It does offer video, audio, and remote control features as standard.

Epson ELP-3000

Price $9,579

Ranking 1

The Epson America company is well known as a maker and marketer of printers, computers, scanners, and other electronic devices. Their customer service program is unique in the industry. If an Epson projector fails, they will provide whole unit exchange in the continental U.S. and Canada for free, and in most cases overnight. They only offer one LCD projector, the ELP-3000, but it's top-of-the-line, offering 16.7 million colors and 300-inch image size, with a healthy brightness of 250 ANSI lumens.

In Focus LitePro 560

Price $6,999

Ranking 10

The LitePro series is the only line of LCD projectors offered by In Focus. Both the 560 and the 570 are highly recommended because of the features they share: bright images at 300 ANSI lumens and 16.7 million colors. Both use halogen lamps. The 560 was ranked lower because it doesn't offer audio or video capabilities.

In Focus LitePro 570

Price $7,499

Ranking 4

The LitePro 570 is similar to the 560 but with more features. In addition to the bright 300 ANSI lumens and 16.7 million colors, the 570 features audio and video capabilities. One unique aspect of the In Focus LCD projectors is its LiteShow option which allows for electronic presentations without a computer.

NEC Multisync MT

Price $9,995

Ranking 6

NEC is a well-known manufacturer of computers and computer peripheral equipment. Their only entry into the LCD market is the Multisync MT (Multimedia Theatre). The MT features a moderate 150-inch image size and 16.7 million colors and comes with audio and video capabilities. One problem with the unit is that the control panel doubles as a remote, which is fine until loss or damage to it results in an inoperable unit.

nView Luminator L115

Price $4,995

Ranking 9

The nView Luminator L115 is a suitable choice for the budget-minded business looking for a projector with all the features but no standout strengths. The L115 comes with audio and video capabilities. The image size of 180 inches is in the middle of the spectrum and with 1.4 million colors, the L115 is at the low end in that category. The 100 ANSI lumens makes it rather low in brightness.

Proxima 2810

Price $7,495

Ranking 7

The Proxima 2810 comes with standard audio and video capabilities and an optional remote control. Its image size of 128 inches is rather small, but it is bright, projecting at 300 ANSI lumens. It can handle 2.1 million colors and projects at a resolution of 640 by 480. Proxima Corporation's solid reputation for progressive support and service should be considered also.

Sharp XV-H37UP

Price $4,695

Ranking 3

The Sharp XV-H37UP is a feature-loaded model that weighs in at a moderate 25 pounds. It features audio and video capability, an image size of 300 inches, a full complement of 16.7 million colors, and a moderate price. Unfortunately, the Sharp Electronics record of service and technical support has suffered but is improving.

CONTACT INFORMATION

Refer to the end of the chapter titled "LCDs, Overview of Panels and Projectors," where a list of manufacturers and their telephone numbers is provided.

PROJECTORS, MOBILES FOR MULTIMEDIA

Presentations aren't what they used to be. No longer do you have to fumble with overhead transparencies or bore your audience with static slides; you're not limited to giving your presentation in a certain room that's equipped with audio-visual equipment. With a notebook computer, presentation software, a mobile projectors and, of course, a little imagination and creativity, you can give presentations with pizzazz, almost anywhere.

Mobile projectors give you the flexibility of giving a top-notch multimedia presentation anywhere. These devices go beyond the LCD panel and special overhead projectors that have been used in the past. These portable projectors have capabilities for playing sound and incorporating video into your presentation. The projectors included in this chapter weigh between nine and 23 pounds. The devices range in price from $5,995 to over $9,000 and use either the Liquid Crystal Display (LCD) or Digital Light Processing (DLP). LCDs use the liquid crystals of the display to either let light pass through (the un-

One of the best projectors on the market, the Epson PowerLite 5000, offers a bright display of 450 ANSI lumens and superior SVGA image quality.

charged phase) or the liquid crystals absorb and redirect light (the charged phase). DLP systems use thousands of mirrors to reflect light. DLP projectors produce a brighter display and have better sound quality. Most units have common features like remote controls, connectors for Macs and PC computers, and jacks for connecting additional monitors, sound, or video sources.

Below are various projectors with their overall ratings.

OVERALL RATINGS

Epson PowerLite 5000	★★★1/2
InFocus LitePro 720	★★★1/2
Polaroid PV-222	★★★
ASK LCD Impression A4	★★★
Lightware VP820	★★★
NEC MultiSync MT800	★★★
Telex Firefly P250	★★★
Proxima Lightbook LB-20	★★1/2

EXPLANATION OF RATINGS

Projectors were scored one to four stars on these features: *Mobility* refers to how easy it is transport; *Display* refers to the brightness of the display (display brightness is measured in ANSI lumens, the higher the number the brighter the display); *Image quality* refers to the resolution of the image; and *Sound* refers to the projector sound capability. The overall rating is the result of averaging the four aforementioned facets of each projector.

ALPHABETICAL DESCRIPTIONS

ASK LCD Impression A4
Price $9,750
Overall Rating ★★★
Mobility ★★
Display ★★★★
Image Quality ★★★

The ASK LCD Impression A4 is touted by its manufacturer as the World's Smallest and Brightest Projector. It is almost the same size as an A4 or letter size sheet of paper and weighs 11 pounds. The Impression A4 is a three-panel LCD projector with a bright display, 500 ANSI lumens. Images can be displayed in resolutions from 1152 x 870 down to 640 x 480. The replaceable lamp has a life up to 2,500 hours. Other features include two computer inputs, a lighted remote, keystone correction and a soft carrying case. Sound is available through one watt stereo speakers. The company has a 48-hour repair policy.

Epson PowerLite 5000
Price $9,399
Overall Rating ★★★1/2
Mobility ★★★
Display ★★★★
Image Quality ★★★★

One of the best projectors on the market, the PowerLite 5000 offers a bright display of 450 ANSI lumens and superior SVGA image quality. This 14.1-pound, three-panel polysilicon projector has a manual focus and zoom, two computer and video inputs, but no keystone adjustment. There are built-in 2W+2W stereo speakers. Images are displayed in the default resolution of 800-by-600. Epson's SizeWize can produce 1,024-by-768 images interpolated. For repairs there is a quick exchange. The projector is covered by a two-year warranty.

InFocus LitePro 720

Price $9,199

Overall Rating ★★★1/2

Mobility ★★★

Display ★★★★

Image Quality ★★★★

The compact InFocus LitePro 720 is a three-panel LCD that weighs 12 pounds. Its display produces a very bright image with an ANSI lumens rating of 450, which puts it in the top tier among the other projectors. You can use the projector in normal room light with the help of its 150-watt metal-halide lamp, which lasts about 2,000 hours. This projector can fill up a 4-foot to 14-foot screen from 5 to 18 feet and is capable of virtual 1,024x768 resolution. Keystoning can be adjusted up to 17 degrees.

The projector is easy to set up. There are icons for easy assembly. The included Cable Wizard gives you 10 feet of cabling for connecting monitors, monitor pass-through, mouse, and audio. You can also use the rotating dial to switch between PC and Mac connectors. You can control the device from backlit buttons on the projector or from the infrared remote. These controls can be used to adjust sound and video, adjust images, or switch sources. There are also jacks for S-video, composite- video/audio jack, and jacks for additional speakers. Stereo drives are conspicuously absent from this device. There is only one three-watt speaker.

Despite this the LitePro's high quality images and brightness make it a good choice. InFocus has a companion product with this projector called the Presentation Player ($1,799 list). This is a six pound device that is designed to attach to the projector. The player comes with a 1.2 gigabyte hard disk and a zip drive, so you can install your presentation on the player and leave your notebook at home.

Lightware VP820

Price $6,495

Overall Rating ★★★

Mobility ★★★★

Display ★★1/2

Image Quality ★★★

The Lightware VP820 has a 6.5-inch active-matrix LCD and weighs in at 9.3 pounds. This lightweight projector can fill a 40-inch (diagonal) screen from five feet and can handle virtual XGA 1,024x768. The display was dim, with 270 ANSI lumens as compared to other projectors. Its lamp uses a 400-watt halogen bulb that can last 40 to 60 hours. Included is an internal replacement bulb. The projector includes three-watt speakers and there are connectors if you need additional powerful speakers. The device comes with an infrared remote control and hard carrying case (which adds five pounds to the weight). You can't beat the weight of this projector, but you can find projectors that produce brighter images.

NEC MultiSync MT800

Price $7,495

Overall Rating ★★★

Mobility ★★★

Display ★★★

Image Quality ★★★

MultiSync MT800 is a 16-pound, three-panel polysilicon projector. The projector's display has 350 ANSI lumens. Image can be displayed in 24-bit at a 800-by-600 resolution. Features include a power zoom lens, a 2Y/4Y electronic zoom, and a Infrared Receiver that plugs into the mouse port. There are also built-in stereo speakers (1.0w x 2.8 ohm). The projector is covered by a one year limited, parts and labor warranty. There is also InstaCare service available, which will replace your projector within 24 hours.

Polaroid PV-222

Price $9,495

Overall Rating ★★★

Mobility ★★

Display ★★★1/2

Image Quality ★★★★

Designed for professional presenters, the Polaroid PV-222 is a one-chip DLP (Digital Light Processing) projector with SVGA image resolution. Images displayed are exactly what you have on your computer's screen. At 23 pounds, it is one of the heaviest projectors of the group. The Polaroid's PV-222 brightness rating is 410 ANSI lumens. The lamp uses a 270-watt bulb that lasts for 250 hours. The projector can fill a five-foot screen from 5.8 to 8.7 feet.

Images are displayed in 800 x 600 SVGA resolution. Sound comes from the three-inch, 5-watt stereo speakers. Features include four input sources for composite videos, S-Video, and either a PC or Macintosh computer. You can connect two computers and two video sources simultaneously and switch between the sources quickly. All four sources have stereo inputs; additional speakers can be used via a stereo-out connector. There is a power zoom and focus and an infrared remote. Other features include keystone correction to 17 degrees and a built-in control panel with an interactive menu for setup, image, and sound selections.

You can control the projector from the wireless remote or the projector. A laser pointer is built into the remote. The infrared receiver is in a separate unit, making it easy to conveniently place it where you want it so you're not confined to one part of a room during your presentation. This wireless remote control has a 50 foot range. This projector also offers operation in other languages besides English, including Spanish, German, and French. This projector delivers superb performance.

Proxima Lightbook LB-20

Price $5,949

Overall Rating ★★1/2

Mobility ★★★

Display ★★1/2

Image Quality ★★

The Proxima Lightbook weighs 11.4 pounds with dimensions of 13.5 x 9.25 x 5 inches. For easy mobility this projector can be folded down to five inches for easy transport. Howeve,r the display is dim, only 200 ANSI lumens. Images can be displayed in SVGA 800 x 600 and VGA 640 x 480. Other features include built-in Kensington Security and two remotes— one is a standard remote and the other can substitute for your mouse. There are two two-watt speakers and keystone correction.

Telex Firefly P250

Price $5,995

Overall Rating ★★★

Mobility ★★★★

Display ★★1/2

Image Quality ★★

This active-matrix LCD projector scored well on mobility. The FireFly P250 is a lightweight 9.8 pounds, which can scrunch down to just three inches, making transportation easy. Images can be displayed in SVGA (800x600) high resolution. Now for the downside. Display brightness is only 220 ANSI lumens, making it one of the dimmest projectors. There is no zoom or height adjustment. There are built in three-watt speakers. For a few pounds more you can find a better projector.

CONTACT INFORMATION

ASK LCD Inc.
(800) 275-5231
www.ask.no.com

Epson America Inc.
(800) 463-7766
www.epson.com

In Focus Systems
(800) 294-6400
www.infocus.com

Lightware
(800) 445-9396
www.lightware.com

NEC Technologies Inc.
(800) 632-4636
www.nec.com

Polaroid Corp.
(800) 662-8337
extension 801
www.polaroid.com

Proxima Corp.
(800) 447-7692
www.proxima.com

Telex Communications Inc.
(800)
828-6107
www.telex.com

BUSINESS PLANNERS

Whether you're going into business or planning strategy for an existing business, you're taking a big risk, but with a little planning, risks can be minimized. A business plan is a good tool that gives you a roadmap of your business idea and gives potential investors a better sense of how viable your business idea is. There are numerous ways to write a business plan: you could get someone to write it for you (and pay them big bucks) or you could do it yourself. There are software programs on the market that can help you with the latter.

These programs either use templates or are interactive. Templates offer a fill-in-the-blank approach with sample business-plan templates that you can use by replacing the sample text with your information. Interactive programs offer more help by asking you different questions about your business, then filling in some of the data for you. Both forms can provide you with a concise business plan. No matter what type of software program you choose to generate your business plan, it won't guarantee your success of obtaining financing, but it can help you be better prepared.

Listed below are six popular business plan programs and their ratings.

OVERALL RATINGS

Plan Write 4.0	★★★ 1/2
Business Plan Pro 2.0	★★★
Smart Business Plan 5.2	★★★
BizPlanBuilder 5.0	★★★
Business Plan Writer 6.0	★★ 1/4
PlanMaker 2.0	★★

EXPLANATION OF RATINGS

Each program was evaluated on four aspects: ease of use, style (template or interactive), help functions, and results. Each aspect could potentially earn up to four stars, with one star being the lowest rating. The ratings of these four aspects were then averaged, resulting in the overall rating.

ALPHABETICAL DESCRIPTIONS

BizPlanBuilder 5.0

Price $129

Overall Rating ★★★

Ease of Use ★★★

Style (template or interactive) ★★★

Help Functions ★★★

Results ★★★

BizPlanBuilder 5.0 has word processing templates and spreadsheet templates in various formats. The word processing templates are several generic formats, including rich text format (RTF), ASCII, Microsoft Word 2.0 for Windows, and WordPerfect 5.1 for DOS. Spreadsheet templates are in Lotus 1-2-3 Release 2.0 for DOS (WK1) and Microsoft Excel version 4 (XLS). Also included is a reference manual which should be read prior to completing the templates.

To build your business plan, you complete a separate template for each component of your plan. Templates include the Vision/Mission template, Company Overview, Product/Service Strategy, Market Analysis, Market Plan, and Financial Plan. There are also sample nondisclosure and cover letters included, along with a list of key business questions. Spreadsheet templates have one- and five-year balance sheets, income statements, breakeven analyses, cash flow statements, budgets, gross-profit analyses, a personal financial statement, and working capital worksheet.

BizPlanBuilder gives you the basic tools to build a business plan, but no polish. There are a lot of templates but they are not formatted. To get a more polished-looking plan you have to do all the formatting, but that is not all that difficult.

Business Plan Pro 2.0

Price $149.95	
Overall Rating ★★★	
Ease of Use ★★★	
Style (template or interactive) ★★★	
Help Functions ★★★	
Results ★★★	

Business Plan Pro uses an interactive split screen that creates detailed business plans. The top half displays the instructions and the lower panel is where you enter in the information for your plan. You are able to toggle between the two panels, cutting and copying sample text into your plan when

necessary. The word processor and spreadsheet applications are built-in.

Topic headings are displayed in a pop-up window. You can work in sequence or jump to any topic you wish by clicking on it. As you move through each topic, if there is a spreadsheet or graph template associated with it an icon is displayed in the upper right corner. Clicking on this icon takes you to the related template. After entering in the appropriate data, you can then return to where you left off. The charts look nice, but you cannot modify them. Also the spreadsheet does not have a "Copy Cells" option. However, the text, charts, and tables are professionally formatted and well-integrated with the rest of the plan.

Business Plan Writer 6.0

Price $49.99	
Overall Rating ★★1/4	
Ease of Use ★★	
Style (template or interactive) ★★★	
Help Functions ★★	
Results ★★	

This program uses nine text files and four spreadsheet files that include instructions and sample data. These templates are in formats compatible with Word, WordPerfect, Excel and Lotus 1-2-3. The business plan templates consist of eight topics: Executive Summary, Description and Origins of the Business, Products or Services, Marketing Plan, Sales Plan, Manufacturing or Services, Performance Plan, and Financial Analysis. To use each template you read through the italicized Guidance text, which explains how to complete each section, then modify the sample data in each template.

The text is not formatted and no graphs or charts are automatically integrated in the plan. Spreadsheet templates offer financial statements, organization charts, a competitive analysis and business projections. A few drawbacks are that the italicized instructions are hard to read, cells are not protected from accidental deletion, and there are no charts or powerful formatting tools to give the spreadsheets more pizazz.

PlanMaker 2.0

Price $129

Overall Rating ★★

Ease of Use ★★

Style (template or interactive) ★★

Help Functions ★★

Results ★★

PlanMaker 2.0 offers a three-pronged interactive approach which is awkward to use. The program uses Worksheets that ask questions about your business idea. Data is recorded on these Worksheets, then you move on to the Instructions/Notes section, which gives you more detailed instructions on the same topic. You have the ability to toggle back and forth from your Worksheet to the Instructions/Notes screen. But in an effort to aid you in entering financial data, Plan-Maker takes an even more awkward approach with a 33-screen process which

consists of an instruction page and an entry page. You constantly have to toggle between the two pages, which is cumbersome and frustrating. Finally, after plenty of jumping back and forth, the printout quality is poor. The program has the capability of projecting three years into the future, but the formatting is lacking. Overall there is a lot of useful information in the program, but its cumbersome navigation makes it tedious to use.

Plan Write 4.0

Price $129.95

Overall Rating
★★★1/2

Ease of Use ★★★★

Style (template or interactive) ★★★★

Help Functions ★★★

Results ★★★

Plan Write 4.0, the number-one rated planner.

Plan Write guides you step-by-step through the business plan process. Using a split screen, each topic displays the Rationale and an example at the top of the screen. The bottom of the screen is the text area where the business plan is created. The information in the top part can be copied to the text area for use in your plan.

Entering financial information is even easier. An explanation for each entry is provided and you enter data one-by-one on some of the screens. As you enter this data a summary spreadsheet will consolidate all of the data. If you need to change a value just click on it in the summary spreadsheet and it takes you to where you entered it. After the data is changed, you are taken back to the summary. The financial data is charted and you can toggle between the chart and the financial screen where the data was entered. This program also has an Internet feature that links you to over 100 web sites with tips and techniques focusing on the program, and the business plan and offers help for finding investors.

Smart Business Plan 5.2

Price $149

Overall Rating ★★★

Ease of Use ★★★

Style (template or interactive) ★★★

Help Functions ★★★

Results ★★★

Smart Business Plan is an interactive program with a built-in text editor. There are two modules: business planning and spreadsheet. The split screen format is used in the planning module with instructions and samples displayed on top, and a text work area below. The text editor is used to create your business plan and includes a spell-check and can include graphics. Printing and formatting is above average.

Ten major topics and 50 subtopics are included with this program. As you work on your plan, you can flag each section as In Progress, Complete, or Exclude. Spreadsheets can be used in Table/Graph mode. The sample spreadsheet is displayed on the top half of the screen, and

the bottom is reserved for your data. Once the data is entered, you click on the graph and the program formats a chart with your data. You can select which sections to include in your plan by using the "Included in This Section" box which is displayed if a graph or chart was associated with a certain section.

CONTACT INFORMATION

PlanWrite
Business Resource Software
(800) 423-1228
www.market.com/PlanWrite/pwrite5.html/

Business Plan Pro
Palo Alto Software
(800) 229-7526
www.pasware.com

Smart Business Plan
American Institute for Financial Research
(800) 791-1000
www.aifr.com/smart/9.htm/

BizPlanBuilder 5.0
JIAN Tools for Sales
(800) 346-5426
www.jianusa.com

Business Headstart
Planet Corporation
(800) 366-5111
www.planet~corp.com

Automate Your Business Plan
Out of Your Mind...And Into the MarketPlace
714 544-0248
www.business-plan.com

Business Plan Writer 6.0
Graphite Software
PlanMaker 2.0
POWERSolutions for Business
(800) 955-3337
www.planmaker.com

COMPUTER NETWORKS,
DEDICATED SERVER LANS

If your company has or plans to install more than 10 to 25 computers or has offices in multiple locations that need to share computer data, you should be considering installing a network.

In this chapter, we look at network operating system software that supports server-based networks that will support up to 100 computers on a network.

A computer network would connect all of the computers to each other letting your people share expensive resources such as printers, CD-ROM drives, and modems. While you may have considered or even installed a "peer-to-peer" network (see next chapter), you may need a server-based network to improve network performance, control loading and sharing of expensive software packages, better manage network resources, improve security, or run network-centered applications such as shared databases. The industry term for a personal computer network is a *local area network (LAN)*.

A dedicated server LAN has one computer set up to contain shared files and applications and to attach shared printers and other peripherals. A network operating system (NOS) is installed on the server. Other computers in the network are called "nodes" or "clients" using the shared resources and possibly sharing their resources with others as well. The client computers have software to communicate with the NOS installed, a network interface card (NIC) and a cable connecting it to the server or other clients. The advantages of a server-based network versus a peer- to-peer network are central data management and backup, improved security over the resources, and more flexibility for growth. Shared software on the server can be updated in one place, ensuring that all users have the same level. And often the client computers can be slower models and have less features because a lot of the processing and networking workload is transferred to the server, resulting in lower overall network costs.

Selecting, buying, and installing a server-based network is not a "do-it-yourself" project for companies who do not have dedicated technical staff. Because making a mistake in selecting the NOS and network hardware can become costly if it later must be replaced, it is worthwhile to get help from experienced network installation experts. The NOS manufacturers can often recommend experienced specialists in your area for their products, and local computer stores and consultants can be asked to bid on your LAN project. Value Added Resellers (VARs) make money by selling you the network equipment and software, so you can get a lot of advice from them for little money; however, they usually only deal with a couple of network types so it pays to get several VARs to bid on your project. Be sure to check their references and probe their ability to support your LAN for several years after installation.

In addition to the NOS, there are a number of hardware options and technical terms you will encounter for connecting your computers into a network.

Topology is a computer term for how your network is connected together. The simplest and least expensive is a "bus" topology where your computers are on one cable that goes from computer to computer with connectors for each one; however, bus topologies tend to bog down with network traffic as your network grows. A slightly more expensive alternative is a "star" topology with all computers connected to a central device called a "hub" on the server. Token Ring networks are similar to the "star" but have a "ring" topology with the computers connected in a ring within the central hub.

Ethernet is the most common network type for small networks because it is inexpensive and easy to install. Speed and distance between computers is indicated in the type of Ethernet network you choose. 10Base2, for example, means 10 million bits per second with a maximum of 200 meters for a cable segment in the network. It is the most common type for small peer-to-peer networks; however, you may want to buy a 10BaseT network if you expect much growth. NICs can be purchased that also have an option for 100BaseT operation for a higher speed network. The "T" in these types indicates they only work in a star topology. Other higher-speed network types include "Token Ring," "100VG-ANYLAN," and "FDDI". If you need to prioritize data on the network to ensure it arrives quickly regardless of network traffic, you need to consider the 100VG-ANYLAN topology. The fastest is FDDI, but because it is so expensive most companies only use this topology for connecting LANs to each other.

Network Interface Cards (NICs) must match the type of expansion slots that are in your computers. Older computers may have VESA, MicroChannel, or EISA slots, while the newer ones will have ISA or PCI slots. Another consideration is the network type and speed that the card can handle: 10Base2, 10BaseT, and 100BaseT are the most common.

Cabling is used to connect your computers to each other. Coaxial cable is used in 10Base2 networks and costs about 25 cents a foot plus labor to install. Twisted pair cables are less expensive per foot but are only used in 10BaseT, 100BaseT, Token Ring, and other higher speed types of networks.

Hubs are required in star and ring topology networks. They can range in price from approximately $50 to more than $2,000 for intelligent hubs. The intelligent hub can identify network problems and help in managing large networks or those that are scattered over several floors or locations and are highly recommended in networks with over 15 computers.

Switches or Bridges are used to break a large network into several smaller ones, but let the entire network still function as one network.

Routers let your network clients send and receive data from remote computers, such as Internet servers, remote offices, or traveling employee laptop computers.

Protocols are like languages that are spoken on the network to send files and other information to other computers or printers. They are implemented by telling your NIC which to use. The important thing is that all the computers speak the same language on the network. Common protocols are NETBIOS, NETBEUI, TCP/IP, IPX (Internetwork Packet Exchange), DLC (datalink control), and SNMP (Simple Network Management Protocol).

Symmetric Multiprocessing Systems (SMP) are multiple processors within a single computer to provide better performance for a task that cannot be subdivided across servers.

Below are network operating systems that support server-based networks that will support up to 100 computers on a network. Data for these packages was obtained from the publishers.

OVERALL RATINGS

IBM OS/2 Warp Server 4	★★★ 3/4
Novell Netware 4.1	★★★ 3/4
Microsoft Windows NT	★★★ 1/2
Banyan VINES 7.1	★★★ 1/4
Novell IntranetWare for Small Business (IWSB)	★★ 3/4

EXPLANATION OF RATINGS

Server-based network operating systems were selected for review from currently available products at their current release level. The overall rating was arrived at by giving individual scores on scalability, ease of use, and features. These scores were then averaged to arrive at the overall rating. The highest rating possible is four stars; the lowest is one.

ALPHABETICAL DESCRIPTIONS

Prices indicated below are an approximate price-per-workstation for new software.

Banyan VINES 7.1

Overall Rating ★★★ 1/4	
Price $2,995 for 10 users	
Scalability ★★★	
Ease of use ★★★ 3/4	
Features ★★★	

VINES can be used for networks of all sizes, with up to 1000 clients per server and multiple servers to support even the largest of companies. And it includes support for SMP systems and parallel processing for fast network performance. Clients supported are DOS versions 4 through 6, OS/2 2.0 and Warp 4.0, Windows 3.1, Windows for Workgroups 3.11, Windows 95, Windows NT, and Macintosh (System 7 or later). There is support for multiple languages including English, German, French, Spanish, Japanese, Korean, and Chinese. Connectivity is via VINES IP or TCP/IP, and SMTP.

The StreetTalk Directory and Explorer make it easy for users to find and use network resources such as files and printers. No matter how big the network may be, there is a single system image for the network and single point of administration from any computer on the network. Printing can be from one queue to multiple printers to avoid problems when a particular printer fails, or multiple print queues can be used to prioritize jobs. Features included are Server-to-Server LAN, Security, Time Synchronization, VINES File Store System, Print, and ENS MT. Other popular networking features are available separately from Banyan or a number of other companies and these include messaging, software license controls, backup and restore, and additional network management utilities.

IBM OS/2 Warp Server 4

Overall Rating ★★★ 3/4

Price $559 server; $749 for server and 10 clients

Scalability ★★★★

Ease of use ★★★ 1/2

Features ★★★★

This product supports up to 1,000 active users per server sharing files and printers, and there is no practical limit on the number of servers that can be included in one network. And for critical application performance, it can run in an SMP environment with up to 64 processors. Other servers in the network can run NetWare 3.x/4.x, Windows NT Server 3.51, LAN Server 4.0, or OS/2 Warp Server. Clients can run DOS 6-7, Windows 3.1, Windows for Workgroups 3.11, Windows 95, Windows NT Workstation 3.51, OS/2 Warp, AIX, and Macintosh. Protocols include NETBIOS, IPX, and Internet access via

enhanced TCP/IP. Ethernet, Token Ring, FDDI, and ATM LAN topologies are supported. Users can easily share files, applications, printers, and modems. Administration is via the integrated Tivoli systems management tools instead of relying on "add on" products. The graphical interface makes administrative tasks easy to do. And there is a sophisticated security capability. Features include comprehensive backup and recovery facilities, remote connectivity, mainframe connectivity, and secure Internet access. And it supports "WorkSpace On-Demand" to let you load both client operating systems and applications from the server to any computer in the network for true mobility of your work force. For high volume workloads, it supports mainframe-type high-speed printers.

Microsoft Windows NT

Overall Rating ★★★ 1/2

Price $999 for server and 10 clients

Scalability ★★★ 1/2

Ease of use ★★★ 1/4

Features ★★★ 1/2

Adding users to a server and servers to your network is easy, but without a strong network management tool, it is difficult to manage a large network. It does support SMP for up to four processors and it can interact in networks containing most other NOS's. Clients supported are Windows 3.1, Windows for Workgroups, Windows 95, Windows NT Workstation, Macintosh, DOS, OS/2, and UNIX. Microsoft describes the ease of use as being like "Windows for your network." Little or no user training is needed to share printers, files, applications, and modems. The same interface is on both the server and the workstations, reducing training and support costs. It extends W95 features, like long file names, to the server environment. While it has graphical network management tools there is no "directory" like NetWare and Vines. Security is set up by individual or group and can get complicated. Features include built-in e-mail, remote user dial-in, a web browser, a web server capability, and support for the Microsoft BackOffice Suite of server-based applications.

Novell IntranetWare for Small Business (IWSB)

Overall Rating ★ ★ 3/4

Price $895 for five clients; $65 per addition or $325 for five client addition.

Scalability ★

Ease of use ★ ★ ★ ★

Features ★ ★ ★ 1/4

This product can support a maximum of 25 users per server; however, migration to their larger IntranetWare product is very easy and inexpensive and you can then expand to up to 1000 users per server. Hardware requirements are modest—a 486 with 24MB RAM, CD-ROM drive, and a 1 gigabyte hard drive are recommended. Clients can run DOS, Windows 3.1, Windows for Workgroups, Windows 95, and Macintosh OS; however, administration can only be done from a Windows-based system. New quick setup and the NetWare Easy Administration Tool (NEAT) appeals to companies installing a network for the first time; however, some functions still require the use of a command-line NetWare Console, which is not very intuitive. There is a feature called "QuickStart" to coach you through the process of setting up users, groups, and shared applications. Printers can be set up using this or NEAT. For users, it contains the highly regarded Network Directory Services (NDS) features that are in the full NetWare product line, with some limitations. NDS screens are similar to File Manager or Windows Explorer, displaying the network resources in a familiar layout. Using NDS, users can share files, printers, modems, and network applications without any formal training. Features include Netware Connect to let users dial in from remote locations and Netscape Navigator 3.0 to let you use the on-line documentation or surf the Internet. Multi-site LAN management and website hosting capabilities are in the full IntranetWare product. Note that there is no direct free technical support other than what is on their Internet site and CompuServe.

Novell Netware 4.1

Overall Rating ★ ★ ★ 3/4

Price $2,495 for server and 10 clients

Scalability ★ ★ ★ ★

Ease of use ★ ★ ★ ★

Features ★ ★ ★ 1/4

This product can handle up to 1,000 users per server. An SMP option is available for improved application performance. Clients can use Windows NT, Windows 3.1, UNIX, OS/2, Mac OS, or DOS. Users can easily share files and printers using the Novell Directory Services (NDS) which has a single network-based view of all network services. It is the easiest NOS to manage from an administrative perspective, as security and access rights can be set at hierarchical points rather than having to deal with each individual resource. Features include integrated resource accounting, software licensing management, web server capabilities, e-mail, faxing, voice mail, and paging services. Known for its stability and reliability in the file and print sharing areas, it has a "mirroring" facility to maintain two copies of critical files, with the copy being made on a second disk driver, if one is available. File compression can result in less disk space required on the server.

CONTACT INFORMATION

Banyan Systems Incorporated
800-222-6926
www.banyan.com

IBM Corporation
800-426-2968
www.ibm.com

Microsoft Corp.
800-426-9400
www.microsoft.com

Novell, Inc.
800-346-6855
www.novell.com

COMPUTER NETWORKS, PEER-TO-PEER LANS

If your office has more than one personal computer in it and does not have a "network," you are probably experiencing productivity problems! Employees are running around the office sharing information on paper or carrying files on diskettes between computers to share them or get them printed on your only printer. A computer "network" would connect all of the computers to each other, letting your people share expensive resources such as printers, CD-ROM drives, and modems. And they could share or exchange files such as customer address lists, standard formats for letters or forms, and faxes received. The industry term for a personal computer network is a *local area network (LAN)*.

The least expensive and easiest to install option for a LAN is a *peer-to-peer Network Operating System (NOS)*. In this type of network, every computer has the same status as a "peer" on the network. Each computer has the NOS, a network interface card (NIC), and a cable connecting it to the other computers. Each computer can share its resources with the others in the network—there is usually no central administrative control over this. And, often the network can be installed without outside assistance—there are "kits" available that include everything you need to set it up for from two to 10 computers. Without considering labor, you should expect to spend from $50 to $150 per computer for the NIC and cables and up to $150 per computer for the NOS.

There are some disadvantages to peer-to-peer networks that you should be aware of before deciding to install one. First, consider your potential for growth in the number of computers on the network. This type of NOS tends to slow down at 10 computers and can rarely support more than 25 computers being used simultaneously. Second, security is left up to each user to both protect and backup critical company information. Third, if your resources are scattered around on various computers, you must have all of these computers turned on to use them, even if some of the users are not in the office at all. And fourth, there are often no tools to support electronic mail within the office, dial-in support for traveling employees, or efficient connections to the Internet. If these things are important to your company, a *server-based network operating system* should be considered instead.

Buying a NOS is not complicated — in fact you already have one if you have Windows 95 or Windows NT Workstation installed on your computers. If you have Windows 3.1, it is a simple upgrade to install Windows for Workgroups because there is no retraining required for your users other than the resource sharing procedures. For users of IBM's OS/2 Warp, you should consider IBM OS/2

Connect V 3 for your NOS, or an upgrade to OS/2 Warp four which has networking totally integrated. And there are other products available from computer retail stores, mail order houses, and the manufacturers. Most NOS software and NICs can be purchased in single computer quantities, but there are significant savings if you buy in quantity. But if you do not have the technical skills in-house to install and support your network, you should consider hiring an expert to help you. The NOS manufacturers can often recommend experienced installation specialists in your area for their products, and local computer stores and consultants can be asked to bid on your LAN project.

In addition to the NOS, there are a number of hardware options and technical terms you will encounter for connecting your computers into a network:

Topology is a computer term for how your network is connected together. The simplest and least expensive is a "bus" topology where your computers are on one cable that goes from computer to computer with connectors for each one. A more expensive alternative is a "star" topology with all computers connected to a central device called a "hub" on one of your computers. Other topologies exist but are not appropriate for peer-to-peer networks.

Ethernet is the most common network type for small networks because it is inexpensive and easy to install. Speed and distance between computers is indicated in the type of Ethernet network you choose. 10Base2, for example, means 10 million bits per second with a maximum of 200 meters for a cable segment in the network. It is the most common type for small peer-to-peer networks; however, you may want to buy a 10BaseT network if you expect much growth. NICs can be purchased that also have an option for 100BaseT operation for a higher speed network. The "T" in these types indicates they only work in a star topology. Token Ring is another network type that is rarely used in peer-to-peer networks because it is more expensive to install.

Network Interface Cards (NICs) must match the type of expansion slots that are in your computers. Older computers may have VESA, MicroChannel, or EISA slots, while the newer ones will have ISA or PCI slots. Another consideration is the network type and speed that the card can handle: 10Base2, 10BaseT and, 100BaseT are the most common.

Cabling is used to connect your computers to each other. Coaxial cable is used in 10Base2 networks and costs about 25cents per foot plus labor to install. Twisted pair cables are less expensive per foot but are only used in 10BaseT, 100BaseT, Token Ring, and other higher speed types of networks.

Hubs are required in star topology networks. They can range in price per connected computer from approximately $20 to more than $300 for the higher speed networks.

Protocols are like languages that are spoken on the network to send files and other information to other computers or printers. They are implemented by telling your

NIC which to use. The important thing is that all the computers speak the same language on the network. Common protocols are NETBIOS, NETBEUI, TCP/IP, IPX(Internetwork Packet Exchange), DLC (datalink control), and SNMP (Simple Network Management Protocol).

We look at network operating system software that supports peer-to-peer networks and that is not limited to two or three computers in the network. Data on these packages was obtained from the manufacturers. Prices indicated are an approximate price-per-workstation for new software when the software was reviewed.

OVERALL RATINGS

Microsoft Windows for Workgroups V 3.11	★ ★ ★ 1/2
IBM OS/2 Warp 4	★ ★ ★ 1/4
Mango Medley 97	★ ★ ★
Microsoft Windows 95	★ ★ ★
Novell Personal NetWare	★ ★ ★
Artisoft LANtastic 7.0	★ ★ 3/4

EXPLANATION OF RATINGS

Peer-to-peer network operating systems were selected for review from currently available products at their current release level. The overall rating was arrived at by giving individual scores for Ease of Installation, Ease of Use, and Features. The highest rating possible is four stars. These scores were then averaged to arrive at the overall rating.

ALPHABETICAL DESCRIPTIONS

Artisoft LANtastic 7.0

Overall Rating ★ ★ 3/4

Price $119 for one user, $499 for 10 users

Ease of installation ★ ★ 1/2

Ease of use ★ ★

Features ★ ★ ★ 3/4

This product, while rated rather low overall, deserves serious consideration because of its network management and security features and ease of converting to a server-based network when needed. It is a little more complicated to install and use than some of the others reviewed because it is an add-on for a computer that already has an operating system such as DOS, Windows, or Windows 95. To make it easy to match up the hardware and software, there is a Starter Kit for two PCs that costs $249 and includes a 25-foot cable and two NICs as well as the NOS software. Add-On Kits are available for $149 with cable, NIC, and NOS license. Features include the ability to share applications, files, printers, CD-ROM drives, modems, and phone lines. Internet access is via the included Netscape Navigator Client to let several computer users share a single Internet connection at the same time. Network users can communicate directly using an interactive chat, feature or send messages to each other very easily. There is also a network administration feature for adding new users and groups from a single computer instead of having to do this from each computer on the network. Protocols are limited to NETBIOS and TCP/IP, with the latter able to connect to Windows NT, NetWare, or

UNIX servers. Free technical support is available weekdays for 30 days from the first call. Fee-based support options are available. Their Internet site also contains installation tips and support materials.

IBM OS/2 Warp 4

Price $249 for one; discount for volume or upgrade version

Overall Rating ★ ★ ★ 1/4

Ease of installation ★ ★ ★

Ease of use ★ ★ ★

Features ★ ★ ★ 1/2

While this option rated highly in our review, it is a complete operating system for your computer. If you have Windows installed currently, there may be other conversion issues such as current software compatibility that would raise the cost of this option. But if you have a prior release of OS/2 installed, there is a $200 option to install OS/2 Warp Connect to get similar networking features added in. This NOS is relatively easy to install and use as each computer in the network can see all the resources available to it in one network window. Eash user can share files, printers, and modems with other Warp, Windows for Workgroups, Windows NT, Windows 95, and LANtastic 6.0 users .Protocols are limited to NETBIOS and TCP/IP to connect to larger server-based networks. Support is available worldwide and their Internet site has extensive support information and product fixes available for download.

Mango Medley 97

Price $249 for two users, $899 for an additional five users

Overall Rating ★ ★ ★

Ease of installation ★ ★ ★ ★

Ease of use ★ ★ ★ ★

Features ★

Medley has a slightly different concept for sharing on a network. They call it a "pool," in that a common "Medley drive" is created for file storage using a portion of every computer's disk space, which looks like a local hard drive to the users. They boast of a one-button installation with literally no user training or network administration required. Information is moved physically to where it is being used, lowering network traffic and improving response time. Every file is saved in at least two computers to ensure availability in case any one computer fails. A major limitation is that it works only on computers with Windows 95 and a minimum of 16MB RAM using an Ethernet network with a hub. Users can share files, printers, and other peripherals, as well as set up simple security for restricting file access. Support includes 90 days of Internet access to their support team and the ability to connect to "Mango Central" via a modem for direct assistance.

Microsoft Windows for Workgroups V 3.11

Price $139.95 each or $49.95 upgrade from DOS or Windows 3.1

Overall Rating ★ ★ ★ 1/2

Ease of installation ★ ★ ★ 1/2

Ease of use ★ ★ ★ 1/2

Features ★ ★ ★ 1/2

For those of you still using Windows 3.1, this is the easiest and least expensive way to set up a network. And you probably already have sufficient hardware to run it as the minimum computer is a 386 with 4MB RAM. It is easy to install—just like installing Windows 3.1, plus giving your computer a unique name on the network. Sharing of resources is done using the Control Panel for printers and the File Manager for files and it is very easy to do just by selecting the share option from the menu and giving the resource a name. Directories or files shared by other network users are easy to connect to, and they then appear as additional disk drives in File Manager or additional printers when you want to print something out. It is also a good option for companies who still have DOS installed or plan to migrate to Windows 95 because this NOS can interact with computers running DOS (using Workgroup Connections software), Windows 3.1, or Windows 95. To accommodate network growth, this NOS can attach to a variety of server-based systems easily. Users cannot share modems or COM ports, but they can share files, printers, and CD-ROM drives. It also includes Chat for communication between users immediately, Microsoft Mail for network e-mail and messaging, and Schedule+ for group scheduling and calendaring. While there is no central network management facility, each user has the use of Net Watcher, which is a way to monitor which users are using your resources and terminate any users, if desired. NETBEUI, TCP/IP, IPX and DLC protocols are supported. Support is available by phone for 90 days from your first call for free. Fee options are available after that time. The Microsoft Internet site has extensive support capabilities.

Microsoft Windows 95

Price $179.95 each or $89.95 upgrade from any other operating system

Overall Rating ★ ★ ★

Ease of installation ★ ★ ★

Ease of use ★ ★ ★

Features ★ ★ ★

With many new computers shipping with Windows 95 pre-installed, this may be the simplest option for those installing computers for the first time because the networking operating system is already installed. Otherwise, upgrading all of your computers to run Windows 95, because this NOS does not support any other connecting system types, can be expensive as it requires a minimum of 8MB RAM, lots of disk space, and your older software may need to be upgraded. Folders (files) and printers can be shared easily by each user just by going into My Computer and changing the properties of each resource to be shared. Users can see the resources available from others by using the Network Neighborhood Icon on the desktop, but you must know which computer in the network a folder or file is on in order to find and open it. Security can be via assigned passwords for each shared resource or by setting up user or group access privileges. There is a facility called Net Watcher to find out who is using your computer's resources and disconnect them, if necessary. NETBEUI, TCP/IP, IPX, and DLC protocols are supported. Support is available by phone for 90 days from your first call for free. Fee options are available after that time. The Microsoft Internet site has extensive support capabilities.

Novell Personal NetWare

Overall Rating ★★★

Price $99 for one user, $395 for five users

Ease of installation ★★ 1/2

Ease of use ★★ 1/2

Features ★★★★

NetWare is a popular networking option because of its relative ease of installation and use with some user training, and its central setup and administration capabilities. It is also an inexpensive option, with minimal hardware requirements for computers running either DOS or Windows. For network growth, it is upward compatible to as many as 50 peer workstations and can connect to server-based NetWare versions. Users can share printers, hard disks, and CD-ROM drives with encrypted passwords and data transmission to protect information from misuse. A designated network administrator can set up "Login controls" for only one Login ID per user having defined rights to access network resources. Audit trails are maintained on network activity. The NOS contains a "Single-Network View," which is a distributed database storing information about every object on the network to simplify network use and management from one computer. Network problem solving diagnostic tools are also included. For additional network management and control capabilities, there is industry standard SNMP agent support to make it easy to manage your network with Novell's ManageWise or other compatible software packages. Support is widely available and their Internet site contains support information.

CONTACT INFORMATION

Artisoft, Inc.
800-846-9726
www.artisoft.com

IBM Corporation
800-426-2968
www.ibm.com

Mango Soft Corporation
888-88-MANGO
www.mango.com

Microsoft Corp.
800-426-9400
www.microsoft.com

Novell, Inc.
801-861-7000
www.novell.com

Databases Programs

FOR CLIENT/SERVERS

Database programs for "client/servers" are a step up from database software that most desktop users are used to. The latter is discussed in the next chapter. Client/server databases involve a system that can share data using personal computers on a local-area network. The computer where the user accesses the database is a "client" and the computer where the database is stored is a "server" and the network of users and database is a "client/server" computing environment.

As the number of users of a set of databases grow, there are economic and performance considerations that must be addressed. Giving every user a "power desktop" computer and a full set of database software is expensive. Client/server database software moves much of the database processing and analysis work to a more powerful shared server computer and provides the users less software on more economical systems—called the "thin-client" approach. Second, the management and reliability needs of the databases become more important as the company comes to depend on it to operate smoothly. Better backup and recovery tools that are not dependent on someone remembering to do the backups are

needed. And often maintenance of a part of the database needs to be done without shutting down the entire network, so a feature called "partitioning" is needed to let a part of the data be isolated for repair or change.

There are increasing needs for portability of databases to run on various computer types, operating systems, and even on the Internet as needs change. "Universal access" is the term used for the portability factor and "scalability" means that the database can grow both in size and the number of users smoothly and without redesigning or converting to another product. Finally, there is new pressure on databases to store information other than text and numbers. Complex data types include images, video, audio, time-series, and spatial data — even fingerprint data!

Client/server database products are usually purchased directly from the manufacturer or from a reseller/systems integrator who may offer product recommendations, network design, system installation, programming, and other services. Demonstration or evaluation copies of the software are often available for review; however, the software is often not a major part of the expense of this type of database system. For a large network, it would probably be a good idea to get several bids from experienced resellers if you do not have in-house expertise to evaluate the options directly.

In this chapter we look at five prominent client/server database software packages. Data on these packages was obtained from the manufacturers. Prices indicated are both for the software package and approximate price-per-user.

The following are some concepts and terms you will need to know about when evaluating client/server database software packages:

SQL stands for Structured Query Language which is a standard procedural language, used to interact with a database.

Rapid Application Development is a technical term for "ease of use," but it implies that there are features and tools in the package to make it both quick and easy to build a relatively complex database system.

Programming Tools to do complex calculations and record handling arean important feature of database packages. High-level procedural or "query" languages can be easy to learn—even for people with no computer programming experience. Lower-level programming languages do most of the work in these packages, meaning you will need experienced programmers to implement your databases.

Internet Features are relatively new in the marketplace. They can range from just creating screen equivalents from your database for your web pages to more comprehensive web-site database management.

Integration is the term used to indicate that a feature is included in the main package as an integral part. Often, integration means that the feature will be more efficient in operation than those features that are called "extensions" or "plug-ins."

OVERALL RATINGS

IBM DB2 Universal Database V5.0	★ ★ ★ ★
Oracle 8	★ ★ ★ 3/4
Sybase Adaptive Server V 11.5	★ ★ ★ 1/4
Informix-Universal Server	★ ★ 1/2
Microsoft SQL Server 6.5	★ ★ 1/4

EXPLANATION OF RATINGS

Client/server database software packages were selected for review from currently available products at their current release level. The overall rating was arrived at by giving individual scores on features, portability, scalability, and tools (management, backup, etc). These scores were then averaged to arrive at the overall rating. The highest rating possible is four stars; the lowest, one.

ALPHABETICAL DESCRIPTIONS

IBM DB2 Universal Database V5.0

Overall Rating ★ ★ ★ ★

Price $999 (workgroup edition)

Features ★ ★ ★ ★

Portability ★ ★ ★ ★

Scalability ★ ★ ★ ★

Tools ★ ★ ★ ★

While every product we reviewed could still be improved and extended, we found that the features offered by IBM are noticeably better than the other products. Databases can be partitioned for maintenance and even replication can be done without interrupting the users of the databases. There is integrated support for complex data types (image, video, audio, and fingerprint) with an "extender" method for other types to be added. Queries run quickly using dynamic bitmap indexing with multidimensional results presentable as rollups or "cubes." Their Internet tool Net.Data is integrated and has all the web publishing and database management features included. Portability ranges from small servers running NT, UNIX, or OS/2 thru OS/400 and up to mainframes with OS/390 or VM/VSE. Scalability also runs the entire range from a single server up through multiple parallel processors of the mainframe class. Tools include automatic backup while in-use, reorganization and administration utilities that are easy to use, and optimization that takes into consideration server speed as well as table characteristics. There is also world-wide support and training, and many resellers and systems integrators available to help get your databases up and running quickly.

Informix-Universal Server

Overall Rating ★★ 1/2	
Price $50,000 per server (or $2,500 per user)	
Features ★★	
Portability ★★ 1/2	
Scalability ★★★	
Tools ★★ 1/2	

This upgrade to Informix Online adds support for complex data types for multimedia applications to proven relational database technology. Complex data types are added using "DataBlades," software modules that plug into the server software to support any type of data. Many DataB-

lades are available, including a primitive one for web publishing. Some partitioning is supported, and replication runs without impacting the database's users. Portability is limited to Sun Solaris and Silicon Graphic's SGI systems — Hewlett-Packard, NT, Siemens, Sequent, and AIX versions are planned. Scalability is based on "Dynamic Scalable Architecture (DSA) technology, across five Informix database products, with the Universal Server at the top of the set. Tools are non-graphical and pretty basic, with backup and other standard data management utilities included. Education and implementation services are widely available.

Microsoft SQL Server 6.5

Overall Rating ★★ 1/4	
Price $1,895 (10 user version)	
Features ★★ 1/2	
Portability ★	
Scalability ★★	
Tools ★★★	

While this is a popular product, it appears that Microsoft is lagging in adding features that have been in other client/server products for a while. But it is very simple to install and get a database running quickly. There is no partitioning and replication is provided in a limited fashion. No support for complex data types is mentioned in their product literature. Analytical processing does include multidimensional rollup and "cube" operators. And Internet publishing is only able to be done by the database administrator (DBA) or webmaster for the target site. (Other Microsoft Internet products can be used to extend this capability.) Portability is limited to the NT operating system running on a PowerPC, Intel x86 or Pentium, the DEC Alpha AXP, and MIPD Rx400 computers. Scalability at present is limited to four-processor SMP servers maximum (SMP stands for standard symmetric multi-processor), and there is no mainframe capability. Microsoft was the first company to include a fully graphical set of tools called the SQL Enterprise Manager, which includes being able to back up your databases while they are being used. There is world-wide support and education for this product.

Oracle 8

Overall Rating ★★★ 3/4	
Price $1475 (for server and 5 users)	
Features ★★★ 3/4	
Portability ★★★ 1/2	
Scalability ★★★★	
Tools ★★★ 3/4	

Coming in a close second in our review is the relatively new release of Oracle's product. They have partitioning but there are some restrictions not in the IBM product. Replication is supported, but when used it impacts performance of the data involved. Complex data types are loosely coupled with the main software using modules called Data Cartridges, which can be added if needed. Multidimensional analysis is supported. Internet support is via their Web Server product, which is similar in function to IBM's Net.Data. Oracle has a very high level of portability to more than a dozen platforms including servers running NT or Unix, and on mainframes, and it is scalable up to massively parallel processors. Tools include backup, recovery, and reorganization utilities, but they all must be run without anyone using the database. To reduce backup times, Oracle can optionally copy all the records or just the ones that have changed since the last backup was run. Database management tools are excellent, but the event and performance monitoring tools are not included in the Oracle 8 package. Oracle has training and support worldwide, and there are many resellers and consultants available to help you get your data up and running quickly.

Sybase Adaptive Server V 11.5

Overall Rating ★★★ 1/4	
Price $995 per NT server, $195 per user	
Features ★★★	
Portability ★★★	
Scalability ★★★	
Tools ★★★ 1/2	

This is a new release of the widely known Sybase SQL Server, renamed and with a focus on improved performance and better manageability. There is still no partitioning and replication is available with a separate Replication Server product. Complex data types are implemented with each type in a separate external database, which may be a performance problem in multimedia applications, and they are not supported by the replication product. Query speed has been dramatically improved by an architecture change to use parallel processing more extensively. Portability is only across servers running IBM AIX, Digital Unix, HP-UX, Sun Solaris, and NT on Intel CPUs. The Unix version is approximately four times more expensive than the NT product. This product is not scaleable to the extent that the IBM and Oracle products are. Tools include an excellent Central Management console that simplifies server administration. Performance management is carried a step further than simple server load balancing using a Resource Governor to restrict users, applications, or sessions to a maximum percentage of server capacity within a priority scheme. Support and education are widely available and many resellers specialize in implementing Sybase databases.

CONTACT INFORMATION

IBM Corporation
800-426-2968
www.ibm.com

Informix Software
800-331-1763
www.informix.com

Microsoft Corp.
800-426-9400
www.microsoft.com

Oracle Corporation
415-506-7000
www.oracle.com

Sybase Inc.
800-879-2273
www.sybase.com

DATABASE PROGRAMS

FOR DESKTOP USE

"Databases" are simply organized collections of related information—address books, inventory cards, customer invoices, payment records, and the like. Check your personal computer—you may already have desktop database software on it as part of the software bundle that came with your computer! If you have Microsoft Office 97, for example, the Access database package may be already installed on your system. Many IBM systems ship with Lotus SmartSuite 97 on them, which would include the Approach package. And if you got the Corel Wordperfect Suite, you will find Paradox ready to use. And many computers come with software with "Works" in the title, which usually include a basic word processor, spreadsheet, and database capability.

If you have a database package installed on your computer, why would you want to change to another? Perhaps the one you have is too basic or too complex or you have reached some limits of its capability. Or you have seen new features in another package that you want to use. Relax! Most of these products have the ability to either read each other's underlying data tables or import your data into their table structures. Just make sure you are not getting trapped into a proprietary package with formats that will not let you export your data easily.

Desktop database products can be purchased from computer and software retail outlets or by mail-order, but there are no places to shop and actually try out the software before you buy it. This makes the ability to try it and return it if not satisfied a very important consideration. In addition, most vendors offer "upgrade" versions of their product at significantly reduced prices to entice you to replace a competitor's product or upgrade your favorite package to a newer version.

In this review we looked at six desktop database software packages, including all of the major packages and a couple that are not as well known. Data on these packages was obtained from the manufacturers. Interestingly, recent reviews of desktop databases in PC World magazine rated some of the ones we reviewed highly. Prices indicated are approximate "typical street prices" for a new copy (without an upgrade rebate) when the software was reviewed.

OVERALL RATINGS

Lotus Approach 97	★★★★
Microsoft Access 97	★★★ 3/4
Corel Paradox 8	★★★ 1/2
Claris FileMaker Pro 4.0	★★★ 1/4
Alpha Five 3.0 Professional	★★★
Borland Visual dBASE 7	★★★

EXPLANATION OF RATINGS

Desktop database software packages were selected for review from currently available products at their current release level. The overall rating was arrived at by giving individual scores on ease of use, performance, features, and support (including warranty). The highest score possible for each is four; the lowest, one. These scores were then averaged to arrive at the overall rating.

ALPHABETICAL DESCRIPTIONS

Alpha Five 3.0 Professional

Overall Rating ★★★
Price $99
Ease of Use ★★★ 1/4
Performance ★★★ 1/4
Features ★★★
Support ★★ 3/4

Alpha Five has an intuitive interface and is very easy to use. Creating a database from scratch is easy and there are "Genies" that help you easily perform complex tasks like building queries and summarizing data. Eight application templates are ready to use as is or to modify. Since this product was just released, there is no performance data available, but the prior product versions were good performers. In addition to the basic table and screen definition capabilities (more Genies), there are unique features such as conditional sections on forms that, for example, could display one set of information if Gender = "male" and another set for "female. Tabbed forms that look like the tabbed panels in Windows dialog boxes are another unique feature. Action

Scripting is a new feature useable by even a novice to create a series of actions, such as creating a new record and switching between screens. And for the experienced developer, Xbasic has been dramatically improved over earlier versions. Scripts can be translated into Xbasis too. Support by phone is available weekdays free for installation questions and at about $2 per minute afterward. The Internet site is a disappointment as there is so little support information available.

Borland Visual dBASE 7

Overall Rating ★★★
Price $350; $200 upgrade version
Ease of Use ★★★ 3/4
Performance ★★★
Features ★★ 3/4
Support ★★★

This product has a new interface—the Borland RAD Workbench (RAD stands for "Rapid Application Development") which includes helpful Wizards and an excellent Report Writer, but it is oriented more toward the experienced database developer. Performance is reported to be excellent because your design generates program code that can be optimized for speed and the resulting application can be distributed freely to anyone without requiring the user to buy the product. It has all the basic table and screen features, but no cross-tabulation or charting capabilities. Internet features include saving reports as HTML and some limited web publishing Wizards to help set up a live web site. Support is available by phone weekdays as a toll call, but free of other charges for only 90 days. Fee support options are then available. No return policy is included in their warranty statement. Their Internet site is informative, but does not come up to the level of others reviewed.

Claris FileMaker Pro 4.0

Overall Rating ★ ★ ★ 1/4	
Price *$199; $99 upgrade version*	
Ease of Use ★ ★ ★ 3/4	
Performance ★ ★ 3/4	
Features ★ ★ ★	
Support ★ ★ ★ 1/4	

FileMaker Pro is known for its ease of use for simple applications. It has 48 ready to use templates for home, business, and education databases and web-oriented templates for shopping cart, guest book, employee database, and Internet URL register applications. It it the only product reviewed that has versions for both the IBM-compatible and Macintosh computers. Performance can be improved by indexing on fields used for common queries, but otherwise it is relatively slow. Experienced developers will like the scripting programming feature, but there is no debug mode to help with error correction. All of the basic table and screen building features are included but there are no helpful assistants to help you step through these tasks. Telephone support is available weekdays with unlimited calls for installation assistance via a toll call. You only get one other call free, but you can purchase support. The warranty includes refunding the purchase price for 90 days. Their Internet site has a lot of information, forums, and files including a download-able copy of this product for evaluation purposes.

Corel Paradox 8

Overall Rating ★ ★ ★ 1/2	
Price *$129; $99.95 upgrade version*	
Ease of Use ★ ★ ★ 1/2	
Performance ★ ★ ★ 1/2	
Features ★ ★ ★ 1/2	
Support ★ ★ ★ 1/4	

Corel has added many new helpful agents, called Experts, to walk you through database design, but it can be intimidating to a novice. Fortunately there are many predefined applications which can be used as is or as a starting point and the PerfectExpert help system pops up with helpful suggestions pertinent to the task being performed. Programming terminology is used throughout and the interface is complicated. For experienced database developers, however, Paradox has a robust programming language called ObjectPal. Performance on single-table databases is excellent, but multi-table queries are relatively slow. Paradox has all the standard features and experts to help you define tables and screens, and a new query editor that is easy to use. Internet features include a web server for publishing your data, but building a real web application requires the use of ObjectPal. A run-time version costs $299. Support by phone is available at no charge toll-free. Corel will refund your purchase price within 90 days if you are not satisfied. The Corel Internet site is very helpful and informative and it has downloadable files and product discussion forums.

Lotus Approach 97

Overall Rating ★★★★	
Price $99.95	
Ease of Use ★★★★	
Performance ★★★★	
Features ★★★ 3/4	
Support ★★★★	

Approach has won many industry and magazine awards for its intuitive interface, generally naming it the "easiest to use" and we agree. Over 50 SmartMasters are provided to get you started quickly with simple table templates and a set of functioning applications you can use as is or as a starting place. Creating new screens, reports, and queries (called "finds") is easy to do with various "assistants" that walk you through each process. Terminology used thruout is non-technical too. It also scores high in performance by optimizing queries and sorts using SmartIndexes that it maintains as you enter and update your data. And you do not need to tell Approach which fields to index! It has all the standard features needed to build applications using common industry standard data formats, like dBASE and Paradox. Programming tools include a high-level "macro" language and a BASIC-like scripting facility common to Lotus products— LotusScript, and you can create macros or scripts by just recording your actions using the keyboard or mouse. Applications can be distributed to non-Approach users only as read-only files. And you can develop live Internet database applications using IBM's Net.Data with DB2 or simply upload static views of your data as HTML files. Support by phone is available weekdays free for 60 days and is toll-free. There is a 90-day limited warranty that includes a refund if the product is returned within 30 to 60 days of purchase. Lotus' Internet support site is excellent with forums, technical information, and downloadable files available. Training on this product is widely available.

Microsoft Access 97

Overall Rating ★★★ 3/4	
Price $299.95; $94.95 upgrade version	
Ease of Use ★★★ 1/2	
Performance ★★★ 3/4	
Features ★★★★	
Support ★★★★	

Access has many helpful agents called "Wizards" to help you design tables and screens, but the terminology it uses is often too technical for a novice database designer. The interface is just not intuitive, forcing the new user to the "Help" facilities often to do even simple tasks. For the experienced programmer, however, Access provides excellent control over every aspect of the application being developed. And programming can be done using a rather limited macro facility or the popular Visual Basic for Applications. All of your data and screen designs are stored together in a proprietary format. Performance can be a problem on large databases in multi-table queries. Access is feature-rich with all the standard table and screen types available and their query facilities are powerful and easy to use. A run-time capability for application distribution is built into the product. It is the first product of its type to offer replication to keep multiple copies of your database synchronized. Internet support includes outputting tables and screens to HTML files for display, or you can send your database to a web server and Access will give you live web interaction using the Microsoft Internet Information Server or Personal Web Server. Support by phone is available weekdays for a fee, after two free calls, and it is a long-distance number. The warranty covers a refund within 90 days of purchase if you are not satisfied. Microsoft's Internet site offers comprehensive information, forums, and downloadable files such as sample databases and tools. Training on this product is widely available.

CONTACT INFORMATION

Alpha Software Corp.
800-451-1018
www.alphasoft.com

Borland International Inc.
408-431-1000
www.borland.com

Claris Corp.
800-544-8554
www.claris.com

Corel Corp.
800-772-6735
www.corel.com

Lotus Development Corp.
800-426-7682
www.lotus.com/approach.nsf

Microsoft Corp.
800-426-9400
www.microsoft.com/access/

Desktop Publishing Programs

Desktop publishing software is used to create high-quality documents including simple newsletters, catalogs, and even web pages. Documents created with desktop publishing programs can not only be printed but converted to electronic formats such as the Adobe Acrobat PDF (Portable Document format) and HTML files for web pages.

The list below displays the overall ratings of the five desktop publishing programs included in this review.

OVERALL RATINGS

Adobe PageMaker 6.5	★ ★ ★ 1/2
Corel Ventura 7	★ ★ ★ 1/2
Microsoft Publisher 97	★ ★ ★ 1/2
Adobe FrameMaker 5	★ ★ ★ 1/4
QuarkXpress for Windows	★ ★ 1/2

EXPLANATION OF RATINGS

Desktop applications were rated in 5 categories: ease of use, page layout, document handling, print quality, and Web tools. Each category could potentially earn up to four stars, with one star being the lowest rating. The ratings were then averaged, resulting in the overall rating.

ALPHABETICAL DESCRIPTIONS

Adobe FrameMaker 5

Price $895	
Overall Rating ★ ★ ★ 1/4	
Ease of Use ★ ★ ★	
Page Layout ★ ★	
Document Handling ★ ★ ★ ★	
Print Quality ★ ★ ★	
Web Tools ★ ★ ★ ★	

If you create a lot of long text documents, you should take a look at Adobe FrameMaker 5. Its tools help you control content cross-references, auto-numbering, indexing, versioning and table of contents generation. The Table Designer easily lets you create custom rules and format text for tables. FrameMaker files can be converted to electronic documents with ease. Files can be exported to the Adobe Acrobat PDF format or to an HTML document. To create an HTML document, you will have to use Adobe's export filter HoTaMaLe. This filter can be downloaded from Adobe's website. Limitations in this program include the lack of column guides, rules, predefined elements and drop-down lists. Creating simple elements such as paragraph rules or hyperlinks can be a major undertaking. Also CIE Lab, PhotoCD and JPEG images can't be imported, and two facing pages can't be printed on a page without a third-party utility. Process separations can be generated from imported CMYK objects, but there are no color management features for accurate screen representations of documents.

Adobe PageMaker 6.5

Price $895
Overall Rating ★★★1/2
Ease of Use ★★★★
Page Layout ★★★
Document Handling ★★★
Print Quality ★★★★
Web Tools ★★★★

Adobe PageMaker 6.5 not only has a new look, but includes new functionality. The addition of frames, layers, web tools and redesigned palettes are the most significant changes in the popular program. The interface has been redesigned to make it more consistent with Adobe's other graphics packages, PhotoShop and Illustrator. Experienced PageMaker users will have to readjust to the new interface, but should be able to get the hang of it in a couple of days. This version of Page-Maker now includes frames, which can help control the appearance of a document. Frames can now contain text or graphics, and any object created in Page-Maker can be converted to a frame. Links can be created between frames to give you more precise control over text. However, PageMaker frames aren't on par with QuarkXPress frames.

Other significant upgrades are layer support and electronic publishing tools. Layers give you control over complex documents and are simple to use, and text and graphics can easily be attached to different layers. You can reorder layers and move objects between them by dragging and dropping. Layers can also be turned off and on to create different versions of your document. Also the layout-adjustment features automatically readjust a document when its size or orientation is changed.

PageMaker documents can also be turned into electronic documents. Documents can be exported to a HTML file for publishing on the Web or converted to the Adobe Acrobat PDF (Portable Document Format) file. You can create hyper links that are retained in your electronic document. With hyperlinks you can create internal links within your document, like a link from the table of contents to the corresponding page or external links to a URL, e-mail address or FTP site. However, there are some limitations in creating HTML files for web pages. Some PageMaker elements that don't convert well are irregular text wraps, images that run across a spread and Page-Maker-created graphics.

PageMaker is a great desktop publishing tool for short documents—images are handled well. In fact, its the only application of the ones reviewed that supports CIE Lab images. Process separations are also no problem for PageMaker. One drawback is that it does not manage long documents well. Despite this, with this versions inclusion of electronic publishing tools PageMaker is now also a good application for electronic publishing.

Corel Ventura

Price $895
Overall Rating: ★★★1/2
Ease of Use ★★★
Page Layout ★★★ 1/2
Document Handling ★★★★
Print Quality ★★★
Web Tools ★★★★

Ventura's strongest suit is its ability to handle long documents, hence it is the choice for books or manuals. This version offers a customizable interface with easy access to many of its features. Automatic functions include chapter and page numbers, headers and footers, indexing, cross references, conditional text and table-of-contents generation. Documents can now have multiple master pages. With this feature, you can have different layouts on different pages. Handling elements has gotten easier with MDI support (Multiple Document Interface), which allows you to drag and drop elements in documents. Color management is a little archaic. Hexachrome separations can't be generated by the CMS engine and CIE Lab Images are also not supported. Four-color separations generated large PostScript files that were unmanageable.

Ventura documents can be exported to several different electronic formats— Envoy, Java, PDF and HTML. Documents converted to Envoy (Corel's proprietary applications) produced good results if the document was mainly text. Graphics-intensive documents produced only fair results. Documents converted to Java using Corel's Barista Technology retain all document formatting except for hyperlinks. PDF and HTML document conversions retain table-of-contents entries, cross references, and index markers as hyperlinks. Documents converted to HTML with hypertext table-of-contents and indexes are placed in separate frames when converted.

Corel Ventura 8 is bundled with a lot of extras: Corel WordPerfect, Corel Data-Base Publisher, Corel Capture, Corel Script Editor, Corel Photo-Paint 6, Corel CD Creator 2, CorelDepth, CorelMemo, Envoy 7 Reader, Adobe Type Manager Lite, and clip art and font galleries.

Microsoft Publisher 97

Price $79.95	
Overall Rating ★★★ 1/2	
Ease of Use ★★★★	
Page Layout ★★★ 1/2	
Document Handling ★★★	
Print Quality ★★★★	
Web Tools ★★★	

This program lacks the sophistication of some of the others, but for those who want to easilty create professional looking documents easily, Microsoft Publisher 97 may be the choice. Geared toward less demanding needs or the personal user, this application makes creating all types of documents a snap. Larger projects, however, such as books, will not play as well on this low priced software.

Publisher guides you step-by step with its PageWizard design assistants. From the main menu you simply select the type of publication you want to create, then the PageWizard will guide you through. Editing text is easy with the Word Story Editor, which allows you to toggle back and forth between Microsoft Word and Publisher. There is also support for frames for text, images and tables. Frames are used to place information anywhere in your publication. Frames and objects can be linked to each other.

Besides creating paper-based documents you can create a simple website with the Web Site Wizard. There is also a Postcard Page Wizard that can help you create postcards, which are ideal marketing tools for a small business. This feature will setup your postcard with the correct font for the U.S. Postal Service's scanning equipment. Other features include a 5,000 piece Clip Gallery and Clip Gallery Live which gives users access to more clip art on Microsoft's website for Publisher 97. In addition to clip art you can also find video and audio clips for your web pages. Publisher has added a mail merge feature that allows users to create address lists or import them in from other applications such as Word, Word, FoxPro and other databases. Templates for Avery mailing labels are included for printing addresses. Print quality is excellent. For professional printing, the Outside Printing Assistant prepares your files correctly. Also there is image color matching which makes sure your printed color publications match your screen display. PaperDirect templates are also included. Publisher is a great program that is powerful enough for novices to create top-notch basic publications.

QuarkXPress for Windows

Price $895	
Overall Rating ★★1/2	
Ease of Use ★★★	
Page Layout ★★★	
Document Handling ★★★	
Print Quality ★★★	
Web Tools ★	

QuarkXpress is known for its powerful features. It offers precision layout tools which include its flexible master pages. To apply a master page simply drag the icon to the page where it is to be applied. Elements are live instead of static and can be edited. Special effects, like automated drop caps and gradient files, are also included. However document management features such as table-of-contents generation, indexing, table editor and conditional text are not supported. A third-party utility can remedy this problem. Quark also has color management problems: its EFI Color engine doesn't support CIE Lab color, space, separate RGB EPS images or generate Hexachrome separations. With other desktop publishing packages moving towards electronic publishing, Quark is lagging behind. HTML is not directly supported by Quark. You can, however, get a third-party Xtension, HexWeb, for converting Ventura files to HTML files. The Macintosh version of Quark does support its own proprietary online document format, QuarkImmedia. Creating Adobe Acrobat PDF files caused problems. Using the Acrobat PDFwriter printer driver produced unreadable files. To create a usable PDF file you have to run Quark's PostScript output through Adobe's Acrobat Distiller instead. There is not much new in this version. The next version promises greater enhancements and features.

CONTACT INFORMATION

Adobe Systems Inc.
800-843-7263
www.adobe.com

Corel Corp.
800-772-6735
www.corel.com

Microsoft Corp.
800 426-9400

202-882-8080
www.microsoft.com

Quark Inc.
800-676-4575
www.quark.com

FLOWCHARTING PROGRAMS

Flowcharting software gives you the ability to create simple flowcharts to complex diagrams such as a LAN network. Flowcharting software has been improved to not only offer diagramming capability but to integrate with third-party software to create dynamic applications. The list below compares flowcharting software. See Explanation of Data for criteria of ratings.

RANKING & OVERALL SCORES

1 Visio Professional   93.8

2 FlowCharter 7   62.5

3 SmartDraw 3.0   43.8

4 Flow Charting PDQ   37.5

EXPLANATION OF RATINGS

These programs were scored in these categories: Interface, which refers to how easy the program is to navigate; Symbols and Templates refer to the amount of these tools included in the program; Customization options refer to the programs ability to create custom applications; and HTML Output refers to the program's ability to generate files for use on the web. The highest score possible is 100.

ALPHABETICAL DESCRIPTIONS

Flow Charting PDQ

Price $125; upgrade $69; Limited version $49 (download from website)

Rank 4

Interface 75

Symbols/Templates 25

Customization Options 25

HTML Output 25

Flow Charting PDQ is a a simple program that lacks the powerful features found in other programs. You can create, edit and move objects easily enough by clicking and dragging. Adding text to an object is straightforward but you have to resize the object to accommodate the text size. Other programs do this automatically. Objects can be linked to one another, but they can't be rotated. Neither can text. Also there is no print preview available. PDQ can support OLE but can't create Visual Basic programs. If you only create simple diagrams and flowcharts try the $49 version of this program and save money.

FlowCharter 7

Price $299; upgrade $129

Rank 2

Interface 100

Symbols/Templates 100

Customization Options 25

HTML Output 25

FlowCharter 7 (formerly ABC FlowCharter) has solid diagramming and flowcharting tools and an unsurpassed library of symbols— 3,800 in all. FlowCharter has also incorporated tools from Micrografx's Designer which can be used to create and save custom shapes. FlowChart 7 has a number of versatile features. The Layer Manager allows you to create layers of elements. These layers can be locked in place or hidden. The CoolSheets feature automatically created templates through a question-and-answer method. Once you've completed the questionnaire, add your test, colors, backgrounds and the template is done.

One unique feature is the Living Flow-Chart, which is designed to help users navigate complex diagrams and flow-charts. Dialog boxes are linked to objects and guide the users through the flowchart by a questions-and-answer format. Your answer determines how you move through the flowcharts. This feature can be used to demonstrate procedures.

Another feature is Web Charter, which can create intricate diagrams of web sites. FlowCharter objects can be linked directly to any web page or any other program. However, charts and diagrams can't be converted to HTML code.

SmartDraw 3.0

Price	*$49*
Rank	*3*
Interface	*75*
Symbols/Templates	*50*
Customization Options	*25*
HTML Output	*25*

If you have trouble drawing a straight line SmartDraw may be the program for you. The program has an easy-to use interface that is geared towards novices. New-use fonts display when you make a mistake or when you are using a tool for the first time. Diagrams can be created easily by dragging lines and shapes from the toolbar or dragging symbols from the library. The symbol library contains 1,500-objects. Text and connectors can be added via the pull-down menu or with a right mouse click that pops up a menu. New shapes can

be created and saved, rotated and exported to GIF and JPEG file formats. SmartDraw can act as an OLE 2.0 server, but does not support OLE automation or Visual Basic Applications (VBA). Drawings can be created in compatible programs but stand-alone applications can't be generated.

Visio Professional

Price	*$350*
Rank	*1*
Interface	*100*
Symbols/Templates	*75*
Customization Options	*100*
HTML Output	*100*

Visio Professional is a powerful easy-to-use program with a flexible drag-and-drop interface. This version now includes Microsoft's Visual Basic Applications (VBA) 5.0. Visio Pro adds automation tools and the ability to integrate with other applications. This capability gives you the ability to use Visio Pro to create graphical front-ends to your databases. This would be useful for tracking products sales. You could have diagrams of your product line linked to information in your database. When orders are placed, macros could be run that would generate orders and track sales. Visio Pro can link to Excel to track pricing information. This Excel data can be shown in Visio Pro.

Visio Pro includes 2,100 symbols that can be used for creating simple organization charts to complex computer networks. Also included are shapes for documenting a Windows 95 application user interface. If you need help in creating diagrams there are wizards that can guide you through the process. There are wizards that can help you diagram a web site or quickly diagram almost any LAN. Any diagram created in Visio Pro can be converted to HTML code for use on the web. Visio Pro is a full-feature program that can be used by novices and advanced users alike.

CONTACT INFORMATION

FlowCharter 7
Micrografx Inc.
716-873-0906

Flow Charting PDQ
Patton & Patton
800-525-0082
www.patton-patton.com

SmartDraw
SmartDraw Software Inc.
800-501-0314

Visio Professional
Visio Corp
800-248-4746
www.visio.com

ILLUSTRATION/ DRAWING PROGRAMS

Programs such as these are perfect to create original images like logos, product illustration or other types of images. Illustration software gives you the capability of creating images by drawing outlines that you fill with a pattern rendered to any size. The images that are created are vector graphic images and can be perfectly resized because they use algorithms for points and curves etc. Illustration program now offer more than drawing tools. They have added functionality to create designs for the Internet. The list below rates most of the major illustration programs.

OVERALL RATINGS

Macromedia Freehand 7	★ ★ ★ 1/2
Adobe Illustrator 7.0	★ ★ ★ 1/4
CorelDraw 7	★ ★ ★
Canvas 5	★ ★ 3/4

EXPLANATION OF RATINGS

Illustration programs are scored for Ease of Use, Drawing Tools, Output (pertaining to color matching and hardcopy quality) and Web Tools. The highest score possible for each category is four; the lowest, one.

ALPHABETICAL DESCRIPTIONS

Adobe Illustrator 7.0

Price $495	
Overall Rating ★ ★ ★ 1/4	
Ease of Use ★ ★ ★	
Drawing Tools ★ ★ ★	
Output ★ ★ ★ ★	
Web Tools ★ ★ ★	

Adobe Illustrator was the pioneer in vector graphics-based programs. When it first appeared on the scene it started a new era in graphics software. This version is a rebirth of Illustrator with new features. The Mac and Windows platforms now have the same interface and files can be shared across both platforms. The tabbed palettes in the interface are also consistent with PhotoShop and PageMaker. An added feature is the ability to drag-and-drop files between PageMaker and PhotoShop. There is added precision control with new grids, align palette and transform palette, and the ability to create vertical text and set tabs. With the push on for publishing on the web, Illustrator can create liked web graphics with built-in URLs. Also included are over 1,000 clip art images, which include templates, patterns, gradients, textures, and stock photographs. There are also 300 Adobe Type 1 fonts and 50 PhotoShop-compatible special effects filters. Illustrator supports other file formats such as CorelDRAW, Freehand, EPS, CGM, PhotoShop, TIFF and PDF (Portable Document Format). Color matching is still tops and now Kodak's precision Color Management System is included. Illustrator is a good program no matter how simple or complex your illustration needs are.

Canvas 5

Price $599.95

Overall Rating ★★3/4

Ease of Use ★★1/2

Drawing Tools ★★★

Output ★★★

Web Tools ★★

Canvas 5 from Deneba Software offers illustration, photo editing, and page layout capabilities in one program. To create an illustration you first select the type of image you want to create, either Presentation, Publication, or Illustration. One drawback is files don't integrate easily with one another. Drawing is straightforward, especially the technical tools. Document dimensions can be set precisely in the ruler dialog box. Canvas offers pixel-level editing for bitmaps. A few drawbacks are no PhotoShop plug-ins or special effects are offered. However it does support some PhotoShop plug- ins. Images can be exported to JPEG and GIF files for use on the web. However there are no plug-ins for web browsers. There are over 30 import/export filters and file support is available for PhotoShop, CorelDRAW, Illustrator, GIF, EPS, and TIFF files. Also included is a CD which contains 20,000 clip art images and 2,000 TrueType and Postscript fonts.

CorelDraw 7

Price $695

Overall Rating ★★★

Ease of Use ★★★

Drawing Tools ★★★

Output ★★★

Web Tools ★★★

Coreldraw 7 is a graphics suite with a simple interface and lots of tools. PhotoShop plug-ins are supported including 2D and 3D effects. Other tools include the Corel OCR-Trace that can convert bitmaps to vector images; Corel Texture creates simulated natural textures, CorelDEPTH creates 3-D logos and text, Corel Capture 7 is a capture utility which can capture full screen, the current window or a rectangular, elliptical or specific area. Other nice capabilities include the lens feature which can zoom in on part of an image. Text is handled easily and there's no need to edit the default kerning. Editing an image's pixels is easy. CorelDraw automatically launches PhotoPaint where you can edit, save the image then return to CorelDraw.

Color matching varied between the screen to print to the web. Kodak's Color Management System is included with the program.

Bundled with Coreldraw 7 is Corel Photo-Paint 7 for creating bitmaps and editing photos, Coreldream 3D 7 is a 3D modeling and rendering program. Also included are 32,000 clip-art images and symbols, 1,000 high resolution photos, 250 3-D models, 1,000 Type 1 and True Type fonts, and over 400 CorelDraw and Paper Direct templates. This full-featured program has plenty of tools for your drawing needs.

Macromedia Freehand 7

Price $400

Overall Rating ★★★1/2

Ease of Use ★★★

Drawing Tools ★★★

Output ★★★★

Web Tools ★★★★

Macromedia Freehand 7 lets you create graphics for both print and the Internet. This program integrates easily with other programs such as PhotoShop, Page-Maker, Macromedia Xres, QuarkXPress, and CorelDRAW. You can drag and drop files, cut and paste, or run and edit images between all of these programs. The improved interface offers tabbed and dockable palettes, full-color auto-trace to convert bitmap images to vector. There are special effects such as envelop distortions, blend along a path, and multi-color fills. Paragraph text handling is great. This powerful feature lets you control how text flows either around or inside of an object. Freehand's 7 forte is its color output which is perfect to the screen, the web, or to print. There is new support for Color Sync compatible, Color Matching and Hi-Fi-Color.

Web tools offer the capability to export files to GIF or JPEG file formats with associated URLs. Freehand 7 includes Macromedia's Shockwave, which is a utility that helps you seamlessly move your creation to the web. The Afterburner plug-in will compress your web graphics at up to 75%. This powerful program can give novices and more seasoned graphic professionals the tools they need to create great illustrations.

CONTACT INFORMATION

Adobe Systems Inc.
800-843-7263
www.adobe.com

Corel Corp
800-772-6735
www.corel.com

Deneba Systems Inc.
800-622-6827
www.deneba.com

Macromedia Inc.
800-288-4797
www.macromedia.com

IMAGE EDITORS,

ADVANCED LEVEL

Image editing software gives you the capability to manipulate, modify and enhance images. With these programs you can create simple images or completely morph an image or photograph into something or even "someone" else. The list below rates image editing programs based on data compiled from the publishers and the opinions of our editors.

OVERALL RATINGS

Adobe PhotoShop 4.0	★★★1/2
Corel Photo-Paint 7	★★★1/2
Fractal Design Painter 5.0	★★★
Picture Publisher 7	★★3/4

The number-one rated image editor Adobe PhotoShop 4.0 (screeen capture shown below) is a powerful, precision image editing tool. Its high-end features and prepress capability have made it an industry standard for quite a while, for both in Windows and Mac formats.

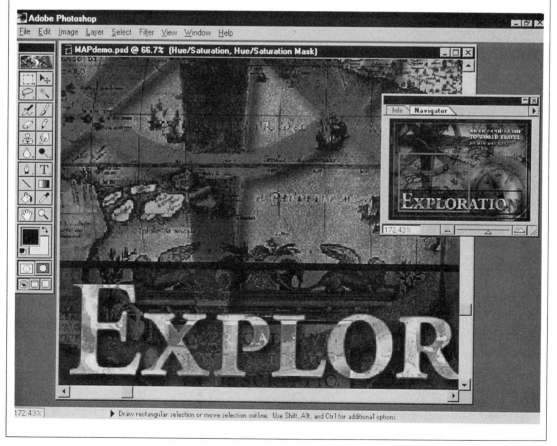

EXPLANATION OF RATINGS

The following aspects of the programs are rated: Ease of Use; Tools, which refers to the painting and drawing tools available to manipulate and edit the image; Advanced Features, which refers to mask and alpha channel functions; Web Graphics, which pertains to the ability to create images for use on the web, and Printing Output, which refers to the quality and efficiency of outputting a printed image. Four stars is the highest score possible for each aspect; the lowest is one star. The overall score is the average of the five aforementioned aspects which are rated.

ALPHABETICAL DESCRIPTIONS

Adobe PhotoShop 4.0

Price $550
Overall Rating ★★★1/2
Ease of Use ★★1/2
Tools ★★★★
Advanced Features ★★★★
Web Graphics ★★★★
Printing ★★★

Adobe PhotoShop 4.0 is a powerful, precision image editing tool. Its high-end features, and prepress capability have made it an industry standard for quite a while, both in Windows and Mac format. Very popular among Mac users, PhotoShop needs quality equipment to get the best from the program. This is a professional program; therefore, the learning curve is rather high. The interface has been made simpler with the addition of preview windows for filters that show the effect the filter will have on the image. The Variations window displays thumbnail images that display how certain adjustments such as brightness, contrast, shadows and midtones will effect the image. This version adds support for new Web file formats including PNGs (Portable Network Graphics), Progressive JPEGs and PDFs (Portable Document Format). Image files can be processed in batches, definable guides, and grids, which give you more control over image-editing. This version also gives you 48 filters including a Multicolor Gradient Tool, a digital watermarking feature. Printed output is accurate each time. PhotoShop continues to be the standard in photo design and production tool for images.

Corel Photo-Paint 7

Price $495
Overall Rating ★★★1/2
Ease of Use ★★★
Tools ★★★★
Advanced Features ★★★
Web Graphics ★★★★
Printing ★★★

Corel Photo-Paint 7 offers many features including web publishing and integration with Corel Draw. It can handle layers and objects effortlessly by giving you the ability to add and modify different elements of an image by making each one independent of the others. Functions are easily accessible through Roll-up palettes, menus and a context-sensitive Property bar. The Photo-Paint web publishing features lets you create indexed color GIFs and JPEG images and clickable image maps. You can also convert digital movies into animated GIFs and export image maps (from the server or client side) with

URLs. One drawback is that printing prepress separations cannot be done. One added plus is the large library of customized brushes and thousands of clip art images. Learning is relatively easy with the Interactive Corel tutor.

Fractal Design Painter 5.0

Price $549

Overall Rating ★★★

Ease of Use ★★★

Tools ★★★★

Advanced Features ★★★

Web Graphics ★★★

Printing ★★

Fractal Design Painter is unique, right down from its paint can packaging to its hundreds of useful brushes. It uses the MetaCreations' patented Natural-Media technologies along with its extensive set of image-editing features which offers the ability to customize textures and brushes of which there are over 100 including Photo Brushes for retouching, a Scratch Remover Brush that cleans up your scans, a Hue Brush for re-coloring and tinting photographs, Gooey Brushes, which stretch, pinch, pull, twist and bulge images and Super-Cloners, which can transform an image into a hand-rendered painting, and can mirror, scale, skew and twist an image. The Layer Brushes simulate painting on a sheet of glass, letting you paint on transparent layers. These are only a few of the incredible effects you will find in this application.

The PhotoPainter tool offers support for the Web. There is also a Net Painter feature and the capability to collaborate on

Painter images via the Internet or a network.

Painter 5.0 also supports multi-frame GIF animation. Creating it is simple. Either open any QuickTime/AVI movie or create the animation in Painter, then save the file as a GIF animation file.

Some other unique features include reflection mapping, Image Warp, Page Rotate Tool and Mosaic in which each tile is a separate object that can be reshaped. Masks and channels are industry standard, with up to 32 alpha channels.

Painter 5.0 can also read and write Adobe PhotoShop 4.0 files with layers, channels and paths in tact. There is also support for CMYK and HIFI Hexachrome output and a full color management system by Kodak. Even if you use another image-editing program, Painter can be used as a compliment program to other image-editing programs allowing you to create unique one-of-a kind images.

Picture Publisher 7

Price $349.95

Overall Rating ★★3/4

Ease of Use ★★★

Tools ★★★

Advanced Features ★★

Web Graphics ★★★

Printing ★★★

Picture Publisher 7 by Micrografx is a pixel editor that uses only objects. It is simple to use, however, printed and online documentation is lacking. One of the program's interesting features is The Command Center that tracks and records your edits. These edits can be saved in folders for use later. Objects that have been merged into the background can be re-edited. The mask function is very good, but an object is limited to one mask. Wizards and macros are available to automate your repetitive tasks. Web features let you create GIF and JPEF images. Images and objects with masks can be exported to a web page. You can even access web sites from within Picture Publisher by adding the web address to the help menu. Text can be typed right on the screen instead of in a dialog box. To edit text, just select it, then make your changes. There's a special effect library in which you can add and preview effects. Plug-ins include Digimarc Corps. PictureMarc, a copyright watermarking system.

CONTACT INFORMATION

Corel Corp.
800-772-6735
www.corel.com

Fractal Design Corp.
800-846-0111
www.fractal.com

Micrografx Inc.
800-676-3110
www.micrografx.com

IMAGE, EDITORS

ENTRY-LEVEL

If you don't need all the bells and whistles of a professional-level image-editing program, there are programs that can provide more than adequate image-manipulation tools that are easy to use and that produce top-quality results. These programs cost less than professional-level programs, which is good if you're on a budget, and many are compatible with other programs. The following list rates four entry-level image-editing programs and their overall ratings.

OVERALL RATINGS

Adobe PhotoDeluxe 2.0	★★★1/2
PhotoSuite 8.0	★★★1/2
Micrografx Small Business and Print Shop	★★★1/4
PhotoImpact with Extentions	★★3/4

The number-one entry-level editor, Adobe PhotoDeluxe 2.0 (screen capture below) is an easy-to-use program with a simple interface. It's based on Adobe PhotoShop and offers a wizard-like interface that guides you through the program's functions.

EXPLANATION OF RATINGS

The programs were evaluated on the following aspects: ease of use, drawing tools, templates and special effects. Each of these aspects could potentially earn up to four stars, with one star being the lowest. The ratings of these four aspects were then averaged, resulting in the overall score.

ALPHABETICAL DESCRIPTIONS

Adobe PhotoDeluxe 2.0

Price $50	
Overall Rating ★★★ 1/2	
Ease of Use ★★★★	
Drawing Tools ★★★	
Templates ★★★★	
Special Effects ★★★	

Adobe PhotoDeluxe is an easy-to-use program with a simple interface. It's based on Adobe PhotoShop and offers a wizard-like interface that guides you through the program's functions and holds your hand while you create documents, manipulate images, touch-up photographs, or apply special effects to an image. As you're taken step-by-step through a function, Cue Cards are displayed to give you more assistance. There are photo-editing tools such as the Clone Tool and One-Step Red-Eye removal and there are over 500 templates, clip art images and photos included. Built-in to this program is the PictraShare(TM) software, from Pictra Incorporated, which gives you the ability to create and share digital photo albums with others via the Internet.

Since this program is from Adobe, of course it supports PhotoShop plug-ins. One drawback to this program is that you can only open one image at a time, but for the low price tag, most users could live with the hitch.

Micrografx Small Business and Print Shop

Price $50	
Overall Rating ★★★1/4	
Ease of Use ★★★	
Drawing Tools ★★★★	
Templates ★★★	
Special Effects ★★★	

Don't let the low price tag fool you into thinking this is not a powerful program...it is. It's actually a watered-down version of two powerful programs, Micrografx Picture Publisher, a higher-level image editing program and Instant 3-D, a 3-D creation program. With this program you can create simple or complex images. If you want to have your creations printed at a print shop, there is support for the four-color process CMYK and spot color separations. If you're lacking in artistic skills there are plenty of templates included with the program. There are over 18 different categories of templates and there are numerous graphics for use on a Web site. For novices on a limited budget this program is a good place to start.

PhotoImpact with Web Extensions

Price $139	
Overall Rating ★★3/4	
Ease of Use ★★★	
Drawing Tools ★★★★	
Templates ★	
Special Effects ★★★	

PhotoImpact with WebExtensions is a robust program for the business user. It has enough tools to accomplish the simplest of tasks to the more complex. The simple interface gives you three ways to work; Basic, Intermediate, and Advanced mode. In Basic mode you can use the AutoProcess tool to guide you thorough image editing and enhancement tasks such as brightness and contrast adjustments. Intermediate mode gives you access to more editing tools and Advanced mode has the features with access to the Color panel and Easy Palette, which can apply up to 38 effects. The Easy Palette contains the Effect, Gradient and Texture gallery which can be used for special effects. One nice feature is the Try button, which lets you preview how your effect will look when applied to an image. If these effects are not enough you can add more through plug-ins, such as Kai Power Tools. PhotoImpact also has web functionality with a web utility, WebExtensions. You can create great web sites complete with animations, special effects, and eye-catching graphics. With this functionality you can generate HTML code for BODY and IMG tags and generate Image Map tag coordinates, create GIF animation, designer custom backgounds and buttons and create numerous gradients and textures. One drawback: there aren't any templates to help the novice users along, but the inclusion of powerful web tools is a major plus.

PhotoSuite 8.0

Price $50

Overall Rating ★★★ 1/2

Ease of Use ★★★

Drawing Tools ★★★

Templates ★★★★

Special Effects ★★★★

PhotoSuite has a paint-like interface that's simple to use. PhotoSuite is a digital darkroom that lets you retouch photos, eliminate red eye, change photos into cartoons and even create multimedia slideshows. There are a wide variety of paintbrushes and selection tools that can be customized. Its greatest strength is the massive template library, with over 700 design templates. Wizards guide you in using the templates. In addition to using your own photographs, PhotoSuite includes a "virtual camera" that can take a snapshot of any image or sound on your PC and immediately store it for your use later. The catalog function manages photos and images and the quick thumbnail views let you find an image quickly without a hassle. PhotoSuite integrates with the web allowing you to post your images on a web site or send them to others via the Internet.

CONTACT INFORMATION

PhotoDeluxe 2.0
Adobe for You
800-888-6293
www.adobe.com

Small Business and Print Shop
Micrografx
800-671-0144
www.micrografx.com

PhotoImpact
Ulead Systems
800-858-5323
www.ulead.com

PhotoSuite 8.0
MGI Software
888-644-7638
www.mgisoft.com

INTERNET BROWSERS

The Internet is changing the way businesses communicate. Businesses are now setting up web sites on the Internet to disseminate information to their customers and find new clients. They are also using the Internet and intranet to communicate with their staff. To take advantage of all that the Internet offers you need a browser, which allows you to connect to web sites, FTP sites and gopher sites. Today's browsers now offer more features that let you view video, listen to audio and collaborate with team members. The two leading products in this category are Microsoft Internet Explorer 4.0 and Netscape Navigator 4.0. Features of these browsers were compared and scored. (See chart below and Explanation of Data)

OVERALL RATINGS

Netscape Navigator 4.0   ★ ★ ★ 1/4

Microsoft Internet
   Explorer 4.0   ★ ★ ★ 1/4

EXPLANATION OF RATINGS

Browsers were rated in six categories; interface/navigation, e-mail, multimedia extensions, multi-platform support, push technology and collaboration tools. A four-star rating was used with four being excellent and one star being the lowest rating. Category scores were averaged resulting in the overall score.

ALPHABETICAL DESCRIPTIONS

Microsoft Internet Explorer 4.0

Price: Free with various software purchases
Overall Rating: ★ ★ ★ 1/4
Interface/navigation ★ ★ ★ ★
E-mail ★ ★ ★ ★
Multimedia extensions ★ ★ ★ 1/2
Multi-platform support ★ ★
Push technology ★ ★ ★
Collaboration tools ★ ★ ★ 1/2

Internet Explorer 4.0 (IE4) gives us a glimpse into the future . . . as Microsoft sees it. Explorer's interface is based on the shell-integration feature, which will change the way your desktop looks. With shell integration all of Microsoft's interfaces will look like a web page. Applications on your computer and web-based applications will have the same look and feel. Internet Explorer 4.0 runs on Windows 95, Windows NT and Mac platforms.

IE4 has some outstanding enhancements such as toolbars that can be customized as well as turned off individually or removed to give you a full-screen display. Another is the automatic URL fill-in feature that fills in the address for you as you type. Explorer does this by keeping track of your most visited sites. If Explorer enters the wrong address you have to delete it and retype the correct one. This could get annoying after a while, however, this feature can be disabled if desired.

Searching forward and backward has gotten easier. If you select the forward or backward buttons, a list of your visited sites is displayed and you can choose the page you want to go to. If you need to search the entire web, click the search button and you'll find something new. Search engines will be displayed in a left frame on the screen. Enter your search terms, select a search engine and the search hits are also displayed in the left search frame. Select the hit you want and the corresponding web page is shown in the right frame. You can switch to another hit by just clicking on it in the left frame.

Explorer can help eliminate returning to web sites that have not been updated. There is a task scheduler that will search your favorite sites and notify you when they have been updated, either by e-mail or a notification will appear on the toolbar. You can also have portions of these updated sites downloaded to browse off-line.

NetMeeting is a newly added collaboration tool that offers whiteboarding, chat, audio, full-motion video and application sharing support. If you need web broadcasting, NetShow is available to act as a broadcast client so you can access web broadcast programs in a streamed format using IP technology.

Other features include an authoring tool, FrontPad, which is a watered downed version of FrontPage, Microsoft Personal Web Server, and a HTTP server, which lets you publish web pages to your own computer.

Netscape Navigator 4.0

Price: $39

Overall Rating: ★★★1/4

Interface/navigation ★★★★

E-mail ★★★★

Multimedia extensions ★★★

Multi-platform support ★★★

Push technology ★★★

Collaboration tools ★★★

Netscape Navigator 4.0 is the cornerstone of Netscape's new suite of Internet tools, Communicator. This application includes the elements for real-time collaboration, calendaring and scheduling, HTML authoring, e-mail and other functions.

Navigator 4.0's interface can be customized in various ways. For example, links you access often can be placed on the toolbar and the Bookmark list is now located on the toolbar. Shortcuts can be created to web pages (like in Windows 95). The backward and forward buttons now show you a list of previously visited sites that you can choose from. No need to cycle back through every page you've visited to get where you want to go. Searching the Internet is easier. Just click the search button and you can access all the leading search engines.

Collaboration tools include a teleconference option with whiteboarding and audio. Netscape has also added a calendar function which can track group or individual schedules.

Push technology is the ability to send customized information from the web to a user's desktop. Netscape has included this new technology in this browser with the inclusion of Netcaster. Using an onscreen remote control you can select content from channels and have the information downloaded to your desktop while you're on- or off-line. Content providers include CNET, CNN, HotWired, ABC News and others. If you're online you can continue working while your desktop is constantly being updated with the information you requested, like news headlines, stock quotes or sports scores.

Other benefits in this package are support for HTML in e-mail messages, support for multimedia such as video, and audio and authoring tools. The SmartUpdate option automatically installs new multimedia plug-ins. There is also support for ActiveX documents (OLE) which will allow you to directly link to other ActiveX applications.

CONTACT INFORMATION

Microsoft Corp.
800-426-9400; 206-882-8080
www.microsoft.com

Netscape
415-937-3777
www.netscape.com

MAPS AND STREET FINDERS

Do you know the way to San Jose . . . or anywhere else for that matter? If you're a business traveler and need a quick and convenient way to get directions to almost anywhere, then Street-mapping software could provide a solution. This software can map out your route from starting point to destination, then print out a map. Some programs can even generate driving or walking directions. Most of these programs come on CD-ROM and are easy to use. The Internet also has mapping web sites. Listed below are six street-mapping programs.

OVERALL RATINGS

Rand McNally Street- Finder Deluxe 1998	★★★★
MapQuest	★★★1/2
Pro CD Select Street Atlas Deluxe 2.0	★★★1/2
Microsoft Automap Streets Plus Deluxe 1997 Edition	★★★
TravRoute Road Trips Door-to-Door 1997 Edition	★★★
DeLorme Street Atlas USA 4.0	★★1/2

EXPLANATION OF RATINGS

Three aspects of maps and street finders were rated: *Ease of Use*, which takes into consideration setup, program navigation, and features; *Printing*, which pertains to the printed quality of maps and printing controls, and *Routing Capabilities*, which evaluates customization of routes, zoom levels on maps, and annotation tools. Four stars is the highest rating for each category; one is the lowest. Overall ratings were achieved by averaging the three aforementioned ratings.

ALPHABETICAL DESCRIPTIONS

DeLorme Street Atlas USA 4.0

Price $45

Overall Rating ★★1/2

Ease of Use ★★

Printing ★★★

Routing Capabilities ★★

This CD-ROM not only offers mapping features but demographic data also. To view demographic data for an area just right-click on a zipcode to display information about that area. This is a great feature for small business owners who want to target a new area for marketing their product or opening a new office. DeLorme's other product, Phone Search USA, works with this program and phone listings can be imported into Street Atlas then displayed on a map. Maps cover the entire U.S. and annotation tools are available for further customization. Printed output of maps are clear and detailed. Some drawbacks are the lack of hotels and restaurants in the database and that no driving or walking directions are generated.

MapQuest

Price Free (downloadable on the Internet)

Overall Rating ★★★1/2

Ease of Use ★★★1/2

Printing ★★★1/2

Routing Capabilities ★★★1/2

If you want to see if mapping software is for you, go to the Internet at www.mapquest.com and try it out. MapQuest is a free web site that can produce complete, customizable road maps. The site has three main sections: *Interactive Atlas* lets you find locations anywhere in the world; *TripQuest* can generate driving directions to almost any destination in the U.S.; and *Personalized Maps* is a map storage area for registered users. To generate door-to-door driving directions go to the *TripQuest* section. You then complete a form with the starting and destination point. Customization options can be selected including route preference; avoidance preferences (so you can bypass certain roads if possible); and display preferences, which set print options for text only, overview map with text and turn-by-turn maps with text. Driving directions are generated with each map. Your route is displayed on the screen and you can print it out or save it in the *Personalized Maps* area. (To do this you'll need to register first, which is free.) Maps that you store here can be retrieved anywhere you have a web connection. One unique feature is "Hot Coupons," an electronic coupon service. You can download and print money-saving coupons from all over the United States. So if you're going to an unfamiliar city, search Hot Coupons for bargains in car rentals, dining, dry cleaning, photo processing, and other useful services. This is a novel idea. Whether you only need maps occasionally or want to have a mapping source for your staff, the MapQuest site can get you there.

Microsoft Automap Streets Plus Deluxe 1997 Edition

Price $69.95

Overall Rating ★★★

Ease of Use ★★★

Printing ★★★

Routing Capabilities ★★★

Automap is a slick program with great graphics, easy navigation, and high-quality map printouts. Bundled with this package is the *American Yellow Pages* directory. Listings from this program can be imported into Automap and their locations marked with pushpins. Routes can be outlines with the Highlight- a-Route feature. There are no extensive map annotation tools and only lines can be drawn. You can search for locations by street address or specific places but not on zip-codes or area codes. Information on hotel and restaurants, addresses, and phone numbers can be displayed for your specific location. There are no driving or walking directions generated with your map. One bonus—you can make travel reservations for your location through a link from Automap to Microsoft's *Expedia* website. There will be a new version of this program, the *Expedia Streets 98*, on the market by the time this book goes to press.

Pro CD Select Street Atlas Deluxe 2.0

Price $79

Overall Rating ★★★1/2

Ease of Use ★★★1/2

Printing ★★★

Routing Capabilities ★★★1/2

ProCD has a lot of data that can be manipulated in a variety of ways. There are twenty categories of locations that can be selected. You can search by zipcode, addresse, state, city, county, area code and prefix. Map annotation tools are available and custom labels and clip art icons can be added to your map. Map zoom levels are infinite and you can display varying

Rand McNally StreetFinder Deluxe is the top-rated map/street finder.

levels, from street-level to county, state, multistate, regional, and national views. Printed output can be adjusted to varying geographic areas. Also included is the *Pro CD SelectPhone Business Deluxe* that contains 15 million listings. No driving or walking directions are available.

Rand McNally StreetFinder Deluxe, 1998

Price $49.95

Overall Rating ★★★★

Ease of Use ★★★1/2

Printing ★★★★

Routing Capabilities ★★★★

Rand McNally brings their map making expertise to software. The program's Map-Style Guide lets you quickly generate customized maps. Once you select a map style then you can search for locations by street addresses, zipcodes, area codes, or intersections. After the area is selected, Streetfinder will display a detailed map. If you are a business traveler use the Business Out-of-Towner option that will display information about car rentals, hotels, and other relevant business traveler information. Map annotation tools include drawing tools for lines, circles, and polygons, clipart, and labels. Maps can be printed in different views with the 14 map zoom levels. Map data covers the entire United States except Alaska. Streetfinder can give you walking directions but not driving directions,

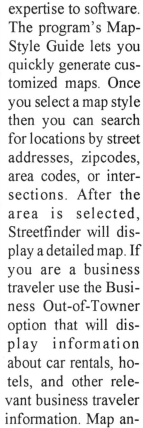

which would make this great program even better.

TravRoute Road Trips Door-to-Door 1997 Edition

Price $49.95

Overall Rating ★ ★ ★

Ease of Use ★ ★ ★

Printing ★ ★

Routing Capabilities ★ ★ ★1/2

This program can take you from here to there—doorstep-to-doorstep with ease. Map data covers the United States. To run your trip, you specify starting and destination points, then your door-to-door route will be generated automatically. It even includes driving and walking directions. Now for the bad news. The quality of the maps are sub-par, more so when you zoom down to street-level. Map annotation tools are absent and there's not of lot of information on places of interest like dining or hotels. If you need a program that will produce high-quality maps, then look elsewhere; however, if you need accurate driving directions then you could get this program, or, just go to the MapQuest website and save a few dollars.

CONTACT INFORMATION

Rand McNally
847-982-0944
www.randmcnally.com

DeLorme
800-452-5931
www.streetatlasusa.com

Microsoft Corp.
800-936-3500
www.microsoft.com/automap

Pro CD
800-992-3766
www.procd.com

TravRoute
800-297-8728
www.travroute.com

NEWSREADERS
FOR USENETS

When people think about the Internet they tend to consider only the World Wide Web. Most people are unaware of one of the other parts of the Internet, Usenet Newsgroups, which are the bulletin boards of the on-line world. They are used to discuss virtually any topic you can think of, and probably a few you would rather not.

Newsgroups are broken into categories that are defined by the first letters of their name. The main categories you are likely to run into are *alt* (alternative), *comp* (computer), *sci* (science), *rec* (recreation), and *soc* (society). You can also find categories for most cities and countries. Under these headings are myriad sub-categories, ranging from *alt.abuse.recovery* to *utexas.zoo* and virtually everything in between.

In order to read and respond to messages posted on newsgroups you need a newsgroup reader. Both Netscape's and Microsoft's web browsers have newsgroup reading capabilities, but there are several stand-alone newsgroup readers that have enhanced functionality and are available on the World Wide Web as both shareware and freeware.

All posts to newsgroups scroll off the groups a few days to a few weeks after they are posted, but there is a service, DejaNews that saves all messages posted to news groups. If you need to find a particular message, or if you want to see what has been said on a topic, DejaNews can help you find them. You can even post messages to the news groups if you have no other access to them.

Below are some of the most common newsreaders.

OVERALL RATINGS

Agent	★★★★
Anawave Gravity	★★★★
FreeAgent	★★★
News Xpress	★★★
WinVN	★★★
Microsoft Outlook Express	★★
Netscape Discussion Groups	★★
Microsoft Internet Mail and News	★

EXPLANATION OF RATINGS

The ratings above are based on evaluations of one primary aspect, features. This is an amalgam of several things: One of them is the ability to use the readers in an off-line mode, which involves retrieving message headers and tagging them to allow the program to retrieve the whole message at a later time. Features also takes into account the ability to watch and ignore various message threads, as well as the ability to filter messages from certain individuals. E-mail support is yet another aspect that was evaluated under the blanket of features. The Overall Ratings were determined by taking the scores in each of the categories and then averaging them.

Anawave Gravity

Overall Rating ★ ★ ★ ★

Price $39.95 (Free 30 day evaluation)

It is easily configurable, but the window layout is a bit static. Gravity has a rules based filtering system that allows users to automate mundane newsgroup reading. Rules can be built to mark articles containing certain keywords as urgent, to ignore articles by authors you don't like, and perform many tasks automatically. Gravity ships with several standard rules so you can avoid creating them yourself. Unfortunately, it is only available for Windows 95.

Agent

Overall Rating ★ ★ ★ ★

Price $29.00 ($40.00 for shrink wrapped version)

Published by Forte Inc., which has two newsgroup readers, it is popular and efficient. The first, Agent, costs $29.00 for a downloadable program; the other, a shrink-wrapped version costs $40.00 for this disk-based version with a printed manual. The program is feature-packed and allows for easy off-line reading, a must if you connect via a dialup connection. Agent has two features that you will come to love, the Kill and Ignore filters. These allow you to avoid many off-topic and spam messages. Agent's help file is good, but its speed is average. It is available in both 16-bit and 32-bit versions.

FreeAgent

Overall Rating ★ ★ ★

Price Free

FreeAgent is a pared down version of Agent. While it has many of the same features, it is missing a few. For example, it cannot be used as an e-mail program like Agen, and it does not have the filtering capabilities. It can, however, be used as an off-line reader. It is available in versions for Windows 3.x and Windows 95/NT.

Microsoft Internet News and Mail

Overall Rating ★

Price Free

When Microsoft released Internet Explorer 3.0 last year, they did not include a newsgroup reader. You must download a separate program to read newsgroup articles. While it is free, it lacks many features that other newsgroup readers include as standard equipment. For example, it does not have support for off-line reading. If you want to read newsgroup messages, you must be connected to the Internet. There are neither kill lists, nor any way to watch particular threads. You may want to look at a more full-featured program.

Microsoft Outlook Express

Overall Rating ★ ★

Price Free

Microsoft has replaced Internet News and Mail with Outlook Express. The new program, while allowing off-line reading of news groups, still lags behind the competition when it comes to features. Outlook Express does not allow you to watch or ignore particular message threads, nor can you set it to ignore posts from people you don't want to see messages from.

Netscape Discussion Groups
Overall Rating ★★

Price $ 40.00 (free for individual evaluation)

This reader works in conjunction with the Netscape Internet browser. It allows for off-line reading, watching and ignoring threads and e-mail support. The program is better than the two Microsoft offerings, but lags behind the other readers. Nonetheless, if you use Netscape and you don't want to hassle with another program you can make do with it.

News Xpress
Overall Rating ★★★

Price Free

News Xpress has message filtering, sorting, and e-mail capabilities and is one of the fastest newsreaders available. However, it lacks some features that are present in other readers, such as watching/ignoring threads, efficient online/off-line switching, and the ability to catch up with subscriber newsgroups. It is available in both Windows 3.x and Windows 95 versions.

WinVN
Overall Rating ★★★

Price Free

WinVN used to be the leader of the Windows newsreaders. When Anawave Gravity and Forte's Agent and FreeAgent hit cyberspace, they quickly knocked it out of the top spot. Since then, they have added new features and improved on the effi-ciency and ease- of-use that have always been WinVN's strongest assets. Its interface is different from the others in that it uses individual tiled-windows listing newsgroups, article lists, and individual articles. It is one of the easiest to use newsreaders available. Like many of the others, it has built-in UUdecoding, hypertext support, and e-mail sending capabilities. One of WinVN's strong points is its ability to sort articles in almost any order. WinVN's features compare well with the other newsreaders, but still fall short in some areas. This is a good newsreader to get started with, but after time, you may want to upgrade to a more powerful one.

CONTACT INFORMATION

Anawave Software, Inc.
(714) 250-7263
http://www.anawave.com

Forte Inc.
(760) 431-6400
http://www.forteinc.com

Microsoft
(206) 882-8080
http://www.microsoft.com

Netscape
(650) 937-2555
(650) 937-3777
http://www.netscape.com

WinVN
http://www.ksc.nasa.gov/software/winvn/winvn.html

OFFICE SUITES

"Office Suites" are software collections and are intended to be all-in-one solutions to your business computing needs. Suites offer word processing, spreadsheet, presentation, database, and other programs for one price. Office suites are money savers. If you were to buy these software packages individually it would cost considerably more. While you may not use all of the programs, they are still a sweet deal.

The top office suites selected for review are from the three companies that have the lion's share of the market of these sorts of collections: Microsoft, Corel, and Lotus. The overall scores for them are below.

OVERALL RATINGS

Microsoft Office
  Professional 97   ★★★★

Lotus SmartSuite 97   ★★★1/2

Corel Office Professional 7   ★★★

EXPLANATION OF RATINGS

Each office suite was rated for the following facets: the Interface, Core Applications, Web Publishing Tools, Work Group Tools, and Custom Options. The highest rating possible is four stars; the lowest is one star. The overall score is the average of the ratings in the five aforementioned categories.

More in-depth reviews of each office suite's core applications can be found in elsewhere in this volume in various chapters that pertain to Word Processing, Spreadsheets, Presentation Software, and Database Programs for Desktops.

ALPHABETICAL DESCRIPTIONS

Corel Office Professional 7
Price $695; upgrade $229
Overall Rating ★★★
Interface ★★★
Core Applications ★★★
Web Integration Tools ★★★1/2
Work Group Tools ★
Custom Options ★★★

Corel Office Professional is made up of many impressive applications and is the first office suite to allow you to publish Java versions of documents. Corel Office includes WordPerfect 7—word processor, Quattro Pro 7—spreadsheet, Presentations 7—presentation graphic program, Paradox 7—relational database, InfoCentral—information manager, and a host of other applications.

The applications in this office suite have been compiled from various companies; WordPerfect, (previously owned by Novell), Paradox, and Quattro Pro are former Borland products. Because of this, there is no consistent interface between applications. Each application has a different interface to navigate, which can be confusing at times. You can write macros across applications to automate tasks and make navigation easier.

Web publishing is well integrated in this package. Links to web pages can be placed in documents and files can be saved as HTML documents or the Envoy portable document format. However, only WordPerfect can open pages directly from the web.

Corel's Barista WYSIWYG web publishing tools let you create HTML pages and Java applets. Netscape Navigator is also included.

Lotus SmartSuite 97

Price $399; upgrade $149

Overall Rating
★★★1/2

Interface ★★★1/2

Core Applications
★★★1/2

Web Integration Tools ★★★1/2

Work Group Tools
★★★

Custom Options
★★★

Lotus SmartSuite 97 offers updated versions of Word Pro, which is a word processor; a 32-bit version of Lotus' 123 spreadsheet; Freelance Graphics, which is a presentation program; Approach, which is a relational database and Organizer, an information manager. Other versions of this suite include NotesSuite, which incorporates a Notes client and OS/2 suite, which has 32-bit version of Word Pro and Freelance Graphics. The workgroup tools in this suite are the best around. There is

also support for OLE 2.0 automation and a bunch of cross-application templates. The learning curve is low for this application. The interface is consistent and the main menu bar is always in view.

The integration of the web allows you to convert Freelance Graphics presentations to web pages or use Word Pro's publishing templates and HTML tables for creating web documents. You can use the included Webster Web browser or your default browser to surf the net. Predefined buttons located in the Internet Draw give you access to Headlines, Stock Quotes, Weather, Reference, and a free online service — Bookmarks.

Microsoft Office Professional 97, the top-rated office suite.

Microsoft Office Professional 97

Price $599 (Professional Edition, upgrade $309); $499 (Standard Edition, upgrade $209)

Overall Rating ★★★★

Interface ★★★★

Core Applications ★★★★

Web publishing tools ★★★★

Work Group Tools ★★★★

Custom Options ★★★★

Microsoft Office is the leader in the office suite race. With over 80 percent of the market, Office has become a standard in most corporate and home settings. Office Professional 97 brings together top-notch applications that include Word 97—word processor, Excel 97—spreadsheet program, PowerPoint 97— presentation program, Outlook 97—information manager, and Access 97—relational database. The Standard version of Microsoft Office includes all of these programs except Access 97, which is included in the Professional version.

Office is based on the familiar Windows interface, which gives a consistent look and feel to all of its applications. This consistency makes the applications easy to learn and use. All applications work seamlessly with each other. You can organize and exchange data effortlessly. Hyperlinks link documents to each other no matter where they are located on your computer. You can create a report in Word, then create a hyperlink in the report to an Excel spreadsheet or to a web site.

Web Publishing tools allow you to create web pages without having to know HTML (Hyper Text Markup Language), the code that creates web pages. The tools are basic and easy to use but there is no support for frames. All of Office's major applications are Internet-ready, allowing you to gather information from the Internet for use in your documents or web pages.

Office 97's newest features include an information manager and e-mail client, an Office assistant that gives you tips to maximize productivity, and Visual Basic for Applications.

CONTACT INFORMATION

Corel Corporation
(800) 772-6735
http://www.corel.com

Lotus Development Corp.
(800) 343-5414; (617) 577-8500
www.lotus.com

Microsoft Corp.
(800) 426-9400; (206) 882-8080
www.microsoft.com

PERSONAL FINANCE PROGRAMS

The software contained in this chapter gives you the tools necessary to organize your personal finances. These applications can help you balance your bank accounts, manage your investments, aid you in tax and financial matters, help with your budgets and offer you access to electronic banking services. In this review we looked at five personal finance packages. The chart of the overall ratings are listed below.

OVERALL RATINGS

Quicken Deluxe Version 98 ★★★★

Microsoft Money 97 ★★★1/4

Managing Your Money 3.0 ★★★

Smart Home Manager 1.5 ★★

The top-rated program, Quicken (screen capture below), monitors the success of your investments, as well as tracks almost every other financial transaction.

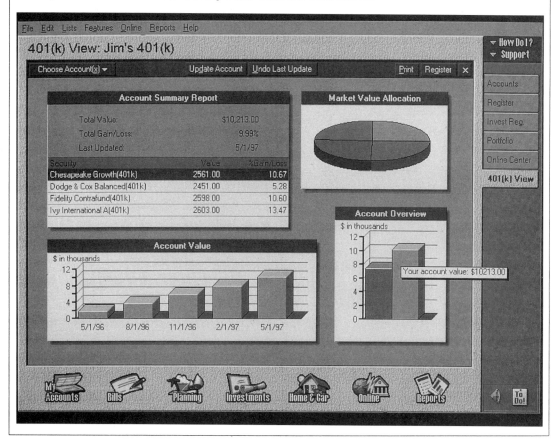

SOFTWARE

EXPLANATION OF RATINGS

Each of these programs were evaluated based on the following five categories: account management, budgeting and financial planning, tax planning, investment management, and online capabilities. Each category was rated on a four-star scale with one star being the lowest rating. The ratings of the five categories were then averaged, resulting in the overall rating.

ALPHABETICAL DESCRIPTIONS

Managing Your Money Version 3.0

Price $79.95
Overall Rating ★★★
Account Management ★★★1/2
Budgeting and Financial Planning ★★★
Tax Planning ★★★★
Investment Management ★★★
Online Capabilities ★★

Managing Your Money has always had stellar financial planning and tax features. However, the program's awkward budgeting features and limited electronic options are its Achilles heel. Using Managing Your Money is simple enough. Its SmartDesk feature uses a graphic of an office as the main interface. Clicking on labeled icons takes you directly to the different areas. For example if you want to write checks, you click on the checkbook.

Information can be imported from other versions of Managing Your Money or other personal finance programs that support Quicken's .QIF format, or data can be entered from scratch. The Electronic Checkbook, which looks like a real checkbook, is the place where you enter checks and deposit transactions. The check register is at the top of the screen and the checks are at the bottom, eliminating the need to toggle between screens. Data entered is automatically recorded in the register along with a running balance. The Check-Free feature allows you to pay bills online directly from your checking account. There is no electronic banking available as in other programs.

Budgeting features are adequate. Budgets can be created from previous spending data. The Financial and Tax Planning features are stronger. The Financial Snapshot feature gives you a monthly overview of your finances as well as a long range look at your financial situation. This debt reduction tool helps you devise a plan to reduce your debt. This program was the first personal finance program to offer such a feature. Investment management allows you to create multiple portfolios and download stock prices and information from QuoteLink through CompuServe. This program may not be as powerful as others on the market, but it does offer basic financial tools.

Microsoft Money 97

Price $35
Overall Rating ★★★ 1/4
Account Management ★★★★
Budgeting and Financial Planning ★★★
Tax Planning ★★
Investment Management ★★★
Online Capabilities ★★★★

Microsoft Money 97 has improved this version especially in the area of electronic banking and the home banking arena. The interface is intuitive and easy to navigate. The main screen displays a chart and tip of the day along with icons of the programs main areas. It's an easy-to-use program that accepts data from other packages in ASCII or Quicken's .QIF format. There is a Conversion Wizard for Quicken users that takes you step by step through converting existing Quicken data. Data can be assigned to different categories and given designations such as "tax related" to make preparing your tax forms easier. Setting up accounts is easy with the Account Wizard. You enter data for each account on a checkbook-like screen with the register at the top of the screen and forms below. The forms are separated by tabs for each type of transaction. Bills can be paid online with Check-Free or Visa e-pay, and 58 banks support online banking.

Portfolio management in Money 97 can help you manage mutual funds, stocks and bonds. Stock quotes can be downloaded from the Internet into your portfolio. You can also link the program with the Money Zone, the product's web site. Money 97 has made minimal changes to its program but it still remains a high-quality personal finance program.

Quicken Deluxe Version 6.0 for Windows

Price $60

•Organize your finances
•Manage your investments
•Help reduce taxes

Quicken Deluxe, the number-one rated personal financial manager.

Overall Rating
★ ★ ★ ★

Account Management
★ ★ ★ ★

Budgeting and Financial Planning
★ ★ ★ ★

Tax Planning ★ ★ ★ ★

Investment Management ★ ★ ★ ★

Online Capabilities
★ ★ ★ ★

Quicken Deluxe Version 6.0 leads the pack with its overhauled version of the popular finance program. All of Quicken has been revised, making it a more streamlined and better performing application. Quicken still offers an easy-to use interface. You can start with the EasyStep feature, which gives you step-by-step assistance, or get right to it by clicking the summary tab. Data can be imported in either .QIF or ASCII format. Account management is as easy as it's always been. Checks and deposits can be entered either in the register or on a blank check and each can be flagged to be printed, transmitted online, or just recorded. ATM transactions and transfers can also be entered. Transactions can be assigned to multiple categories and Quicken's tools can help you budget and reconcile your checkbook.

Financial planning features include the Debt Reduction Planner which can help you in managing and eliminating your debt. Other tools help you obtain your credit report, produce reports, and minimize future taxes. This program embraces the online technology with its numerous online features. You can pay your bills through CheckFree or Intuit Financial Services. Also there is online banking support for 38 banks. Microsoft Money 97 is the only other program to offer more (58 banks). Quicken monitors the success of your investments by looking at price histories and current prices of your portfolio. With the included Netscape Navigator web browser and an Internet connection, financial information can be obtained via the Internet from the Quicken Financial Network (QFN) and Intuits web site Quicken Live. You can download free stock quotes, news and program fixes, and obtain a list of web-based financial sites. Mutual funds prices can be updated and researched with the Mutual Fund Finder. Quicken's Investor Insight gives you access to online investment information and, for an extra $9.95, a Watch List of securities can be established for regular price downloads. Quicken Deluxe gets high

scores in all categories making this a top choice for everyone.

Smart Home Manager 1.5

Price $59.95
Overall Rating ★★
Account Management ★★
Budgeting and Financial Planning ★★
Tax Planning ★★
Investment Management ★★
Online Capabilities ★★

Smart Home Manager is the newest personal finance programs on the market. There are no online banking features and you can't pay your bills online, but it does have simple financial tools plus some extras. It also offers task list management, and tracking tools for medical records and household items. The interface is outdated and the financial tools are not as powerful as other programs, but if your financial needs are simple this program will suffice. Users can't import data from other financial programs and there is no automatic setup for new users. The standard data entry screen for check and deposit transactions is just that, a screen. It does not resemble a checkbook as in other forms; you enter the necessary data then use the Payment Scheduler to request a reminder or posting of the transaction. Checks are printed one at a time or in a batch, but you can't pay the bills online. Other tools, such as budgeting, financial planning and investment management, are adequate. Budget creation uses previous data or you can enter data monthly; however the program does not reconcile differences. You can track investment information but stock prices have to updated manually. SmartHome Manager is geared more toward the home users with its household features than for those who need powerful financial planning tools.

CONTACT INFORMATION

Managing Your Money
MECA Software
(203) 452-2600
www.mym,net.com

Microsoft Money 97
Microsoft Corp.
(800) 426-9400
(202) 882-8080
www.microsoft.com

Smart Home Manager
Surado Solutions
(800) 478-7236
(909) 682-4895

Quicken Deluxe Version 6.0 for Windows
Intuit Inc.
(800) 446-8848
(415) 944-6000
www.intuit.com
☐

PERSONAL INFORMATION MANAGERS

Our daily lives are packed with information. We have to keep track of business and personal information such as appointments, addresses, phone numbers, and shopping lists. Personal Information Managers (PIMs) can give order to this information. Designed somewhat like a dayplanner you can record names, addresses, phone numbers, e-mail notes, to-do lists, appointments, and other vital information. This chapter evaluates some of the more popular PIMs on the market today. Below are their overall ratings.

OVERALL RATINGS

Janna Contact Personal	★★★★
Now Up-To-Date	★★★★
On-Schedule 3.0	★★★★
Day-Timer Organizer 2.1	★★★
Ecco Pro 4.0	★★★
Ascend 97	★★★
Microsoft Outlook 97	★★★
Lotus Organizer 97	★★ 1/2
AnyTime Deluxe	★ 1/2

EXPLANATION OF RATINGS

These PIMs were rated in the following five categories; Ease of Use, which considers how easy it was to set up the program and use it immediately; Data Handling, which evaluates how well data can be entered and manipulated; Scheduling, which pertains to appointment and group scheduling features; Mail Merge, which evaluates the program's ability to generate multiple or individual correspondence and import or export it; and Customization, which refers to how customizable the program is. Each category was given a one-to-four star rating. The overall score was attained by averaging the ratings in the five categories.

ALPHABETICAL DESCRIPTIONS

AnyTime Deluxe
Price $49.95

Overall Rating ★ 1/2

AnyTime Deluxe is a simple program, but it lacks the powerful features found in other packages. It's easy to use and data entry is straightforward. The address book is very basic and data is placed in one field, making mail merges impossible. There are templates included, but you can create your own correspondence. There is no linking capability to attach letters to their recipients. Also, there is no spell checker included.

Ascend 97
Price $99.95

Overall Rating ★★★

Ascend 97 goes beyond managing information; it is designed to manage your life. Developed by the Franklin Quest people who make the popular Franklin Planners, this program gives you features to set your goals, keep you inspired, and manage your information. You can enter data into one of the following sections: Prioritized Daily Task List, Appointment Schedule, Daily Record of Events, Address and Phone Book, Values and Goals, Master Task List, Journal, Favorite Quotes, Turbo Files, and Red Tabs. It also allows you to create records with vital information such as name, address, and phone number in the notes area. Each record has a contact history section for tracking phone calls. There is no autofill feature, which would have made entry even more simpler. Appointments are created on the calendar easily by clicking on the data and entering the appointment. The makers of Ascend want this program to be a integral part of your life, which is why there are seminars around the country on how to use this PIM to enrich your life.

Day-Timer Organizer 2.1

Price $60; CD-ROM deluxe edition $80

Overall Rating ★ ★ ★

This personal information manager greets you with the Day-Timer Daily Pop-up, which displays a tip on using the program. The program features a daily, weekly and monthly planner; a scheduler; and an address book. You can record phone calls, expenses, and tasks and enter information in the notebook, timeline and message board. The global list feature shows all of your information in a list. The contact database includes fields for up to six phone numbers and four e-mail addresses as well as the usual name and address information. You can customize the program and create your own categories to fit your needs. Contact information can be dragged and dropped to the task list or scheduler. This creates a link to the contact information. Day-Timer had a problem importing information

into its program. Other features include a timer to track billable hours in the Task List. Day-Timer supports IntelliLink transfer protocol so you can exchange data with a PDA. Day-Timer also has excellent Internet capabilities that allow you to enter a contact's e-mail or web address and then access those sites directly from the program.

Ecco Pro 4.0

Price $99

Overall Rating ★ ★ ★

Ecco Pro is more powerful than a standalone personal information manager. It's group scheduling features can schedule single or recurring group meetings, as well as search for group members who have free time and can book meeting resources. For group scheduling, the program works with cc:Mail, Lotus Notes, Microsoft Exchange, and Z-Mail Pro. Mobile computers can easily use Ecco Pro while traveling and synchronize the data from their notebooks or handheld computers. Data exchange support is available for U.S. Robotics' Pilot and the Timex Data Link watch. Ecco Pro also has Internet/intranet capabilities. The Ecco Internet Address Book contains a directory of over 1,000 World Wide Web, FTP, and Gopher sites in over 30 categories, such as computers, software business, and sports. You can get information from the Internet quickly with the Ecco Pro Shooter just by selecting the information on the Internet, then sending it to Ecco Pro or another Windows application.

Time management features include a calendar that can display appointments in day, week, month or yearly views. There are to-do lists, unlimited notes, and customizable alarms for appointments or tasks. Other features include project management capabilities, which include Gantt charts, team tracking, and cross-reference capabilities with calendar and phonebook. Contact management uses drag-and-drop ease to schedule and update appointments. The address book is customizable so you can create fields for the information you need. The entire contact history can be viewed. E-mail and faxes can be sent from within the program and mail merges are automatic when using Microsoft Word and WordPerfect.

Janna Contact Personal

Price $49

Overall Rating ★★★★

Janna Contact Personal is a top-notch personal information manager with powerful features ,which is why it ranked as tops in this category. The address book is simple and straightforward. It's divided by three tabs— Contact, Profile and Notes. Basic contact information like names, addresses, and phone numbers are entered under Contact. Other information such as favorite restaurants,and birthdays are placed under Profile. The Notes section lets you attach documents such as letters, and invoices. A big plus for this program is its ability to import from other programs such as Act!, Ascend, and Lotus Organize. In sum, it's simple, easy to use and just wonderful if you want to spend more time working at your professional life than working with the program.

Lotus Organizer 97

Price $99

Overall Rating ★★1/2

Lotus Organizer has a simple interface that resembles a dayplanner. Data entry is a no-brainer, but there are a few drawbacks. Street addresses are entered as one field, so if you have contacts with multiple address lines this could be a problem. There is no field for a web page address. Scheduling appointments is as easy as clicking on the program's calendar. Select the day you want, click on it, then enter the appointment. The program will alert you if you have a scheduling conflict. Lotus Organizer can track your phone calls and even dial for you. You can also link your to-do list to calls you need to make and contacts can be linked to each other. The Organizer cannot do mail merges or keep a history of your contact interactions. Since it comes bundled with Lotus SmartSuite 97, it supports SmartSuite's team-mail, but it cannot act like an e-mail client. Lotus SmartSuite users will find this program useful but there is no compelling reason to buy it, particularly since you cannot merge data.

Now Up-To-Date

Price $69.95

Overall Rating ★★★★

Now Up-To-Date not only lets you record contact information on your computer, you can also publish your calendar and address book on the Internet for others to view. If you work in teams, this program can help your team collaborate. Calendars and address books can be dragged from the web into Now Up-to- Date. You can store a contact's e-mail address and URL activate it easily with one click. The interface is easy to use. You can access any information from the floating toolbar without launching the program. The daily schedule can be viewed at a glance and there are reminder alarms for upcoming events. Another unique feature is the Quick Pad, which can be accessed without starting the program itself. Use Quick Pad to record phone calls, appointments, and other notes and the information is entered into your contact database automatically. The calendar is easy to use. Your schedule can be viewed the way you want, monthly, weekly, etc. Changing your schedule has drag-and-drop ease and data entry is just as easy. The AutoType feature saves you time by automatically typing familiar words, thus eliminating repetitive data entry. Business cards can be easily scanned with the included

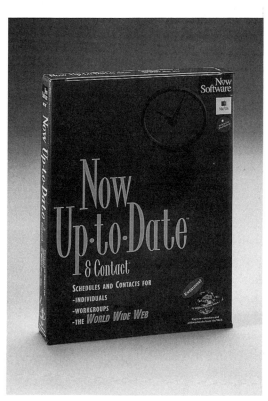

Now Up-to-Date, the number-one rated application.

support for the Visioneer Paperport. Information from the business cards is automatically placed into the database. Now Up-To-Date imports information from ACT! Sidekick, Schedule+ or text files. For travelers, this program gives you easy access to data even when you're on the road. Changes made to data while traveling can be easily synchronized with your main program. The US Robotics' Pilot is supported, but you need an additional software program, Now Synchronize. Now Up-To-Date is also available in a Macintosh version. This is a powerful program that can give you everything you need to manage your information.

On Schedule 3.0
Price $89.95

Overall Rating ★★★★

On Schedule has powerful features often found in a contact manager program. You can create various phone books, making it easy to categorize your contacts. Besides the standard contact data, you can enter company names, positions, departments, up to four e-mail addresses, Internet addresses, birthdays, spouse's name, pager, and cell phone numbers. The autofill feature is great and eases the pain of repetitive data entry. Phone books can easily be linked if you need to have the same contact information in multiple phone books. This program excels for those who have over 50 contacts to deal with.

Microsoft Outlook 97
Price $129

Overall Rating ★ ★ ★

Outlook 97 incorporates e-mail with its main information features. Contacts are entered into the contact database, which supports customizable fields. Contacts can be grouped together, making it easy to manage data. If you want to send an e-mail message, just drag a contact name to the e-mail icon, enter your message then send. Word for Windows can be set up as your e-mail text editor with the use of OLE edit-in-place function. The program's mail merge is a mixed bag. Creating letters for one contact is easy, just select the contact, then Word's letter creation wizard launches and the letter is automatically addressed. Multiple merges aren't as straightforward. You have to select all the contacts you want to include in the mail merge, export them to a separate file, then set up the mail merge in another application, like Word. Group scheduling is setup with point-and-click simplicity—select all the contacts you want to include in the meeting and the program sends notification to everyone by e-mail. One nice feature is Outlook's Journal, which tracks your communications with contacts. It records email sent and other interactions. The Outlook application is included as part of Microsoft Office 97.

CONTACT INFORMATION

AnyTime Deluxe
Individual Software
1-800-822-3522
www.individualsoftware.com

Ascend 97
Franklin Quest
1-800-975-1776
www.franklinquest.com

Day-Timer Organizer 2.1
Day-Timer
1-800-225-5005
www.daytimer.com

Ecco Pro 4.0
NetManage
206-885-4272
www.netmanage.com

Janna Contact Personal
Janna Systems Inc.
1-800-268-6107
www.janna.com

Now Up-To-Date
Now Software
800-237-2078
www.nowsoftware.com

On-Schedule 3.0
Odyssey Computing Inc.
1-800-965-7224
www.odysseyinc.com

Lotus Development Corp.
800-343-5414
617-577-8500
www.lotus.com

Microsoft Corp.
800-426-9400
www.microsoft.com

Corel Corporation
800-772-6735
www.corel.com

PRESENTATION GRAPHICS

Presentation Graphics programs give you the ability to create hard copy or electronic presentations. Your presentations can have more impact when you use these programs' drawing, charting, outlining, and multimedia features. Some programs offer the ability to distribute presentations via the Internet. Listed below are six presentation graphics programs and their overall scores.

RANKINGS AND OVERALL SCORES

1	Microsoft PowerPoint 97	95
2	Astound 4.0	85
3	Lotus Freelance Graphics 97 Edition	80
4	Adobe Persuasion 4.0	75
5	Corel Presentations 8.0	73
6	Harvard Graphics 4.0	70

EXPLANATION OF RATINGS

Five aspects of each application were scored: *Multimedia Effects*, which refers to the integration of audio, video, animation, and interactivity in presentations; *Design and Content*, which pertains to templates, auto-content features, clipart, and on-line help; *Output*, which rates electronic and paper-based presentations; *Ease of Use*, which refers to the program's learning curve and usability; and *Internet Tools*, which involves how well the program interfaces with the Internet. The maximum score for each category is 20. The five scores for each application were added, resulting in the overall score, which has a potential of 100 total points.

ALPHABETICAL DESCRIPTIONS

Adobe Persuasion 4.0

Price $395; $129 upgrade

Rank 4

Ease of Use 10

Multimedia Effects 10

Output 20

Internet Tools 20

Design and Content 15

Adobe Persuasion 4.0 is a cross-platform application that comes with a set of disks for both Windows and Macintosh computers. The graphics tools are first-rate and offer high-precision, like other Adobe products, Illustrator and Photoshop. This package is not as simple to use as the others. It lacks on-line help, wizards, auto-content, and other hand holding features. Beginners will have to stumble along until they find their way. Presentations are created in layers, with different objects like text on one layer, graphics on another, and so on. However, there is an ample collection of 125 templates for on-screen and web presentations, 500 clip-art files, movies, and sounds on a CD-ROM, which can streamline the creation process. The finished presentation can be presented on screen, color 35mm slides, overheads, black-and-white hardcopy, 8-bit (256 color) and 24-bit (true-color) web presentations. The multimedia effects in the electronic presentation may not be as robust as other programs but it does support chart builds. The precision graphics tools give you the ability to drag and drop graphics from other Adobe programs, use keyboard shortcuts and various palettes, on screen ruler guides, automatic pair kerning, and 24-bit color options. Color matching is easy with the eyedropper or you can type in color values or select colors from color libraries. Adobe Persuasion is for those users who want more precision control over color in their presentations.

Astound 4.0

Price $249.95; $99.95 upgrade	
Rank 2	
Ease of Use 15	
Multimedia Effects 20	
Output 20	
Internet Tools 15	
Design and Content 15	

Astound 4.0 has the look and feel of PowerPoint; it can even import PowerPoint presentations. The interface is easy to navigate and Astound's head-start templates can automatically create presentation on a variety of topics, such as presenting a marketing plan or training. Despite these templates, there is not much in the way of step-by-step help in creating presentations or auto content for business presentations. Astound's strength is in its sizzling animation tools. Included are over 100 pre-animated templates, over 1,800 clip-media files, and about 300 animated actors—from businessmen that can walk on your screen to animated animals—that can bring your presentation to life. Astound's animation wizard includes options like grow, bounce, fly-in charts, spinning text, flying bullets, and animated chart segments. Controlling this animation is made simple with a visual time-line window where you can speed up, slow down, or pause animation without programming. Freeform path animation is also supported. Any object can be made to move along a line that is fine tuned with a Bezier path tool. Interactivity is another strong suit here: any object can be linked to an action, including jumps to other parts of the presentation or a web site. There is also a mouse roll-over feature that can add interactivity. This is when the mouse rolls over an interactive object and a text box appears or sound plays. No programming is needed for this option either. This feature is associated with higher-end multimedia products. Delivery of your presentation is simplified with the distribution wizard. Your presentations can be delivered via disks, computer, e-mail, master on a recordable CD-ROM, 35mm slides, overheads, and converted to HTML for use on the web. Astound 4.0 is a great application for creating dazzling on-screen shows. If you create on-screen shows on a regular basis and don't need a lot of hand-holding, this application can deliver the results you would find in higher-end multimedia programs.

Corel Presentations 8

Price $99; upgrade, $49.95	
Rank 5	
Ease of Use 20	
Multimedia Effects 15	
Output 13	

Internet Tools 10

Design and Content 15

This is a simple straightforward program with an easy-to-use interface, web integration tools, and 10,000 clip art images. As in other presentation graphics program's, you can select a template or create your own background for your presentation. The programs Perfect Expert leads you while you create a presentation by asking you to select a goal, type of audience, or purpose. Corel only provides a limited amount of content templates on certain business topics, but it does have a ton of clipart and 40 new screen transitions. Graphics tools include tracing tools that convert bitmapped graphics into vector graphics, which resize without distorting. The Quick 3D feature creates three-dimensional objects from any object. Presentations lets you play sound but not video. Video playback is only supported through OLE (object linking and embedding) which is hard to use. Interactivity for your onscreen presentations can be added by simply right-clicking on an object which displays a quick menu where you can choose animation or sounds or movement. Keystrokes can also be programmed to perform move functions. You can convert your presentation to a portable format by creating a runtime version for use on other computers. There is a runtime module for those who do not have Corel Presentations 7 installed on their system. This version does not allow remote viewing of presentations. Your completed Corel presentation can be converted to HTML for use on the web. Your presentation can contain frames, multiple pages, and links to other web sites. The presentation retains its links after conversion to HTML, but the slide transition effects will not display in the web browser. Despite all the multimedia bells and whistles being added to presentation packages, many presentations are still produced on paper, making the printing function of a program important. Corel did have trouble when printing backgrounds. Some of the text did not appear because the gray-scale contrast did not alter correctly, and it prints slower than other products in this review. Overall, Corel Presentations contains many features the other packages do and is an adequate program. If you are on a budget and need a presentation program, this one should suffice, but if you're already using another presentation program there's no compelling features that would make you switch.

Harvard Graphics 4.0

Price $289

Rank 6

Ease of Use 15

Multimedia Effects 20

Output 15

Internet Tools 5

Design and Content 15

This version of Harvard Graphics includes new functionality and enhancements that can help you create good-looking presentations with more ease. The new Advisor feature gives users design tips for creating presentations. The Advisor also has a Check design option which checks your presentation against a set of design guidelines and provides feedback on how to improve your presentation. This design checker can be run on one slide or an entire presentation. If you know what you want to say but have no idea how to say it, Harvard Graphics has a set of predesigned presentation templates for you to edit to fit your needs. However, Harvard Graphics templates are not as extensive as other programs, but they are of good quality. There are also 15 ready-made animation samples and a clip art gallery of about 500 symbols, but it's not very diverse. While you are working on your presentation you can preview updates before you implement them; transition effects can also be previewed and you can edit directly in the Slide Editor. New File formats are supported, including Lotus 1-2-3 version 4 (WK4), Encapsulated Postscript (EPS), Kodak PhotoCD (PCD) and CorelDraw (CDR). Printed output is excellent but the onscreen slide transitions run slower than other programs. Harvard Graphics does not support web publishing and only allows presentation conferencing over NETBIOS-compatible LANs. However this program is one of the few (besides Corel Presentations) that can break a pie slice into a column chart, and it has extensive drawing effects. This presentation program offers a good set of design tools for those with design experience. Harvard Graphics has stood the test of time and is still a viable presentation program.

Lotus Freelance Graphics 97 Edition

Price $355; upgrade, $105	
Rank 3	

Ease of Use 20	
Multimedia Effects 10	
Output 15	
Internet Tools 20	
Design and Content 15	

This version of Freelance Graphics supports HTML frames and saves files directly to a web server. Presentations can include links to web sites and multi-point presentation conferencing is now included. This version still supports the electronic filing cabinet function and now has workgroup capabilities, namely the TeamReview feature that is found in Lotus' other applications. To create a presentation you can select from one of over 130 SmartMasters templates, with some having multimedia capabilities. This is a simple process that lets you quickly add data, format text, and switch between the slide, sorter, and outlining views. If you need a starting point for your presentation, Freelance provides content advice on a variety of topics from leading business authorities like Zig Ziglar. One strong feature of Freelance is its business diagramming. There are over 80 shapes and connectors and over 100 predesigned business diagrams you can select. It also has an extensive clipart gallery. Freelance can incorporate sound and video into slides. You can add interactivity to slides by right-clicking on slides or objects then assigning a function from the pop-up menu. Where Freelance stands out is in its workgroup capability. TeamReview lets groups view presentations via a network, Lotus Notes, e-mail, or floppy disks and then add comments for revisions. Team-

Show displays presentations remotely. Your presentation can be delivered on screen, remotely, on the Internet, placed on floppies, 35mm slides, or printed out as hard copy or transparencies. Printing was effortless and straightforward. If you're looking for workgroup prowess, then Freelance should be your presentation program.

Microsoft PowerPoint 97

Price $340; upgrade, $110

Rank 1

Ease of Use 20

Multimedia Effects 20

Output 20

Internet Tools 15

Design and Content 20

Microsoft PowerPoint 97 is the latest version of this popular presentation program. This version offers more animation effects, interactivity, web integration, and online help. It continues to have an easy to use interface as in previous versions. The new Office Assistant offers context-sensitive help in the form of an animated character. This cartoon-like helper appears when you are incorrectly trying to perform a function. The Office Assistant will then show you what you are doing wrong. The Office Assistant is a slick feature but, for those who find him a bit annoying after a while, he can be disabled. PowerPoint has added new multimedia features that include the ability to animate text and objects and move them at specific times. These animations can be previewed in a thumbnail slide. There are also new AutoShapes including banners, block arrows, stars, callouts, action buttons, and

flowcharts. AutoShapes can now be automatically connected by a line, which will readjust if the AutoShapes are moved. You can also add interactivity to your presentation with hyperlinks and buttons that look as if they are depressed when a user clicks on them. Custom shows can be created in one presentation to gear parts of a presentation to different audiences, eliminating the need to create multiple presentations. Design and content templates have been expanded and include a bunch of new backgrounds and content templates from Dale Carnegie. Web integration is easier with this version. No additional add-on is needed. The PowerPoint 97 presentations can be converted to HTML and placed on the web with links to URLs. A person needs the PowerPoint Animation Player to view the web presentation. This add-on comes with the program or can be downloaded from Microsoft's web site. site. In addition to viewing your presentation on a computer and the web, PowerPoint 97 has the ability to show presentations on a remote computer and the Pack and Go Wizard copies your presentation so you can send to others or take it on the road with you. In addition to electronic presentations, PowerPoint 97 can output your presentation to overheads or paper in either black-and-white, color, or 35mm slides. Files created in PowerPoint 97 can be saved in PowerPoint 95 format if needed, but some of the new features you have incorporated into your presentation will lose some of their sizzle in the 95 version. An added bonus, though, is the ability to save multiple versions of a presentation in one file and automatic file compression to nearly 50 percent. PowerPoint 97 still comes out a winner with this program. Beginners and experienced users alike will be comfortable creating dynamic presentations with this program.

CONTACT INFORMATION

Adobe Persuasion
Adobe Corp.
(800) 843-7263
(408) 536-6000
www.adobe.com

Astound
(888) 4ASTOUND
(415) 845-6200
http://astoundinc.com

Corel Presentations
Corel Corporation
(800) 772-6735
(6130 728-3733
www.corel.com

Freelance Graphics
Lotus Development Corp.
(800) 343-5414; (617) 577-8500
www.lotus.com

Power Point
Microsoft Corp.
(800) 426-9400; (206) 882-8080
www.microsoft.com

Harvard Graphics
Software Publishing
(800) 336-8360
www.spco.com

REMOTE CONTROL SOFTWARE

Imagine you're on a business trip and have discovered you left your presentation on your office computer. . . and the office is closed; there is no one there to send you the file. What do you do? You fire up your notebook, and with your remote-control software you can access your office computer and transfer the presentation to your notebook.

Remote control software allows a remote computer (called the client) to connect to another computer (called the host) via either a dial-up, Internet, or LAN connection. The client computer then takes over the host computer's operations and can then transfer files or run applications. This

The number-one rated application LapLink (screen capture below) stands out from the crowd with its intuitive interface, great features, and online help system.

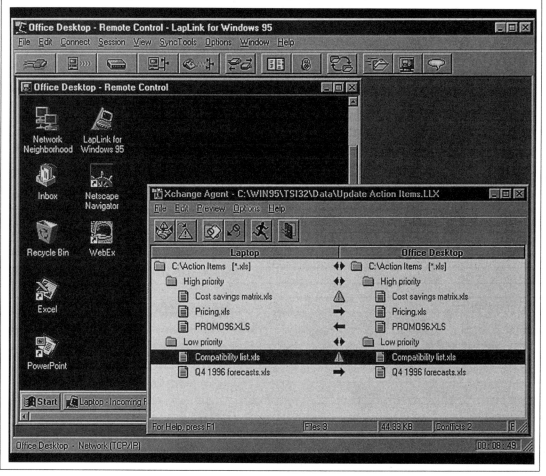

type of software is routinely used by sales reps, help-desk staff, trainers, business travelers, and telecommuters.

Listed below are six remote control software programs and their ratings.

OVERALL RATINGS

LapLink For Windows 95   ★ ★ ★ 1/2

ReachOut   ★ ★ ★

pcAnywhere 32   ★ ★ ★

Carbon Copy   ★ ★ ★

InSync CoSession Remote 7.0   ★ ★ ★

Remotely Possible/32   ★ ★ ★

EXPLANATION OF RATINGS

Each program was evaluated on the following four criteria: ease of use, remote control capabilities, file transfer, and security. How well these features performed distinguish the different packages from each other. Extra features may include wallpaper suppression, color scaling and printer redirection. Wallpaper suppression disables the wallpaper bitmap, thereby preventing this large file from being transmitted needlessly. If you want to reduce colors, the color scaling option allows you to. Printer redirection can print files stored on the host computer to a remote client printer.

Remote access is established either through remote control or remote node. Remote control sets up a remote client computer to take control of another computer (the host). The host does most of the processing, which is useful if the remote computer has less power and storage space. Remote mode treats the remote computer as if it were connected to the LAN. The remote client does most of the processing. File transfers and application processing occurs via an ISDN line, Internet link, or modem.

ALPHABETICAL DESCRIPTIONS

Carbon Copy for Windows

Price $129

Overall Rating ★ ★ ★

Ease of Use ★ ★ ★

Remote Control Capabilities ★ ★ 1/2

File Transfer ★ ★ ★

Security ★ ★ ★

Carbon Copy is an easy-to-use program for Windows 95, Windows 3.1 and DOS. Setup can be accomplished in a matter of minutes. The point-and-click interface lets you quickly access the software's functions. Besides the basic features of remote control and file transfer, Carbon Copy offers remote printing, a Netscape Navigator plug-in and two-way drive mapping. The drive sharing option allows the host and remote client access to each other's hard drives. But there is no role-reversal feature which gives the host control of the remote computer.

For remote viewing you can suppress the host's wallpaper, reduce screen resolution, auto-pan screens, or reduce screens. However, when the host computer screen is reduced to fit the remote clients, the display is hard to read.

Transferring files is as easy as dragging and dropping them. You can also restrict access to host files and synchronize files. If your transfer is interrupted there is a crash recovery feature. Files can be stored locally to increase display speed.

Security features include the basic user name and password plus the ability to password-protect directories and files, host confirmation using Caller ID and remote dial-back, and the ability to limit log-in attempts, session time, and restrict user access.

This program lacks data encryption, virus scanning, and support for long file names, TAPI and Windows 95 Dial-UP Networking.

InSync CoSession Remote 7.0

Price $79 (two-user pack)

Overall Rating ★★★

Ease of Use ★★★

Remote Control Capabilities ★★1/2

File Transfer ★★★

Security ★★★

This no-frills application offers you key features found in more expensive applications, for less than half the price. CoSession is a Windows 3.1 program, but runs well under Windows 95. A separate DOS version lets DOS-based computers take control of Windows 3.1 or Windows 95-based computers. Its icon-based interface makes it easy to use.

LapLink for Windows 95, the number-one rated application.

The interface supports drag-and-drop file transfer similar to Windows 95 Explorer. There is support for long file names, tracking of remote-client connections and delta-file transfer support. There is a transfer-interrupted safeguard which will start your transfer where it was interrupted. Synchronization of directories is also available.

Security features include a log-on notification on the host, and the ability to set a master password and users' rights. The host computer can be configured to wait for a call either by modem or via a network.

CoSession cannot disable wallpaper, shrink the host screen or host multiple simultaneous connections. It also does not support TAPI. (A Windows NT Workstation 4.0 version will remedy this.)

LapLink for Windows 95

Price $149

Overall Rating ★★★1/2

Ease of Use ★★★★

Remote Control Capabilities ★★★★

File Transfer ★★★

Security ★★★

LapLink stands out from the crowd with its intuitive interface, great features, and online help system. The help system is like a trainer in a box, offering you assistance at each step. LapLink can access Windows 95 built-in Dial-Up Networking option. Windows 3.1 users will find a separate product for them included with this software.

Remote screens can be displayed at full size. File transfers were simple with drag-and-drop on a split screen interface. This same split-screen is used for file synchronization.

If you need to set up connections with far-away users, LapLink allows 11 simultaneous connections and supports a number of Internet connection options.

Additional options include wallpaper suppression, screen-scaling, and role reversal features. LapLink does not have remote drive-mapping or remote printer redirection. LapLink is a great tool to use for support, training, or other collaborative efforts.

pcAnywhere 32

Price $149 (two-user version)
Overall Rating ★★★
Ease of Use ★★★
Remote Control Capabilities ★★★1/2
File Transfer ★★★
Security ★★★1/2

pcAnywhere 32 offers a lot of features, including multiplatform compatibility, Internet connections, Windows 95 integration, automatic file synchronization, and session recording.

Configuration is easy, with wizards and TAPI support. Its Dial-Up Networking interface imitates Windows 95's, and connection icons can be dragged onto the desktop for easy access. Host screens can be viewed full screen, windowed, or scaled to fit. Colors can be limited to speed-up performance.

All the pcAnywhere products work together over a variety of connections, but there is no support for multiple concurrent connections.

File transfers can be confusing. The interface does not follow the Windows 95 Explorer, making it difficult to navigate directories. Also, browsing is not allowed when setting up automated file synchronization. You have to know the file's exact location. LapLink has LAN support, supporting more network protocols than other products. A gateway feature allows an administrator to install pcAnywhere 32 on a server so users can dial out to online services, a BBS, or pcAnywhere host.

Security options include data encryption, session limits, host notification, master password protection, and drive access restrictions, as well as the basic user ID and log-on password. It does not offer intruder detection, but failed log-on attempts are logged. Added features include Norton Anti-virus which scans over the Internet and terminal modules for connecting to online services or bulletin boards.

ReachOut

Overall Rating ★★★
Ease of Use ★★1/2
Remote Control Capabilities ★★★

File Transfer ★★★

Security ★★★

With its fast performance, network support, and other features, ReachOut supports multiple platforms. If you're technically savvy this program is a good choice. ReachOut uses the Windows 95 built-in networking features. File transfers are fast, and remote viewing performance was good. One great feature is the way ReachOut maps drives. Its two-way drive mapping allows both the host and client to access each other's drives. Its good security features, flexible network support, and anti-virus scanning makes this package a one-stop solution for multiple platforms.

Remotely Possible/32

Price $169 - Windows 95 version;

$199 Windows NT Workstation version

Overall Rating ★★★

Ease of Use ★★★

Remote Control Capabilities ★★★

File Transfer ★★1/2

Security ★★★

Remotely Possible is available for the Windows 3.1, Windows 95, and Windows NT platforms, but has no support of DOS. There are several Windows 3.1 versions for different communication protocols.

Performance on remote control was good, but file transfer performance was only fair. Remote viewers can disable wallpaper, set remote printing options, and navigate the host using auto-pan mode, which controls the screen according to mouse movements. There is no scaling feature available.

File transfers are done via drag-and-drop; however, files are not automatically transferred. Instead, the files are placed in a queue, then the file transfer is executed. This allows you to select multiple files from various directories and transfer them simultaneously. Remotely Possible security features data encryption, access limits, tracking log for transaction, host notification option, and the basic user name and password.

CONTACT INFORMATION

Remotely Possible/32
Avalan Technology Inc.
800-441-2281
508-429-6482
www.avalan.com

ReachOut
Stac
www.stac.com

Norton pcAnywhere32
Symantec Corp.
800-441-7234
408-253-9600
www.symantec.com

LapLink for Windows 95
Traveling Software Inc.
800-343-8080
206-483-8088
www.travsoft.com

InSync CoSession Remote
Artisoft Inc.
800-846-9726
520-670-7100
www.artisoft.com

SPREADSHEETS

Today's spreadsheets still do basic calculations and charting but now also have collaboration features and Internet integration. This chapter takes a look at the major spreadsheet programs. The following table shows the overall score for each application.

OVERALL RATINGS

Corel Quattro Pro 7	★★
Lotus 123	★★★
Microsoft Excel 97	★★★★

EXPLANATION OF RATINGS

Spreadsheets were scored for the following facets: *Data Manipulation*, which refers to processing, analysis, and charting of data; *Programming*, that is, the ability to customize spreadsheets; *Collaboration Tools*, which pertains to the ability to share data with a group; and *Internet Integration*, which involves the ability to get information to and from the Internet. The highest rating for each categories is four stars; the lowest is one star. The category ratings were then averaged into the overall score.

ALPHABETICAL DESCRIPTIONS

Lotus 123 97
Price $329; upgrade $105

| *Overall Rating* ★★★ |
| *Data Manipulation* ★★★1/2 |
| *Programming* ★★★ |
| *Collaboration* ★★★★ |
| *Internet Integration* ★★★ |

Lotus 123 97 is the first 32-bit version of this program. New features include an improved interface, Internet integration and LotusScript (a cross-application scripting language).

The interface has been enhanced with customizable menus for common tasks and the inclusion of the Lotus InfoBox, a floating toolbox that gives you access to all formatting tools. Another neat enhancement is the totaling feature, which lets you type the word "total" into a cell and the corresponding rows or columns will then be added up. There is also a feature which consolidates different versions of a spreadsheet into one final version. The different versions can be stored in one file and you can keep an audit trail of spreadsheet changes. If you need to create your own functions, LotusScript can help you do this. LotusScript is a scripting language similar to Basic that can be used across applications. One drawback is that some older macros do not convert. Internet support includes the ability to read files and write files to the web and FTP sites. You can also mine data from the Internet with LotusScript programming. Collaboration tools are the best you can find in this program. Files can be sent to co-workers with security features to limit editing, and can include custom instructions for routing files. TeamMail sends messages with embedded current files. TeamReview will send ranges and merge comments and edits from recipients back into the original spreadsheet. TeamConsolidate stores individual worksheet pages in Lotus Notes 4.1 or later for replication or reconciliation. Established Lotus 123 users will find this revamped version a better product. For others, if you have a direct Internet connection and have the need to work with a team, this package gives you to power to do that.

Microsoft Excel 97

Price $340; upgrade $110

Overall Rating ★ ★ ★ ★

Data Manipulation ★ ★ ★ ★

Programming ★ ★ ★ ★

Collaboration ★ ★ ★

Internet Integration ★ ★ ★ ★

Excel still ranks as one of the best spreadsheet programs, around. Like other programs it has made Excel 97 Internet-ready with support for workgroups with collaboration tools. Excel can do web queries to gather data from the Internet or intranet and place it into a spreadsheet. You can also write to web sites and read files on the web. Links to web sites or local files can be placed in a worksheet. Workgroup tools allow multiple users to view and edit the same worksheet simultaneously. Conflicting changes to worksheets are reconciled by Excel by either accepting the last change made or displaying a dialog box and letting the user choose which change to accept. There is also an audit trail feature that records all user's edits to a worksheet. Shared workbooks can now be merged. Other features include the ability

of Excel's PivotTables to calculate fields, a streamlined charting feature, automatic correction for common formulas, and formatting tools all in one toolbar.

Corel Quattro Pro 7

Price $99.00; upgrade $49.95

Overall Rating ★ ★

Data Manipulation ★ ★ ★ 1/2

Programming ★ ★ ★

Collaboration ★

Internet Integration ★ ★

Since being acquired by Corel and included in its Corel Office Suite, Quattro Pro 7 has undergone some changes. The interface has been changed to keep in line with other Office Suite applications. Quattro Pro 7 has moved into the Internet arena by offering Internet features. You can open files from the web, FTP or Gopher sites, but you cannot write files to these areas. Files you download from the Internet lose hyperlink data. Links can be created by typing the URL into a cell. You can also create web queries with the PerfectScript language, which updates worksheets with data from the Internet. PerfectScript is Quattro Pro's programming language that writes macros and other custom functions. If programming is not your thing, there are about 100 new library functions you can choose from to help automate your work. Corel gets a thumbs down on their collaboration tools. You can send a workbook as an mail attachment, but you can't send a specific worksheet range or mail sequentially. Work groups can use the consolidate command to merge their various worksheets, but it is complex and frustrating.

CONTACT INFORMATION

Lotus Development Corp.
800-343-5414; 617-577-8500
www.lotus.com

Microsoft Corp.
800-426-9400; 206-882-8080
www.microsoft.com

Corel Corporation
800-772-6735; 613-728-3733
www.corel.com

UNINSTALL UTILITIES

Uninstall utilities are used to completely remove software applications from your hard drive. Uninstalling software is not an easy process. It takes more then just deleting the folder where the program's files reside. Even using the Windows 95 uninstall feature does not remove all of an application's files. When software is installed it makes itself at home and places all types of files all over your hard drive. Uninstall utilities can help you get rid of unwanted files and help keep your hard drive clean and tidy. One word of caution: when using an uninstall program pay careful attention to what you are doing, especially if you are not technically savvy. If you're not an experienced user, even with all the safety features you could end up deleting something you did not mean to. All of the following programs do have a feature that keeps compressed backups of applications in case they need to be reinstalled.

Using Remove-It, the number-one rated utility, (screen capture below) is easy. From the main panel you can select one of 10 buttons to access Remove-It's tools.

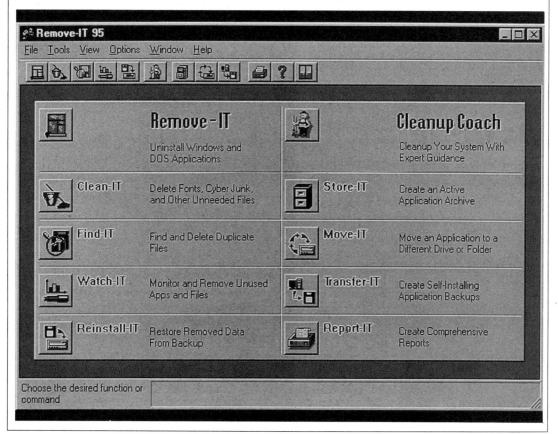

Listed below are nine popular uninstall products followed by their overall ratings.

OVERALL RATINGS

Remove-It 95	★★★★
CleanSweep 3.0	★★★
Power Cleaner	★★★
Uninstaller 4.0	★★★
WinDelete	★★1/2

EXPLANATION OF RATINGS

Each product was evaluated on three aspects: ease of use, safety features, and removal functions. Each aspect could potentially earn up to four stars, with one star being the lowest rating. The ratings of these three aspects were then averaged, resulting in the overall rating.

ALPHABETICAL DESCRIPTIONS

CleanSweep 3.0
Price $39.95
Overall Rating ★★★
Ease of Use ★★★
File Removal Functions ★★★
Safety Features ★★★

CleanSweep is an easy-to-use program which does an above average job of removing software applications. It safely removes 16- and 32-bit programs. After you install CleanSweep, it keeps watch over your hard drive for all new Windows installations. Wizards are available to guide you through the process of removing an application. You can select files to delete or keep and the program makes compressed backups of applications it deletes. The Safety Sweep features protect you from accidentally deleting a file. This safety feature helps prevent users from accidentally deleting something they need.

Additional utilities for reinstalling, archiving and moving applications are also included. Other features include Update-It, which will update CleanSweep via the Internet. CleanSweep has an application knowledge base of more than 1,000 programs. In addition to removing unwanted applications and files, CleanSweep can move programs to other locations, copy files to another computer, and get rid of unused and duplicate files. Its Registry Sweep gets rid of invalid registry entries. This is a thorough and powerful program.

Power Cleaner
Price $29.95
Overall Rating ★★★
Ease of Use ★★★
File Removal Functions ★★★
Safety Features ★★

Power Cleaner can remove unwanted applications on your hard drive—even preexisting ones. It's easy to use and offers features such as Program Mover, which moves applications and files to another location or computer (this only works for 16-bit applications); Program Archiver, which compresses programs to give you more space; and Orphan Tracker, which finds files that are not associated with any program. Files found for deletion are color-coded to tell you what will happen if a file is deleted. The safety feature is not automatic. The user must mark each file to be deleted so as to not delete an essential file accidentally. This is not a good thing, especially for novices.

Power Cleaner's advanced algorithms are not merely limited to monitoring new installations; they are excellent at removing pre-existing applications.

Remove-It 95

Price $39.95

Overall Rating
★ ★ ★ ★

Ease of Use ★ ★ ★ ★

File Removal Functions ★ ★ ★ ★

Safety Features
★ ★ ★

Remove-It is an excellent uninstaller program that easily removes software applications, even pre-existing ones. Using Remove-It is easy. From the main panel you can select one of 10 buttons to access Remove-It's tools. After Remove-It is installed, it acts as a monitor for your hard drive, keeping track of all installations you make.

Remove-It 95, the number-one rated uninstall utility.

There are two ways to remove files, the Custom or Express format. The Custom format allows you to select the file you want to delete while Express automatically removes the program. Both formats remove files efficiently and fast. It even removes pre-existing software with no

problems. Remove-It's safety features mark questionable files and won't remove executable files or system folder files. It also saves compressed backups of software that has been removed. Other features include the ability to move applications to other locations on your hard drive or to another computer. It also finds and deletes orphaned files. Thanks to the thoroughness with which this program carries out its removal tasks, it truly does live up to its name.

UnInstaller 4.0

Price $39.95

Overall Rating ★ ★ ★

Ease of Use ★ ★ ★

File Removal Functions ★ ★ 1/2

Safety Features
★ ★ ★

UnInstaller 4.0 is a little pokey, but it's easy to use. The opening screen gives you five choices: Application Cleanup, File Cleanup, Quick Cleanup, Restore, and Reports. Once UnInstaller is set up on your computer, the program prompts you to install all new software using UnInstaller's setup monitor. UnInstaller keeps track of all software applications on your computer and has SmartLinks, which tracks your system for related files. Your entire hard disk is examined to determine what applications share files and other file associations. This examination takes longer than other programs.

There are also wizards to help you through the file removal process. The File Cleanup feature searches for disconnected files. When Uninstaller finds files to delete, it color codes them—green means you can delete the file, yellow means be careful, and red indicates do not delete.

UnInstaller has other features which compress applications for moving to other hard-drive locations or computers, and find and remove duplicate or orphaned files.

Even with Uninstaller's meticulous examination of the hard disk, it can fail to delete files during the removal process. Another drawback is its process of removing suite software. Each executable file must be selected and deleted individually. What a pain.

WinDelete

Price $39.95

Overall Rating ★★1/2

Ease of Use ★★

File Removal Functions ★★1/2

Safety Features ★★★

WinDelete not only has uninstall capabilities, but includes full virus protection and Internet management, which helps get rid of litter from cyberspace (i.e., the Internet or online services). However, the program can be difficult to use. The interface forces you to manually select individual files in order to remove applications. For Win-Delete to monitor installations, software has to be installed through WinDelete, or

you can activate the Windows 95 Add/Remove program and select the Install with WinDelete box. Even if applications are installed with WinDelete, parts of the applications are still left after Win-Delete supposedly removed them. Suite applications have to be deleted file by file through a time-consuming process of selecting files one by one then deleting them. However, the color-coding feature allows you to mark which files you want deleted and which to leave alone.

This program does have a few nice features, such as saving compressed backups of deleted applications, moving applications to different drives or other computers, and looking for and deleting orphaned backup and duplicate files. It also includes other software such as MacAfee's VirusScan and Office Central, a file viewing utility. But these extras do not make up for WinDelete's lackluster performance in removing files. Delete this program from your list.

CONTACT INFORMATION

CleanSweep 3.0
Quarterdeck
(800) 282-0866
(310) 309-3700
www.quarterdeck.com

Power Cleaner
Alpha Software Corp., (Division of SoftQuad).
(800) 451-1018; (617) 229-2924
www.alphasoftware.com

Remove-It 95
Vertisoft
(800) 466-5874
(415) 956-5999
www.vertisoft.com

UnInstaller 4.0
MicroHelp
(800) 777-3322
(770) 516-0899
www.microhelp.com

WinDelete 3.0
IMSI
(415) 257-3000
www.imsi.com

Virus Utilities

Virus utilities—sometimes called antivirus utilities—are software programs designed to protect you from computer viruses. A computer virus is simply a self replicating program that can infect and often cripple data on magnetic media, such as your hard drive. Virus programs are written by programmers who, for unknown reasons, create and unleash these destructive programs onto the computing community.

Virus utilities detect and remove computer viruses from your hard drive and diskettes. When installed on your computer, virus utilities set up a type of security system that runs in the background, checking for a large variety of viruses. When one of those nasty bugs try to infiltrate this security system, the virus utility issues a warning on your computer screen allowing you to take immediate action.

In order to infect your system, the virus must attach itself to an executable program you are currently using. There are many different types of viruses, but they all fall into two classes: "executable viruses" and "boot sector viruses," the latter being viruses that attach files where your system files reside. Executable viruses infect executable codes, so any of your files are vulnerable. The only way this kind of virus can replicate is through executing a program. Boot sector viruses are more dangerous because they replicate by placing a copy of the particular virus in memory. When a diskette is formatted by an infected computer, replication is transparent to the user. On the other hand, boot sector viruses can remain undetected for long periods of time.

Use your antivirus utility at all times. Once you've installed it on your system, keep it active. If you deactivate the memory resident module, you have actually turned off your PC's security system and have exposed your computer to viruses.

In addition to installing and regularly using an antivirus utility here are other steps you can take to keep your computer healthy:

1) Backup your PC often. Mishaps occur and if you have not had any PC disasters, just wait, you will. You should back up your system after you have installed an antivirus utility and vaccinated your system.

2) Password protect your computer to keep others from using it and inadvertently infecting your system.

3) Scan your diskettes, especially if you exchange data with others. Viruses can easily be transferred from a diskette to your PC. Also, make sure your write-protect tab is on when not writing files to your disks. Don't leave disks in your diskette drive.

4) Scan all files that you download from the web or from e-mail. Infected files can be inadvertently sent to you as an attached e-mail file. The sender may not know it is

infected, but to be safe you should check for viruses regardless. Even though most commercial on-line sites check for viruses, you can't be sure of everything, so scan your downloaded files, even compressed ones, before using them on your PC.

5) Keep your antivirus utility program updated. To keep your system current with new virus information you should obtain virus updates from the manufacturer.

Below are six major virus, or antivirus, utilities, along with their overall ratings. Specifications pertaining to them were gathered from their publishers.

OVERALL RATINGS

Dr. Solomon's Anti-Virus
Toolkit ★★★ 3/4

Inoculan AntiVirus for
Windows 95 ★★★ 1/2

Norton AntiVirus 2.0 for
Windows 95 ★★★ 1/2

F-Prot Professional ★★★ 1/4

Touchstone PC-Cillin II ★★★ 1/4

IBM Antivirus Version 2.5 ★★★

McAfee VirusScan for
Windows 95 ★★★

EXPLANATION OF RATINGS

The virus utilities were scored for Ease of Use, Performance, which refers to virus detection and Availability of Updates. A four-star rating system was used with four stars being the highest possible and one the lowest. An overall rating was computed by averaging the three previously stated scores.

ALPHABETICAL DESCRIPTIONS

Inoculan AntiVirus for Windows 95

Price $69
Rating ★★★1/2
Ease of Use ★★★
Performance ★★★★
Update Availability ★★★

This program, published by Cheyenne, performs excellently and is easy to install and use. It automatically secures your computer, providing total Internet protection. The National Computer Security Association (NCSA) certifies that Inoculan AntiVirus will protect your computer from 100% of the viruses in actual circulation. These viruses are also known as "viruses in the wild." All files are scanned, including compressed and executable files. For emergency situations, the Rescue Disk Wizard can create a backup of your computer's vital system files to a floppy.

Signature file updates are available online free for one year and can be downloaded to your computer every 30 days. One unique feature is the Cheyenne Virus Information Center (www.cheyenne.com/virusinfo. Here you can receive information on virus alerts and other security issues, access a virus encyclopedia, and have your files scanned for free. Online software updates are free for one year. There is also a 30-day money-back guarantee and 24-hour online support.

Dr. Solomon's Anti-Virus Toolkit

Price $95

Overall Rating ★★★3/4

Ease of Use ★★★★

Performance ★★★★

Update Availability ★★★

Dr. Solomon's Anti-Virus Toolkit is a superior performer and is said to detect more viruses than other programs— 11,000 in all. This easy-to-use program includes a virus encyclopedia that contains information on all known viruses. Also included is a bootable diskette for scanning and removing viruses on other computers. Toolkit can scan networks, local drives, and diskettes. It can scan inside all files, including compressed and archived files. This utility comes in a single-user version or License Packs of 5, 10, 25, 50, 100, and 250 users. License Packs will cost you more. You can receive monthly or quarterly updates free from the manufacturer. There is also a more streamlined version of this software, Dr. Solomon's Anti-Virus. This version does not scan network drives, but it basically has the same great features as the Toolkit version. In this version you can receive monthly updates for $29.95 a year.

F-Prot Professional

Price $99

Rating ★★★1/4

Ease of Use ★★★★

Performance ★★★1/2

Update Availability ★★

This is only an average performer when it comes to detecting viruses. It allows you to select which drives, folders, and files you want to scan as well as send an e-mail virus warning. It will also send a warning to a LAN administrator. This is the only program that has this feature. One big problem with this program is the way virus updates are obtained. You can get the updates over the web, but you must call the company for a password. Once you get the update, the entire program has to be reinstalled to add the update file. This is the only program that requires a complete reinstall.

IBM Antivirus Version 2.5

Price $100

Rating ★★★

Ease of Use ★★★

Performance ★★★

Update Availability ★★★

IBM's Antivirus Version 2.5 has good virus detection. When a virus is detected, it will not remove it unless it is positive it will not damage the infected file. When this happens you will have to manually delete the file and then reinstall it from backup disks. One drawback is the way the emergency bootable disk is created. One is created during the initial install, but, if you want subsequent ones, you have to go back and use the installation diskettes. Some advantages are that virus updates are available on their Website, which has versions for different operating systems including Windows 95, Windows 3.1, DOS, and OS/2. Overall, however, the program has limited virus removal capability.

McAfee VirusScan for Windows 95

Price $45

Overall Rating ★ ★ ★

Ease of Use ★ ★ ★

Performance ★ ★ ★

Update Availability ★ ★ ★

VirusScan is an easy-to-use package, allowing you to customize options and scan all files, including compressed files. It also includes versions for all operating systems: Windows 95, Windows 3.1, Windows NT, DOS and OS/2. Performance is good. However, you have to pay for support. Virus updates can be obtained via the web, but they are not guaranteed to work unless you are a subscriber. For the first 90 days registered users can get one free program update, but after that you have to pay $49 per year for unlimited free virus and program updates and 24-hour support.

Norton AntiVirus 2.0 for Windows 95

Price $70

Overall Rating ★ ★ ★ 1/2

Ease of Use ★ ★ ★ ★

Performance ★ ★ ★ 1/2

Update Availability ★ ★ ★

Norton AntiVirus is one of the best virus utility programs. The program is simple to use and install. Features can easily be customized to scan individual drives, directories, files, and compressed files can be scanned. Advanced options that let you detect file size changes, automatic scanning, and reporting scanning results are also available. Another feature, the Virus Repair Wizard, shows you the virus detected, gives you detailed information about it, then shows you the options for getting rid of it either automatically or through a step-by-step procedure. Program and virus updates are available through LiveUpdate, a feature that connects to the web to download updates to your computer.

Touhstone PC-Cillin II

Price $50

Overall Rating ★ ★ ★ 1/4

Ease of Use ★ ★ 1/2

Performance ★ ★ ★ ★

Update Availability ★ ★ ★

PC-Cillin II has good performance; however, the interface is kind of drab and hard to use. Included in this package is the SmartMonitor feature that displays viruses it finds along with a history of scans and viruses found on your computer. Virus updates can easily be obtained from the company's website with just a single mouse click. There are also other customizable options where you can set your scans and removals to your liking.

CONTACT INFORMATION

Cheyenne (Division of Computer Associates)
800-243-9465
www.cheyenne.com

Dr. Solomon's Software Ltd.
888-377-6566
www.drsolomon.com

F-Prot Professional
Command Software Systems
800-423-9147
www.commandcom.com

IBM
800-742-2493
www.av.ibm.com

McAfee Associates
800-332-9966
www.mcafee.com

Norton AntiVirus 2.0

Symantec
800-441-7234
www.symantec.com

PC-Cillin II
TouchStone Software
800-531-0450
www.checkit.com

WEB AUTHORING TOOLS

Web Authoring Tools are applications that create web pages and take most of the work out of creating them. With these tools there is no need for a user to have extensive knowledge of HTML (Hyper Text Markup Language—the language that makes up a web page) since the code is automatically generated. Businesses today are using the web to communicate not only with their customers but also with their employees.

There are two types of web authoring tools: WYSIWYG graphic editors, which allow you to visually create pages by placing text and graphics where you want, and code editors, where you have to type in the HTML code to create pages. For this review we took a look at web authoring tools that can help you design web pages

The number-one rated application Microsoft FrontPage97 (screen capture below) is a versatile web authoring tool with an array of features for both web page creation and site management.

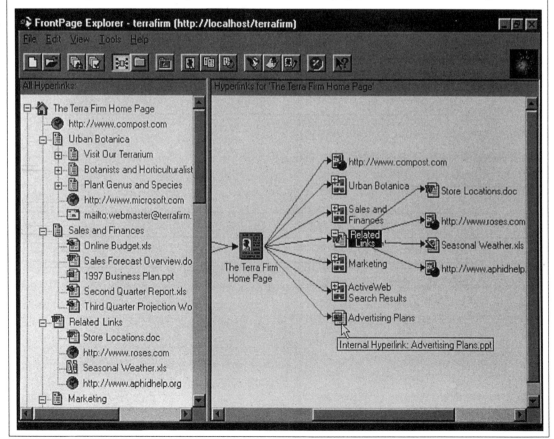

quickly. This review focused on WYSI-WYG tools, which are easier to use because you do not have to have an in-depth knowledge of HTML, though sometimes it is helpful to have some basic knowledge so you can tweak your pages if necessary. The list below gives the ratings each product received. If you want to find out more about web publishing visit the web Developers Journal on the Internet (see Additional Information below.)

EXPLANATION OF RATINGS

Microsoft FrontPage 97 ★★★★

Macromedia Backstage
Designer Plus ★★★1/2

Adobe PageMill 2.0 ★★★

AOLpress 2.0 ★★1/2

Claris Home Page ★★1/2

Corel Web.Graphics Suite ★★1/2

Quarterdeck TotalWeb ★★1/2

Netscape Navigator Gold ★★

EXPLANATION OF RATINGS

Each application was evaluated in six categories: *Ease of Use*, which looks at how quickly a user can build a page, the interface, available templates, preview options and on-line help; *Graphics and Text Handling* refers to how the program manipulates these two elements; *Page Layout* concerns elements such as forms, tables, frames, borders, and image maps; *Advanced Features* concerns CGI, Java and database support; *Miscellaneous Tools* includes the program's capability to edit HTML tags and multi-file, site-wide

search and replace; and *Site Management Options* concerns how the program handles multiple web pages and broken links. A four-star rating is the highest possible for each category; one is the lowest. An overall rating was achieved by averaging the ratings of the six categories.

ALPHABETICAL DESCRIPTIONS

Adobe PageMill 2.0

Price $99

Overall Rating ★★★

Ease of Use ★★★★

Graphics and Text Handling ★★★1/2

Page Layout ★★★★

Advanced Features ★★

Miscellaneous Tools ★★★★

Site Management Options ★

Adobe PageMill 2.0 has versions for the Mac and Windows 95/NT. The interface resembles a web browser that lets you view how your pages will look in finished form. There's a spell checker with custom dictionary, search and replace tools, and basic editing tools. Text and graphics can be dragged and dropped onto the page. Text is easily aligned with borders and can be wrapped around graphics. Advanced features such as forms, tables, and frames are easily handled. Tables are created by just dragging the mouse and you can create nested tables. Tables can also be imported from applications such as Microsoft Excel. Frames are easy—just drag them anywhere on the page, as many as you like. If you need to tweak your page a bit, just switch to code mode to edit HTML tags, which are shown in various colors. Multimedia elements such as animated GIFs and Macromedia's Shockwave can be placed on your page with drag-and-drop ease. Some drawbacks to this program are its lack of support for advanced features such as CGI, Java, and streaming multimedia like RealAudio and VDOLive. Adobe PageMill is an entry-level program that you may outgrow as your web site grows.

AOLpress 2.0

Price Free

Overall Rating ★★1/2

Ease of Use ★★★

Graphics and Text Handling ★★★

Page Layout ★★★

Advanced Features ★★

Miscellaneous Tools ★★

Site Management Options ★★1/2

If you just want to try your hand at creating a web page without spending a lot of money, try AOLpress 2.0. This web authoring tool is free for the asking—you just download it from America Online or the Prime Host web site www.primehost.com. AOLPress creates a web page quickly and easily. It has an easy-to-use interface that allows you to create forms, tables, and frames quickly and efficiently. AOLPress 2.0 is a WYSIWYG editor and web browser all in one interface. You can browse the web with it or design your own creations. It supports all HTML 3.2 and Netscape Extensions and you can save your finished web pages directly to the Internet from within the program. HTML code editing is allowed for those who need to fine-tune their pages and color-coded tags make editing easier. Advanced fea-

tures such as Java applets are also supported. One drawback: it has a nasty habit of hanging up if it encounters an unsupported HTML tag. Besides that, you can't beat the price and it's a decent program.

Claris Home Page

Price $99

Overall Rating ★★1/2

Ease of Use ★★★1/2

Graphics and Text Handling ★★★1/2

Page Layout ★★★

Advanced Features ★★

Miscellaneous Tools ★★1/2

Site Management Options ★

This WYSIWYG tool is one of the easiest programs to use with its drag-and-drop ease for graphics text and URL links. It can also directly manipulate frames. Images are automatically converted into smaller GIF or JPEG files and interlaced. The Object Editor lets you easily manipulate graphics and text and edit HTML tags. Pages can be previewed in an external web browser or displayed as text only. Advanced features such as CGI and Java support were lacking and inline table editing was not impressive. Despite this, we found Home Page to be an decent starter package for beginners, but it lacks the advanced features that are now standard in other packages.

Corel Web.Graphics Suite

Price $299

Overall Rating ★★1/2

Ease of Use ★★★1/2

Graphics and Text Handling ★★★

Page Layout ★★1/2

Advanced Features ★★

Miscellaneous Tools ★★

Site Management Options ★★

Corel takes an all-in-one approach by combining all of their web products into one "suite package" that is supposedly designed for beginners and experienced web designers alike. The Web.Graphics Suite includes CorelWeb.Designer, CorelWeb.Transit, CorelWeb.Move, CorelWeb.Draw, CorelWeb.World and CorelWeb.Gallery. The CorelWeb.Designer is the web authoring tool that is as easy to use as Claris Home Page. There are a variety of templates to help in designing pages and the CorelWeb.Gallery contains tons of backgrounds, buttons, borders, and clip art. You can easily create tables and forms. Animation can be added with CorelWeb.Move, an animation program. Other useful programs are Corel-Web.Draw, a version of Corel's Draw! graphics package; CorelWeb.Transit, which converts word processing or graphics files into HTML; and Corel-Web.World, a 3-D VRML editor. With all these applications you can create polished web pages. However, CorelWeb.Designer is limited in its functionality. Some of the drawbacks are that it does not support frames or newer HTML tags, has no HTML code editing, and for advanced features, its two-page manual tells you to buy Macromedia Backstage Designer.

Macromedia Backstage Designer Plus

Price $99

Overall Rating ★★★1/2

Ease of Use ★★★1/2

Graphics and Text Handling ★★★★

Page Layout ★★★★

Advanced Features ★★★★

Miscellaneous Tools ★★★★

Site Management Options ★★

This well-designed program is simple to use and has enough advanced features to help you manage a growing web site. Backstage Designer has a WYSIWYG intuitive interface that includes a spell checker, thesaurus, and a text-based search and replace tool. Wizards and tool bars help you out with more complex design features such as frames, tables and forms. You can also incorporate Java or Shockwave applications into your web pages. PowerApplets, which are predesigned templates that use Java and Shockwave elements, are included. The PowerApplets can be customized to your needs. Other features include a large clip art gallery, which can be accessed by the included graphics editor Macromedia's xRes 2.0 Special Edition. Site management options include the ability to view, edit, and retrieve pages from the web server. This application is part of Macromedia's Backstage Web design products and is a good choice for novices who want to get started on the web and keep going.

Microsoft FrontPage 97

Price $149

Overall Rating ★★★★

Ease of Use ★★★★

Graphics and Text Handling ★★★1/2

Page Layout ★★★★

Advanced Features ★★★★

Miscellaneous Tools ★★★★

Site Management Options ★★★★

FrontPage97 is a versatile web authoring tool with an array of features for both web page creation and site management. It provides database access, the Microsoft Image composer add-on, Internet Explorer, Microsoft Personal Web Server, browser previewer, Microsoft Word RTF converters, global spell checker and thesaurus, SSI security, and scripting support among other features. This application can handle simple page layout to more complex designs. Tables, forms, frames and multimedia effects can be incorporated into your pages. One major improvement is the addition of an HTML code editor and image editor. Templates, a clip art gallery, and sample web pages are included to aid you in designing your site. The Microsoft Image Composer, a tool

Microsoft FrontPage97, the top-rated application.

for creating and customizing on-screen graphics is also included. FrontPage 97 is a high-end web authoring tool and site management application for those who need to establish a presence on the Internet or intranet.

Netscape Navigator Gold 3.0

Price $79

Overall Rating ★★

Ease of Use ★★★

Graphics and Text Handling ★★1/2

Page Layout ★★

Advanced Features ★★

Miscellaneous Tools ★

Site Management Options ★★

Navigator Gold is an add-on WYSIWYG program that is really a web editor. With this program you get the Netscape Navigator web browser and a very basic web authoring tool. Its features do not match the other authoring tools reviewed here, but it can do a basic job of web page editing. To create web pages you click the pencil icon to switch from browser mode to edit mode, where you do all your designing. You can insert and edit tables, wrap text around images, create links, and save your pages directly to the web server. To create features such as forms or frames you need to know HTML because you have to hand-code these elements by inserting HTML tags. Codes can be added with an outside source such as Windows Notepad or Microsoft Word. If you have no clue about what HTMLs are all about, forget this program. There are plenty of other simple web authoring tools on the market that would better fit your needs.

Quarterdeck TotalWeb

Price $99
Overall Rating ★★1/2
Ease of Use ★★★
Graphics and Text Handling ★★1/2
Page Layout ★★★
Advanced Features ★★
Miscellaneous Tools ★★
Site Management Options ★★1/2

Quarterdeck takes a suite approach by combining all of its Internet products into one product. TotalWeb includes what the company says is "Everything you need to start publishing on the web!" This application includes Web-Author Pro, Mosaic, WebImage, 16- and 32-bit web servers and FTP, IRC chat, and Telnet clients. The inclusion of the additional Internet client and server applications can help beginning web designers publish their work faster. Web-Author Pro is a WYSIWYG editor with a familiar interface for this type of program. It supports HTML 2.0, 3.0, and 3.2 tags and Netscape and Microsoft extensions. Basic design elements are supported. There are bundled templates for you to use which conform to WebAuthor's recognized tags, but some strictly adhere to either HTML 2.0 or 3.0, making your pages viewable through less-advanced browsers. The WebImage program is an image-editing and conversion tool that can convert images into GIF, JPEG, and PNG formats. It also supports UUencoding and UUdecoding. Web-Image can also be used to create client-side, NCSA-, or CERN-compliant image map files. This product is a good starting point, but lacks some advanced multimedia elements.

CONTACT INFORMATION

Adobe Corp.
800 843-7263
408 536-6000
www.adobe.com

Claris
800 544-8554
www.claris.com

Corel Corp.
800 772-6735
613 728-7733
www.corel.com

Macromedia Corp.
415 252-9080
wwww.macromedia.com

Microsoft Corp.
800 426-9400
202 882-8080
www.microsoft.com

Netscape Corp.
415 937-2555
www.netscape.com

Prime Host
888 AOL-1111
www.primehost.com

Quarterdeck
800-282-0866
310 309-3700
www.quarterdeck.com

WORD PROCESSORS

Today's word processing software offers far more than editing. Word processors now can correct your typos, automatically format documents, build web pages, and, in some cases, type for you. Of the applications reviewed, each offers desktop publishing tools, wizards, and automated templates. There used to be at least a dozen different word processors on the market, but now only three are vying for market share. We reviewed the top three word processors from Microsoft, Corel and Lotus Corporations. Below are their overall ratings.

OVERALL RATINGS

Microsoft Word 97	★★★★
Corel WordPerfect 8	★★★
Lotus Word Pro 97	★★★

EXPLANATION OF RATINGS

Each application was rated in seven categories; Page Layout, Text Handling, Document Handling, Desktop Publishing, Collaboration Features, Automation Tools, and Web Integration. Each category was rated on a four-star scale with four stars the highest score possible; one the lowest. Overall ratings were achieved by averaging the seven category ratings.

EXPLANATION OF RATINGS

Corel WordPerfect 8

Price $395 (only sold as part of WordPerfect Suite 8); upgrade $129

Overall Rating ★★★
Page Layout ★★★★
Text Handling ★★★
Document Handling ★★★★
Desktop Publishing, ★★★★
Collaboration Features ★★
Automation Tools ★★★★
Web Integration ★★★

WordPerfect has undergone several changes. Originally owned by WordPerfect Corporation, this product was acquired by Novell, then sold to Corel Corporation, which has made major changes to the popular word processing software. WordPerfect 8 is now a 32-bit version, but it still uses the previous file formats so earlier versions of WordPerfect will be compatible.

The interface has been streamlined so you don't have to navigate through several menus to format your documents. The QuickSpot option allows you to click on its button and select formatting options on the fly. You can also adjust your document's margins, headers and tables right on the screen by dragging on-screen lines to new locations on the page. WordPerfect 8 still is superior when it comes to handling long documents and precise formatting.

If you need to build a simple web site, WordPerfect's wizard will automatically create a home page with tables and links to other pages. Included in this application is Corel's Barista technology that lets you save any WordPerfect document as a Java applet. There are a few drawbacks; you cannot create forms or open files directly from the Internet. Internet files can be viewed in WordPerfect but you have to save the file to your hard drive first, then open it in WordPerfect. WordPerfect 8 is sold as part of the WordPerfect Suite 8 for Windows. In addition to WordPerfect, the suite includes Corel Quattro Pro 8, Corel Presentations 8, Envoy 7 viewer, Netscape Navigator, and plenty of clip art, fonts, and photos.

Lotus Word Pro 97

Price $105; upgrade $105	
Overall Rating ★★★	
Page Layout ★★★	
Text Handling ★★★	
Document Handling ★★★	
Desktop Publishing, ★★★★	
Collaboration Features ★★★★	
Automation Tools ★★★★	
Web Integration ★★	

Users of Ami Pro will be relieved to know that this application has been completely overhauled. Word Pro 97's best feature is its collaboration tools that make sharing and editing documents with a group a snap. If you're looking for work group tools this application should be your choice.

Document Handling is more flexible, with Word Pro's documents divider interface. You can move chapters, sections or objects by dragging its tab to a new location. Text can be flowed into frames either on the same page or on different pages.

Word Pro's Internet features allow you to create web pages and build HTML forms, but they can't automatically generate an entire site with links. Files can be opened and saved on FTP or web sites. Despite its revision, Word Pro 97 is not in danger of overtaking other word processors on the market.

Microsoft Word 97

Price $340; upgrade $85	
Overall Rating ★★★★	
Page Layout ★★★★	
Text Handling ★★★★	
Document Handling ★★★	
Desktop Publishing, ★★★★	
Collaboration Features ★★★	
Automation Tools ★★★	
Web Integration ★★★1/2	

Word 97 is the best-selling word processing software. Its speed and features have been greatly enhanced, making it even more powerful. Word 97 still uses the same consistent interface found in other Microsoft applications, so new users will find it easy to use while experienced Word users will have no problem in upgrading.

Word is now Internet ready. Files on the Internet can be opened in word and edited. Web pages can be created effortlessly, from simple layouts to the more complex. Forms can be created with just a click from the toolbar. However you will need to understand HTML forms processing to use this feature effectively. Word does not support frames or Java applets.

This application has all the basic text editing tools, plus enhanced drawing and border tools, desktop publishing features which include the ability to flow text into frames on different pages, and a table-drawing pencil tool that creates tables on the screen. Also multiple versions of a document can be stored in one document.

If you use macros, Word 97 now uses Visual Basic for Applications instead of WordBasic for creating macros. Older macros are automatically converted when you open a template or document. Macintosh users can also experience the power of Word 97. There is a version of this software for the Mac with all the same power and versatility.

CONTACT INFORMATION

Lotus Development Corp.
800-343-5414; 617-577-8500
www.lotus.com

Microsoft Corp.
800-426-9400; 206-882-8080
www.microsoft.com

Corel Corporation
800 772-6735
613 728-3733
http://www.corel.com

LES KRANTZ is an author and book developer who has produced reference books for many major U.S. publishers in the past decade. He is best known for books that provide analyses based on statistical information, particularly those which culminate in rankings. Some of Krantz's books that have dealt with statistical treatments or rankings include *The Jobs Rated Almanac, The Best and Worst of Everything, What the Odds Are, CD-ROMs Rated, The Definitive Guide to the Best and Worst of Everything*, and other books. In addition to his books, he has written articles on the everyday significance of statistical information for various print media, which have included *Reader's Digest* and the *Wall Street Journal*. He is a graduate of the University of Missouri School of Journalism and currently heads Facts That Matter, Inc., a publishing company in Chicago that produces nonfiction books for major American publishers.

ADRIENNE BROWN is president of Media Artists, a computer consulting firm that designs software for businesses and schools. Brown specializes in information retrieval systems and has over 15 years experience in the computer field. She is a former teacher in the California school system and has a master's degree in education. She has been a senior editor for *CD-ROMs Rated* and research director of several of Krantz's books, which include *The Jobs Rated Almanac* and *The Definitive Guide to the Best and Worst of Everything*. Brown also has written for World Almanac Books, contributing material pertaining to business- and computer-related fields. She works with various organizations, consulting on business applications related to computers and productivity.